"Valuable . . . Clark has conducted impressive research and selects quotes from it well, for insight and intensity, from both sides." —*America in WWII*

"Outstanding . . . Brings an immediacy to one of the war's legendary episodes." —*Oxford Times*

"Excellently written and researched . . . Clark depicts the tension between the British and Americans fastidiously, backing up his arguments with diligent research. His depictions of the hopes and fears of paratroopers before the battle are as eloquently rendered as his examinations of the power struggles of the Allied leaders. It is this descriptive talent which sets this book apart from other military accounts. This is an engaging account of warfare, told from an extremely detailed and strategic point of view. It is a fine addition to the many excellent tomes on WWII, written with impressive clarity and providing an interesting insight into the build-up, execution, and aftermath of two of the mightiest airborne operations ever conducted." —*Sunday Business Post*

Praise for *Anzio*:

"Masterly . . . A heartbreaking, beautifully told story of wasted sacrifice." —*The Washington Post*

"Lucid . . . Elegantly written . . . Clark has succeeded in producing a fast, enjoyable narrative . . . Absolutely first class."
—Alex Kershaw, *The New York Times* best-selling author of *The Longest Winter* and *The Few*

"A rich account . . . Highly readable . . . Clark does much to disprove the Italian campaign's reputation as a sideshow."
—*Kirkus Reviews*

CROSSING THE RHINE

Also by Lloyd Clark

1918 – Flawed Victory

The Fall of the Reich (with D. Anderson)

The Eastern Front Iwith D. Anderson

World War One – A History

The Orne Bridgehead

Operation Epsom

Anzio: Italy and the Battle for Rome – 1944

CROSSING THE RHINE

2008   343 pp

BREAKING INTO NAZI GERMANY
1944 AND 1945–
THE GREATEST AIRBORNE BATTLES IN HISTORY

LLOYD CLARK

Grove Press
New York

First published in 2008
by HEADLINE REVIEW

ISBN-13: 978-0-8021-4430-0

Grove Press
an imprint of Grove/Atlantic, Inc.
841 Broadway
New York, NY 10003
Distributed by Publishers Group West
www.groveatlantic.com

09 10 11 12   10 9 8 7 6 5 4 3 2 1

Contents *3 43 pp*

For the girls: Catriona, Charlotte, Pauline, Caroline, Betty, Lorna, Dariel, Isobel, Sophie, Alicia and Ciara. Formidable.

Acknowledgements

I count myself extremely fortunate to have a job that I enjoy so much and which frequently brings me into contact with so many extraordinary and generous people. This book could not have been written without their assistance, and I am delighted to acknowledge them here. A list of those veterans whom I interviewed, corresponded with, and who provided me with their diaries and papers, can be found in the bibliography, but I should particularly like to thank the late Geoffrey Powell, the late Len Wright and Major-General Anthony Deane-Drummond, a remarkable man from a remarkable family who continues to be an inspiration to all who are privileged to meet him. I feel immensely honoured to have spent so much time in the company of old soldiers, and remain humbled in their presence.

I should also like to express my gratitude to the hardworking staff of the following archives, libraries, museums and other institutions who have gone out of their way to make my job as easy and as enjoyable as possible: the National Archives, Kew, London; the Imperial War

Museum, London; the Liddell Hart Centre for Military Archives, King's College London; the Airborne Forces Museum, Aldershot; the Museum of Army Flying, Middle Wallop; the Royal Historical Society, University College London; the Institute of Historical Research, University of London; the University of London Library; the London Library; Dr John S. Duvall at the Airborne and Special Operations Museum Foundation, Fayetteville, North Carolina; Dr Adrian Groeneweg and the staff of the Airborne Museum Hartenstein, Oosterbeek, Holland; the National Archives, Maryland; the Donovan Research Library, US Army Infantry School, Fort Benning, Georgia, and Das Bundesarchiv, Freiburg and Koblenz. I am also grateful to Mr Derrick Randall for permission to quote from his *Experiences of a Medical Officer at Arnhem* from the BBC WWII People's War Archive. Whilst I have endeavoured to trace the copyright-holders of other material that I have quoted in this book, I have either failed to track them down or found that my letters have not been answered. I would, however, be pleased to rectify any omissions if copyright-holders should wish to contact me.

My particular thanks, as always, go to Andrew Orgill and his patient, jolly and highly professional team at the Central Library, Royal Military Academy Sandhurst: John Pearce, Gareth Bellis, Ken Franklin, Stuart Robinson and Mel Bird. Sandhurst is an excellent, vibrant and stimulating place to work, and without the support of this august institution I would not be able to write. Sean McKnight, Yoland Richardson, Dr Duncan Anderson and my colleagues in the Department of War Studies have all played their part in making this book possible. My military colleagues are also deserving of my appreciation, with a special mention due to Majors Laurence Bedford and Sid Keyte, with whom I have worked closely over the last year, much of it abroad. Their sense of humour, focus and companionship have been much appreciated. Laurence, I forgive you for getting me lost so often and for making me go out for runs along beaches in blizzards. I also owe my officer cadets considerable thanks for their thirst for knowledge, intelligent questions, encouragement and sense of fun: they make my job worthwhile and have my admiration. I am also indebted to Debbie Fields, Leo Berger and Michael Roberts, who assisted me with research and the translation of important texts; Charlie Viney, my ever supportive agent; and my patient and kind publishers, Martin Fletcher and Lorraine Jerram at Headline, and Jofie Ferrari-Adler and Morgan Entrekin at Grove Atlantic. Thanks also to Margaret Wallis for her copyedit and Alan Collinson at Geo-Innovations for the maps.

Finally, my deepest gratitude goes to my longsuffering family. I have now written several books and each one has impacted on them more than I would like and they deserve. My wife Catriona and children Freddie, Charlotte and Henry have tolerated my long absences abroad, my preoccupation with 'the book' and all that goes with being a busy writer and academic, with great fortitude and understanding. Thank you.

Lloyd Clark
Wigginton Bottom and Camberley, April 2008

Maps

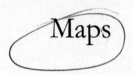

Introduction

There are thousands of eyes keeping watch on the Rhine; thousands of German eyes . . . It has the feel of the last barrier, and I know that when the Allied armies cross this brown river, it will be the end of Nazi Germany.
(War Correspondent R.W. Thompson, 24 November 1944)

The River Rhine has been at the centre of the lives of those living within its reach ever since man could harness its potential, but over the centuries it attained a significance and influence that affected the entire Continent. From its source in the Swiss Alps to its emptying into the North Sea, the Rhine not only carved its way through 820 miles of Europe's heartland, but also deep into its people's psyche. As an important boundary, trade route and symbol of strength, it quickly became the subject of passionate political disagreement and military violence. Indeed, its blood-soaked shoreline has moved one commentator to write: 'In every century great armies have fought for possession of its banks, its bridges, its crossings, its cities, in a way that no other river has ever been fought for.' Its long and troubled history helped to define the river, and although today's travellers cruising along its calm waters may delight in the aesthetic charm of the castles and ruins on its banks, they are the physical evidence of the Rhine's turbulent past. These fortifications enhanced the river's natural defences, encompassed notable breadth, depth and current, and allowed few successful aggressive crossings from the West. Consequently the Rhine developed a reputation as not only a great physical barrier but also a psychological one. It was a situation that Julius Caesar recognized when his troops breached the river in 56 BC. He later wrote that his offensive motivations were in part to give the Germans 'reasons of their own for anxiety when they realized that an army of the Roman people could and would cross the Rhine'.

The River Rhine was never more of a military impediment than when it was faced by the Western Allies in months during the autumn of 1944. For them it was a known obstacle that had to be overcome if their forces were to take and hold vital ground at the heart of Germany and gain access to the enemy's capital city. For the Germans, meanwhile, the Rhine remained a bulwark, a liquid security blanket behind which their shattered nation could cower, a line which, if breached, would mark the end of their fragile hope. In such circumstances General Dwight Eisenhower, Supreme Commander of the Allied forces in Europe, had to face the question of how and where to cross the Rhine – and who would carry it out, a situation that could not be dealt with by merely waving a large hand across a small map. Indeed, the challenge of crossing the mighty Rhine highlighted a sensitive feature of Eisenhower's seemingly irrepressible military machine: Anglo-American rivalry. This friction was fast approaching its third trying year, and far from abating, looked to be increasing with every step towards the Fatherland. It was a situation personified, and also exacerbated, by British Field Marshal Bernard Montgomery, commander of the British Twenty-First Army Group, who seemed to be in permanent conflict not just with the Germans but also with American commanders. In such circumstances the submissions forwarded by these senior commanders in their rush to be chosen as the man to make the Rhine attempt were laced with skulduggery, hidden agendas and coated in a rich polemic. Even so, Eisenhower –

under intense pressure and scrutiny – had a responsibility to decide which commander, and therefore which nation, was to be favoured with the strike across the Rhine. He also had to bear in mind that in so choosing, that commander would be set fair to forge on to Berlin and steal a pre-eminent place in the history books.

One of the many influences on Eisenhower's decision to award Montgomery the prize was the Field Marshal's desire to use the newly formed First Allied Airborne Army to help achieve a Rhine crossing. By applying a new solution to an old problem, there was an opportunity to avoid a much-feared, protracted and costly slogging-match on the banks of the river. Nevertheless, the airborne method was not without its critics, who in 1944 pointed to its mixed success thus far in the war. They argued that it was a complicated, vulnerable, expensive and prof-ligate form of warfare whose potential was outweighed by the massive risks associated with it. To others, however, airborne warfare was exactly the sort of dynamic, flexible and bold form of fighting in which the Allies should be engaging. They reasoned that by inserting troops into areas that were otherwise inaccessible, the enemy could be surprised, dislocated and outmanoeuvred with the possibility of an advantageous strategic impact. However, both opinions on this new form of warfare tended to lack objectivity, with personal loyalties and assumptions often undermining their helpfulness. Of course, airborne operations had the same basic requirements as any other form of warfare: they needed to have achievable aims, be adequately resourced and carefully planned to ensure that their risks were deftly managed. However, because airborne operations were by their nature more risky than most other types, they should only be employed in very specific circumstances if those risks were not to become fatal vulnerabilities. It is the applicability of these specific circumstances that needs to be considered if two separate but inextricably linked Montgomery schemes to cross the Rhine using airborne forces are to be fully understood.

Of these two remarkable operations: Market Garden, conducted during September 1944 in Holland, and Operation Plunder Varsity, conducted in March 1945 in Germany, the former is by far the better known and is one of the most famous engagements of the Second World War. There have been scores of books, articles and documentaries produced over the last 30 years about this dramatic attempt to 'bounce the Rhine', with many inspired by the success of the 1977 film *A Bridge Too Far*, which was based on Cornelius Ryan's book of the same name. Indeed, in recent years a Market Garden-based computer game has been a bestseller proclaiming: 'From war-room strategy to gritty trench combat, battlefields come to life as you command Allied or Axis powers. It's a desperate fight – bridge after bridge – where every second counts.' The phrase 'a bridge too far' is in common usage on both sides of the Atlantic as a descriptive shorthand for overstretch. But while it is tempting to say that the fascination of Market Garden is based on the controversy surrounding it, the reality is that it has come to be seen as an Aunt Sally operation. There has grown around it an overwhelmingly dominant perception, summarized by British historian Ronald Lewin, who writes that it was 'a British disaster where naked courage lacked the bodyguard of competent planning, competent intelligence, competent technology'. Dissatisfied with such a damning verdict, he goes on to add spitefully: 'war's objective is victory, not only the Victoria Cross, and it was shameful that by the autumn of 1944 we could still be so amateur'. But these glib criticisms signally fail to provide a full and empathetic account of the circumstances in which the operation was conceived, planned and conducted. Moreover, it is not only disrespectful but unworthy of Lewin to argue that Allied commanders in the autumn of 1944 needed to be reminded that 'war's objective is victory, not only the Victoria Cross'. Such facile statements are extremely misleading as they make it seem as though critical decisions were taken in a strategic vacuum rather than in a heady atmosphere dominated by competing interests.

Yet whilst Market Garden has been subjected to many harsh

words that have served to raise its profile, Plunder Varsity remains little known. When compared to Market Garden it has attracted scant attention from authors, its commemorations are muted and far less well attended by the public, and battlefield tours to its important sites are rarities. However, it remains an operation highly deserving of close attention for it was a remarkable undertaking and surrounded by controversy all of its own. Plunder Varsity was the largest single airborne lift operation in history, which reflected the massive material advantages that the Allies enjoyed at the time, but it was not, of course, without risk. The resultant battles were dramatic, intense, involved some heavy casualties and were not without mistakes or great drama. Indeed, there seems to be a misconception that the Battle of the Ardennes in December 1944 was the last great battle of the Western Allies in Europe, and that the fighting that followed was little more than a walkover. But Plunder Varsity underlines the need to re-evaluate such easily accepted notions, for although it is undeniable that the Germans were already unstitched by the final months of the war, the story of them being pulled apart demands to be told.

Together the stories of these two great airborne operations provide the ideal opportunity to investigate the unfurling of Eisenhower's strategy, along with Germany's struggle to sustain its war effort. They also provide an insight into the development of Allied fighting methods and, in particular, the audacious art of airborne warfare. Never before or since has the world seen such a grandiose and romantic use of the air flank, and although Market Garden and Plunder Varsity differed in many ways, they also had much in common. Chief among the similarities was the importance of high-quality fighting troops. An airborne soldier who lacked physical or mental strength was ill-equipped to contend with the many demands that being lightly armed and dropped behind enemy lines entailed. The story of these operations is, therefore, not only about rivalry and friction in the higher echelons of command but also about the rigours of small-unit actions and the motivations of the individual. It is about the comradeship, professionalism, courage and tenacity displayed by the airborne soldiers that remains peerless in the history of warfare.

Dramatis Personae

BRITISH

Field Marshal Sir Alan Brooke – Chief of the Imperial General Staff

Field Marshal Sir Bernard Montgomery – Commander British Twenty-First Army Group

Lieutenant-General Sir Miles Dempsey – Commander British Second Army

Lieutenant-General Frederick Browning – Commander I British Airborne Corps and Deputy Commander First Allied Airborne Army during Operation Market Garden

Major-General Richard Gale – Commander 6 British Airborne Division during the opening phase of Operation Overlord

Major-General Roy Urquhart – Commander 1 British Airborne Division during Operation Market Garden

Major-General Eric Bols – Commander 6 British Airborne Division during Operation Plunder Varsity

Lieutenant-General Sir Brian Horrocks – Commander XXX Corps

Major-General Allan Adair – Commander Guards Armoured Division

Major-General Pip Roberts – Commander 11 Armoured Division

Major-General Ivor Thomas – Commander 43 (Wessex) Division

AMERICANS

General George C. Marshall – Chief of the Army Staff

General Dwight Eisenhower – Supreme Commander of the Allied Forces in Europe

General Omar Bradley – Commander US Twelfth Army Group

Lieutenant-General William Simpson – Commander US Ninth Army

Lieutenant-General Courtney Hodges – Commander US First Army

Lieutenant-General George Patton – Commander US Third Army

Lieutenant-General Jacob Devers – Commander US Sixth Army Group

Lieutenant-General Lewis H. Brereton – Commander First Allied Airborne Army

Lieutenant-General Matthew B. Ridgway – Commander XVII US Airborne Corps during Operation Plunder Varsity

Major-General James Gavin – Commander 82 US Airborne Division during Operation Market Garden

Major-General Maxwell D. Taylor – Commander 101 US Airborne Division during Operation Market Garden

Major-General William Miley – Commander 17 US Airborne Division during Operation Plunder Varsity

POLISH

General Stanislaw Sosabowski – Commander 1 Polish Independent Brigade

GERMANS

Field Marshal Gerd von Rundstedt – Commander-in-Chief West during Operation Market Garden

Field Marshal Albert Kesselring – Commander-in-Chief West during Operation Plunder Varsity

Field Marshal Walter Model – Commander of Army Group B during Operation Market Garden

Colonel-General Kurt Student – Commander First Parachute Army during Operation Market Garden

Lieutenant-General Alfred Schlemm – Commander First Parachute Army during Operation Plunder Varsity

Lieutenant-General Wilhelm Bittrich – Commander II SS Panzer Corps

General Eugen Meindl – Commander II Parachute Corps

SS-Obersturmbannführer Walter Harzer – Commander 9 SS Panzer Division during Operation Market Garden

SS-Gruppenführer Heinz Harmel – Commander 10 SS Panzer Division during Operation Market Garden

Prologue

The wood is misty when I arrive, but shafts of sunlight cut their way through the canopy of leaves to illuminate the scene. 'The Hollow' is less distinct than I had expected and would not normally warrant a second glance. It's just a collection of eroded leaf-covered holes in the ground; the deepest is 15 feet from the bottom to its lip and the largest can be walked around in seconds. They are defended by tall, straight, elegant beech trees which stand like pristine Guardsmen, but look carefully and you can see their battle scars. I pull out a map to get my bearings, to help me in the imaginative leap that I need to picture the scene 50 years ago when British para-troopers gave battle here. The Germans were in the trees on the other side of the lane, intent on blocking the way to the edge of a pocket containing the shattered remnants of the 1 British Airborne Division. A brisk hour's walk eastwards would bring me to the division's main objective, the road bridge over that most mesmerizing of water obstacles, the Lower Rhine. I was lying prone on one of The

Hollow's damp banks trying to get a paratrooper's perspective when Colonel Geoffrey Powell arrived. He had fought here as a company commander in 156 Para and now gives me an encouraging smile, offering approvingly: 'That's it exactly.' With those few words I notice a transformation in the previously quiet, elderly gentleman whom I had met yesterday: his back is straighter, he has a glint in his eye, he looks younger.

I had travelled from England with some military colleagues, Geoffrey Powell and Sir James Cleminson, for a reconnaissance of the Arnhem battlefield prior to a visit by the British Army Staff College. I felt immensely privileged being in the company of these veterans of the battle, having first read about their dramatic exploits as a 9-year-old boy. Powell, the intrepid leader whose bravery seemed to know no bounds, and Cleminson, the 3 Para platoon commander whose own remarkable story included being forced to take refuge in an attic with the divisional commander, Major-General Roy Urquhart, when they were surrounded by the enemy. I was desperate to learn from these men, but on our journey we merely made polite conversation, as the British do so well, in an attempt to get to know each other. But now, standing in the woods just outside Oosterbeek where his men had fallen, Geoffrey is back in 1944. Looking me in the eye, he begins to relive his experience. 'We took this place,' he says in a voice that still boasts considerable resonance, 'after a good old-fashioned charge.' An intensely modest man who would rather be remembered for his considerable postwar literary achievements than for his exploits as a soldier, Geoffrey is understating the achievement of an action that could so easily have ended in his death. He led the charge with his close friend Major Michael Page at his shoulder, a man who had cropped up in conversation several times yesterday. As it turned out, the sight and sound of a body of paratroopers screaming feverishly as they hurtled towards the Germans was enough to make the stunned defenders withdraw. I help Geoffrey down into a sandy hole: 'I organized things from here,' he recalls, 'we were expecting the Germans to counterattack before too long.' He pauses and gathers his thoughts before continuing with a wave of his hands: 'Michael defended the right side of the Hollow, and Corporal Rosenberg the left. It was a tight, contained position.' He points out an area of ground equivalent to the size of about one and a half football pitches and describes the location of the enemy, their weapons and, touchingly, the personalities of some of the men. Geoffrey offers an intimate and loving portrait of Michael Page whom he describes as a large, dependable and caring man with whom he had a close affinity.

We wander around the position and each step that Geoffrey takes seems to trigger a memory of that tumultuous day in September. Here is the place where wounded Germans were searched for ammunition; here the site where an enemy self-propelled gun was silenced by an anti-tank round and there where the man that fired the round was hit by a stream of machine gun bullets; over there is the nook where a soldier with a mortal stomach wound asked quietly to be put out of his misery. He talks about the dead in a semi-detached manner, discussing each in a way that reveals that neither the officer nor the civilian can afford to dwell on them without encouraging a distorted perspective on events. We stop for a moment to comment on the clearing mist, and then retrace our steps before coming to a halt. Geoffrey says: 'Brigadier Hackett and I discussed our little situation here. Hackett was a cool customer. He had saved his friend's life shortly before.' I know the story. During enemy shelling and mortaring, a jeep loaded with ammunition caught fire and threatened another bearing a severely wounded officer on a stretcher. Seeing the danger, Hackett leapt up, ran over to the casualty's jeep through a small arms barrage and, shielding his face from the flames, started the engine and sped away. That wounded man was Lieutenant-Colonel Derick Heathcote-Amory, a future Chancellor of the Exchequer.

Continuing our exploration, Geoffrey seems distracted and is quiet for a minute or two. Then, for the first time that morning, he speaks without looking at me: 'Snipers were a real threat', he states warily, 'and it was around here that Michael was killed.' Page was shot through the forehead while trying to locate the position of a German machine gun. 'I could not bring myself to look at his body. It was a difficult thing to reconcile. He had been so alive just minutes before.' He quickly changes the subject and begins to talk about his diminishing band of fatigued soldiers who were running dangerously low on ammunition after hours of being pinned down by the Germans. 'Time was not on our side'. Geoffrey reflects, 'and the Brigadier decided that he would lead a charge out of The Hollow and through the enemy to break into the divisional position.' There was nothing more to be done here, and Powell disengages. The mist had burnt off, it was a bright sunny day and we had an appointment at the Hartenstein Hotel.

Note: Geoffrey Powell died in 2005, but his experiences live on not only through his book, my favourite wartime memoir, *Men at Arnhem*, but also through what he told me that day. I have passed on his experiences and wisdom to many military and civilian groups over the years, and I make a point of visiting Michael Page's grave in the Arnhem Oosterbeek Military Cemetery whenever I am there.

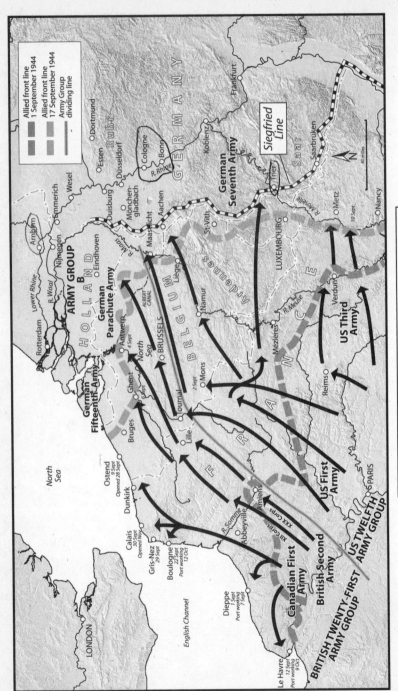

Map 1: Allied Advance to the Dutch Border
July to September 1944

CHAPTER 1

The Strategy of Exploitation

(The Allies: 25 August–17 September 1944)

Private Wally Parr broke the tension by bursting into song with all the Cockney gusto that he could muster. Perched on wooden benches bolted onto either side of the cylindrical fuselage, the platoon followed his lead, their voices battling against the creaking and whining made by the flimsy plywood glider and the throbbing engines of its bomber tug. Up front in the cramped cockpit, the pilots, Staff-Sergeants Jim Wallwork and John Ainsworth, concentrated on the red-hot glow of the Halifax's exhausts to maintain their position as they cut through the night sky. Their passengers – five sappers and 23 men from D Company, 2/Oxs and Bucks Light Infantry – were part of a *coup de main* force. They were supremely well prepared for every conceivable scenario, but some still believed that they were on a suicide mission. The men's singing helped mask their anxieties, and company commander Major John Howard, seated at the front of the aircraft opposite one of the exit doors, knew and respected it. He peered down the aircraft's dark interior at the ungainly shapes of his men, their blackened faces occasionally illuminated by the moonlight. Exchanging reassuring smiles with Den Brotheridge, he tried to forget that this young platoon commander had so recently found it necessary to hide from his pregnant wife the possibility that he would never see her again.

Wallwork spotted waves breaking on a beach and signalled to Howard who gave the order for silence. Seconds later, six miles from their objective, the tow-rope was released with a jerk and the glider dropped into a stomach-churning dive below the scattered clouds. When levelled out, Brotheridge released his safety belt, stood up and, stabilized by Howard, opened the exit door. Fresh air flooded into the stale compartment and the recognizable shapes of buildings, fields and hedges could be seen scudding past the void at 90 miles per hour just 200 feet below. Then Wallwork recognized the sparkling Caen Canal on his left and, reassured that he was on course, gave a thumbs-up to Howard. On the officer's command, the soldiers automatically prepared to land by linking their arms, interlinking their fingers, raising their knees and tensing up. The glider slammed hard into the ground throwing up a shower of sparks from its metal skids. The arrester parachute was briefly deployed and the contraption slowed a little before coming to a sudden bone-crunching halt against a small embankment. When the cockpit collapsed, both pilots were catapulted through the Perspex windscreen whilst still in their seats and their passengers were thrown violently around the fuselage. It was, nevertheless, a successful landing, with Wallwork managing to deliver the platoon just 85 yards from its goal, the bridge over the Caen Canal. It was 0016 hours on 6 June 1944, the Allies had arrived in Normandy and D-Day had begun.

The glider-borne assault on the bridges over the Caen Canal and River Orne and the subsequent operations conducted in Normandy by 6 British Airborne Division were a great success. By taking and holding the left flank of the Allied beachhead, a defensive flank was established which helped the invaders to establish themselves in France. Major-General Richard 'Windy' Gale's division then fought hard throughout the subsequent battle of Normandy, spending 12 weeks in the line, three times longer than the 82 and 101 US Airborne Divisions which were also inserted on D-Day. Gale's men returned to England having suffered 4,457 casualties. Among them was Den Brotheridge, killed by a German sentry whilst leading his men across the bridge over the Caen Canal within minutes of his glider landing. But even as the division was preparing to sail back home, a new phase in the campaign in north-west Europe was opening, with Allied ground forces striving to exploit their success in Normandy by striking eastwards. Drawing the attention of his troops to this, the chief of the Allied Land Forces and commander of Twenty-First Army Group, General Bernard Montgomery (or 'Monty' as he was popularly known) sent a personal message to his troops: 'The German armies in north-west France have suffered a decisive defeat . . . there are still many surprises in store for the fleeing remnants. The victory has been complete, definitive and decisive.'

By the last week in August, the Germans were disintegrating, having suffered losses of at least 450,000 men and 1,500 tanks and self-propelled guns in Normandy. The formations and units that survived were battered, their organization and morale severely damaged, and although continuing to fight rearguard actions, they were in no position to stem the Allied offensive. After Paris fell without a fight on 25 August, it soon became clear that fears of a problematic crossing of the River Seine were unfounded. After the claustrophobic and protracted battle for Normandy, the sense of relief for the Supreme Commander of the Allied Expeditionary Force, General Dwight 'Ike' Eisenhower, was palpable, and he urged his force on towards Germany. In northern France that force consisted of Montgomery's British Twenty-First Army Group advancing along the coast, with General Omar Bradley's US Twelfth Army Group on his right flank and Lieutenant General Jacob Dever's US Sixth Army Group – which had landed on the Mediterranean coast in mid-August – advancing up the

Rhone Valley from the south. Leading the charge for the German border for the British in late August was Lieutenant-General Sir Miles Dempsey's Second Army, with Lieutenant-General Sir Brian Horrocks's XXX Corps in the vanguard with XII Corps on its left. Horrocks was in an ebullient mood, racing across France; he later wrote: 'This was the type of warfare I thoroughly enjoyed. Who wouldn't? I had upwards of 600 tanks under my command and we were advancing on a frontage of fifty miles ... like a combine-harvester going through a field of corn.' It was a measure of the man that Horrocks, wanting to keep his finger on the pulse of the battle, commanded his corps from a modified tank close to the front line. The charismatic 49-year-old 'Jorrocks', as he was known, was extremely well liked, with Major-General Allan Adair, the commander of his Guards Armoured Division, attesting:

> Brian Horrocks was the best war-time commander I ever came across. He was a great leader and I found him much more impressive than Monty. When giving orders, he was very clear, and he was always right up with one and helping one along. He was full of grip and insisted on pushing us along as much as possible.

That notorious grip, however, was not always as tight as it might have been, for in June the previous year in North Africa, Horrocks had been badly wounded in the chest and leg by a strafing German fighter which had laid him up for over a year. Still weak and in some pain, it is doubtful that having been enticed from his convalescence by Monty to take command of XXX Corps in August, he was strong enough to weather the stresses and strains associated with the demanding position. Indeed, within weeks of taking up the post he succumbed to a recurring bout of illness which forced him to his bed as his corps crossed the Seine. In such circumstances it was as well that the enemy was in such disarray. One young officer wrote in his diary that Germans were 'surrendering *en masse*' and 'greeted our troops like long-lost family members'. Moreover, an Intelligence Summary issued on 26 August by Major-General Kenneth Strong, Ike's British head of intelligence, revealed:

> Two and a half months of bitter fighting, culminating for the Germans in a blood-bath big enough even for their extravagant tastes, have brought the end of the war in Europe within sight, almost within reach. The strength of the German armies in the West has been shattered, Paris belongs to France again, and the Allied armies are streaming towards the frontiers of the Reich.

For XXX Corps, this allowed Adair's Guards Division to strike out towards the Somme, with 38-year-old Major-General Pip Roberts' 11 Armoured Division on its left. There was little to hold them up, and even the terrain was friendly. Guardsman Jim Hetherington, of 2/(Armoured) Irish Guards, had been concerned that after the Seine the countryside:

> would be like Normandy all over again, small fields, heavy fighting and very little progress. [But] nothing could have been further from the truth! ... We were just tearing along ... ignoring what was happening on the flanks, and passed through, or by, town after town ....The few Germans who were about got out of our way ...

Horrocks noted much the same, reporting that 'German rearguard actions were swiftly brushed aside allowing huge columns of vehicles – lorried infantry, tanks, armoured cars – to rumble forward along roads lined with locals.' 'Club Route', as the Guards called their pathway, became a high-speed road. Indeed, 2nd Lieutenant Robert Boscawen, an Eton, Cambridge and Sandhurst-educated tank troop commander in the Coldstream Guards, wrote in his diary: 'We had enough maps to reach Moscow, but in two days we had run over them all.' The Guards Armoured Division was gaining a head of steam and was determined to use its momentum to throw Second Army forward, as Boscawen notes:

> Still we raced on, regardless of bogie-wheels and tracks. One of my tanks sheared off all the nuts on one side of the sprocket but I decided to keep it going . . . In front the Grenadiers had practically no opposition until the Somme, except shooting up an occasional convoy. The Recce Welsh . . . were well out in front shooting up Germans struggling vainly to escape.

The fact that the armoured Guardsmen were driving through the old battlefields across which their fathers and regiments had struggled a generation before was not lost on them. Captain James Osborne of the Irish Guards reflected: 'It took us two hours to cross the Western Front that had been fought over for four years in the 1914–1918 War.' It was not unusual, as the battalion War Diary notes, for the unit to advance 60 miles a day during the last week of August, and the Germans were shocked. Horrocks came across an incongruous sight on entering the city of Amiens on 31 August, later recalling:

> And from behind one of the lorries was led a scowling, unshaven and very ugly German officer dressed in a black uniform. I would have disliked him at sight, even if he had not looked like a senior SS commander (which he wasn't). Roberts was exactly like a proud farmer leading forward his champion bull. He told me that his prize exhibit was General Eberbach [Heinrich Eberbach, commander of Seventh Army] . . . whom the 11th Armoured had captured in his pyjamas during the night advance.

And still the advance continued, with the first day of September being particularly successful. As the War Diary of the 3/Irish Guards recorded: 'A long day of movement ... We travelled 70 miles and reached Arras as it was getting dark, to receive a great reception from the inhabitants.' The Coldstreamers, Robert Boscawen recorded, enjoyed the same welcome:

> As soon as we were well into the town ... every door and house was thrown open and out from every street alleyway the liberated people of Arras flooded and swarmed around the tanks ... They completely abandoned themselves, rejoicing, shouting and cheering. Old men and young girls dancing down the street climbed onto my tank kissing and embracing me, shouting 'Vive les Anglais' and 'No more Gestapo' ... The bells pealed and Arras was free.

The tumultuous advance continued into Belgium, with Montgomery, Dempsey and Horrocks all keen to ensure that the Germans were not given any opportunity to rest and reorganize themselves. XXX Corps now had some key objectives in its sights which included 11 Armoured Division capturing Antwerp. The senior officers of the Guards Armoured Division, meanwhile, were gathered together by Adair on 2 September for a briefing. Lieutenant-Colonel J.C. Windsor Lewis, commanding the Welsh Guards Group, recalls:

> It was pouring with rain as the Brigadiers and Commanding Officers, with their staffs, assembled in the General's tent to receive orders. Most of us expected to be told about maintenance and the general enemy situation; few could have guessed their sensational character.

General Adair's 'Intention' paragraph cut through the air like a swishing sword. 'Guards Armoured Division will advance and capture Brussels [still some 80 miles away] – and a very good intention, too,' added the General, wearing a mischievous smile. This was greeted with roars of laughter from the keyed-up and astounded officers.

The 2/Household Cavalry Regiment, the reconnaissance element of the Guards Armoured Division, led the way to the Belgian capital, supported by RAF fighter-bombers. They scythed through the patch-work enemy defences leaving dead Germans, burning vehicles and hordes of prisoners in their wake. By the evening of 3 September, they had penetrated into Brussels and as darkness fell were followed by the rest of the division. Windsor Lewis says of the breakthrough:

German machine guns, anti-tank guns and snipers barked at us. We barked back ... The opposition was soon overpowered, and the crowds emerged excitedly and over-ran the tanks ... The last time I had been in Brussels was in July 1940, as a fugitive escaping from the Germans. On that occasion I had entered the city from the east in a tram. Today I entered it from the west in a tank.

Captain Michael Bendix of 5/Coldstream Guards recalls arriving in Brussels at 2300 hours that night: 'I can remember being kissed endlessly by girls, but fell asleep as I was so worn out. On waking up, to our great joy, there were some public baths opposite and I hadn't had a bath for a month. The noise of the cheering crowds was deaf-ening.' That night the Irish Guards sat down to dine in the largest café in the main square. As they ate, news arrived that some Germans were still holding a house a short distance away. Lieutenant-Colonel J.O.E. (Joe) Vandeleur, commander of the Irish Guards Battle Group remem-bers:

Everybody was having much too good a time to be disturbed so a combined Officers' Mess party went off to deal with the matter, assisted by a Honey tank. We shot the place up and found some miserable little Huns in full marching order ... praying in slit-trenches. They were fixed up quickly and we returned to dinner. The night was uproarious and we could not get any work done on our tanks and vehicles.

With Brussels in British hands and Roberts' 11th Armoured Division taking Antwerp on 4 September, Horrocks was immensely proud of his corps' achievement. It had covered nearly 250 miles from the Seine in less than one week. The newspapers jubilantly reported the advance with *Daily Mail* correspondent Alexander Clifford writing: 'This mad chase is getting crazier by the hour ... You can't digest it in the least as you go along. It is so big and so swift that you almost feel it is out of control ... Our columns just press on and on and on ... The atmosphere is heady and intoxicating.' The American headline writers, meanwhile, were equally delighted with progress as Lieutenant-General George Patton's US Third Army made a swift advance towards the Saar. On 30 August, under the headline 'U.S. TANKS RACE ON', *New York Times* correspondent Drew Middleton declared:

Sweeping northward and eastward at a speed of better than twenty-five miles a day, the American offensive east of Paris has crossed the River Aisne at Soissons and the Marne near Chalons-sur-Marne, threatening on the one hand the main German forces northwest of Paris and on the other the security of the enemy's frontier, now less than a hundred miles from the armoured spearheads ...

The Allies were carried along on a wave of optimism, as illustrated by a diary entry of Winston Churchill's Private Secretary, John Colville:

'There is a feeling of elation, expectancy and almost bewilderment, and it may well be that the end is now very close.' The Combined Allied Intelligence Committee in London believed that the Germans were incapable of recovery and that 'organized resistance under the control of the German high command is unlikely to continue beyond December 1, 1944'. For planning purposes, the British War Cabinet used 31 December as the date for the end of the war in Europe, whilst in the United States a Gallup poll taken in the first week of September revealed that 67 per cent of Americans questioned expected the fighting to be over by Christmas. In Washington, meanwhile, General C. Marshall, Chief of the Army Staff, was already looking to redeploy certain American formations from the European theatre to the Pacific whilst cancelling some military contracts.

The foundation for this optimism was not difficult to explain when examining a map – particularly if one equated the taking of ground with success – but alarming cracks, caused by the rapid advance, were beginning to show in the Allied logistical infrastructure. The planners quite simply had not prepared for such a precipitous sweep across France and had relied on a bloody fight for every field and street to allow them to build up the stores of supplies required for a push into Germany. Indeed, logisticians at the Supreme Headquarters Allied Expeditionary Force (SHAEF) had assumed that the Western Allies would not reach the German border until D+360. Thus, although the two divisions in the vanguard of XXX Corps were in excellent positions to push their advantage home, they were stymied by the need to allow supplies to catch up. The decision to halt Adair's Guards Armoured Division in Brussels and Roberts' 11 Armoured Division in Antwerp was later deeply regretted by Horrocks, who wrote:

To my mind 4th September was the key date in the battle for the Rhine. Had we been able to advance that day we could have smashed through this screen and advanced northwards with little or nothing to stop us. We might have succeeded in bouncing a crossing over the Rhine ... I believe that if we had taken the chance and carried straight on with our advance instead of halting at Brussels the whole course of the war in Europe might have been changed.

For want of sufficient resources at the fighting front, operations were being undermined. The problem was that the Allies could not transport an adequate tonnage of the supplies that they were landing at Cherbourg the 450 miles by road to the fuel-hungry forward formations. In such circumstances, with the French railway system badly damaged by earlier Allied bombing raids and transport aircraft at a premium, Eisenhower was desperate for an adequate forward port. Although Dieppe had been captured on 1 September, it did not have the capacity that the Allies required, whilst other ports along the coast, including Le Havre, Boulogne, Calais and Ostend, were still in German hands. The seizure of the port of Antwerp intact by Roberts' division was, therefore, a great coup as it was one of Europe's largest cargo terminals. However, to make it operational the Germans needed to be cleared from the 54-mile estuary leading up to it, and then its mines cleared. The German troops deployed around this estuary were part of Lieutenant-General Gustav von Zangen's retreating Fifteenth Army. This formation, consisting of some 150,000 men, had left some of its strength to defend the Channel ports and the Antwerp estuary against the Canadian First Army's attack up the coast, while the remainder withdrew in an attempt to escape encirclement by the British Second Army. The failure of 11 Armoured Division to push on just another 15 miles after taking Antwerp, though, meant that the pocket was not closed and allowed a significant proportion of von Zangen's force to escape and turn the nearby Albert Canal into a strong defensive line. Horrocks later wrote self-critically of the failure to block the German escape route: 'I realise now that it was a serious mistake. My excuse was that my eyes were entirely fixed on the Rhine, and everything else seemed of subsidiary importance.'

Horrocks' eyes may have been fixed on the Rhine, but his feet were immobilized by the Allies' logistical difficulties. With not enough fuel finding its way through to Montgomery and Bradley for them to continue with their impressive advances, Eisenhower needed to determine how to develop his offensive. It was a decision influenced primarily by military factors but also, out of necessity, the politics of the Allied forces and Anglo-American rivalry in particular. British influence within the Western alliance had been waning ever since late 1943, by which time its Mediterranean strategy had failed to make a decisive impact on the Germans. The subsequent invasion of France had been launched from English shores and with full British support, but being dominated by American resources an American was installed as Supreme Commander. Recognizing this important departure, Winston Churchill later wrote: 'Up to July 1944 England had a considerable say in things; after that I was conscious that it was America who made the big decisions.' But Eisenhower was not an arrogant man and nor was he so insensitive to Britain's contribution to the war effort that he dismissed the nation from his complex strategic calculations. Ike was also a patient man, but none tested that patience more than Bernard Montgomery. Monty personified a perceived British arrogance towards the Americans and seemed unwilling to accept the strategic consequences of his country's diminishing military importance.

Monty, the victor of El Alamein, was the most haughty of British generals, but he was also developing into the nation's greatest military hero since Wellington. Eric Larrabee has written that the shrew-like officer had become something of a military deity by the autumn of 1944:

He walked in the company of the great captains, his every step a vindication of their living presence. Crowds followed him, yearned to touch his sleeve. He had become a rule unto himself and could do no wrong. He wore non-regulation uniform of sweater and beret even in the presence of the monarch, who smiled.

The man believed that he was irreplaceable and was therefore untouchable – a view reinforced by the sycophantic support of key military colleagues in London. It nurtured an unseemly cockiness and self-confidence which made Montgomery as unpopular with the British as he was with the Americans that he so overtly derided. As Robin Neillands has written: 'Montgomery was detested because, in many ways, he was indeed detestable. He was vain, dictatorial, obsessive, a sore trial to his peers and superiors and not above tinkering with the truth.'

One senior British officer who disliked Monty and thought him unworthy of the attention that he was attracting was Eisenhower's deputy, Air Chief Marshal Sir Arthur Tedder. He told the equally difficult George Patton, who had himself clashed with Monty during the invasion of Sicily, that the contrary British general was 'a little fellow of average ability who has had such a build-up that he thinks of himself as Napoleon'. Field Marshal Sir Alan Brooke, the Chief of the Imperial General Staff and Britain's top soldier, was a supporter but, aware of Monty's lack of political tact, deplored some of his subordinate's behaviour. Brooke was even moved to write to his unruly charge when Monty was antagonizing all and sundry in the Mediterranean that he should recognize 'the importance of your relations with allies and other Services, it is so easy to create impressions through which you may be misjudged and completely misappreciated'. But the general continued to speak his mind, continued to upset colleagues and did not stop doing so when the war moved to northern Europe. Writing to the Secretary of State for War, Sir James Grigg, Montgomery opined: 'The real trouble with the Yanks is that they are completely ignorant of the rules of the game we are playing with the Germans. You play so much better when you know the rules.'

Montgomery's belligerent stance had nothing to do with an unprofessional strain of patriotism or a petty one-upmanship, but an uncompromising belief that he had all the solutions to the various problems of the campaign. As this immense self-confidence was combined with a distinctly anarchic streak in his personality, Monty could be argumentative and had no compunction in taking on all comers. He was, consequently, a nagging headache for Eisenhower, whose protective British chauffeur and confidant, Kay Summersby, later wrote: 'I grew to dislike the very name Montgomery. In my personal opinion, he gave the Supreme Commander more worry than any other one individual in the entire Allied Command . . .' But Eisenhower appreciated Monty's talents, and whilst his boss in the Mediterranean during 1943 wrote:

> General Montgomery is a very able, dynamic type of army commander . . . He loves the limelight; but in seeking it, it is possible that he does so only because of the effect upon his own soldiers, who are certainly devoted to him. I have great confidence in him as a combat commander. He is intelligent, a good talker, and has a flare for showmanship. Like all other senior British officers, he has been most loyal – personally and officially – and has shown no disposition whatsoever to overstep the bounds imposed by Allied unity of command.

Ike certainly gave Montgomery a remarkable degree of autonomy whilst the latter was acting as Land Forces Commander during the first phase of the campaign in Normandy. During this period of 'the break-in battle' the British general was relatively placid because he was in control, but as soon as the battle of Normandy was won and Eisenhower's planned assumption of the land role became imminent, the piqued Monty became disruptive. Montgomery, desperate to remain Land Forces Commander, believing that he was the best man for the job, argued that Ike had too many competing priorities to devote the necessary time to the role. He was not overstating the case, for at SHAEF Eisenhower had to handle all aspects of war-fighting in Western Europe, including the civil administration of the liberated nations, and was an important link between the theatre and political and military superiors in Washington and London. But what Montgomery failed to see was that the American people would not countenance their massive military force in Europe being commanded by a Brit. As Major-General Francis ('Freddie') de Guingand, Montgomery's Chief of Staff, later wrote of his boss:

> He was, I think, apt to give insufficient weight to the dictates of prestige and national feelings, or to the increased contribution of America, in both men and arms . . . it was obvious, however, to most of us that it would have been an impossible situation for a British General and a British Headquarters to retain command of these more numerous American formations indefinitely.

Eisenhower subsequently explained the situation in his official report on the campaign after the war:

> [T]he size of our forces and the extent of our front made it necessary for me to take direct control of the land forces operating on the Continent . . . [A] change in the command set-up was necessary . . . due to the diverging lines of operation and the need for having a commander on each of the main fronts capable of handling, with a reasonable degree of independence, the day-to-day operations in each sector. These operations were to be guided by directives issued from my Headquarters.

Monty was replaced as Land Forces Commander by Eisenhower on 1 September, but was tactfully elevated to the rank of Field Marshal that same day. Churchill believed that promotion, Brooke noted in his diary, 'would mark the approval of the British people for the *British* effort that had led to the defeat of the Germans in France through the medium of Montgomery's leadership'. Nevertheless, Monty's obvious pleasure at his new appellation was severely undermined by his frustration at having lost his influential role. Even so, he was determined to remain vocal about the development of strategy, and remained critical of Ike's ability to be an effective land commander. Over and above the Supreme Commander's distractingly broad portfolio, Montgomery was particularly disapproving of the location of Ike's headquarters. The main body of SHAEF remained in London, but a forward headquarters had recently been established at Granville, a safe seaside-resort town north of Mont-St-Michel at the southern end of the Cotentin Peninsula in Normandy. Being so far behind the front line it afforded the Supreme Commander a broad view over the front, was within easy reach of southern England and was situated amongst the forward elements of both the Allied naval and air forces, but it was hardly ideal. With the battle moving further east with every passing day, Eisenhower needed first-class communications in order to follow the latest operational developments; yet Granville had no liaison officers, telephone links or radiophone capability with its subordinate commands, and thus Ike was forced to communicate by telegraph or letter. It was a situation that infuriated Montgomery who felt that the headquarters could not exercise proper command and control of operations, and he later wrote: 'This was possibly a suitable place for a Supreme Commander; but it was useless for a Land Forces Commander who had to keep his finger on the pulse of his armies and give quick decisions in rapidly changing situations.' The forward headquarters was little more than a public relations façade which fulfilled the home front's expectation, and Eisenhower's desire, for a high-level presence on the Continent.

The location of Eisenhower's headquarters, however, was a mere bagatelle when compared with what Monty perceived to be Ike's lack of the experience and skill to develop the ground war successfully. This, Monty argued, was because Eisenhower had not enjoyed the fighting command experience that he himself had, and it had left the American 'deficient'. It was a situation that so irked the British commander that he wrote to Alan Brooke in August 1944: '[Eisenhower's] ignorance as to how to run a war is absolute and complete; he has all the popular cries, but nothing else. He is such a decent chap that it is difficult to be angry with him for long.' Brooke sympathized, lamenting in his diary that Eisenhower's taking command of the ground forces was likely 'to add another 3 to 6 months on to the war!' He also failed to understand why the long-suffering Eisenhower did not put his subordinate firmly in his place. Montgomery was a thoroughly disruptive influence who had made a habit of pushing the Supreme Commander's patience to its limits. It was a situation that reached a head during the first weeks of September when the new Field Marshal made it clear that he did not support Ike's 'broad-front' strategy. This broad-front approach sought to advance the Allied forces eastwards with the main thrust north and south of the Ardennes towards the crucial industrial Ruhr region. In practical terms this meant the army groups advancing together in a coordinated fashion, with no one formation outrunning its logistics or its fellow formations. A slow but sure way of advancing. However, with Patton's rapid progress towards the Saar catching the eye, Montgomery believed that the Ruhr thrust was being demoted, and later complained: 'we had no fundamental plan which treated the theatre as an entity. Our strategy was now to become "unstitched".' Instead he advocated a 'narrow front' of concentrated Anglo-American forces which, he believed, would be far more efficacious.

Writing to Ike on 22 August, Monty opined: 'The quickest way to win this war is for the great mass of the Allied Armies to advance northwards' and, moreover, 'single control and direction of the land operations is vital for success. This is a WHOLE TIME job for one man.' Whilst advocating the narrow front as a more efficient and effective strategy for the Allied forces, there is little doubt that Montgomery also saw it as a way for Britain to punch above her weight. Stephen Hart has written that this strategy:

> sought a high military profile for Britain's limited – and diminishing – forces within a larger Allied effort that eventually would defeat the enemy without incurring a bloodbath of the last of Britain's fit young men. If the British army defeated the enemy in such a manner, this would ensure Britain a prominent British influence on the emerging postwar political structure of Europe.

The narrow front would do the pugnacious commander's ego, profile and desire for influence over strategy no harm either.

Montgomery's justification for an 'advance northwards' was based in his assessment that to the south neither Bradley's US Twelfth Army Group nor Dever's US Sixth Army Group offered as fertile prospects for a strategically influential offensive as that of his own command. Twenty-First Army Group, he was convinced, could smash through the West Wall (known to the Allies as the Siegfried Line), which ran for nearly 400 miles from Holland and along the western German border to Switzerland. Originally constructed in the 1930s and consisting of an outdated series of bunkers, trenches, strong-points and anti-tank defences in need of repair, it could nevertheless prove a considerable obstacle to the Allied advance if well-manned. As a consequence, Montgomery's desire was for Eisenhower to facilitate an Anglo-American force under his command 'which would be so strong that it need fear nothing' to smash the German defences. This mass of 40 divisions, its right flank protected by an element of the US Twelfth Army Group, would thrust north-east through Holland, directed on Aachen and Cologne 'to secure bridgeheads over the Rhine before winter began and to seize the Ruhr quickly'. With such major objectives secured, Montgomery would then look to exploit across the north German plains to Berlin and end the war in Europe. It was a strategy that General Günther Blumentritt, the Chief of Staff to Field Marshal Gerd von Rundstedt, the sometime German Commander-in-Chief West (OB West), believed sound, later reasoning that:

> The best course of the Allies [was] to concentrate a really strong force with which to break through past Aachen to the Ruhr area. Strategically and politically, Berlin was the target. Germany's strength is in the north. He who holds northern Germany holds Germany . . . There were no German forces behind the Rhine, and at the end of August our front was wide open.

On 23 August Monty met up with Eisenhower to articulate his case:

> I said that if he adopted a broad front strategy, with the whole line advancing and everyone fighting all the time, the advance would inevitably peter out, the Germans would be given time to recover and the war would go on all through the winter and well into 1945. I also said that he, as Supreme Commander, must sit on a very lofty perch in order to be able to take a detached view of the whole intricate problem . . . Someone must run the land battle for him.

The entire scheme was rejected for many reasons, not least the risk inherent in placing so many resources in a single attack, but also because of the potentially explosive political consequences of a Montgomery-led advance to glory. But in an attempt to assuage the obvious inference that he was trying to place his own interests ahead of strategic primacy, Montgomery offered to serve under Bradley's command. Eisenhower was still unimpressed, but he did make some concessions to the British call for more resources, and by 29 August Lieutenant-General

Courtney Hodges' US First Army – whilst remaining under Bradley's command – was sent into Belgium to temporarily assist Twenty-First Army Group. Moreover, the newly formed First Allied Airborne Army (FAAA) was placed at Montgomery's disposal, and he was encouraged to develop a plan to utilize this powerful and flexible force to support his offensive. It was a victory of sorts, and Monty believed that the allowances Ike had made showed that there was still a hope that his boss might be made to see the innumerable errors in his flawed strategic thinking.

Unmoved by the optimism that was washing over Eisenhower's command during the last week of August, the pragmatic Montgomery instead pointed to the various challenges that still had to be faced: the logistic difficulties, the attainment of a Rhine crossing, the breaching of the West Wall and the problems which would be caused by the onset of winter. Monty did not expect the enemy to fold just as the Allies were approaching Germany and interpreted the recent Allied territorial gains as evidence that the Germans were preparing to defend their border in numbers and with tenacity. He was far from alone in this view, with Colonel Oscar W. Koch, Patton's astute intelligence officer, writing: 'It is clear that the fixed determination of the Nazis is to wage a last-ditch struggle in the field at all costs . . . the German armies will continue to fight until destroyed or captured.' Churchill agreed, and wrote in a minute: 'It is at least as likely that Hitler will be fighting on the 1st January [1945] as that he will collapse before then. If he does collapse before then, the reasons will be political rather than purely military.'

With the strength of the German defence noticeably increasing against them and a lack of supplies forcing Dempsey to halt in northern Belgium and Patton at Verdun, Eisenhower's advance had reached a tipping-point. Yet out of touch with developments at the front, and laid up with a painful knee injury, the new American Land Commander was not in a strong position to influence matters; and so his subordinates took events into their own hands. At a meeting attended by

Montgomery, Bradley, Hodges and Dempsey on 3 September, the Americans made their desires abundantly clear. Here the US Twelfth Army Group Commander eschewed any further vacillation and said that he wanted to limit the US First Army support that he was providing to Montgomery to just two corps and intended to push Patton across the Rhine to Frankfurt just as soon as the logistics allowed. Bradley, whom Ike called, 'the best-rounded combat leader I have yet met in our service', was clearly using Ike's incapacity to strike a blow for the prospects of his southern offensive. He later justified his thinking by writing: ·

[The] principal advantage of the American plan with its primary thrust toward Frankfurt lay in the directness of its route to the enemy's homeland across the undefended front that stretched beyond Third Army. A main effort there would not only carry us past the fortifications of Metz and through the Maginot Line, but it might even penetrate the unmanned defenses of the Siegfried Line. And if in the event it went all the way to the Rhine, it would deprive the enemy of his important Saar basin.

So confident was Bradley that the attack would succeed, that his aide de camp, Major Chester Hansen, noted that his boss sought 'to be on the Rhine on 10 September'. The meeting was clearly another setback for Twenty-First Army Group but, resolved to promote his Second Army offensive, Monty signalled Freddie de Guingand that Dempsey was to advance from the line 'Brussels–Antwerp on 6 Sep directed on Wesel [the end of the West Wall] and Arnhem and passing round the North side of the Ruhr'. It was a route that the planners had rejected in the past due to its difficult terrain, which included numerous water obstacles, but with FAAA available to him to help overcome such challenges, the Field Marshal was able to add: 'Require airborne operation – Operation Comet – of one British Division and Poles on evening 6 Sep or morning 7 Sep to secure bridges over Rhine between Wesel and Arnhem.'

The two corps FAAA was formally established on 8 August. Eisenhower, General Henry 'Hap' Arnold, the commander of the US Air Force, and General George Marshall, were all keen to see what the new army could achieve before the war was over. Operation Comet was the fifteenth airborne operation that had been considered to assist the Allied advance since 6 June, but none had taken place largely due to the ground units having swept forward so fast that the intended objectives had already been taken. But now Comet was being prepared in order to throw the British Second Army across the Rhine, with 1 British Airborne Division and the 1 Independent Polish Parachute Brigade being inserted behind enemy lines in Holland to seize the bridges that Dempsey's force would need to cross. The problem was, however, that the transport aircraft used to relay the parachute and glider forces were also such valuable supply carriers that the RAF could not afford to take risks with them. Thus, as soon as air force commanders learned that their aircraft would have to over-fly German anti-aircraft guns in the Ruhr area after delivering the airborne troops, they protested. The result was that the entire direction of the operation was altered, and a new Rhine-crossing location was chosen which put the transporters out of the reach of the Ruhr's anti-aircraft: Arnhem. The choice of this quiet Dutch town on the Lower Rhine necessitated a Second Army advance along a single highway via Eindhoven, Grave and Nijmegen. It was a bold concept, particularly considering the narrow attacking frontage of the ground troops and the relatively few lightly armed airborne troops involved, but an early launch date of 7 September was chosen in order to exploit continued German disarray.

As the planning for Operation Comet progressed, Montgomery continued to badger Eisenhower for the resource priority he needed to develop his northern offensive. Consequently, on 4 September he telegraphed the Supreme Commander:

1. I consider we have now reached a stage where only one really powerful and full-blooded thrust towards Berlin is likely to get there and thus end the German war.
2. We have not enough maintenance resources for two full-blooded thrusts.
3. The selected thrust must have all the maintenance resources it needs without qualification and any other operation must do the best it can with what is left over.
4. There are only two possible thrusts, one via the Ruhr and the other via Metz and the Saar.
5. In my opinion, the thrust likely to give the best and quickest results is the northern one via the Ruhr.
6. Time is vital and the decision regarding the selected thrust must be made at once . . .
7. If we attempt a compromise solution and split our maintenance resources so that neither thrust is full-blooded we will prolong the war.
8. I consider the problem viewed as above is very simple and clear-cut.
9. The matter is of such vital importance that I feel sure you will agree that a decision on the above lines is required at once. If you are coming this way perhaps you would look in and discuss it . . . Do not feel I can leave this battle just at present.

When Eisenhower received the message on the evening of 5 September, he was exasperated: didn't the man know when to stop struggling? Was Montgomery so naïve as to believe that a 'full-blooded thrust towards Berlin' was politically viable? It did not help that Monty's signal had crossed with a new directive sent by Ike to his commanders to reiterate and clarify his position. In it the Supreme Commander emphasized his desire to stretch the Germans and provide two alternative routes into Germany by striking at both the

Ruhr *and* the Saar. Although he said that the Saar operation 'should be started as soon as possible to forestall the enemy in this sector', he also emphasized that the element of US Twelfth Army Group 'operating north-west of the Ardennes against the Ruhr must first be adequately supported'. Although this was not so very different from what had been decided in Ike's absence at the 3 September meeting, there was one important difference: whilst SHAEF perceived the two thrusts as a coordinated Allied effort, both Montgomery and Bradley recognized that they were becoming increasingly disassociated with US Twelfth Army Group paying little more than lip-service to the priority that the Supreme Commander attached to the British Ruhr thrust. As a result, Montgomery hoped that Eisenhower would reinforce the northern advance in a reply to his latest signal.

As the battle over strategy moved into a new phase, so did the fighting, and on 6 September British Second Army resumed its attack towards the Dutch border. Within a few short hours it became clear that the German defences had been strengthened over the previous few days and with Operation Comet just a few hours from being launched ahead of XXX Corps, there was a new fear that the ground forces would not be able to link up with the airborne forces quickly enough. Thus, with Montgomery still awaiting clarification from Ike that this Ruhr thrust was to receive the priority that he desired, Comet was cancelled. Horrocks' force struggled on, nevertheless, hoping that by maintaining pressure on the enemy, cracks would appear in the defences. In fighting of an intensity that was more reminiscent of the confrontations in Normandy than the heady days of late August, 11 Armoured Division stalled on the Albert Canal whilst the Guards Armoured Division, although having crossed the water obstacle by 9 September, could only manage to push on a few miles to the village of Helchteren. Reviewing the situation with officers at his forward headquarters, Major Peter Merchant, a Twenty-First Army Group Staff Officer, recalls that Monty again grumbled that Ike's 'mismanagement of the campaign had again made the task of his men more difficult and dangerous than it needed to be'. His mood did not improve when Eisenhower's reply to his call for a drive on the German capital eventually arrived. Trying once again to make his position clear, Ike wrote:

While agreeing with your conception of a powerful and full-blooded thrust towards Berlin I do not agree that it should be initiated at this moment to the exclusion of all other manoeuvres ... The bulk of the German Army that was in the West has now been destroyed. Must immediately exploit our success by promptly breaching the Siegfried Line, crossing the Rhine on a wide front, and seizing the Saar and the Ruhr. This I intend to do with all possible speed. This will give a stranglehold on two of Germany's main industrial areas and largely destroy her capacity to wage war, whatever course events may take ... No reallocation of our present resources would be adequate to sustain a thrust to Berlin.

However, in his final paragraph, the Supreme Commander once again gave hope to Montgomery by stating:

I have always given and still give priority to the Ruhr [Repeat] Ruhr, and the northern route of advance ... Locomotives and rolling stock are today being allocated on the basis of this priority to maintain the momentum of the advance of your forces, and those of Bradley north-west of the Ardennes. Please let me know at once your further maintenance requirements for the advance.

Bent on finding out what exactly the 'priority' that the signal referred to would mean in practice, the irascible Field Marshal wrote to Brooke on 9 September: '[Eisenhower] keeps saying that he has ordered that the northern thrust to the Ruhr is to have priority; but he had NOT ordered this.' Nevertheless, Montgomery began formulating a new attack to give his supposedly 'higher-ranking' advance a deft shove through Holland and across the Rhine. It was an offensive that he wanted to carry out before the enemy had further reorganized and because he had received word that two V2 rockets, launched from the Dutch coast, had recently landed in England. As Montgomery later wrote: 'So far as I was concerned that settled the direction of the thrust line of my operations to secure crossings over the Meuse [Maas] and Rhine: it must be towards Arnhem.' By pushing the Second Army from Eindhoven to Arnhem and following it up with a short jab to the Ijsselmeer in northern Holland, the British could potentially accomplish a great deal: cut off all German forces in the west of the country; capture the V2 sites; assist in the clearance of the Antwerp estuary and overrun Rotterdam. Grabbing a Rhine crossing would also provide a perfect launch-pad for a further attack to outflank the West Wall and continue on to the Ruhr.

Montgomery's new offensive plan – Operation Market Garden – included a greatly enlarged airborne operation based on Comet. It was a plan at the forefront of his mind when he met Ike aboard an aeroplane on a Brussels airfield at noon on 10 September to talk about strategy, logistics and the next steps towards the Reich. It was the first meeting between the two men since the Supreme Commander had taken control of the Land Forces and Monty immediately lost his self-control, and poured out days of frustration in a loud and aggressive tirade against his superior's lack of grip and the consequences of his flawed strategy. Clutching a batch of directives that he had recently received from SHAEF and adopting an aggressive posture, the Field Marshal screeched: 'They're balls, sheer balls, rubbish!' The American general, in considerable pain from his injury, was in no mood for such histrionics, but he kept his cool and listened stoically before suddenly putting his hand on Monty's knee and saying, 'Steady Monty, you can't speak to me like that. I'm your boss.' It was a withering interjection which elicited an immediate apology from Montgomery, who quickly regained his equilibrium and assumed a more professional stance. The result was a fruitful discussion about the northern advance on the Ruhr during which the British commander outlined his plan for Operation Market Garden. Eisenhower was interested: SHAEF wanted to take a Rhine crossing before winter and the plan would not only ameliorate some of Monty's concerns about the Ruhr thrust but also provide a chance for FAAA to show what it could do. However, whilst revealing his support for the operation, Ike also made it clear that the offensive would only be part of a limited attack to cross the Rhine, and he would not stop Patton to facilitate it. This, the Supreme Commander emphasized, was in line with his recent communiqué to Montgomery. When the meeting broke up, the Field Marshal felt that he had won an important victory, but he still needed more detailed information about the resources that he could expect from Ike. Even so by the evening of the 10th, Lieutenant-General Frederick 'Boy' Browning, the deputy commander of the FAAA and commander of I British Airborne Corps, started the detailed planning of the airborne element of the plan – Operation Market – back in England, whilst Miles Dempsey began his preparations for the ground element – Operation Garden – in Belgium.

As critical decisions were being made by the high command on 10 September about the next phase of the push to the Rhine, the Guards Armoured Division pushed on past Helchteren in an attempt to gain a bridgehead over the Meuse–Escaut Canal. Leading the way was Joe Vandeleur's Irish Guards Battle Group, which was tasked with seizing the de Groot bridge near Neerpelt on the road to Eindhoven. It was critical that the crossing was taken quickly so that the Germans were not given the opportunity to destroy it, hold up the British attack and reinforce their defences there. However, advancing well ahead of the rest of the division and its supporting guns, Vandeleur recognized that tactical success on this occasion would depend on the speed and guile of his troops rather than firepower. Following the Household Cavalry, which was scouting ahead of the main group, the Guards sped up a road not marked on their maps to the village of Overpelt just short of the objective. The Irish Guards history reveals that their arrival was unexpected, for 'the leading troops ran straight into a large black Mercedes staff car, going hell-for-leather. They shot the car and its contents, a smartly dressed officer, to bits, with the added pleasure of knowing that they were evidently not expected from this direction.'

Observing the bridge from the top of a slag-heap, Vandeleur was pleased to see that the stucture was still intact, but was concerned that it was defended by a clutch of fearsome 88mm guns which were capable of destroying an armoured attack. With his options limited, Vandeleur turned to the hapless commander of the leading squadron and said confidently and with a smile: 'Obviously boldness is the thing. We will rush the bridge.' Shortly afterwards, a troop of three Sherman tanks, commanded by Lieutenant Duncan Lampard, and a platoon of infantry, led by Lieutenant John Stanley-Clarke, pushed up to a crossroads just short of the canal covered by the machine guns and high explosive shells of the remainder of the squadron. A tractor caught out in the open and towing one of the 88mm guns towards the bridge was hit and exploded into flames just as the infantry moved into position. Then, having completed their preparations, the platoon fired a red Very light, the supporting fire stopped and Lampard's troop drove for the bridge, closely followed by Stanley-Clarke's men. The leading tank was commanded by Sergeant Steer and driven by Corporal Claude Kettleborough who recalls:

When the order came from Sgt Steer to lead on we emerged from the side road, and there it was – the bridge. A small lorry [actually the tractor which had been set on fire] was blazing half way up the slope to the bridge, alongside an 88 millimetre ... I never got into top gear; speed wasn't an advantage as the anti-tank weapons were straight ahead of us ... We stopped at the [north] end of the bridge and all was quiet; we didn't see the enemy at all. I think they were disorganised and frightened – they had done a nip.

The infantry, however, did stumble across a few stunned German soldiers as they mopped up. These surrendered immediately and one shouted with noticeable relief, 'Well done, well done!' As the prisoners were rounded up, sappers climbed over the bridge cutting cables and removing the detonators from charges attached to its wooden frame-work. The crossing had been fully prepared for demolition and it was later learned that the NCO tasked with carrying out the bridge's final destruction had run away as soon as he had witnessed the arrival of enemy troops at Overpelt. This dereliction of duty had important consequences, for after the bridge had been made safe, the remainder of the tank squadron and infantry company crossed to the north side of the canal, expanded the bridgehead and quickly established their defences. The attack had been a great success, and an ecstatic Vandeleur toured the Irish Guards' newly won position to congratulate his men and oversee the organization of its defences. From that moment on the crossing became known as 'Joe's Bridge', and numerous German coun-terattacks to retake it over the next few days were valiantly thwarted.

Having seized the bridge over the Meuse–Escaut Canal, the Guards Armoured Division instinctively wished to exploit its success, but was not in a strong position to do so. Dogged by chronic supply problems that were undermining the fighting elements of the entire Second Army, Adair's men needed time to build up their stores of supplies for their next move forward. That move, Monty hoped, would be in Operation Market Garden, but on 11 September he signalled Ike that, lacking supplies, 'the large-scale operations by Second Army and the Airborne Corps northwards towards the Meuse and Rhine cannot now take place before 23 Sep. at the earliest and possibly 26 Sep.' Warming to a favourite theme of the Allies failing to exploit advantageous situations, he continued, '[t]his delay will give the enemy time to organise better defensive arrangements and we must expect heavier resistance and slower progress ...' On receipt of the message, Eisenhower, still in discomfort from his swollen knee and feeling the need to reach a compromise with the British commander, noted in his diary: 'After discussing ways and means of supporting left flank, sent Beetle [his Chief of Staff, Major-General Walter Bedell Smith] off to see Monty to find out just what we had to do. Monty's suggestion is simply – give him everything. This is crazy ...' It seems the meeting with the sharp Bedell Smith reassured Montgomery, for on the evening of 12 September he wrote to Brooke:

> The Saar thrust is to be stopped. Three American divisions are to be grounded and transport used to give extra maintenance to 21 Army Group. The whole of the maintenance of 12 Army Group is to be given to First US Army on my right and that army is to cooperate closely with me and I am to be allowed to deal directly with Hodges ... As a result of these changed conditions I have now fixed D day for [Operation Market Garden] for next Sunday 17 Sept. So we have gained a great victory. I feel exhausted by it all but hope we shall now win the war reasonably quickly.

Monty was feeling relieved, but on the following day he received a signal from Ike which indicated that he had misinterpreted Bedell Smith's offer. In it, the Supreme Commander reiterated the highly temporary nature of the priority that had been proposed by saying:

> Naturally, these measures are emergency ones and must be temporary, but I am willing to give effect to them for a limited time to enable you to cross the Rhine and capture the approaches

to Antwerp ... I understand this arrangement will meet your minimum requirements. The arrangement can continue until about the first of October; by then it is anticipated you will have reached your initial major objective.

If any further underlining of Ike's intentions was required it came in the form of news on 14 September that SHAEF had agreed to Patton continuing his attack towards the Saar. Being pulled in two directions by the British and American commanders who both argued convincingly for extra support for their offensives, Eisenhower had decided to try to please both by using his broad-front strategy which, in Monty's eyes, revealed all the indecisiveness, inexperience and muddled thinking that was so deleterious to the Western allies' advance. Even so, the news did not dissuade him from continuing with his own plan, and that same day he directed that Operation Market Garden should be a 'rapid and violent' thrust: XXX Corps was to attack out of the Neerpelt bridgehead and advance up a single road through Holland, where 35,000 airborne troops were to be inserted to assist its passage to the Lower Rhine at Arnhem.

Although conceived at a time of strategic wrangling, Allied friction and personality clashes, Operation Market Garden was a concept that suited both Montgomery and Eisenhower – although for different reasons. Whilst Eisenhower wanted a Rhine crossing to help keep his broad attacking options across the front wide open, Montgomery's intention was to use the bridge as a springboard for a powerful narrow-fronted offensive on the Ruhr and beyond. The Arnhem plan was not, therefore, conceived in a strategic vacuum: it was generated in response to a developing campaign that had reached a watershed. The question was, had the Western allies already missed their great opportunity to capitalize on German post-Normandy disorganization? Operation Market Garden would find out.

CHAPTER 2

Withdrawal

(The Germans: 25 August–17 September 1944)

At the door of the wrecked wooden chalet the obsequious Field Marshal Wilhelm Keitel embraced a small, smouldering, stumbling figure and sobbed: 'My Führer, you are alive, you are alive'. Twenty-four people were in the room when the bomb exploded. Adolf Hitler was bent over a heavy oak table, leaning on his elbow, his head in his hand, studying positions on a map, when there was a flash of blue and yellow flame and an ear-splitting blast. Two pounds of high explosive had detonated just six feet away from him. Windows and doors were blown out in an instant, shards of glass and splinters of wood sliced through the air, whilst papers whirled in all directions. There was a silence, soon broken by whimpering pleas for help, gasps of pain and mumbled moaning. As clouds of smoke billowed from the devastation, those deafened and blinded by the explosion staggered through the burning room and, choking on the dust, tried to find the exit. Hitler and Keitel were the only two men to have avoided concussion and serious injury. Although plaster covered his torn uniform and blood trickled out of his ears and down his legs, the Führer was still able to walk when supported. Leaving the scene to the medics and security personnel, Hitler was escorted by his bodyguard Otto Günsche slowly to his bunker, where he was attended by his personal physician, Dr Theo Morell. His injuries were minor: cuts to his forehead, burst eardrums, a painfully swollen right arm, lacerations to his left arm and burns to his hands and legs that had been scorched and peppered by wood splinters. 'You have been spared,' said Morell, whilst cleaning the Führer's blood-smeared brow, 'a lucky escape.' Hitler's face remained fixed in a look somewhere between rage and excitement, with his fists clenched tightly shut. Moments later Heinze Linge, Hitler's valet, hurried into the room. The Führer raised his head slowly, and fixing the panting figure with a stare said coldly: 'Linge, someone has tried to kill me.'

The bomb at Hitler's Wolfsschanze (Wolf's lair) headquarters in East Prussia on 20 July 1944 came closer to success than any of the other numerous attempts on his life. Carried out by Colonel Claus Schenk von Stauffenberg, the life of the 55-year-old dictator had very nearly been snuffed out. The stress and strains caused by a war that was turning increasingly against him were etched all over Hitler's colourless, wizened face. He was in poor physical condition, with a trembling left arm and leg that sometimes refused to work, which led to the Führer dragging his foot when walking. He complained of stomach cramps, headaches and various other ailments. Specialists who had not examined the hypochondriacal Hitler began to talk in hushed tones about the possibility of Parkinson's Disease and syphilis. Others, however, merely pointed to the lifestyle of a man who pushed himself too hard, refused to delegate and would not relax. In reality Hitler found it impossible to relax, and even when alone endlessly turned over in his mind the people, places and issues that dominated his life. To help him sleep, and to address the maladies that apparently afflicted him, he took an ever-growing number of drugs, supplied and prepared by the man upon whom he depended and whom he therefore despised: Theo Morell. Seen by other doctors as an uncouth and inarticulate quack, Morell was very probably, if inadvertently, poisoning his patient.

Hitler's feeble health reflected Germany's ailing strategic situation. Ever since the failure to knock the Soviet Union out of the war in 1941, Germany had been ground down in a war of attrition for which it had not prepared and which it could not win. By the summer of 1944 the Reich was under intense and growing pressure. In the east the Red Army had surged forward in a series of massive offensives which put Joseph Stalin close to Warsaw, deep into East Prussia, and on the verge of a campaign for east central Europe. At sea, meanwhile, the U-boat fleet had failed to recover from its losses in the second half of 1943, and Allied convoys were crossing the Atlantic with near impunity. In such circumstances, Hitler recognized that a cross-Channel invasion was likely in 1944 and believed that its defeat would change Germany's fortunes. Richard Overy has written of this conviction: 'He sought a psychological shock from which British and American opinion would not recover. Victory would free German forces for a renewed offensive on the eastern front.' The battle of Normandy that summer was in fact a turning-point of the war, but not to the advantage of the Third Reich: the confrontation revealed the devastating effect of the Anglo-Americans' quantitative superiority which led to the German armed forces haemorrhaging men and *matériel* whilst making the much-dreaded two-fronted war.

There was little good news with which to console the German population during mid-1944. The picture of the war that could be collated from snippets of information was bleak. Their own lives told them as much, as they became gripped by total war as never before. The touchstone of this was the impact of the Anglo-American strategic bombing across the Reich. What was to become an awesomely powerful Allied weapon had humble beginnings when the British sought an offensive outlet in the wake of the Dunkirk evacuation in 1940. Yet the bombing developed rapidly, and particularly so after the United States entered the war in late 1941. Within two and a half years German towns and cities – including Berlin – were subjected to raids which sought to undermine production and morale by dehousing the population as well as destroying the nation's infrastructure. The impact of the bombing was witnessed by Gefreiter Hans Jungbauer of 188 Infantry Division during three of the five days that he was home on leave in Munich during July 1944. After being taken prisoner by the Allies later that summer, he was questioned about the raids and his interrogators noted that:

> when he arrived the whole town seemed to be one mass of flames, and the conflagration increased during the following attacks . . . He states that the fires were never extinguished during his stay in Munich, and when he left the town, two days after the final raid, the fires were still burning.

Having picked their way through the debris and with the flames licking at their heels, the Germans became increasingly fatalistic. A proud people had their hope blasted from them and they grew unwillingly adept at standing in queues outside shops to obtain their increasingly meagre rations whilst enduring the never-ending anxiety that a loved one might become a casualty. As if to compound the agony that summer, Reich Propaganda Minister Joseph Goebbels extended the working week to 60 hours and announced a 'temporary ban' on holidays. It was all such a long way from the brave new world that Hitler had promised. Any ripples of euphoria that had greeted his military success had by the summer of 1944 been replaced by waves of fear and doubt which further pounded a war-weary nation. In the space of a few short years, Germany's *raison d'état* had shifted from conquest and occupation to protection and survival. Like a body in acute trauma, Germany was just trying to stay alive; attempts to do anything more merely diminished its chances of success, and both its people and armed forces seemed to recognize this. Michael Hirsch, a survivor of the 1916 Battle of the Somme and father of a soldier fighting in France, reflected Germany's pain when he wrote in his diary on 12 August 1944:

> I pray every morning and every evening that this war will end ... The village is in mourning for its lost sons and yesterday bombs fell just 2 miles from the church ... We have not heard from Steffan for eight weeks. I fear the worst but cannot talk about it with his mother and sister ... This war must end before long – but when? How much more suffering can the German people take?

Hitler dealt with Germany's increasing distress by closing his mind to the reality of the situation. He refused to visit any bombed towns and, unable to look the population in the eye, refused to give any morale-boosting speeches. Martin Bormann, his personal secretary, even went to considerable lengths to ensure that bad news was kept from the Führer. This task was made considerably easier by the fact that Hitler had been living in his isolated Wolfsschanze headquarters in East Prussia since June 1941. Colonel-General Alfred Jodl, Chief of the Operations Staff of the Armed Forces High Command (OKW), said of the place: 'The whole site is resplendent with luscious greenery. The woods breathe magnificent tranquillity ... We feel well at ease here. It's become a second home to us.' To others, however, it was a dark, dank, dreary place hidden within a forbidding forest. One senior OKW officer who spent a considerable amount of time there described it as:

> a mixture of cloister and concentration camp. There were numerous wire fences and much barbed-wire. There were far-flung

outposts on roads leading to it, and in the middle was the so-called Security Zone No. 1. Permanent passes to enter this security zone were not even given to my Staff. Every guard had to inspect each officer whom he did not know. Apart from reports on the military situation, very little news from the outer world penetrated this holy of holies.

Hitler's days at the Wolfsschanze were largely taken up with meetings. Rising late in his simply furnished bunker, he breakfasted alone before holding his 'noon' war conference. This gathering was attended by his critical staff and was the main event of the day. It could last several hours. A series of reports were made by experts on the military situation and pronouncements were made by Hitler. It was not uncommon for the Führer to go off on flights of fancy during these conferences, and to deliver long-winded monologues. Such rants troubled the stenographers as well as those officers looking for a systematic analysis of the issues leading to a judicious decision. One of Hitler's favourite subjects recently had been the defeatism that he believed was being exhibited by certain senior officers at the fighting fronts. One such man was Field Marshal Gerd von Rundstedt, who in June, whilst Commander-in-Chief West, was asked by Keitel, the Chief of Staff of OKW, what should be done to stop German forces from being overwhelmed by the Allies. His reply, 'End the war, you fools. What else can you do?' helped to earn him the sack. For Hitler, such pessimism undermined the strategic difficulties faced by the armed forces in the summer of 1944, and it was not uncommon for him to lecture on the 'sickening and unwarranted undermining of morale' during lunch. After this mid-afternoon break, the Führer held more conferences which often went on late into the evening. Dinner was rarely served before midnight, and was taken alone or with his secretaries, who were under strict instructions not to mention the war. Further discussions with colleagues might then take place in the early hours of the morning, with Hitler ending his day at around 0400 hours with tea in the company of his flagging secretaries and sometimes Morell and Julius Schaub, his adjutant. Once again, there was no talk of the war and Hitler instead reminisced about the past, and held forth on society, religion, history and other weighty subjects dear to his heart. His sycophantic guests smiled and nodded approvingly whilst their host petted his beloved Alsatian bitch, Blondi, who considerately offered unconditional love and asked for very little in return.

The Wolfsschanze became a bulwark against reality, providing an artificial world that sustained Hitler, and it was here that Colonel Claus von Stauffenberg sought to kill him. Over the years the Führer had survived numerous attempts on his life, several of which were perpetrated by the military. With the armed forces at the sharp end of the sacrifices that Hitler was demanding, it was logical that some should be highly critical of his leadership. Yet it was a gigantic step from passing judgment over a coffee amongst trusted colleagues about the Führer's decision-making, to working actively to remove him from power. Nevertheless, a conspiracy grew around Colonel Henning von Tresckow, a staff officer on the Eastern Front, who in late 1941 began planning Hitler's assassination which was to be followed by a coup. Various attempts to carry out his schemes failed – although some came very close to success – with the greatest problem being the difficulty of getting within striking distance of the target. But in Claus von Stauffenberg the conspiracy found a man able to get within the necessary proximity of Hitler, and who was also willing to carry out the task. Born into an old noble family from southern German, von Stauffenberg had served with distinction as a staff officer in Poland, France and Russia, but having encountered the atrocities carried out by the SS on the Eastern Front along with the brutality of the fighting there, he allowed himself to become dangerously outspoken about Hitler. Sent away to North Africa for his own safety, he was severely wounded whilst in Tunisia by a strafing American fighter-bomber during April 1943, and was not expected to live. Nevertheless, defying his doctors, he left hospital after three months having lost the sight in his left eye and most of his right hand, and was appointed Chief of Staff to the head of the General Army Office, General Friedrich Olbricht, in Berlin. Olbricht was a recent convert to the anti-Hitler conspiracy and with von Stauffenberg having been given access to Hitler as a specialist military adviser, it was not long before the two men had developed a plot to kill the Führer and follow it with a coup based around a domestic unrest mobilization plan. Von Stauffenberg's first two assassination attempts had to be aborted, but the opportunity soon arose for a third when he was asked to make a report about the reserve army during a war conference at the Wolfsschanze. In preparation Olbricht began to mobilize troops which began moving towards the centre of Berlin on 20 July 1944, just as the disabled assassin hurriedly armed his briefcase bomb and set its timer before entering the meeting. The conference was held in a single-storey chalet, as construction of a suitable underground bunker had not yet been completed. The room was dominated by a heavy rectangular oak table covered with maps and surrounded by 24 chairs. Hitler was positioned in the middle of one of its long sides, and von Stauffenberg was shown to a seat on one of the short sides, to the right of the Führer. Having placed his briefcase against the outside of a solid table-leg, von Stauffenberg lost no time in making an excuse to leave the room – a not uncommon occurrence when telephone calls needed to be made – and left the building. As he was preparing to leave the complex, there was a crunching explosion. Convinced that Hitler had been killed, the bomber began his two-hour flight back to Berlin from a nearby airfield. Meanwhile, a swiftly organized investigation into events made von Stauffenberg prime suspect as the coup faltered, and then was crushed. By midnight von Stauffenberg, Olbricht and two other officers had been executed.

The aftermath of the failed assassination was brutal and bloody with several thousand arrests and scores of executions. Hitler, meanwhile, sought to draw strength from the unsuccessful attempt on his life, not only because it reinforced his belief that his life was 'specially protected', but because it led to the expunging of what he perceived to be 'a canker of unreliable officers'. Indeed, talking to the Wolfsschanze wounded in hospital a few days after the blast, he remarked with great emotion:

> There are you, seriously injured – yet you were not the one that was marked down for assassination. These gentlemen were after me and only me: yet I escaped entirely. Four times in this war my enemies have tried to take my life, and now the Almighty has stayed their hands once again. This can have only one historical interpretation, that Providence has elected me to lead the German people.

Hitler's survival ensured that the battle of Normandy was played out under a new Commander-in-Chief West, Field Marshal Günther 'Hans' von Kluge. Yet even the optimistic von Kluge became severely disheartened after just a short time in the job. Having visited exhausted troops in below-strength formations which lacked essentials and complained about being consistently outnumbered and attacked from the air, his perspective changed rapidly. Then, with his force having been gradually worn down, a crisis developed in mid-August when around 100,000 of his men were threatened with encirclement at Falaise. At its height on 15 August, the day that the Western Allies invaded southern France, a paranoid Hitler lost faith in von Kluge when he could not contact him and feared that he was negotiating a surrender.

The reality was very different. Von Kluge, his radio destroyed by enemy fire, had entered 'the pocket' and was trying desperately to command his troops in the van of battle. Nevertheless, he was immediately recalled and replaced by one of Hitler's most trusted officers: 54-year-old Field Marshal Walter Model. But if Hitler expected the arrival of his monocled substitute to immediately turn around the deteriorating situation, he was to be disappointed. Indeed, the German position was so desperate that it was all that Model could do to try to save as many troops as he could from the crushing Allied pincer at Falaise, albeit at the expense of almost all of his armour and heavy weaponry. What little hope there was that the German army might be able to hold the Allies in the West died in the 'Falaise Pocket'. Kay Summersby travelled across the battlefield in late August and later recalled:

> It was a soldier's nightmare of retreat and defeat. German equipment – splintered wagons, smashed tanks and lorries, banged-up and burned staff cars – jammed the sides of every roadway so tightly that it overflowed into the adjacent fields. Horses, swollen in death, covered the area, each in a grotesque position. The litter, the gigantic, awful litter, was unbelievable. Hundreds of distorted German bodies testified to the sudden power of the Allies' trap; some covered the ground for hundreds of yards in all directions, others hung limply from tanks and lorries; some were only grotesque parts. I was glad when we emerged from the Falaise section, leaving the sickly odour and sight of death far behind.

Of the approximately 50 German divisions that had fought in Normandy, only a fifth were of a reasonable quality by late August when a fighting withdrawal began. Initially this retirement was well organized and disciplined, but by the time that Paris fell on 25 August it was becoming ragged and panicked. Nevertheless, setting the standard for professionalism and resolve when crossing the River Seine near Rouen were the two divisions of II SS Panzer Corps: 9 SS Panzer Division 'Hohenstauffen' and 10 SS Panzer

Division 'Frundsberg'. The former began crossing the river on the 24th in good weather and was immediately targeted by American Thunderbolts which killed SS-Obersturmbannführer Otto Meyer, the commander of the division's panzer regiment, while his adjutant, SS Captain Peter Frolich, had an arm torn off. The following day 10 SS Panzer Division began its crossing, as Wilhelm Tieke reveals:

> All approaches to [the river] are hopelessly jammed, the columns in double and triple rows, radiator to radiator, wheel to wheel . . . We estimated 5,000 to 7,000 vehicles. Rain rules the day and keeps away the enemy airplanes. Beside the roads, in woods and fields, small fires flicker. Boxes, files, apparatus and rubbish are burning. What seemed valuable a few hours ago is now set on fire . . . Officers of the Waffen-SS direct traffic with pistols in hand . . . A clearing group of about eight men stationed on the bridge has the assignment of tipping any vehicle off that has broken down.

The last of the German troops crossed the Seine on 29 August, harassed by Allied ground forces, and on that day Model reported to Hitler:

> The divisions which were taken back from Normandy across the Seine under extreme difficulties and hardest fighting are armed only with a few medium weapons, in general only carbines, etc. The supply of the personnel and *matériel* replacement required is absolutely insufficient . . . The panzer divisions, at present, each have five to ten tanks ready to be employed. In regard to artillery, only isolated guns are left with the infantry divisions and isolated troops with the panzer divisions. . .The low degree of manoeuvrability of the infantry divisions, caused by the fact that they have been made mobile only by temporary

expedients (horses), had a particularly unfavourable influence in the unequal fight with the motorised enemy, all the more as the necessary reserves of assault-guns and other heavy anti-tank guns are completely missing. Consequently, there was an absolute tactical inferiority of the formations still available.

If the Germans were outmanned and outgunned in Normandy, the situation once they had crossed the Seine was far worse, with much of their heavy weaponry abandoned on the river's west bank.

By the end of August, OB West was in turmoil: Army Group G was retreating from the south of France, whilst Army Group B – personally commanded by Model – was weak and badly fractured. As the Americans pushed against the crushed remnants of its Fifth Panzer Army, British Second Army advanced into the 75-mile gap between its Seventh Army and the Fifteenth Army, which was holding the North Sea coast. The lack of cohesion between the major formations withdrawing back towards the German border was a disaster. As regimental commander Lieutenant-Colonel Fritz Fullriede noted in his diary on 31 August: 'The whole west front has collapsed, and the other side is marching about at will.' Even so, Hitler was not about to give up, as he made clear at one of his War Conferences:

If necessary we'll fight on the Rhine. It doesn't make any difference. Under all circumstances we will continue this battle until, as Frederick the Great said, one of our damned enemies gets too tired to fight any more. We'll fight until we get a peace which secures the life of the German nation for the next fifty to a hundred years and which, above all, does not besmirch our honour a second time, as happened in 1918 . . . Things could have turned out differently. If my life had ended [on 20 July] I think I can say that for me personally it would have been a release from worry, sleepless nights and great nervous suffering . . .

By the first day of September the Germans were routed, and a muddle of personnel from different services, arms and units shambled eastwards: the field grey of the Wehrmacht mixed with the blue of the Kriegsmarine, the blue grey of the Luftwaffe and a smearing of paratrooper olive-green. A few wore the 'tiger'-pattern camouflage of the Waffen SS. Occasionally a man or woman in civilian clothing could be seen carrying a suitcase: fleeing collaborators pulled along by the German tide because they had nowhere else to go. Many of the troops carried packs, rifles and side arms, a few lugged machine guns and other weapons and heavy equipment, but a conspicuous few conveyed nothing but themselves. Some marched, but most walked in bedraggled columns, kicking up clouds of dust and occasionally making way for trucks, cars and motorcycles, but rarely for armoured vehicles. Some of the men had commandeered horses, carts and bicycles for their journey. One group was spotted clinging on to an old fire engine, another a bus and a third, led by 19-year-old artillery Lieutenant Joseph Enthammer, a refuse-collection vehicle. The latter crashed into a Luftwaffe staff car, killing 12 men and rendering Enthammer unconscious by the side of the road. Accidents such as this were not infrequent, particularly at night and when the drivers had been drinking, as the increasingly disorganized Germans fell back – to the fury of OKW and the consternation of von Rundstedt and Model. 'There was no order, no leadership and very little supervision of the situation', remembers Obergefeiter Julius Lange, 'for some of the officers had thrown in their lot with their troops, whilst those still trying to organize their men seemed to have lost control.' On occasion a frustrated officer would try to rally a group of men by shouting orders or firing a shot into the air to attract their attention, but sometimes their attempts merely attracted unwanted attention, as Schütze Oskar Bieber remembers:

> A young *Leutnant*, unshaven and with a mad look in his eye, stood by a bridge over a stream. He was shouting at the men who passed him, imploring them to join him and set up a defensive position in a nearby village. Most looked away, trying not to catch his eye. Some even looked embarrassed for him. The troops were tired, frightened and just wanted to get away from the front. As I watched from about 200 metres away, an NCO passed the officer and as he did so pulled a pistol and shot the officer in the head. The men that followed just stepped over the body. Nobody said a word ... The incident has stayed with me because it seems to sum up the German army at the time – a rabble, directionless and drifting along.

As discipline broke down, a number of soldiers sought to desert, and insubordination, looting and drunkenness became rife. For some it was a liberation after months and years of being told what to do, but for others this anarchy was frightening and dangerous. Moreover, the Allies had not gone away but were on their tails, and sometimes their flanks as well. In such uncertain and confusing times it was not uncommon for troops to feel for the first time that Germany was likely to lose the war and that their fate was in the hands of their enemies. Private Fritz Gerber wrote home at this time: 'Our only hope is to be taken prisoner. Now, my dear ones, I send you my last greetings from the West, and should we not see each other again in this world, we must hope to be reunited in another one above.' Gerber's letter was received by his family, but thousands of letters were lost, as they could not be passed through the normal channels because those channels no longer existed. In many cases, even if units had managed to remain intact, the supporting infrastructure upon which they relied for their day-to-day living had collapsed. Thus the soldiers had to live off the land, and learned quickly not to ask where their food came from. Landser Alfred Stoob says: 'We had to scavenge for food. Here a dog without a master, there a few eggs in a chicken coop', whilst SS-Sturmmann Gerhard Keller argues: 'It was the civilians or us and there was no contest. We always offered to pay for what we needed, but if a farmer or household refused to give us what we knew they had, we took it anyway. In this way we survived.' Some found this reversal in the fortunes of the German armed forces hard to digest. As Gunner Helmut Hörner recorded:

> In May 1940 I first set foot on French soil with the best-equipped and best-trained army in the world. Then the German troops overran this land with a victory march without comparison ... Today, four years later, I slip out by the dark of night toward the starting-point, back in the Reich, with a bitter feeling of shame in my soul at the way the rest of my brave division has dissolved, while troops from a continent 4,000 miles away follow close on our heels.

Hounded by the enemy, disorientated and heartily disgruntled with their situation, the withdrawing German troops also found that an increasingly self-possessed local population were intent upon making their lives even more unpleasant. Whilst some of the French and Belgians merely lowered their tolerance towards their unknown itinerant occupiers, others were brazen enough to shout abuse from doorways and ignore requests for assistance. Meanwhile, Resistance groups became more visibly active by, amongst other things, destroying bridges, making escape routes impassable and conducting ambushes. Gunner Hans Blothner noted in his diary that he stumbled across: 'a *Leutnant* shot in the head, a *Hauptmann* with his throat cut'. He went on to say: 'The civilian population is armed and shooting from every house. There's machine gun fire and rifle fire from rooftops, from cellars, from windows, from the church steeple ... The population goads us like cattle.' For one regimental commander, Helmut Ritgen, it soon became clear that the weak and the isolated were vulnerable, and he recalls: 'For stragglers, small groups or single vehicles it was like running the gauntlet through a hate-filled country in an uprising.'

Endeavouring to stabilize the front, Model explored options for building defensive lines, but as one of his staff officers, Major Heinrich Mayer, recalls: 'it was like trying to scoop up water with an open hand.' With communications failing and his headquarters finding it impossible to determine what formation was where and what its strength was, Model was guilty of giving irrelevant orders to units that were not listening. The only instructions issued from Berlin were for Army Group B to 'Hold! Hold!'; but lacking manpower, supplies and leadership the chances of this disintegrating force fulfilling such a task were slim. Lieutenant-General Siegfried Westphal, the astute former Chief of Staff to Field Marshal Albert Kesselring in Italy, later recalled:

> There could be no question of systematic supplies for the Western Army at this time, not only because of the speed of the withdrawal, but because of the destruction wrought by air attack on the rail and telephone network, and the absence of any sort of preparation for a retreat. All such preparation had been forbidden to prevent any thought of the possibility of a retreat. Such lack of providence contained the gravest dangers.

It was a desperate situation, and Hitler looked no further than Model for a scapegoat. Consequently, even though the Field Marshal had latterly been getting the measure of the challenge that had been presented to him, he was removed on 4 September and replaced by 69-year-old Gerd von Rundstedt for his second stint as

Commander-in-Chief West. The Führer believed that the situation required a cool, keen strategic mind and that von Rundstedt was capable of distilling complicated scenarios to their essence and acting decisively, whilst Model, who retained command of Army Group B, was better suited to fighting the sort of defensive battles at which he excelled. Model had not been popular with those who had worked with him at OB West: they complained that he was dogmatic, boorish and overbearing. Von Rundstedt, however, had a reputation as a calm delegator who was very loyal and remained dignified in all circumstances. He was, therefore, in many respects the opposite of Model, whom he saw as a coarse upstart lacking the qualities required of a Field Marshal and was better suited to being a 'good regimental sergeant-major'.

Von Rundstedt's first job on reaching his headquarters in the little town of Aremberg near Koblenz in Germany was to find out more about the forces at his disposal. He was told that he had the equivalent of just 27 divisions pitted against what was believed to be 60 Allied divisions (although in reality they amounted to just 49). The Allies could also boast air superiority verging on supremacy, which gave their ground forces tremendous flexibility whilst severely restricting the German ability to move both strategically and tactically. The failure of the Luftwaffe to counter this dominance infuriated Hitler and on 3 September he ranted at Reichsmarschall Hermann Göring, the head of the service, and his Chief of Staff, Lieutenant-General Werner Kreipe: 'I am considering disbanding the Luftwaffe altogether and tripling anti-aircraft instead.' Kreipe made notes about the meeting in his diary, and in doing so shed light on the strange and rather surreal world that the German High Command were increasingly inhabiting:

[The] Führer spoke first: a tirade against the Luftwaffe. No good, gets worse year after year, he was lied to permanently about

production figures and also about aircraft performances ...
[Then the] Führer promoted me very cordially to full general and
said I had been an excellent representative of the Luftwaffe these
last weeks ... Afterwards I sat a long time with Göring who was
pleased with himself and said the idea of disbanding the air force
was a dead duck. He promised to get Himmler to stop tapping my
telephone.

Von Rundstedt's review of the precarious situation in early
September served only to reinforce the opinion that he had formed
earlier in the summer: that the German cause was lost. But he
reported to OKW:

Our own forces are tied up in battle, and in part severely mauled.
They are short of artillery and anti-tank weapons. Reserves
worthy of mention are not available. The numerical superiority of
the enemy's tanks to ours is incontestable. With Army Group B
at the present there are some 100 tanks [compared with the Allies'
2000] available for action. The enemy air force dominates the
battle area and rear communications deep into the rearward
terrain ...

To make matters worse, the quality of the German force in the west
was deteriorating. This was not only because of a lack of fuel,
ammunition and weaponry, but also because the fighting troops were
tired and rapidly losing their efficiency. Poorly trained replacements
were being drawn from an increasingly shallow and inappropriate
pool of men from within the Reich. Those that made it to the front
were invariably met by understandably disconsolate comrades who
were taking part in a disorganized withdrawal after a miserable
defeat. Lars Hahn was a decorated 30-year-old major who had
fought on the Eastern Front for two years before being transferred

to Normandy in April 1944. Recalling the difficult days after the battle of Normandy he says:

> We had been fighting since 8 June without much time to sleep and only one or two days away from the front. My company was gradually whittled away during the summer. At first we received some young and inexperienced men as replacements, and then some older experienced men still suffering from wounds, but by early August there were none at all. In early June I commanded 123 men, but by the time we had crossed the Somme we were less than a section, 8 men . . . and I was carrying two wounds – one in the thigh and one in the shoulder. But I could not leave my men. They wanted the war to end, and so did I, but we fought on because we had to, because we were told to and because we still had some vestiges of honour left.

Hahn and his comrades were ready to continue their fight in spite of the recent morale-sapping setbacks. Others felt likewise. Young Lieutenant Erich Schneider, for example, had deserted from 553 Infantry Division at the end of August. But when questioned about the fighting spirit of his unit he replied: 'The general opinion . . . was that the war would be over in eight weeks, but the soldiers of the Regt considered that they might as well retain their honour by fighting to the end.' It was by harnessing the seemingly limited potential of such men, whilst strengthening the line with para-troopers, soldiers of the Waffen-SS and others who retained their motivation and combat effectiveness, that von Rundstedt and Model planned to build a defensive line to bring the retreat to an end. This was desperately needed for as Siegfried Westphal, von Rundstedt's new Chief of Staff, later wrote:

The overall situation in the west was serious in the extreme. A heavy defeat anywhere along the front, which was so full of gaps that it did not deserve that name, might lead to a catastrophe, if the enemy were to exploit his opportunity skilfully. A particular source of danger was that not a single bridge over the Rhine had been prepared for demolition, an omission which took weeks to repair . . .

The opportunity to stop the exodus came with the stuttering of the Allied offensive around 4 September. It also coincided with Model's final Order of the Day as Commander-in-Chief West:

With the enemy's advance and the withdrawal of our front, several hundred thousand soldiers are falling back – army, air force and armoured units – troops which must re-form as planned and hold in new strongpoints or lines.

In this stream are the remnants of broken units which, for the moment, have no set objectives and are not even in a position to receive clear orders. Whenever orderly columns turn off the road to reorganize, streams of disorganized elements push on. With their wagons move whispers, rumours, haste, endless disorder and vicious self-interest. This atmosphere is being brought back to the rear areas, infecting units still intact, and in this moment of extreme tension must be prevented by the strongest means.

I appeal to your honour as soldiers. We have lost a battle, but I assure you of this: we will win this war! I cannot tell you more at present, although I know that questions are burning on your lips. Whatever has happened, never lose your faith in the future of Germany. At the same time you must be aware of the gravity of the situation. This moment will and should separate men from weaklings. Now, every soldier has the same responsibility. When his commander falls, he must be ready to step into his shoes and carry on.

These are strong words, but it is doubtful that many troops were aware of Model's exhortations. It is much more likely, therefore, that the formation of an embryonic defensive position at this time came about after some fleeing troops had been successfully stopped and organized into a coherent force. Assisting in this process was the timely but unexpected arrival in southern Holland on 3 September of troops commanded by Lieutenant-General Kurt Chill. Chill had been ordered to move the remnants of his destroyed 85 Division back to Germany, but having seen Model's Order of the Day, and angered by the stifling chaos, decided to merge his men with the remnants of two other divisions and organize a line along the Albert Canal in northern Belgium. Having set up reception centres on innumerable bridges, Chill's officers and NCOs managed in just 24 hours to corall thousands of troops from every arm into new positions. By 5 September Chill's growing force had been joined on its right from Antwerp along the Albert Canal to the junction of the Meuse–Escaut Canal by Lieutenant-General Karl Sievers' 719 Infantry Division. These old men who had been stationed along the Dutch coast since 1940 – and had not fired a shot in anger – were supplemented by one Dutch SS battalion and a few Luftwaffe detachments. Over the days that followed, the newly shored up line was further reinforced by men from Fifteenth Army who had escaped a British Second Army encirclement by crossing the Schelde and reached the mainland north of Antwerp. Over 16 days, 65,000 men, 225 guns, 750 trucks and wagons and 1,000 horses were evacuated to take up defensive positions along the Albert Canal and throughout Holland. Meanwhile, Colonel-General Kurt Student's First Parachute Army was also moving into position. It was activated on 4 September, when Jodl ordered him to collect all available units together and 'build a new front on the Albert Canal', which was to 'be held at all costs!' Göring made 20,000 men available to Student from six parachute regiments and two convalescent battalions, together with a further 10,000 men composed of sailors, Waffen-SS training units, Luftwaffe air and ground crews, along with 25 tanks. Lieutenant-Colonel Friedrich von der Heydte's 6 Parachute Regiment moved quickly into defence with the three-regiment 7 Parachute Division, commanded by Lieutenant-General Wolfgang Erdmann, on its left flank. Completing the German line down to Maastricht was 176 Infantry Division which comprised invalids and convalescents. On 10 September, at his headquarters in Vught (17 miles north-west of Eindhoven), Student analysed the newly created 75-mile-long front that he had been charged with commanding. Spreading out a map on a large carved oak table, he announced in an exasperated tone that it amounted to little more than 'the sweepings from Germany and else-where and the exhausted from France: not many of them and very little armour. But it must remain steadfast.' Student, the talented yet modest creator of Germany's airborne forces, recognized that his men would very soon be confronted with a renewed Allied thrust and that if he was to provide time required for the defences on the Rhine and along the West Wall to be reinforced, his army could not afford to crumble at the first blow.

It was the earliest arriving of these newly tasked German troops that the British clattered into as they resumed their offensive on 6 September. Immediately offering resistance to XXX Corps, 11th Armoured Division was held on the Albert Canal, whilst the Guards Armoured Division just managed to push on to the Meuse–Escaut Canal and to create a bridgehead at Neerpelt. Amongst those initially defending against Adair's Guards was Lieutenant Adi Strauch, a platoon commander in 2 Parachute Regiment who had been wounded whilst fighting in Russia. Just before moving out to the front in northern Belgium he inspected his men:

Standing alongside young volunteers were old NCOs, Luftwaffe men taken away from their company office desks and from head-quarters duties. The nucleus of the company consisted of just eight trained paratroops. We were soon to go into action so there was little time; a few days at the most, in which to give them weapon training.

The company began its journey forward on 5 September. It consisted of 'two heavy machine gun platoons, a mortar platoon, a half-platoon of infantry guns, two Panzerschrek sections and company headquarters'. By the following day, the battalion was preparing itself for an attack on the village of Helchteren near the Albert Canal:

> Our battalion reached the form-up area during the morning of the 7th and was soon involved in fighting against a British armoured division ... On 8 September and for the next few days the British attacked again and again, but each assault was beaten back, although there were now heavy losses to both sides.

As the British bludgeoned their way forward, the Germans struggled to contain them, and suffering prohibitive casualties, Strauch was forced to take command of the company:

> My old comrade, who had led No. 1 Platoon, was fatally wounded ... and enemy tanks began to work round our left flank. Over the field telephone, which was still working, I was ordered to pull back. British tanks were only metres away as I, together with five others, worked our way back to battalion headquarters which enemy tanks were now nearing. Our close-quarters tank-busting teams went into action and the enemy advance on that sector was quickly halted.

This was the type of tenacious defence that the British troops had not experienced since the middle of August. It spelled the end of 'Montgomery's waltz through northern Europe' and the beginning of something far more plodding and fraught. Indeed, the Dutch resistance informed the British that the German line was solidifying, and by the end of the first week in September Twenty-First Army Group was reviewing evidence to suggest that new units and formations were moving into Holland as Fifteenth Army escaped its clutches and a further 20,000 troops were sent into the line by OKW. This latter force consisted of various third-rate troops pillaged from units in training, cadres of veterans supplemented by untrained personnel, and Volksgrenadier divisions. These Volksgrenadier formations not only lacked men and heavy weapons but also suffered from a bare minimum of training, which made them useful only in static defensive positions. Their units were formed around a small cadre of experienced soldiers, but their ranks were filled with the young, the old, those who had previously been deemed unfit for military service and 'unemployed' men from other services and arms. Lieutenant Lingenhole, a platoon commander in the recently formed 553 Volksgrenadier Division, believed that the division was not ready for battle when it received its orders for the front. During that summer 'no long tr[ainin]g marches were made . . . The co[mpan]ys of 1st Bn, GR1120 had a march of approximately 12 km to the range where they fired [their weapons]. About 10 per cent to 15 per cent of the personnel were unable to march that distance, and had to be transported.' Lingenhole also said that the division's troops were aged from 17½ years to 39½ years, the formation was at 60 per cent strength when deployed and 'approximately half were not completely fit for field service'. Moreover, Major Geyer, who was on the divisional staff, reported that 'The personnel of the Division suffered from low morale, not so much because of their lack of desire to fight, but because they felt that they were so poorly equipped with weapons.'

Even so, Model could not afford to be choosy about the men that he took: he understood that such formations were essential if the Germans were to have anything other than Student's thin crust of a defensive line.

Accompanying these new formations through the rear area were those who had been so badly battered that they had been pulled out of the line for rest, refit and reorganization. In Holland this included 9 and 10 SS Panzer Divisions of II SS Panzer Corps, commanded with passion by the highly skilled and well-respected 50-year-old Lieutenant-General Wilhelm ('Willi') Bittrich. The SS (Schutzstaffel, or protection squad) was originally formed as protection for Hitler in the late 1920s and commanded by Heinrich Himmler, who sought to make it racially exclusive. By the mid 1930s it had an armed wing (the Waffen-SS), which was increasingly seen as an alternative army. Highly motivated, fiercely proud and rigorously trained, the SS boasted four divisions by 1941 which sought to have no rival on the battlefield and were given the toughest missions. I SS Panzer Corps' official historian has written: 'The combined effects of brave officers and senior NCOs and brave, dedicated soldiers made for an extremely formidable military machine. Wounds were to be borne with pride and never used as a reason to leave the field of battle; mercy was seen as a sign of weakness and normally neither offered nor expected.' The 9 and 10 SS Panzer Divisions were created in early 1943, and during the remainder of the year were trained at various locations in France. SS-Rottenführer Gerd Rommel of 10 SS Panzer Division recalls:

> Our training was indeed hard . . . These were the last divisions that were able to make use of relative peace in the West for their training, before the D-Day invasion in June 1944. However, it was very intensive. They all received the most up-to-date and modern equipment but, because they were so well

equipped, a great deal was expected of them when they went into action.

The corps saw action on the Eastern Front a year later, suffering such heavy losses that it was forced into reserve after a refit. However, although still desperately needed in Russia, within a week of the invasion of Normandy it was moved to France, where it arrived before the end of June. Here, both divisions were heavily involved in the fighting and, once again, took substantial casualties. Even so, the two divisions remained dangerous antagonists, and during the Allied breakout they held the line, counterattacked and fought stoically in whatever role was required of them. They became such a feared and highly respected opponent that Dwight Eisenhower said of the final phase of the battle of Normandy: 'while the SS elements as usual fought to annihilation, the ordinary German infantry gave themselves up in ever-increasing numbers'. But such was II SS Panzer Corps' sacrifice during the summer of 1944 that both of its divisions were beginning to be referred to as '*Kampfgruppe*' – a battle group which varied in size and consisted of various divisional elements which took the name of its commander. For example, 9 SS Panzer Division had left Russia 18,000 men strong with a fearsome array of tanks, vehicles and heavy weapons, but by late August it consisted of a mere 3,500 men and a handful of vehicles. Nevertheless, it continued to work in close cooperation with 10 SS Panzer Division, and together they took part in operations in the Falaise Pocket to hold open an exit for other units to escape through before managing to break away themselves. In so doing, the two divisions revealed that they remained not only selfless, but highly competent fighting organizations.

Much of the continued vitality of II SS Panzer Corps came from Bittrich's excellent direction and the quality of his subordinates. The 9 SS Panzer Division was commanded by the determined and decisive

32-year-old SS-Obersturmbannführer Walter Harzer, who had very recently taken up the position. Looking older than his years and often scruffily presented, he was a first-class combat soldier who had recently been awarded the Cross in Gold for his superb leadership in Normandy. The 10 SS Panzer Division, meanwhile, was commanded by 38-year-old SS-Gruppenführer Heinz Harmel. The debonair Harmel was also a highly decorated officer who had himself been awarded the Cross in Gold and also a Knight's Cross of Iron with Oak Leaves, a Wound Badge, an Infantry Assault Badge, Tank Destruction Badges and a Close Combat Clasp. He was a popular soldier with his superiors and also his men. SS-Sturmmann Rudy Splinter revealed that Harmel was 'a real soldier's soldier, no airs and graces, and he would do anything for his men. It's no wonder they would follow him anywhere and do anything he asked . . .' Thus, in spite of their recent losses, with men of the quality of Harzer and Harmel at the helm, the two formations remained driven and highly competent. Throughout the last week of August, having crossed the Seine, II SS Panzer Corps conducted several important rearguard actions to slow the Allied advance. The divisions stayed just ahead of the British and American spearheads and continued to suffer casualties. Indeed, losses were taken just getting designated replacements to the front from Germany. Nineteen-year-old Alfred Ziegler, a despatch rider for the staff of a newly raised anti-tank unit for 9 SS Panzer Division, remembers that during the train journey to the front, Allied aircraft constantly harassed them:

> The first company was caught in a very heavy fighter-bomber attack during which our company commander von Brocke was killed. We all fired our machine guns so that no bombs scored a direct hit on the train. Subsequent strafing runs did, however, cause some damage to the tank destroyers and vehicles, and wounded about 10 men. Later we detrained and joined the third

company which had already been in the West for some time. But now the enemy started to chase us.

Ziegler and his unit arrived at the front just in time to fight alongside some German paratroopers. Such actions were always frenetic, with little time for preparation, and exhausting. The division's armoured engineer battalion was commanded by 41-year-old SS-Captain Hans Moeller who said:

> The situation could change by the hour. Every second was vital and called for quick decisions. The engineer battalion was last in the divisional column, and had to look after itself; we had lost radio contact. Should we be struck off as lost already? The weather at this moment was favourable. It had rained and low cloud was hindering enemy air sorties . . . There was always a feeling of uncertainty. Although not openly admitting it, everyone was preoccupied with the thought that chance or the fortunes of war may yet change. I kept my thoughts to myself, but I knew all these sleeping forms, exhausted, wrapped in blankets and tents, were thinking the same. We were absolutely worn out.

It was the norm for the SS troops to be outnumbered and outgunned. Indeed, when Harzer fought at Cambrai on 2 September he was confronted with '200 American tanks and accompanying infantry'. The battle that followed was ferocious and although he later claimed that some 40 of those tanks had been put out of action, by the end of the day his *Kampfgruppe* had lost most of its 88mm guns, and he had to order his men to withdraw. Its move down the Cambrai–Mons road that night has been described by SS veteran and historian Wilhelm Tieke:

The highway was overcrowded with fleeing vehicles. At the end the stream drove the last prime movers of the 4th SS Flak battery with its sixteen survivors, among them many severely wounded. Shortly before Valenciennes, one of the vehicles broke down. The badly wounded were no longer able to endure the torments of the hasty retreat. The courageous battery medical orderly, Gottschalk, remained with those wounded who could no longer be transported and went into captivity with them.

Having been cut off from the main body of his *Kampfgruppe* on becoming surrounded, Harzer and his command group only managed to get away by flying British and US flags on their vehicles and taking several unattended Allied trucks that they found at the roadside. The experience was indicative of the division's role for it fought until the very last moment, and on several occasions they were nearly encircled or overrun. It was by providing such excellent cover for the general withdrawal that Harzer and Harmel stopped more of the German armed forces from being neutralized than eventually occurred. However, such was the intensity of their involvement that the two divisions could not continue in the role indefinitely, and so on 4 September, II SS Panzer Corps received orders to pull out of the line for a rest and refit around the quiet Dutch town of Arnhem, 75 miles behind the front line.

By the time that Bittrich's corps had been given an opportunity to catch its breath, von Rundstedt and Model were on the cusp of bringing their ugly withdrawal to an end on the line of the Albert Canal. As has been described above, by marshalling units already at the front, and supplementing them with new formations from Germany, a new defensive zone was created that was a credit to German improvisation. This reorganization coincided with the damaging effects of overstretch being felt by the Allies, and so by the time that British Second Army lurched forward again, it found the way barred far more formidably than just a few days earlier. Nevertheless, the problems that Hitler faced after a summer of catastrophic setbacks were chronic, and finding a few thousand new second-rate troops to hold a line together with some shattered comrades was never going to alter his strategic prospects. With every passing day Hitler, OKW and the commanders in the West recognized that a major new Allied offensive was increasingly likely. Between 9 and 14 September Model's intelligence officer issued daily warnings about increasing reinforcements coming up behind British Second Army and an imminent breakout, probably towards Nijmegen, Arnhem and Wesel, aimed at the Ruhr. This enlightened soldier was further convinced that Eisenhower would deploy his airborne forces, a known and feared commodity which had led to the Germans seeking some depth to their defences, in order to crack the front wide open. In an attempt to read Allied intentions more clearly and empathize with their ambitions, he went as far as to write a report as though he were Dwight Eisenhower giving orders to Miles Dempsey. His instructions to British Second Army were:

> on its right wing it will concentrate an attack force, mainly composed of armoured units, and after forcing a Maas crossing, will launch operations to break through to the Rhenish–Westphalian industrial area [Ruhr] with the main effort via Roermond [24 miles east of Neerpelt]. To cover the northern flank, the left wing of the [Second British] Army will close to the Waal at Nijmegen, and thus create the basic conditions necessary to cut off the German forces committed in the Dutch coastal areas [the Fifteenth Army].

Allied plans were somewhat different, for although Model's intelligence officer had correctly identified the Ruhr as a medium-term Allied objective, the main effort was to seize a Rhine crossing via Eindhoven and Nijmegen. It was this blow – Operation Market Garden – that was about to fall in depth on defences that had not been there just two weeks before. In such circumstances the role of the airborne forces in the undertaking looked not only more important but also far more risky.

CHAPTER 3

Chasing the Dream

(Airborne Warfare and its Soldiers: The Birth of Parachuting to Summer 1944)

Perched on the edge of the hole – or the 'aperture' as the instructors called it – with his feet hanging in the void and his heart pounding, an ashen-faced Private Davey Jones awaited the command. Some 500 feet below, soldiers were scattered across a large emerald-green field. The 19-year-old hung beneath a captive barrage balloon in a small basket which swayed gently in the light breeze beneath an azure sky. It was a hot July day which had left Jones cuffing the sweat from his forehead just minutes before, but now he was experiencing such a strange feeling of dislocation that his body was only tuned to the need to launch himself through the hole. He was going to do it. His earlier stomach-lurching fears had vanished; he no longer worried that he might funk at the last moment; his thoughts had turned away from his concerns about the diligence with which the Women's Auxiliary Air Force had packed his parachute. He had reached the point of no return.

The instructor barked 'Number One – Go!', and without hesitation Jones pushed himself forward and slipped into nothingness. The young soldier's stomach charged into his mouth, his mind and body reuniting suddenly as he fell, the air rushing past his face. Then a reassuring shock to his shoulders told him that his parachute had deployed. Looking up, Jones' face cracked into a smile as his descent slowed. The usually stoical Welshman found himself whooping for joy, his flesh fizzing with a mixture of relief and pleasure as he began to enjoy the sensation of floating over the gentle English countryside. His reverie ended abruptly with the harsh Glaswegian tones of an NCO below, who demanded that he 'concentrate on landing rather than swanning around'. Jones automatically adopted the landing position: 'Point those toes! Keep those knees and feet together!' The hard ground seemed to rise towards him unfeasibly quickly, but even though he bent his knees and relaxed his body as his boots touched the ground, he failed to execute the roll that he had practised. It was not an elegant landing – 'Classic feet, backside, head' he was later told – but he was down and felt ready to take on the world.

By the time that Davey Jones had qualified as a parachutist in July 1943, airborne warfare was barely a quarter-century old. Whilst embraced by the politically and militarily radical states of Germany, the Soviet Union and Italy, the concept of inserting troops behind enemy lines by air had been rejected by Britain and the United States as expensive and unnecessary at a time of foreign policy conservatism and financial retrenchment. However, on 22 June 1940 Winston Churchill, having learned of the part that airborne forces had played in Germany's successful invasion of the Low Countries, opined: 'We ought to have a corps of at least 5,000 parachute troops.' Within weeks, a parachute training school had been established at RAF Ringway, just outside Manchester, commanded by Lieutenant-Colonel John Rock and named the Central Landing Establishment. Its first intake was personnel from No. 2 Commando whose training as raiders reflected early British ambitions for the new force. These men became 'airborne guinea pigs' upon whom the designers of all the new equipment, techniques and drills associated with parachuting tested their ideas. It was an experimentation, however, that was severely hampered by lack of resources: only six obsolete and crudely converted Whitley bombers were made available for training. These aircraft were hated by parachutists. They were squeezed into the low, narrow fuselage and had to shuffle forward on their backsides to 'jump' through a hole in the floor. Even so, through Rock's determination and improvisation – and not a few broken bones, bruises and sprains suffered with fortitude by his first trainees – by the end of the year nearly 500 men from No. 2 Commando had completed basic parachute training to form what was initially called 11/Special Air Service and was soon to become 1 Para.

British airborne forces grew steadily over the next two years, with three parachute battalions having formed Richard Gale's 1 Parachute Brigade by September 1941. As this expansion was consolidated, small airborne raids were conducted which provided much-needed experience for the troops, their commanders and the developing airborne fraternity. The first was launched in February of that year, when 38 paratroopers dropped in southern Italy destroyed the Tragino Aqueduct before being captured. The second raid took place a year later, when a 2 Para company not only delivered valuable technical information from a German radar station on the north coast of France at Bruneval but also provided a parachuting propaganda coup which proved a welcome boost to British morale. By this time further airborne progress had taken place, with positive tests having been carried out on the heavy lift and precision-landing potential of gliders and the formation of George Hopkinson's 1 Airlanding Brigade. With this new organization in place and both a second parachute brigade and supporting troops *en train*, it became possible to establish an embryonic 1 British Airborne Division. Its commander was the 45-year-old Major-General Frederick 'Boy' Browning, a handsome, dapper and vain Guardsman who had distinguished himself as a junior officer during the First World War and was married to the novelist Daphne du Maurier. Browning, a tireless advocate of the airborne method who was also a qualified glider pilot, had been injured during both of his parachute jumps. He was described by Richard Gale as 'a colourful personality' who had:

> all the qualities of superb leadership. Always with a ready smile, he, nevertheless, had a quick temper, which kept one both attached to him and certainly on one's toes. He had great resolve and determination, characteristics that were called for in all the comings and goings through which airborne forces went in the earlier days.

The well-connected and politically adept Browning was able to deal not only with the various government departments that his new position required but also with the RAF, which continued to view airborne forces with some suspicion. But what the aloof and ambitious general lacked was operational command experience, a deficiency which he was acutely aware of and determined to correct. In the meantime, however, he oversaw improvements in the selection and training of airborne soldiers, which led in April 1942 to Hardwick Hall in Cheshire becoming the Airborne Forces Depot and the creation of the Glider Pilot and Parachute Regiments to administer his new type of troops. Browning had astutely prepared 1 British Airborne Division for action, but when it left England in May 1943 to fight in North Africa it did so commanded by Hopkinson after Browning had been appointed 'Airborne Adviser' to Dwight Eisenhower, the Supreme Commander in the Mediterranean. In this position although he missed leading 'his' division in battle, Browning played a key role in determining the employment not only of British airborne troops but also of the new American parachute forces during the invasion of Sicily.

The man tasked with the development of US airborne forces in 1940 was 43-year-old Major Bill Lee. Whilst remaining in his infantry staff job in Washington, by June he had established a Parachute Test

Platoon at Fort Benning, Georgia, consisting of volunteers from 29 Infantry Regiment. This unit, commanded by Lieutenant William T. Ryder, was also undermined by a lack of resources, but on 29 August it managed a mass jump from B-18 bombers in front of VIPs. It was a defining event that was quickly followed by a burst of activity which saw the creation of a Parachute Training School at Benning and a developmental focused Provisional Parachute Group at Fort Bragg, North Carolina. Commanded by a promoted Lieutenant-Colonel Bill Lee, the Provisional Parachute Group was determined to ensure that the United States could undertake large-scale airborne operations. Lee, convinced that divisional-sized drops could have an impact out of all proportion to their size, wrote in a typically understated manner: 'I think it would be dull of us to say that parchute troops will seldom be employed in units larger than a battalion.' Assisted by a tide of opinion that was in his favour, Lee had overseen the activation of four parachute battalions by the summer of 1941 and, in the military expansion that followed America's entry into the war, four parachute regiments of three battalions each by the following spring. To coordinate this rapidly growing force and integrate an emergent glider element, Airborne Command was established at Fort Bragg, commanded by Bill Lee with the rank of Brigadier-General.

During the summer of 1942 the parachute regiments and their supporting elements successfully undertook major exercises and, later in the year, these also involved glider troops. This training was assisted enormously by the recent arrival of the first C-47 aircraft, a superb transportation aeroplane which was ideal for the airborne role and gave the US airborne forces a massive advantage over their extemporizing British counterparts. The spacious C-47, known to the Americans as the 'Skytrain' or 'Gooney Bird', could carry 20 fully equipped parachutists, who jumped from a rear door in the port of the fuselage. It was so good that the British eagerly placed an order for a number, and named it the 'Dakota'. Anglo-American airborne cooperation had been strong from the outset, with both nations experiencing similar developmental stages and struggles to gain resources and respect. It was the shared common goal that prompted Lee to travel across the Atlantic in the summer of 1942 to discuss all things airborne with Browning, to learn about 1 British Airborne Division and to discuss possible roles for such formations in the projected cross-Channel invasion. It was not surprising, therefore, that on his return to Fort Bragg, Lee recommended the immediate formation of American airborne divisions. Authority was given for the raising of two, each with a strength of 8,321 men, and 82 and 101 US Airborne Divisions were activated in mid-August. An immensely proud Bill Lee was given command of the 101st. Well aware that he was breaking new ground, he said in one of his first orders:

> The 101st . . . has no history, but it has a rendezvous with destiny. Like the early American pioneers whose invincible courage was the foundation stone of this Nation, we have broken with the past and its traditions to establish our claim to the future.

> Due to the nature of our armament and the tactics in which we shall perfect ourselves, we shall be called upon to carry out operations of far-reaching military importance, and we shall habitually go into action when the need is immediate and extreme.

> Let me call your attention to the fact that our badge is the great American eagle. This is a fitting emblem for a division that will crush its enemies by falling upon them like a thunderbolt from the skies.

> The history we shall make, the record of high achievement we hope to write in the annals of the American Army and the American people, depends wholly and completely on the men of

this division. Each individual, each officer and each enlisted man, must therefore regard himself as a necessary part of a complex and powerful instrument for the overcoming of the enemies of the nation. Each, in his own job, must realize that he is not only a means, but an indispensable means for obtaining the goal of victory. It is, therefore, not too much to say that the future itself, in whose moulding we expect to have our share, is in the hands of the soldiers of the 101st Airborne Division.

The 82 US Airborne Division was commanded by 47-year-old Major-General Matthew B. Ridgway, a first-class soldier described by one who knew him as a 'solidly built, hawk-visaged, no-nonsense soldier who turned out to be absolutely fearless, and who demanded the very best from his subordinates and their commands. He could scare the hell out of someone with a glance.' He, Lee and their subordinate commanders had to use all of their leadership, command and organizational skills to help fashion their new divisions in the required form, forge their identities, bond the men and train them for war. Time was short, for in April 1943 82 US Airborne Division set sail for operations in North Africa, and four months later the 101st crossed the Atlantic for England.

The British and American airborne forces embarked on the Mediterranean campaign lacking experience, but with extremely capable personnel. It was not any soldier that had the wherewithal to slip behind enemy lines and fight in a small group against overwhelming odds with light arms and extremely limited support, but some actively sought that challenge and thrived on it. Private David Webster of 506 Parachute Infantry Regiment (PIR) 101 US Airborne Division, who volunteered to be a parachutist in 1943 whilst studying English literature at Harvard, suggested that it was in the 'best airborne tradition . . . [to rely] on madmen instead of firepower'. The historian of 82 US Airborne Division put it another way: 'Every 82nd

Airborne trooper is by the nature of his mode of warfare an individualist of the first rank ... His personality is as unpredictable as his dependability in combat.' Such men required a variety of attributes, but in particular needed to be fit, intelligent, innovative, tenacious and courageous.

In Britain, soldiers were asked to volunteer for the new parachute units, an application that could not be blocked by their Commanding Officer (CO) who was asked to provide a recommendation and to send only those with 'A1' fitness and a good character. Each man had his own reasons for wanting to join: for the glamour of parachuting, perhaps, or to join a unit more likely to see action, or even to benefit from the extra two shillings a day pay. Deciding to become an 'Umbrella Dangler', as parachutists were popularly known, required considerable courage as the concept was new and their role was undeniably dangerous. Indeed, when Alastair Pearson was given a commission in the paratroopers his stunned CO reacted by saying: 'Be your age. What do you know about parachuting?' Pearson admitted that he knew nothing, and so his CO replied: 'Well, it serves you bloody well right.' Each volunteer was put through a medical and some basic military tests before, if passing both, moving on to a gruelling course at Hardwick Hall. The Americans ran a similar volunteering system with the offer of an extra $50 per month for qualified parachutists. Spencer F. Wurst maintains that the extra money was seductive, but he joined the paratroopers because he wanted to be the best: 'If I had to soldier', he said, 'I wanted to soldier in an elite unit, not in an average infantry regiment.' Bill Guarnere concurs:

I was going to enlist in the Marines – they're known as the best of the military, but at the recruiting station I saw a poster, it said 'All New! Paratroopers'. I went to see what it was all about, and I enlisted ... The elite of the Army. If you're going to combat, you want to fight with the best. You're accepting something no one else wanted to do. It was new, untested, people thought you would get killed fast. If you volunteered for that, you're half nuts.

However, volunteering was just the first step towards becoming one of the elite, as those who were accepted and arrived for training soon found out.

The training at Hardwick Hall and Fort Benning sought to put the trainees under immense pressure; any soldier not attaining the required standard was discarded. The aim was not to seek or make supermen, but to select those who had 'common sense and character . . . sufficient strength of will to conquer doubt and fear . . . [and shown] determination and will-power'. Nevertheless, Captain John Frost, Adjutant of 2 Para in the autumn of 1941, recalls:

> Among those who came, nearly half had no documents, a large number could be labelled lame, halt or blind, a good few were hardened criminals in the military and sometimes the civil sense, and some had been arbitrarily detailed as if for an unpleasant fatigue party. Unto us was left the task of sorting the sheep from the goats, of returning most of the goats to their detestable owners and of taking a chance with a few of them.

Captain Colin Brown says that the Hardwick Hall course could hardly have been more exacting, and that 'the object was to break all but the fittest physically and mentally!' The physical tests were punishing and included: running 200 yards in 16 seconds in full equipment; carrying a man 200 yards in two minutes in full equipment; boxing three one-minute rounds with gloves; completing an obstacle course; climbing a 15ft vertical rope; jumping a 9ft 6ins ditch in full equipment and finishing a forced march of eight miles in under one hour 15 minutes. Ernie Rooke-Matthews from the East End of London joined the Parachute Regiment from the Royal Armoured Corps; he remembers dragging himself through the fitness regime:

The physical training was organized and led by a motley crew of physical training instructors . . . all superb specimens of physical perfection . . . We sweated like pigs; the instructors, fit as they were, sweated profusely. We thought they were masochists, but they never asked us to do anything they wouldn't do better or harder or longer.

James Sims says that he expected that his body would be pushed to its limits, but was surprised to have to undergo a psychological test. He writes that a psychiatrist asked him: 'Why do you hate your mother?', a question designed to provoke a reaction:

If you sat there calmly and replied, 'Good heavens, what on earth gave you that idea?' you were out – for lack of aggression . . . You had to jump up, knocking the chair over backwards and shout, 'What the hell are you going on about?' Better still, you should reach across and make a grab for the psychiatrist. Then you were sure of a rifle company.

The American training was equally gruelling, with trainees at Fort Benning passing into the Parachute School under a sign which read: 'Through these portals pass the toughest paratroopers in the world.' The course consisted of four parts with the first – 'A Stage' – largely concerned with physical fitness. The instructors were charged with trying to identify and exploit weakness in their trainees in order to break them. Those holding a commission were treated no differently, indeed Spencer F. Wurst has said that the officers 'took even more verbal abuse [from the instructors] than we did'. Lieutenant Fenton Richards agrees:

We were always tired and hungry and told that it kept us mean and on the edge. It did, on the edge of exhaustion and a couple of my fellow officers couldn't take it and left. If we couldn't take what was being handed out at Benning then we would not have been able to cut it as parachute officers. The regime was for a reason, to get rid of the incapable, and it worked and no doubt saved many lives in combat.

Colonel Robert F. Sink prepared 506 PIR thoroughly at Camp Toccoa, Georgia, for entrance into the Parachute School. Bill Guarnere of 2nd Battalion says that he will never forget the intensity of his 12-hour-a-day conditioning there:

> Camp Toccoa was only about one thing: weeding out the weaklings. Our training schedule was brutal, and the training was brutal – all physical conditioning, led by Captain Sobel [the company commander] . . . If you couldn't take it, you were out . . . Sobel pushed you to the limit, beyond what you thought your body could take. But you *made* your body do it if you wanted to be in the paratroopers, that's all. The man was training us to be killers.

At the end of their time at Toccoa, such was the fitness of the 506th that its 3rd Battalion set a new endurance march record when they covered the 136 miles from Atlanta to Fort Benning carrying full field equipment and their weapons in cold, wet weather in just 72 hours. On arrival at Benning, the 506th was excused A Stage training.

The parachute training course for the British and Americans had two central pillars: testing whether the men could overcome their fear of jumping from platforms of various heights, and teaching them how to jump safely and effectively. At RAF Ringway, the would-be paratroopers were taught the correct way to enter an aircraft with their enormously burdensome equipment, how to hook up their static lines, the method of exiting the aircraft, techniques for controlling the parachute and the correct landing positions. The enthusiastic RAF instructors went about their business in a very different way to the 'sadistic' army trainers at Hardwick Hall, with a deliberate 'move away from beasting and towards encouragement', as one RAF instructor put it. Trainee Ernie Rooke-Matthews immediately recognized the change in tone at Ringway: 'They made small men feel tall, their enthusiasm was infectious.' Even so, it took time for some of the soldiers to warm to their instructors, as one RAF NCO, Alf Card, has admitted:

> The Army and RAF were not exactly bosom buddies, as a lot of the trainees were ex-Dunkirk veterans who used to bemoan the absence of the RAF at Dunkirk and did not think highly of the 'Brylcreem Boys', as we were called. However, it says much for the RAF parachute jumping instructors that they were able to win the confidence of their trainees and develop an amazing rapport with their sections. [We] adopted a friendly kid-glove approach, one of persuasion – not do as I say but do as I do.

Most of the parachute training was done on improvised ground-based apparatus so that the basics could be learned quickly, but also because of the lack of aircraft. In both Britain and America the troops made exits from mock wooden fuselages and the British also had a contraption known as 'The Fan' which simulated the initial fall from an aircraft by using air resistance to slow the release of a steel cable attached to a trainee's harness. Other pieces of equipment assisted the practice of landings – the aspect of parachuting most likely to lead to injury – and included a device that involved a pulley system which transported a man along an off-ground wire from which he dropped at a prescribed point in order to 'land'. The mantra: 'Head well forward, shoulders round, elbows in, and watch the ground', was ingrained in everyone who undertook parachute training at RAF Ringway.

Unlike in England, there was no change in instructing style at Fort Benning during the American parachute training. Indeed, Spencer Wurst says that the instructors deliberately taunted the men: '[The] theme was kept up all throughout our schooling. The instructors always presented the toughness of our training as a personal challenge: "What ya gonna be, a wimp or a man? Are ya good enough to be a trooper or not?"' Moving on to B Stage, during which they learned exiting and landing techniques, trainees leapt from a 10ft high platform and then moved on to jump from a mock fuselage perched 34ft off the ground. Launching themselves from this door, a soldier's fall was arrested by straps on his harness which were connected at the top to a wheel which rolled down a steel cable. It was, according to Ron Reeve, common for some men to 'turn around, go down the steps and never be seen again'. C Stage took the jumps to a 250ft tower, which imitated parachute drops. Whilst a trainee may have passed the previous tests with flying colours, a small but significant number froze when confronted with the tower. Reeve says, 'I saw one guy pee himself after he had spent ten minutes arguing with himself about whether to go ahead or not. Needless to say, he didn't jump.' Others, however, such as Private Howard C. Goodson, revelled in the thrill and the danger:

> The last tower was the best. An actual parachute was hooked up, and when you reached the top, it automatically released you. You were floating along like a regular parachute. The instructor was down below with a bullhorn, and they taught you how to pull on your risers to guide you down. Then you had to land exactly right.

The final part of the training for the Americans (D Stage) and the British was the qualifying jumps themselves. In England the requirement was for two jumps from a balloon and six from an aircraft, all of which took place at nearby Tatton Park. It was the climax of the course, but John Frost's keenness to complete his jump-training was tempered by those who had already been through it:

> Our qualified brother officers were unanimous in their enthu-siasm and even though half of them were damaged in one way or another, we all envied them tremendously. In general I gathered that there was nothing very frightening about it all, that the second jump was worse than the first, that jumping from the stationary balloon was worse than jumping from an aircraft and that one did need to be hard and fit to avoid damage to one's legs and ankles.

As in the United States, some good men could not overcome their fear when asked to jump from a height of more than a few feet. Colin Brown says that 'about 10 per cent chickened out' during this phase of his course. Unlike their American counterparts, the British did not jump with a reserve parachute, which led one gibbering man to ask what would happen if his parachute did not open. His RAF lecturer replied, 'Bring it back and I'll give you another one.' All manner of rumours circulated around Tatton Park about the potential horrors of parachuting, some of which amused instructor Stan Livermore:

> I heard all sorts of facts and figures about parachuting from those that had never done it before – and they were all wrong. I was asked whether it was true that 10 per cent of parachutes failed to open. Of course it wasn't. I was told that casualties caused by jumping always exceeded 50 per cent – way off the mark. I even heard two men chatting over a cup of tea about a chap who became 'strawberry jam' after landing on his head. You ought to have seen the other bloke's face when he heard that! Yes, we had injuries, but the exaggerations were extraordinary.

John Frost made his first balloon jump with the CO of 2 Para:

> Colonel Flavell was cheerful in almost any circumstance, but then
> came the morning when we found ourselves sitting side by side in
> the crazily swinging basket of a balloon which was rising slowly
> ... and we smiled at each other, the learner parachutist's smile,
> which has no joy or humour in it. One merely uncovers one's
> teeth for a second or two then hides them again quickly lest they
> should start chattering.

The first balloon jump was considered by qualified parachutists as the
most nerve-racking – and the most exciting. Ernie Rooke-Matthews
says that 'no jump thereafter gives the same thrill or sense of excitement [because] we were no longer leaping into the unknown'. As a
result the first aircraft jump was something of an anticlimax for
soldiers like Bob Collins:

> We were all worried about flinging ourselves from a perfectly
> good aircraft – it was what we had been building up to – but there
> was nothing to it really. Most of us had already overcome our fear
> of parachuting by that stage – although a few refused at the door
> – and I found it a simple process. Once we were on the ground
> we all wondered what we had been so worried about. That said, I
> do not recall anybody that actually enjoyed military parachuting,
> as the risk of injury remained as great on the tenth jump as it did
> on the first.

American trainees had to make five jumps to qualify. Spencer Wurst
remembers his acute anxiety before his first jump:

> I always had doubts about being successful. I told myself, 'You've
> taken all the crap so far without quitting, even though others have

failed.' My main motivation was to not become less than the men around me. Personal pride, ego, self-esteem – all of it entered into it. What would my friends think if I failed? I had to succeed, I told myself, because failure would be more than I could handle. I *wanted* to be a paratrooper, to walk with the pride and self-confidence of a man who had proven himself a notch or two above the ordinary. But I was scared. I believe 95 per cent of us were, and the other 5 per cent were maybe liars.

The original members of the test platoon were so nervous about their first jump that it was arranged for them to see a 150lb dummy pushed out of an aircraft and float safely to earth prior to it. The platoon gathered excitedly to see the bundle released from the aircraft, but then watched in horror as its parachute failed to open and it smashed into the ground in front of them. On the night of Babe Heffron's last qualification jump, one of the aircraft crashed, killing all 16 on board.

Those who successfully completed the parachute courses on both sides of the Atlantic were rewarded with small but immensely coveted badges – the parachutist's wings. Out of the original 165 men on James Sims' course, just 60 qualified, and so the receipt of their wings, he remembers, was 'one of the greatest moments of our lives and one of the proudest'. Whilst the British received cloth wings which were worn at the top of the right sleeve, American parachutists were given metal silver wings, which they pinned over their left breast-pocket. Bill Guarnere was awarded his by Colonel Robert Sink, and says, 'Those wings made you different, and you never took them off.' Yet these new graduates all recognized that they still had a great deal more to learn before they could call themselves competent paratroopers, and so readily embarked on their next phase of training, which taught them how to think and fight as airborne soldiers. For the British, this meant time on the battle training course at Hardwick Hall, which familiarized the men with their weaponry and equipment, whilst exercises were based around the various missions that they were likely to undertake. It was here that the paratrooper became acquainted with his unique role and, learned, in Richard Gale's words:

> that once on the ground his future lies in his own skills. The gun which he carried down in his drop and the small supply of ammunition on his person are his only weapons for support in either attack or defence. His water and food are what he can carry when he jumps. His sense of direction, his skill in fieldcraft and in mapreading and his physical strength must all be of a high order. He may be alone for hours, he may be injured, he may be dazed from his fall. But it is his battlefield, and he knows it. There is no 'A' Company on his left and 'B' Company on his right. There is no barbed wire and no well-defended defensive line to cling to. There is no close artillery support and there are no tanks. If he is lucky and wins through his first fight, later these things will come to him. But the initial battle is his.

The American paratroopers underwent a similar training regime which, as in England, began with the development of the individual soldier, before progressing on to the squad, platoon, company and battalion. Spencer F. Wurst was sent to Company I in 507 PIR of 82 US Airborne Division, and says that at this time he got a chance to fire a plethora of weapons, developed his endurance, took part in live-firing exercises and solved tactical problems that 'helped us greatly in future operations'. It was quite clear to all concerned that what they were doing was wholly focused on getting the troops ready for battle. Bill Guarnere remembers that as the weeks went by, 'the training got harder and more complicated, more combat-orientated'. During this time each man became more competent, each unit more cohesive, and great strides were taken towards the production of outstanding fighting outfits. 'Through specific small-unit training', says platoon commander Fenton

Richards, 'we got to know each other, trust each other, and dealt with the "what if?" questions using whatever methods we could. We took away as much of the fear of the unknown as we could, and in that way we prepared our boys for battle.'

Whilst the paratroopers were at the heart of the Allies' airborne divisions, the formations were strengthened by gliders which inserted infantry, divisional troops, vehicles, weapons and other equipment. Two British gliders were used operationally: the Airspeed Horsa and the General Aircraft Hamilcar. Tugged by the Albemarle, Short Stirling or C-47, the Horsa was 67ft long and had an 88ft wingspan. Its two pilots were housed in the perspex nose of the aircraft, from where they controlled the ungainly looking plywood contraption. It could deliver 25 fully equipped troops, combinations of jeeps, trailers and 75mm guns, or up to 3½ tons of cargo. Pilot Eddie Raspison says that the Horsa was:

a wonderful aircraft which handled impeccably both on tow and in free flight, heavy or light, and in all conditions. And since it could glide approximately 2½ miles for every 1,000 feet of height, a totally silent approach could be made to an objective without the noise of aircraft engines alerting the enemy – known as a remote release.

The Hamilcar was a much larger aircraft and could only be tugged by powerful bombers such as the Halifax, Stirling and Lancaster. It too was wooden and it measured 68ft in length, with a wingspan of 110ft. Its two pilots were perched above the cargo door, which had a hinged nose to give access to a large, square cargo area. This space could be used to transport various combinations of light tanks, Bren gun carriers, scout cars, 25lb guns or up to 7 tons of cargo. Pilot Andrew Taylor says:

The Hamilcar was a remarkable design, but could be a devil to fly, being so big and heavy. The stresses and strains on the aircraft were immense, and trying to get the crate to stop on landing was always an interesting challenge – particularly as the buggers had a habit of flipping over and crushing the pilots.

The Americans did not have a Hamilcar equivalent, but they did have the Waco CG-4A – known as the 'Hadrian' by the British – which was tugged by a C-47. Described by one pilot as looking like 'a dark green blunt-nosed dragonfly', the Waco was just under 49ft long, with a wingspan of nearly 84ft. Its fuselage was constructed of steel tubing, but its wings and tail were wooden and covered with fabric. Piloted by two men, it could carry 13 men, a Jeep and its crew or carry cargo. John Lowden and his co-pilot felt extremely vulnerable in their flimsy Waco, and were so worried at the lack of protection under the cockpit that they 'scrounged up armoured plate' to sit on. He recalls: 'We did not by any means discount the narrow odds of taking a shot in the foot or leg. But we were even more antsy about taking a slug of silver or shrapnel in the butt or family jewels.'

The importance of having properly trained and motivated pilots to deliver troops and their equipment accurately and in good order was soon recognized by airborne commanders. Be they the pilots of the glider tugs, parachute transporters or resupply aircraft, all needed special skills. The requirement to fly low, slowly and accurately – sometimes in the dark and often attracting enemy ground fire – required not just great technical ability but also nerve and bravery. However, in both the United States and Britain, the 'best' pilots rarely found themselves supporting airborne operations as they were siphoned off for 'more important jobs'. This placed a great responsibility on the RAF and USAAF to work hard to train the airborne pilots to the very highest standards. Piloting of a similar excellence was also required of the glider crews if they were to deliver their cargo and passengers intact. In

Britain these men were volunteers who, after a selection interview and medical, undertook six weeks of soldier training at the Glider Pilot Regiment Depot on Salisbury Plain. Eddie Raspison, who had fought with the infantry at Dunkirk before applying to become a glider pilot, says:

It was felt that those accepted should be not only complete soldiers and airmen but fit, strict disciplinarians, proficient in the handling and firing of all airborne weapons and the driving of all vehicles, *and* capable of acting as infantrymen or gunners, taking their place alongside the troops they carried into battle!

Only after passing this course were the volunteers taught how to fly: first in light aircraft, and then in the small Hotspur training glider. Having attained their Army Flying Badge at the end of the phase, the pilots then moved on to special Horsa and Hamilcar training at the Heavy Glider Conversion Unit. Once qualified, they became members of the Glider Pilot Regiment with the retained rank of Staff-Sergeant, and began to hone their new-found flying skills on exercises and further courses. American glider pilots underwent a similar pattern of training, having volunteered from the Army Air Corps. John Lowden has written that the job attracted 'an odd lot':

The maximum age was thirty-five, rather than twenty-six, as it was for the military power pilots. Minor physical disabilities, such as less-than-perfect eyesight, were not a problem ... In short, we were a mix of men like me who had washed out [he had failed powered aircraft training]; weekend pilots, some over the age limit for power-pilot training; and enlisted men and officers from all branches of the military service, as well as hundreds of civilians, who had no previous flight training but who had the urge to fly.

In the United States there was also a basic flying course, followed by instruction on gliders, an advanced course and then qualification. However, when it came to infantry training there were distinct differences between the British and American approach. The British viewed their glider pilots as an essential ground asset, whilst the Americans believed that their glider pilots were pilots first and foremost, and thus extended their infantry training little further than the basic skills and tactics.

The glider transported infantry not drawn from individual volunteers were provided by units converted from other roles. In England, Albert Blockwell of the Royal Army Ordnance Corps (RAOC) was attached to the 7/King's Own Scottish Borderers (KOSB) when that battalion was re-roled in August 1943. It was a move that shocked everyone, he remembers, when announced by the CO at a parade:

> Well, when he said that I guess anybody could have wafted all of us down with a feather. As I stood there in that hall I could literally feel the whole crowd sway with surprise. We just looked at each other and mouths opened, but not a word was spoken. Not that we were afraid to go into action, oh no! The spirit was there all right, but we just wanted to know what our chances were. Very few of us were afraid to go into the fight, so long as we were given a fighting chance against the other guy. We didn't mind having the odds against us on the ground as long as we had a good chance of getting down to the ground.

Thus it was by chance that the vast majority of glider infantry became airborne troops, as Jimmy Mason of 82 US Airborne Division laments with considerable bitterness: 'We didn't choose the gliders, they chose us. I had to go into battle in a toy plane and then have my ass shot off because I was in the wrong infantry unit at the wrong time.' He tried to argue that he should be rejected on account of his flat feet, but he was passed fit. However, there was potential for considerable unofficial 'local selection' during these medicals, as CSM WO2 J. Swanston of the 7/KOSB remembers:

> A weeding-out process started, and for my own company this process turned out to be satisfactory. The method was an easy one. I marched the men one by one to the Medical Officer. I was to stand just behind the man to be examined and then I would just nod yes or no to the doctor. This resulted in a positive or negative check. I am sure than some never understood why they were turned down.

The glider infantry training covered, as with all the other airborne troops: fitness, insertion techniques, familiarity with weapons and tactics. There was, however, the obligatory 'spit 'n bullshit' phase that was the precursor to all military courses of this type. Len Lebenson remembers clearly that his time at Fort Bragg began with:

> close-order drill, manual of arms, marching in small and large formations, and received instruction in the care and cleaning of the M-1 rifle . . . We [also] did the obligatory washing down of the wooden barracks floor using toothbrushes, and suffered white glove inspections.

Those who were deemed to have the required level of airborne aptitude after the initial stage then moved on to Maxton in North Carolina for a week of specialist training in gliders. Unlike their parachuting brothers-in-arms, there was no need for the glider infantry to spend a great deal of time on their method of insertion, as 'brace up and pray' was far easier to teach than jumping out of an aircraft on a static line. Thus after a brief time practising loading and unloading, landing positions and exiting, the troops moved on to light infantry tactics. The British course was very similar and it was with considerable concern that Albert Blockwell undertook his first flight in a glider:

> So we climbed in, fastened straps, held our breath and said a silent prayer, (at least, I think I did). The roar of the four engines of the bomber rose louder and louder, until the glider shuddered and vibrated in the wind. Then, with a jerk, we were moving – faster and faster! We tore down that runway, then we lifted and like the others [we had watched], slipped from left to right. I could see the green fields flying past the wing – 160 mph! I looked at the bomber, it was still tearing along, and I said under my breath, 'Come on, old pal, get her up', and then we were both airborne and well off the ground. I experienced all of that every time I took off – no wonder we had to have good hearts.

Sitting in the swaying gliders, it was not unusual for the men to feel airsick. Corporal Charles Wilson says: 'Vomiting was part of the deal. Some used their helmet as bowls, but most just did it straight onto the floor – to the anger of the pilots who would have to wash it out.' The vomiting was a major problem as it weakened and dehydrated its sufferers before they had even reached the battlefield. There were numerous attempts to try to find a treatment to stop the symptoms but, as Major Napier Crookenden found out, they did not work: '[I] and 19 volunteers from brigade head-quarters made a dozen flights in Horsas to try out a dozen anti-airsick-ness remedies – and all were sick a dozen times.'

Few men enjoyed riding in a glider. As Corporal Billy Meyers, a former tank-driver from London, says: 'who would like being cooped up in a confined space for hours wearing full kit with vomit sloshing around their feet, providing a nice slow target for ground fire, awaiting the crash landing – and then having to fight a battle?' It was not without good reason that gliders soon earned a reputation for being 'flak bait' and 'flying coffins', and their pilots 'suicide jockeys'. Indeed, in the

United States between May 1943 and February 1944, 17 men were killed and a further 162 injured in crashes, and in England Lieutenant-Colonel John Rock was killed whilst testing a glider. In 1943 a demonstration in front of several generals went badly wrong when a Horsa carrying a platoon of the Royal Ulster Rifles (RUR) skidded into an oak tree at 55 mph. The troops in the rear, who had already released their seat-belts so that they could make an impressively fast exit, were hurled into the bulkhead on impact, whilst the first pilot was thrown through the cockpit windscreen. The pilots often bore the brunt of poor landings because, sitting in the nose, they were vulnerable. Moreover, although the gliders took off on wheels, on operations and on exercise they landed on metal skids, which provided little control over direction or speed and made them liable to crash. On one occasion John Lowden landed his Waco carrying a trailer and eight men safely, but hit a depression in the field whilst still slowing:

> The trailer snapped its mooring lines on impact, came hurtling forward and sheared off the floor-bolts of my seat and the co-pilot's. Both the lieutenant [in the co-pilot's seat] and I were slammed into the instrument panel. Because the skids were buried, the nose couldn't automatically rise up, so the rear of the glider whipped up instead and the fuselage broke away where the nose was hinged. The only thing that saved me from serious injury (I lost some front teeth and banged up my back and face) was the fact that I was wearing my heavy, fleece-lined, leather flying jacket. The airborne lieutenant had on only his combat fatigues and the crash almost broke him in half. Christ! I will never forget his screams. The eight badly battered troops ended up a hundred feet in front of the glider's nose, hanging upside down in the fuselage from their seat-belts.

Even though the glider troops chalked messages on the side of their aircraft such as 'Why march into battle when you can ride?', they knew that there were plenty of sound reasons why a soldier would not want to ride into battle in a glider. They needed a sense of humour, and it was these same men who produced the self-mocking posters that were pinned up around their barracks. One American bill proclaimed 'Join the glider troops! No flight pay. No jump pay. But never a dull moment!' The earnings issue jarred with the US glider men for whilst their British counterparts received an extra shilling a day, they did not receive any supplement until July 1944, when they then became entitled to the same pay as the parachutists. As a result, the glider infantry, although an essential part of the airborne team with a remarkably dangerous job, often felt that they lived in the shadow of their more glamorous and famous parachuting brethren. But it was a situation that they learned to live with, for they understood that their method of arriving on the battlefield made them very special soldiers. Walter Cronkite sympathized with these men and wrote after a combat glider landing whilst a war correspondent: 'I'll tell you straight out: If you've got to go into combat, don't go by glider. Walk, crawl, parachute, swim, float – anything. But don't go by glider!'

Whilst there was an undoubted rivalry between the different cap badges within the airborne forces, it was almost always healthy. Binding the men together was what they shared: tough training, insertion by air, small numbers, high standards, a sublime fighting ethos and the uniqueness of their role. In Britain, the sartorially aware 'Boy' Browning sought to enhance the strong *esprit de corps* that had grown within the airborne forces by providing them with a clear visual identity in 1942. The result was a distinctive maroon (not red) beret which was worn by all airborne soldiers with the badge of their regiment or corps affixed, and a claret and light blue insignia of the Greek warrior Bellerophon – the first airborne warrior – riding his winged horse Pegasus, which was worn on the battledress sleeve. In the United States an airborne identity was created by the wearing of 'jump boots' with 'bloused' trousers. Looking the part was important to Bill Guarnere who says:

> We were 18, 19 years old when we went in. We knew we wanted to be the best and fight beside the best. Be in the Airborne. Be paratroopers. The uniform alone showed the world you were different and special. You put on those silver wings, bloused up your pants, and you were it.

Qualified troops could also wear their own special circular-shaped cloth insignia which was sewn on to their foldable 'overseas' hats. The parachutist's badge, for example, was a white parachute on a blue background within a white circle, whilst the glider infantry wore a red glider on a white background in a red circle. Glider troops were also entitled to wear a glider badge over their right pocket, aping the paratrooper's jump wings. The two US airborne divisions also had their own heraldry, with the men of the 101st wearing a 'Screaming Eagle' patch on their sleeve, and the 82nd the 'Double A' denoting its 'All American' origins. These badges, the shared experience, the sense of being a part of something 'special' all helped to bond the soldiers to their units and, ultimately, to each other.

The success of the conditioning became increasingly tangible as combat drew nearer, as Spencer Wurst of 505 PIR relates:

> Many soldiers who could have stayed back for any number of legitimate reasons . . . did not. They were eager to go into combat, and they made it their business to get there . . . Nothing was more crucial than that bond to our individual will to fight and prevail, nothing more essential to our pride in ourselves as a unit.

Second Lieutenant Harold Watkins, a paratrooper in 101 US Airborne Division, saw his platoon develop into a tightly knit outfit during training. He noted in his diary that they had 'gained the ability to anticipate the moves of others and to work as if as one'. He continued:

> We have become a family with all its strengths and weaknesses. We rely on each other totally. The platoon has become our province and the company our world. Some of the men relish it because it is the first family that they have enjoyed. We can tell by a look or an intonation of the voice how someone is feeling, their innermost thoughts. Like a family we squabble, but mostly we joke about everything and above all – stick together.

Albert Blockwell also recalls enjoying the camaraderie of his glider unit in England: 'we didn't care [about anything] – that was the spirit that was wanted and that was the spirit we had. We took everything with a laugh and a joke, and we always laughed at somebody else's misfortune, but tried to help them if we could, at the same time.'

A good sense of humour was as essential to an airborne soldier as anything else in his personal armoury, but when mixed with a keen sense of identity, pride, competitiveness and physical excellence could result in a remarkable degree of aggression. This aggression had, of course, been deliberately nurtured during training so that it could explode in an organized fashion on the battlefield, but it often spilled out in brawls when not sufficiently tamed. 'It was always E Company versus the whole damn world', says Bill Guarnere, whilst one observer wrote of 505 PIR:

> Every man a clone of the CO, Gavin. Tough? God they were tough! Not just in the field, but twenty-four hours a day. Off duty they'd move into a bar in little groups and if everyone there didn't get down on their knees in adoration, they'd simply tear the place up. Destroy it. And God help the 'straight legs' [regular troops] they came across.

The addition of alcohol to the already heady airborne cocktail was only more likely to lead to a fight between units, formations, arms and, of course, airborne troops against all-comers. John Lowden recalls walking into a bar frequented by paratroopers with some glider pilot colleagues and before long there was a brawl:

> It was a fair fight, with little serious slugging. Mostly contact was wrestling and trying out hand-to-hand tactics learned in training . . . As the futility and foolishness of the encounter sunk in, the fighting spirit petered out. We shook hands all around and returned to the bar, where it was agreed (over quite a few glasses of beer) that paratroopers and glider riders were going to make an unbeatable combination in combat.

In 2 Para there was a Scottish company who, John Frost remarks: 'weren't particular who they fought and if there was no one else available as an enemy, then the English would do very well'.

Sometimes it was the officers who needed to let off steam, as Gavin has written:

> There was this thing they did to show how tough they were. They'd have a few drinks at the Officer's Club and start jumping – off high places, like the balcony onto the dance floor. Then, after a few more drinks, they'd start jumping out of the second-floor bathroom window, which was about the size of a door on a C-47.

The officers were not flawless – their men would not have expected them to be so – and a sense of fun was seen as a worthy characteristic, but they had to set standards and be capable of imposing their will on a situation. An airborne officer could not afford to be flummoxed by events, as Brigadier James Hill told his officers before going into battle:

'Gentlemen, despite your excellent training, preparation and orders, do not be daunted if chaos reigns. It undoubtedly will.' Above all, the officers needed to be strong leaders, as Bill Lee reminded his junior officers: 'When you first lead your men into the valley of the shadow of death they will look to you with pathetic eagerness for leadership, and you had better be ready.' It was not an easy job marshalling the ebullient airborne troops, keeping them keen whilst continuing to develop their skills and making them combat ready. It came as a relief to many officers, therefore, when the time came to put the effectiveness of their troops to the test.

The 1 British and 82 American Airborne Divisions were blooded in the Mediterranean campaign, where they gained valuable experience in both the planning and conduct of operations and a fearsome fighting reputation. North Africa proved a particularly difficult début for 1 Parachute Brigade, which suffered nearly 1,700 casualties in six months of fighting from late 1942, but it was here that the Germans began to refer to them as '*den roten Teufeln*' – the Red Devils. The invasion of Sicily during the summer of 1943 involved both British and American airborne troops with some success, but only after a poor start. Inserted during the night of 9–10 July ahead of the amphibious assault to help them create a beachhead, Jim Gavin's 505 PIR was scattered over hundreds of square miles due to poor weather, and only 52 of 1 Airlanding Brigade's 137 gliders made landfall. To make matters worse, on the following night, 23 of 504 PIR's transporters were shot down having been mistaken for the enemy. Sergeant Len Lebenson of 82 Airborne Division Headquarters watched the spectacle unfold from Sicilian soil, and he later wrote: 'Dozens of planes went down, and I heard that some gunners kept shooting at planes that had splashed in the water. The air armada was decimated . . . It was horrifying to watch.' Yet despite the difficulties caused by their unedifying insertion, the airborne forces managed to scatter and confuse the enemy, take important objectives and undermine counterattacks against the beachhead. The capture of Sicily therefore provided plenty for the Allied airborne commanders to cogitate on, much to feel satisfied with, but also showed up many areas where improvements could be made. Some improvements had already been pushed through by the time that the Allies invaded mainland Italy in early September. Although 1 British Airborne Division was landed by ship at Taranto, 504 and 505 PIR were inserted by air when Fifth Army's landing at Salerno ran into difficulty in the middle of the month. Successfully reinforcing the beachhead and taking the brunt of numerous German blows, the American parachutists were awarded the epithet 'the devils in baggy pants' by the Germans.

With the two divisions back in England by the end of the year – less 504 PIR which was to fight at Anzio that winter – there began a process of soaking up lessons and passing on knowledge to the other formations by swapping personnel, holding study-days and undertaking joint exercises. Yet the Mediterranean campaign had done little to silence the critics of airborne warfare, with Dwight Eisenhower himself writing to General George Marshall: 'I do not believe in the airborne division.' Many observers could not see past – or were disinclined to look beyond – the risk, weaknesses and resources associated with airborne warfare as illustrated by a British War Office report dated 12 December 1943, which stated:

at a time when we are scouring the country to find infantry and transport aircraft remain at a premium, the launching of high-risk airborne operations seems to be a frivolity that this nation is not in a strong position to sustain ... What we have learned from 1943 is that airborne attacks do not offer the decisive impact that some expected.

General Omar Bradley, an airborne supporter, later reflected that events in the Mediterranean 'seriously jeopardized the future of airborne operations; many of my infantry cohorts declared the paratrooper a dead dodo.' Nevertheless, when faced with the challenge of an Allied invasion of Normandy it became difficult for Eisenhower to dismiss the airborne divisions, and they soon became an integral part of his vision.

Following a period of intense training, three Allied airborne divisions launched Operation Overlord in the early hours of 6 June 1944. The 101 US Airborne Division – commanded by Major-General Maxwell D. Taylor after Lee had suffered a heart attack – worked with the 82nd to secure the right flank of the Allied beachhead, whilst 6 British Airborne Division, formed the previous spring and commanded by Major-General Richard Gale, did the same on the left. In spite of problems with scattering once again – particularly in the US sector – the divisions managed to take critical objectives in advance of the ground forces, confused and stretched the German defences, and effectively protected the nascent Allied foothold on French soil. The result was the most effective large-scale Allied airborne operation to date, so effective in fact that SHAEF was soon clamouring for more. In the meantime, the formations returned to England to lick their wounds, rest and reorganize. One of the most pressing jobs was to replace casualties with new men, not a simple task with such heavy losses having been suffered. Private First Class (PFC) Henry Matzelle, a clerk for a rifle company in 505 PIR, recorded: 'Of the 162 [officers and] men who went to Normandy, 23 were killed outright, 94 were wounded and evacuated, and 45 of us returned to England.' Nevertheless, both the replacements and lessons from Normandy had to be absorbed quickly in preparation for the next mission. Bill Guarnere remembers:

we ran through training over and over, again and again. There were mistakes made in Normandy ... The officers saw those mistakes and set out plans to correct them. We went over them in Aldbourne [where they were based] and drilled them into the replacements, too. We started training with live ammo, it was good for the kids who were never in combat. When you see bullets flying, you learn to crawl as low as possible, to move on the ground like a snake. We trained on different types of terrain, trained at night, during the day, in all kinds of conditions. All kinds of exercises, over and over.

By the late summer of 1944, four Allied airborne divisions had gained operational experience and offered SHAEF flexible and dynamic fighting options. FAAA was established in early August to control the divisions, make plans and liaise between ground and air assets. The formation of FAAA made it even more difficult for the high command to ignore the clarion cry of airborne operations and it became the Allied Strategic Reserve. The Army's commander was an airman named Lieutenant-General Lewis H. Brereton, and under his purview came the troop-carrier squadrons consisting of 1,300 C-47 transport aircraft – mostly belonging to US IX Troop Carrier Command, but some to 38 and 46 Groups RAF – along with I British and XVIII US Airborne Corps. The British corps was commanded by Browning, who also served as Brereton's deputy, and was made up of 1 and 6 British Airborne Divisions, 1 Polish Independent Parachute Brigade and the attached air transportable 52 British Lowland Division. The American corps consisted of the newly formed 17 US Airborne Division together with the 82nd and 101st. With Ridgway promoted chief of XVII US Airborne Corps, Gavin stepped up to command the 82nd, becoming at the age of 37 the youngest major-general in the US Army. Born into the heady atmosphere of the Allied breakout from Normandy, FAAA was tasked by Eisenhower to prepare a plan which, Brereton noted in his diary, 'would have as its purpose a maximum contribution to the destruction of the German armies in western Europe. He wants imagination and daring . . .' Urged on by Generals Marshall and Arnold, who wanted to see what FAAA could achieve, Eisenhower wanted a grand plan that would both satisfy Washington and further his advance towards Germany. In such circumstances there was an excitement surrounding Allied airborne warfare, the like of which had never before been experienced, and which led Matthew Ridgway to comment: 'Not since the days when the Greeks of classical mythology abandoned a gigantic wooden horse at the gates of Troy had military forces brought forth such a startling new dimension to the conduct of war.'

Having granted Montgomery the use of FAAA, a series of ideas were taken to various stages of development to help Twenty-First Army Group's 'northern thrust' towards the Ruhr. Some of these never left the drawing-board and others were rendered useless by the speed of the ground advance. Even so, in early September one plan attained a military and political momentum which made it virtually unstoppable – Operation Market Garden.

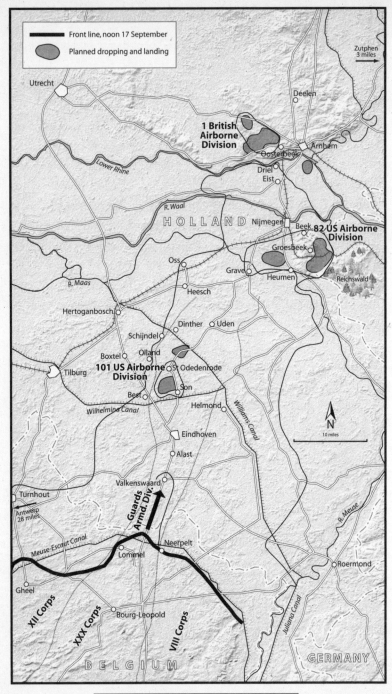

Map 2 : The Market Garden Plan

CHAPTER 4

Stitching Things Together

(Planning: 10–17 September 1944)

The two commanders looked like 'The Odd Couple' standing side by side as the officers entered the room. Lieutenant-General Lewis Brereton was a small, shambling man who, with his steel-rimmed spectacles, receding hair and crumpled clothing, looked more like a tired suburban accountant, or a harassed night-shift newspaper editor than the commander of a mighty airborne army. He was chain-smoking: a man under pressure. By contrast, the handsome Lieutenant-General Frederick 'Boy' Browning was an imposing figure, immaculate and resplendent in his well-cut service dress, gleaming Sam Browne belt, medal ribbons and Glider Pilot Wings: a man of action in full control.

It was 1800 hours on 10 September, and Brereton's office at FAAA Headquarters near Ascot was filling up with a variety of uniforms – Army, RAF and USAAF – all with a plethora of badges. At first it was possible to discern British, American and Polish accents, but they soon blended into an excited hubbub. The voices belonged to the 34 key commanders and staff officers who were to be intimately concerned with the planning of Operation Market Garden and included its three airborne GOCs: Maxwell D. Taylor, Jim Gavin and Roy Urquhart.

Brereton asked the gathering for their attention, and silence fell immediately. In his Pittsburghese he thanked them for coming, but wasted no time in inviting Browning, the commander of the operation, to outline the plan. He spoke animatedly – but carefully – for 15 minutes in his cut-glass English accent, tracing circles with his finger around the key locations on a large, hastily prepared map. His audience were models of concentration, enthralled by the boldness of his proposals: it was just the sort of operation that many of them had been hoping for. When Browning had finished, Brereton shuffled forward, his shoulders slightly hunched, and perched himself on the edge of his cluttered desk. He reminded the room that the scheme provided for 'the largest airborne operation that had ever been mounted' and that planning time would be short in order 'to make use of the advantageous German situation in Holland'. The General wished the officers luck in their endeavours and bade them good evening. As one, them rose to leave.

Earlier that day, Eisenhower and Montgomery had met in Brussels to talk about strategy, resources and plans for the 'northern thrust'. With the vanguard of Twenty-First Army Group on the verge of entering Holland, Montgomery sought to plunge forward and cross the Rhine in order to create a launch-pad for further operations. An advance by the Second Army's XXX Corps – Operation Garden – would be supported by around 35,000 paratroopers and glider infantry of the newly created First Allied Airborne Army landing in Holland – Operation Market: 101 US Airborne Division in the south near Eindhoven, 82 US Airborne Division in the middle at Nijmegen, and 1 British Airborne Division and 1 Polish Independent Parachute Brigade in the north outside Arnhem. It was a stunningly audacious plan and being inter-Allied, inter-service and inter-arm, was also hugely complex and a massive risk. It was now up to the planners, both ground and airborne, to manage those risks and mitigate them: to give the operation the best chance they could of succeeding. These men worked fast and tirelessly to ensure that the various essentials were in place: there was no time for last-minute changes – once a decision was taken it had to be stuck to – for Market Garden was to be launched on 17 September.

There were many challenges facing XXX Corps in its part of the operation. Led by the Guards Armoured Division, followed by 43 (Wessex) Division, it would have to gain sufficient momentum to pass quickly up a narrow 65-mile-long road which, on its route to the Lower Rhine at Arnhem, passed through many towns and villages and over numerous waterways. This single artery was also surrounded by boggy ground, impossible for heavy vehicles to traverse, whilst the few minor roads leading off it were not suitable for military traffic due to fragile bridges over innumerable streams. Thus if the Germans cut the main road or destroyed a bridge, XXX Corps had little option but to stop and create a vulnerable 20,000 vehicle traffic-jam until the blockage was removed. Indeed, Major the Hon. Freddie Hennessy, the operations officer of the Guards Armoured Division, said that advancing up the road would be 'like threading seven needles with one piece of cotton, and we only have to miss one to be in trouble'. With his options severely limited, the XXX Corps commander, Brian Horrocks, decided 'to blast my way down the main road on a comparatively narrow front with as much air and artillery as I could get'. To support his flanks VIII Corps would be on the right and XII Corps on the left but, as the General later said, 'as most of the available resources had been allotted to us, it was realized that they would not be able to advance quickly, and we should be operating on our own for a considerable period'. Nevertheless, a break-out from the Meuse–Escaut Canal was expected quickly, with the first Guards tanks timetabled to reach Eindhoven within two to three hours, and Arnhem in two to three days.

The Operation Garden schedule was so demanding largely because of the need to relieve the vulnerable airborne troops that were to be dropped along the route's length to take bridges, hold open the road and dominate vital ground. To achieve this, Browning's force had to construct a robust plan, but it was necessarily shaped by the requirements of IX US Carrier Command, which had overall responsibility for the airlift. Amongst the first decisions taken was for a daylight insertion to assist accuracy, but at the insistence of Major-General Paul L. Williams, commander of IX US Carrier Command, that insertion would have to take place over three lifts spread out over three days. It was a decision based in the lack of adequate aircraft to fly the airborne force to Holland *en masse*, but he rejected two lifts on the first day due to concerns about air crew fatigue and the time needed to undertake aircraft maintenance and repair battle damage. Just when risks needed to be taken, Williams believed that aircraft survivability outweighed all else, and Brereton, an airman, backed that stance. It was a decision that fundamentally affected the airborne plan with the extra lifts diminishing their surprise and diluting their initial attacking strength to objectives, a problem exacerbated by the need for men to protect the DZs and LZs for subsequent lifts. The plan for three lifts also made the operation more vulnerable to the weather, which could delay the later arrivals. Moreover, the divisional commanders faced the dilemma of deciding what each lift should contain. Taylor was to receive the bulk of the first lift, Gavin the next largest share and Urquhart – despite being dropped the furthest from the front line – the smallest portion. The premise of this 'bottom to top' priority was to ensure that 1 British Airborne Division was reached, rather than ensuring that the formation had the resource to fight the longest. To make the British plight even more precarious – but also affecting the other two airborne divisions and Second Army – Williams insisted that the immensely valuable support offered to troops on the ground by fighters and fighter-bombers was to be prohibited during airborne insertion and resupply due to the fear of collision in congested air space over the battlefield. It was another stunning example of a risk-averse decision which had the potential to undermine the whole operation.

With the fundamentals of the air plan worked out, it was then the job of the airborne divisional commanders to develop their ground plans. The 101st had the task of seizing two major canal crossings, nine road and railway bridges, whilst also holding open a 15-mile stretch of highway. To achieve this, Taylor decided to land his 502 and 506 PIRs along with divisional headquarters at the centre of his sector just 1½ miles north-west of the critical Son bridge over the Wihelmina Canal, and equidistant from Eindhoven and Veghel. Meanwhile, 501 PIR was to land further to the north in order to take its bridges over the Willems Canal and the Aa River. In doing this, Taylor would strike early with his parachute troops, and leave his heavier glider force for the later lifts in the hope that by the time artillery support was required, XXX Corps would be on hand to supply it.

North of Veghel, the 82nd had a string of objectives. Along with the need to defend a 10-mile section of road, the division had also to dominate some high ground and capture a number of bridges. So numerous were the goals that Jim Gavin's Chief of Staff, Colonel Robert H. Wienecke, believed the division needed to be twice as strong to achieve its mission. (After the war his boss admitted: 'I was deeply troubled by the possibility of failing to accomplish some of my objectives.') Even so, both Gavin and Browning decided that the priority was the Groesbeek Heights, overlooking the city of Nijmegen and adjacent to the Reichswald – a forest which ran along the border with Germany. It was thought that this area might provide a launch-pad for an enemy counterattack. Thus landing zones were chosen just 1½ miles from the Heights and three to four miles south-east of Nijmegen. Here, the 508 and 505 PIRs would land on the first day, together with a battalion of air-landing artillery and divisional headquarters, with the rest of the Glider Infantry Regiment following in subsequent lifts. With units to take the high ground allocated, Gavin then assigned 504 PIR to seize the bridges over the Maas River and the Maas–Waal Canal south of Nijmegen with nearby DZs to facilitate this as quickly as possible. There was no detailed arrangement to take the vital road and railway bridges over the wide Waal in Nijmegen immediately on landing due to the other pressing requirements; they would be attacked once the other objectives were safely in the division's hands, and possibly with the assistance of XXX Corps.

In spite of the difficulty of the tasks faced by the two American divisions, it was 1 British Airborne Division that was being dropped over 60 miles behind the German lines that faced the greatest challenge. Browning's Operation Instruction to Roy Urquhart stated:

Your Primary task is to capture the Arnhem bridges or a bridge.

Your Secondary task is to establish a sufficient bridgehead to enable the follow-up formations of 30 Corps to deploy North of the Neder Rijn. [Your third task] During your operation immediately after the landing of the first lift, you will do all in your power to destroy the flak in the area of your DZs, LZs and Arnhem to ensure the passage of your subsequent lifts.

Yet Urquhart's ability to achieve this was put in jeopardy on 11 September when he was informed that enemy flak precluded his troops from being landed near the main Arnhem bridge objective. Some heavy enemy anti-aircraft fire had been witnessed in the area by RAF bomber pilots *en route* to Germany during August, particularly around Deelen airfield to the north, and this was more influential than the new aerial reconnaissance photographs which suggested that the guns had subsequently been replaced with dummies, dismantled or destroyed in subsequent bombing raids. However, the prospect of an early airborne insertion close to the main bridge was unlikely even without the threat of flak, due to the unsuitability of the ground. Although the northern end of the Arnhem bridge was undeniably cluttered with buildings which made a parachute landing impossible, the possibility of a glider *coup de main* was not even entertained. Furthermore, contentions that the southern end was too wet and obstacle-strewn for an airborne landing were contradicted by the plan to land the Polish Brigade there in the third lift. As Major Anthony Deane-Drummond, second-in-command of the division's signals, later wrote:

> There was no doubt that the RAF were dead set on using DZs to the west. They appeared to be mesmerized by their excellence from an airman's point of view. Every possible snag was put in the way of using DZs to the south of the bridge.

Thus the division had to use five DZs and LZs which although perfect for the job – they were large, flat, open spaces with good access to roads – were between six and eight miles from Arnhem bridge. A tight daylight drop, therefore, raised the spectre of the Germans being able to work out what the likely objectives were and having enough time to block the routes to them. It was a situation that led Browning, the US divisional commanders and their senior staff officers to harbour grave concerns about the British plan when Urquhart briefed them on 14 September. They said nothing, however, recognizing the paucity of practical alternatives. The Americans, moreover, had enough to concern them with their own plans without getting involved in what the Brits were up to. As Gavin later stated, with more than a hint of sarcasm: 'I assumed that the British, with their extensive combat experience, knew exactly what they were doing.' The fact of the matter was that the air plan dictated Urquhart's ground plan to such an extent that his hands were tied, and to make matters worse he had the smallest first lift. Caught between the need to attack his objectives and defend his foothold, he decided on an initial insertion of infantry and artillery which consisted of the entire 1 Parachute Brigade and part of 1 Airlanding Brigade. This left the division's 4 Parachute Brigade to arrive with the remainder of the air-landing brigade in the second lift, and 1 Polish Independent Parachute Brigade to arrive in the third lift. If all went well, Urquhart told Major-General Stanislaw Sosabowski, the 52-year-old commander of the Poles, his brigade would arrive in Arnhem at the same time as the Guards Armoured Division.

The problem perceived by many objective observers was that the plan relied too much on 'if all went well'. Richard Gale, the experienced erstwhile commander of 6 British Airborne Division, saw so many flaws in the Arnhem plan that he later said that he would have resigned rather than carry it out. Sosabowski was also concerned, and on hearing its details declared: 'But the Germans, how about the Germans, what about them?' He knew that Model's men had stopped running and had started reorganizing, and this led him to think that the British had fallen into the trap of seriously underestimating the enemy and their restorative powers. Although his wary position was dismissed as being unnecessarily pessimistic, the Pole's instinct that the Germans were quickly regenerating was sound. Even as Sosabowski examined the plan, bivouacked in the woods and farms north-west of Oosterbeek, a suburb to the west of Arnhem, and between the intended British DZs/LZs and their objectives, was SS Panzer Grenadier Training and Reserve Battalion 16, commanded by an ambitious and capable 37-year-old SS-Captain Sepp Krafft. According to the unit's war diary, by 17 September its strength was '13 officers, 73 NCOs and 349 Other Ranks ... mainly composed of half-trained 17–19 year-old personnel, 40% graded unfit for action. [However] the NCOs' enthusiasm and determination can only be described as outstanding.' Its orders were clear. Krafft was to 'prepare for and attack airborne landings' and 'defend the bridges and ferries over the R. Rhine at Arnhem and to prepare them for demolition'. Even so, Field Marshal Walter Model did not believe that such a valuable asset as the FAAA would be frittered away in southern Holland whilst the Ruhr beckoned. Reflecting this belief, he had recently moved his headquarters to the Tafelberg Hotel in Oosterbeek for safety, although he had also alerted troops throughout the region to the threat of an airborne attack and established small mobile counterattacking *Alarmeinheiten* (alarm units) by way of a precaution.

By the second week of September the Germans were in the process of considerably enhancing their defensive potential. Nevertheless, at the same time Twenty-First Army Group was informing FAAA that German morale and motivation was 'minimal' and that it should not expect to be met by an organized force as the enemy's administration was 'chaotic'. Yet even as Brereton's staff acted on this information, a hotchpotch of Model's troops from different services, arms, formations and units were being successfully bound together into fighting formations. In the space of just a few days the Germans found their leadership once more, and with it their discipline and will-power. Although it may have been true that the Army Group B lacked morale, most remained motivated to fight, whether to defend their border, the honour of their country or something else. All that the rabble had needed to become an army again was some direction. As Corporal Wolfgang Amsel says:

> We understood that Germany would probably lose the war, but we were prepared to fight on. Our homeland was being attacked and to have laid down our weapons would have been done only as a final option . . . We had honour and were ready to die; we had told ourselves that we were already dead, it made it easier.

Many of the Germans fought on in *Kampfgruppen*, which in seeking to fulfil their superior's intent by fighting in the manner that they saw fit, were flexible, fast and dangerous. Collected under the command of accomplished soldiers such as First Parachute Army's Kurt Student, stationed near the front line at Vught, and II SS Panzer Corps' Willi Bittrich, based at Doetinchem, just 25 miles to the east of Arnhem, such formations could prove devastating. Bittrich's 9 SS and 10 SS Panzer

Divisions, which had themselves been designated *Kampfgruppen*, had left some units behind to help Student contain the British on the Meuse–Escaut Canal, but by 9 September the majority of both had arrived in the Arnhem area. Together they amounted to just over 6,000 men, with the 9 SS containing some 20 serviceable and unserviceable Mark V Panther tanks, a handful of self-propelled guns, a few armoured cars and 40 armoured personnel carriers; the 10 SS had very few vehicles of any type. Thus when Bittrich received orders to re-inforce one of the formations with assets from the other and to send the weakest back to Germany for a refit, it was not a straightforward decision. Both had shown their capabilities in the recent fighting withdrawal, were well motivated, capably led, offensively minded and had trained in counter-airborne warfare. The commander of 10 SS, Heinz Harmel, later said:

The whole II SS Corps was especially trained over the previous fifteen months via classroom and radio exercises – all directed to countering a landing supported by airborne forces in Normandy. At the lower end, NCOs and officers were taught to react quickly and make their own decisions. NCOs were taught not to wait until an order came, but to decide for themselves what to do. This happened during the fighting all the time.

In the end, the deciding factor was news that Harmel was shortly to receive some new Panther tanks, and so it was that 9 SS was told to pass on its hardware and prepare itself to move back to the Fatherland. Walter Harzer was distinctly unimpressed and, fearing that it would spell the end for the division, determined to consent and evade. To this end his armoured engineer battalion commander, SS-Captain Hans Moeller, says that his unit only 'gave up three APCs. The remaining two were "out of order" and "unroadworthy".' As a result, by using sleight of hand (removing a track here and a gun-barrel there), Harzer kept hold of his armoured vehicles. What was more, he also decided that as a major new Allied offensive was in the offing he would entrain his strongest units last – on the afternoon of 17 September.

The Allies knew that II SS Panzer Corps was in the Arnhem area because they had been tracking its movement for weeks. Through the use of Ultra decrypts of German Enigma radio ciphers, they gleaned a great deal about the enemy's plans, orders of battle and deployments. As a consequence, the British knew not only where Bittrich's corps was, but also all about its strengths and weaknesses. However, this was such a sensitive source of detailed information that, whilst intelligence gathered from enemy personnel, captured documents, aerial reconnaissance photographs and the Dutch Resistance was fully and liberally distributed to units, Ultra information was severely delayed and diluted as it trickled down from Army Group. As a result, Browning was not made aware of the presence of II SS Panzer Corps in the operational area until 10 September, and neither he nor Urquhart were ever made fully aware of all that was known about Bittrich's command and so could not make a considered judgement about its threat. What the I British Airborne Corps commander was told was that the German corps had been badly mauled, was vastly under strength and did not pose a threat to the operation. Nevertheless, Browning's Senior Intelligence Officer, 25-year-old Major Brian Urquhart (no relation to Roy Urquhart), became increasingly nervous about the proximity of armoured SS formations to the British airborne division's objective. Somewhat underwhelmed by the Market Garden plan at the time, Brian Urquhart later argued that the scheme was riddled with dangerous assumptions:

[The operation] depended on the unbelievable notion that once the bridges were captured, XXX Corps' tanks could drive up this abominably narrow corridor – which was little more than a causeway, allowing no manoeuvrability – and then walk into

Germany like a bride into a church. I simply did not believe that the Germans were going to roll over and surrender.

On making his fears known to Browning and senior staff officers, Brian Urquhart was rebuffed: 'They said, as I remember, that I should not worry unduly, that the reports were probably wrong, and that in any case the German troops were refitting and not up to much fighting.'

As a result, all three Allied airborne division commanders were fed intelligence reports from I British Airborne Corps that glossed over any mention of a significant threat posed by II SS Panzer Corps. One such report of 13 September reveals:

The enemy is fighting determinedly along the two water obstacles Canal Albert and Canal Escaut ... His line is held by the remnants of good Divs including Para Divs, and by new arrivals from Holland, Denmark and inside Germany. The total strength of armour is probably not more than 50–100 Tks, mostly Mk.IV. There is every sign of the enemy strengthening the defence of the river and canals through Arnhem and Nijmegen especially with flak, but the tps manning them are of low category. The flak is sited for dual purpose – both A.A. and ground.

Even so, Brian Urquhart was unwavering in his attempts to find out more about the potency of II SS Panzer Corps, and on 15 September he received the photographs from a low-level RAF reconnaissance sweep of the Arnhem area that he had requested. Five images revealed armoured vehicles trying to avoid detection under camouflage close to the intended British insertion points. Urquhart believed that he now had the evidence that he needed to confront Browning, but the photographs were dismissed as showing 'a few armoured vehicles that are probably unserviceable'. A little later the indomitable Major Urquhart was visited by the corps medical officer, told that he was suffering from exhaustion and sent on sick leave.

So it was that 1 British Airborne Division was forced to make its plans with minimal information, which led Roy Urquhart to write later:

> The planning of the operation was not helped by the scanty intelligence that was coming our way. I knew extremely little of what was going on in and around Arnhem and my intelligence staff were scratching around for morsels of information ... Browning himself told me that we were not likely to encounter anything more than a German brigade group supported by a few tanks.

But whilst Corps gave 1st Airborne an accurate assessment of the size of the German opposition that it was to expect, the quality of the enemy was not inferred; they were not even identified as SS troops. Even so, as Roy Urquhart subsequently said:

> in the division there was a certain reserve about the optimistic reports coming through from 21st Army Group concerning the opposition we were likely to meet ... I had no illusions about the Germans folding up after the first blow. I counted on the likelihood that ... retaliation would get fiercer by the hour.

These 'optimistic reports' were not only received by the airborne forces, however, as XXX Corps' detailed orders for Operation Garden, received on 15 September from Second Army, reveal: 'The total German force, including both remnants of formations now quitting France and Flanders and reinforcements from Germany and satellites, is quite inadequate to offer prolonged resistance along any line.' Such grand simplifications of the situation were greeted with furrowed brows by those who had lately witnessed a new German resolve at the front. Brian Horrocks, for example, could not help wondering why what was obvious to him was not obvious to his superiors. After the war he argued:

> I knew that we were opposed by some tough German paratroops under the command of the redoubtable General Student, and I remembered that the essence of Montgomery's plan had been to keep up a continuous pressure and never give the Germans time to recover from their defeat in Normandy. Yet we had been forced to halt in Brussels for three days, and now another week had been taken up with preparations for this battle. Market Garden could not possibly have been laid on any sooner, but these halts had given the Germans time in which to recover, and their resistance had been stiffening ever since we had advanced from Brussels.

Neither Horrocks nor Browning believed that Operation Market Garden would be an easy victory, for they were experienced enough not only to expect the unexpected but also to recognize that a scheme with so many 'moving parts' was vulnerable. Nevertheless, both were also genuinely convinced that they and their troops would prevail. Browning's confidence in Market Garden in particular was central to the operation being launched rather than aborted. There is little doubt that if he as its commander had serious doubts about its continued efficacy, then it would have been cancelled – or at least have prompted his resignation. Yet his want and his need for the operation to proceed blinkered him to the difficulties caused by the air plan and the increasingly worrying intelligence. One commentator has cast aspersions on Browning's competence by arguing that he was not up to the job, and attributes the General's rise to prominence to 'political aptitude and ruthless ambition, for despite received wisdom and his own pretensions Browning had no operational airborne experience at all'. Browning's ruthlessness had been witnessed by many who had served with him during the Mediterranean campaign, prompting Gavin to write that Ridgway 'cautioned me against the machinations and scheming of General F.A.M. Browning . . . and well he should have'.

To the commander of I British Airborne Corps, Operation Market Garden offered a last chance to attain the experience that he lacked, and he was therefore unsympathetic to anything that might trip up the scheme. So keen was he to make a show with his corps headquarters that it was to be inserted with 82 US Airborne Division in 38 valuable gliders. However, with poor communications and no exercises having been carried out in conjunction with the three divisional headquarters, Browning's presence in Holland was likely to hinder rather than help. Even so, this indulgence was of far less significance than the unswerving support that he offered the operation. By doing so, he fell into the front rank of a powerful section of senior figures which included Marshall and Arnold, keen to see what the FAAA could achieve; Churchill, desirous of the destruction of the Dutch V2 sites; Eisenhower, wishing to further his strategy and attain a Rhine crossing; Brereton, who at last had a plan worthy of FAAA, and Monty, who was following his own agenda. As a result, Market Garden assumed a sacrosanct position among Allied designs and drew strength from the great political momentum behind it. What is more, whilst its authoritative enthusiasts believed that it would be marvellous if Market Garden succeeded, they also felt that it would not be fatal if it failed. It was, therefore, a calculated risk which would be interesting and revealing, whatever happened. As Geoffrey Powell has said, 'Montgomery could have cancelled the operation, but he certainly knew that more battles are lost through indecision than by bold action. His reasons for not wavering were sound indeed.'

The senior commanders in 1 British Airborne Division also found the risks acceptable. Shan Hackett, commander of 4 Parachute Brigade, later wrote:

In retrospect, it seems crazy for my brigade to drop on the second day with all the surprise gone, but we realised that we had to get into battle after all those cancellations. You can't go on doing that to troops of quality. They were so good, so fit, so keyed up, so keen to get on, that you had to get into the battle almost at any price. So shortcomings in the plan were readily forgiven as long as we could get in there.

Roy Urquhart was also keen to get the division into action and to win his airborne spurs, but his later ruminations suggest that that adrenaline may have dulled his critical faculties:

By the time we went on Market Garden, we couldn't have cared less. I mean I really shouldn't admit it, but we really couldn't ... we became callous. Every operation was planned to the best of our ability in every way. But we got bored, and the troops were more bored than we were ... We had approached the state of mind when we weren't thinking as hard about the risks as we possibly had done earlier.

The officers of 1 British Airborne Division were concerned that the division was becoming stale and, as a result, losing some of its fighting efficiency. Geoffrey Powell, a company commander in 156 Para, has written that whilst 6 Airborne was winning the plaudits with its work in Normandy, his men were frustrated as their operations were cancelled:

Nerves had frayed and discipline been upset during the summer. More and more men had drifted away, absent without leave, to return when boredom set in or consciences started to bite. Fights outside pubs with GIs from nearby American units had become a regular Saturday night fixture in the Midlands cities and market towns.

Urquhart argued, however, that there was a positive side to the division's seemingly endless state of alert, for the aborted operations 'had the effect ... of sharpening our state of readiness and advancing our planning to a fine art, also creating a common attitude of eagerness to be off. By September 1944 my division was battle-hungry ... we were ready for anything.' But was it? It should be remembered that although the division – with an average age of 27 – contained prewar regulars and some Dunkirk veterans, casualties sustained during the Mediterranean campaign meant that only half had been in action before, and the newly promoted 42-year-old Roy Urquhart was an airborne newcomer. The big Scot had served with distinction in Sicily and Italy as a brigade commander, and had picked up the division on 10 January 1944 after George Hopkinson had been killed in Italy and his replacement, Eric Down, had been quickly moved on. Both Down, a straight-talking and experienced airborne officer, and Gerald Lathbury, the commander of 1 Parachute Brigade, were obvious choices to command the division, but Browning wanted a more pliable man at the helm. Urquhart was the ideal officer; he came with fighting experience, but could be manipulated far more easily by I British Airborne Corps than those with an airborne pedigree. The downside, however, was less constructive criticism and a commander who had to learn so much so quickly about his complex formation that he could spend less time honing it to a sharp cutting edge. Moreover, Urquhart held some damaging and unchecked assumptions such as his belief that 'an airborne division was a force of high-trained infantry ... and once it had descended from the sky it resorted to normal ground fighting. Infantry rules operated, if under rather different conditions ...' The flaws in this argument have been pointed out by 2 Para's Lieutenant-Colonel John Frost:

> The snag with bringing in a complete newcomer was that however good they might be, they were inclined to think that airborne was just another way of going into battle, whereas in fact the physical and mental, and indeed spiritual problems were, when the battle might be fought without support from the

normal army resources, very different . . . It obviously takes time for anyone to adjust to different circumstances and one of the greatest was the realization of utter dependence on another service in the shape of the RAF.

Urquhart may have suited Browning's purpose, but he was far from being a fool and, in common with other new 'non-airborne' officers, immediately recognized that the airborne forces had begun to believe their own publicity and some complacency had set in. Major Philip Tower, for example, a recent arrival as brigade major to the division's artillery commander, remarks: 'We found the airborne boys, with their red berets, etc, hard to convince that other people had done a lot of fighting in the war. They were a marvellous lot but they overestimated their prowess.' Urquhart, meanwhile, opined:

As a whole, the division contained a great collection of individuals. Wonderful material, but the units and the brigades were short of training as formations. Many of the chaps had done well in North Africa and Sicily. But, in many places, there was a slight reluctance to accept that further training was vitally necessary. So the next few months everywhere were very busy.

But whilst life may well have been busy at division headquarters, there was a distinct lack of field training by the two parachute brigades and only 1 Airlanding Brigade focused on its deficiencies by running several taxing exercises. Cutting around southern England, getting to know his units at their disparate locations and settling into his job, Urquhart failed to drive his division as hard as he might have, and, therefore, it only came together for one exercise, and that was in preparation for its likely Normandy role, which required deployment by road rather than by air. As a result 1 British Airborne Division was not only stale, it also ended up distinctly undercooked.

The 82 and 101 US Airborne Divisions, meanwhile, had a different set of challenges confronting them, caused by strenuous fighting in Normandy. In the few weeks available to them between returning from action and the launch of Operation Market Garden, the formations had to rest, re-equip, reorganize, take on the lessons from Normandy, take up replacements and prepare themselves both physically and mentally for their next mission. Having taken a short, sharp furlough, units were brought back up to strength and training began in earnest. The replacements tried to integrate, but it was not an easy job with one later saying of the Normandy veterans in his 82nd Airborne unit: 'These were a bunch of very tough customers.'

Richard Winters, of 506 PIR of the 101st, recalls that those with combat experience were:

> particularly tough on the replacements, cutting them no slack during the two weeks we trained ... [Some] refused to get too close to the replacements, some of whom were no more than mere boys. As for the newly arrived troopers joining the regiment, they were justifiably in awe of the Normandy veterans, who formed a nuclear family of their own. Somehow they stood apart from the newer members of the company. To this day, those who made Easy Company's initial combat jump into Normandy sit at separate tables during the company reunions.

David Webster, a private in Winters' company, underlined the disdain with which the new men were viewed:

> Our ranks had been filled with replacements in whom nobody was interested; we had received a week's furlough, new green jumpsuits, and machine guns with bipods for hedgerow fighting; and our training schedule had been jammed night and day for more than a month with infuriating field problems. We were

ready to go again, but we did not look forward to it, for the adventure was over, the battle was joined, the rest would be brutal.

As Webster contends, the 101st, just like the 82nd, successfully regenerated. Through hard work born of a dogged determination, the two formations quickly prepared themselves for their next assignment under the watchful eye of their commanders, who included the highly experienced and talented Jim Gavin as the new GOC of the 82nd. They transformed themselves quickly and stoically, and the airborne divisions were thus far better placed to confront the next challenge offered by the Germans than the ground forces preparing to undertake Operation Garden.

The British Second Army had fought through Normandy, across France and Belgium to within a few miles of the Dutch border, and the strain was beginning to show. Miles Dempsey's commanders all complained about tired troops, diminishing motivation and morale, and the need for more resources of all kinds, but particularly men, vehicles and fuel. Between 4 and 17 September alone, the Guards Armoured Division had suffered 113 killed, 405 wounded and 80 missing. Consequently it, like many other formations in the corps, had units 25–30 per cent under strength, with NCOs commanding platoons and companies reduced from three platoons to two. The corps' weaknesses found physical representation in its commander, Brian Horrocks, who was struggling with his own fitness, having been wounded in North Africa. He was not on his best form in September 1944. Both Horrocks and his corps were weary, distracted by the prospect of the end of the war and lacking their former bite. Even so, in an event which belied the fragility of both, on the morning of 16 September, 'Jorrocks' arrived at the cinema in the town of Leopoldsburg, some ten miles from the front line, to brief his officers about Operation Market Garden. Waiting for him in the stalls was a colourfully attired audience.

Hubert Essame, a brigade commander in 43rd (Wessex) Division, recalls:

> The variety of headgear was striking . . . No one deigned to wear
> a steel helmet. The Royal Armoured Corps affected brightly
> coloured slacks or corduroys. The Gunners still clung for the
> most part to riding breeches or even jodhpurs. Few retained their
> ties, but wore, in their place, scarves of various colours dotted
> with white spots. Snipers' smocks, parachutists' jackets, jeep-
> coats, all contributed to the amazing variety of costume.

The officers broke spontaneously into warm applause and cheered the
popular Horrocks as he strode down the centre aisle and stepped up onto
the stage. As silence fell in the auditorium, the General's hawk-like features
broke into a smile, and he announced: 'This is a tale that you will tell your
grandchildren – and mightily bored they'll be!' He then proceeded to
outline the plan which elicited looks of amazement from some, including
Joe Vandeleur, the Commanding Officer of the Irish Guards Group
which had been selected to form the tip of XXX Corps' spearhead.

By the time that the officers of XXX Corps headed back to their
headquarters to brief subordinates and make their own plans, the three
airborne divisions were making their final preparations. During the day,
the two American formations completed their move to 16 airfields, a
process that was to be followed by the British to their eight airfields the
following morning. Corporal Hansford Vest vividly remembers his
arrival at one of the 502 PIR camps, for his heart immediately began
to beat faster and his stomach flip as he saw aircraft and gliders 'parked
for miles all over the countryside and guards everywhere'. At that point
Vest became fully aware for the first time that he was part of something massive. All over the southern half of Britain a recent frenzy of
pre-operation activity was reaching a climax as transporters and tugs
were primed, gliders loaded, orders disseminated and briefings held.
Sergeant George Koskimaki of the 101st wrote in his diary:

September 14: Things are mighty hot for us again. We leave for the marshalling area. One officer said that this was positively a 'wet run'.

September 15: I learned we were gonna pave the way for the British 2d Army. Mission is in Holland to capture and hold vital bridges.

September 16: Were briefed today and received our foreign currency. Got ammo and made final checkups. We land in Holland at 1330 tomorrow.

The briefings that Koskimaki mentions took place throughout the day and ensured that each man in each unit of each division knew precisely what the objectives were and what his personal role was in taking and defending them. The thorough grounding received by Company C of the 82nd's 505 PIR is outlined by Lieutenant Jack Tallerday, its executive officer:

[On the morning of the 16th] troops were issued with ammunition, rations, maps, and orders. Detailed briefings at all levels, using sand tables, maps, and air photos were conducted. Every battalion commander knew the other battalion commanders' mission and plan of attack: likewise, company commanders within the battalion knew the other company commanders' missions and plans.

It was the same for Geoffrey Powell in 156 Para who recalls:

The briefings were over, and now everyone should know in exact detail everything which had to be done from the moment of landing. I had pored over the maps and aerial photographs for so many hours that I needed only to close my eyes to visualize the sandy countryside west of Arnhem where we would land.

Once the briefings were over, the men were given time to attend to their own administration. According to the 82nd's History:

> The remainder of the morning was free for men to write letters, visit Red Cross Mobile Units and check personal equipment. The afternoon was spent loading and checking bundle release mechanisms, loading and tying of bundles ... Motion pictures were held in the evening.

Each soldier had to divide his personal kit into what was necessary and could be carried, and the rest which would be left behind. Some, however, indulged themselves: John Frost, for example, asked his batman to ensure that his dinner jacket, shotgun, cartridges and golf clubs followed him over to Holland; Lieutenant Pat Glover of 10 Para prepared to take his pet chicken – the 'parachick', which had been awarded wings after several jumps – tucked into his smock, and Staff-Sergeant, 'Ginger', Green, a PT instructor also of 10 Para, took a deflated football 'in case there was time for a quick game'. As they packed, and whenever there was a quiet moment, the men naturally mulled over their personal concerns: First Sergeant Daniel Zapalski of the 502nd 'sweated out the jump; hoping the chute was packed right; hoping the field was soft; and hoping I didn't land in a tree'; Geoffrey Powell was concerned about 'jamming Stens and Bren guns'; Private James Sims of 2 Para ruminated on the words of Sergeant Hamilton, 'who warned us that if we refused to jump in action we would be shot', whilst Babe Hefron, who was to make his first combat jump, recalls:

> At night, you had your own thoughts. We sat on our beds and thought. And we'd bullshit. Some guys played cards. I never got

into playing cards . . . Some guys played darts. I'd rather sit in the bar and have a beer . . . We tried to keep things light. Every man had his own feelings about going into combat. But we were raring to go. After all, why did we enlist? Some guys were nervous, but we trained for this, we were ready to do what we were trained for. I couldn't wait to jump . . . I wasn't afraid. I wanted that star on my wings. You got one for every combat jump. The guys who were in Normandy had one.

Meanwhile, the senior commanders worried about changes in the variables – and particularly the weather. It was with some relief, therefore, that in the early evening of 16 September the meteorologists announced that apart from some early morning fog the following morning, the weather for the next three days would be fair with little cloud and light winds. On receiving the good news, Brereton signalled his commanders: 'Confirm Market Sunday 17th. Acknowledge', and wrote in his diary: 'At last we are going into action . . . Now that I've made the decision, I've quit worrying.'

That night some of those scheduled for the first lift quickly fell into a deep sleep after the mental and physical exertions of the previous few days; others tossed and turned, prisoners of their own thoughts during the dark, quiet hours. By dawn there was already considerable movement around the tented camps occupied by the American airborne units, but it was masked by a blanket of fog, as if thrown across the scene for secrecy. In Wiltshire, Donald R. Burgett of the 101st remembers: 'The morning was cool, with a thick fog hugging the fields and runways. By mid-morning, it had burned off. The air was very damp and moisture collected on our steel helmets, dripping from the rims as we moved forward, foot by foot, in long lines to receive breakfast.' That breakfast of eggs and bacon, Burgett says, was 'sort of like a condemned man's last meal'. The British also rose and found a hearty breakfast on offer. James Sims of 2 Para remembers: 'Sunday started off just like any other day except for some butterflies in the stomach. "Have a good breakfast," they advised, "as you don't know when you'll get your next meal.'" Nearby, his battalion commander, John Frost, tried to keep to a leisurely routine:

I got up with mixed feelings on 17 September 1944, the day for which we had planned and trained so long ... Owing to the reasonable hour fixed for our take-off there was no need to hurry over breakfast, and I read the papers as usual while eating the last plate of eggs and bacon I was to have for some time to come ... I wandered along to the mess to find everyone else reading and smoking, all in the best spirits and no worries anywhere ... I certainly did not anticipate much difficulty as far as our task was concerned.

By the time that he had left the mess, vehicles, with equipment and weapons piled beside them, were waiting to take his men to the airfields. Lieutenant Len Wright, a platoon commander in 3 Para, says:

We pulled each other up into the trucks and for the first time in days the men were quiet. It was only a short journey, but I was struck by the fact that even the jokers fell silent. I toyed with making a quip to lighten the mood, but decided against it. The quietness seemed natural and necessary.

On their arrival at the airfields, the men of 1 British Airborne Division quickly took in the sight of the massed aircraft, the smell of the aviation fuel, and the noise of shouting voices which were frequently drowned out by the jeeps, motorcycles and scooters that nipped around. Within seconds Wright noticed that the mood of his men had lightened:

It was as though the stimulation of their senses had the effect of forcing them out of their short-lived introversion which, inevitably, led to japes and fooling around. It was quite clear to me, however, that whether in silence or horse-play, most were trying to hide their fear. In a sense, although I had responsibility, I was lucky, my mind was always occupied and I had little time to think about what might happen to me.

The high spirits shown by the airborne troops that morning were a vindication of their successful training, the light atmosphere belying the fact that within a few hours they would be deep behind enemy lines and, possibly, fighting for their lives. James Sim describes the scene:

Someone dished out great mugs of tea and bacon sandwiches, and a camera crew on a truck came along and filmed us. We jumped about and waved our mugs in the air. The excitement was beginning to build up, everyone was laughing and shouting; the atmosphere had suddenly become like a school outing or picnic. All our doubts seemed to be swept away in a sudden surge of confidence. At last we were going, and we somehow knew that this time there would be no stand-down.

Captain George B. Wood, the Chaplain of 505 PIR, was about to make his fourth combat jump and, as usual just before action, found himself much in demand. Holding a church service on a patch of grass in the sunshine, the airborne soldiers prayed together. Wood recalls: 'I sought a spiritual motto to fit the occasion and finally decided on the last words from the Cross. "Father, into Thy hands I commend my spirit".'

Gradually, and as the final part of their preparation, the troops helped each other into their equipment. It was a tiring business. Although different in detail, the British and American airborne troops wore similar specialist clothing: a specially lined helmet with chin-strap, a jacket (or 'smock' as the British called it), which provided protection from the elements, and trousers with usefully large pockets. Over this they wore webbing from which hung pouches for the various essential items which required quick and easy access. Other bags and haversacks contained all of the other items that a soldier needed to do his job and live in the field. American Don Burgett's personal equipment, for example, consisted of the following:

> helmet, boots and gloves, main chute, reserve chute, Mae West [life-jacket], and M1 rifle, a .45 automatic pistol, trench knife, jump knife, hunting knife, machete, one cartridge belt, two bandoleers, two cans of machine gun ammo totalling 676 rounds of .30 ammo, 66 rounds of .45 ammo, one Hawkins mine capable of blowing the track off a tank, four blocks of TNT, one entrenching tool, three first-aid kits, two morphine needles, one gas mask, a canteen of water, three days' supply of K rations, two days' supply of D rations, six fragmentation grenades, one Gammon grenade, two smoke grenades, one orange panel, one blanket, one raincoat, one change of socks and underwear, two cartons of cigarettes, 'and a few other odds and ends'.

Meanwhile, under his parachute harness and parachute, Major Geoffrey Powell wore:

> A haversack containing maps, torch and other odds and ends; respirator, water-bottle and compass; pistol-holder and ammunition case; and on my chest the two pouches crammed with Sten magazines and hand grenades. Across my stomach I then tied my small pack, solid with two days' concentrated rations, mess tin, spare socks, washing kit, pullover, a tin mug, all topped with a Hawkins anti-tank grenade. Slung around my neck were binoculars, while a large shell dressing, a morphia syringe and red beret

were tucked into my smock pockets. Next I wrapped myself in a denim jumping-jacket to hold the bits and pieces in place and prevent the parachute cords snagging on the many protuberances. Over everything went a Mae West life-jacket with a camouflage net scarfed around my neck and the parachutist's steel helmet, covered with a scrim-decorated net, on my head. Onto my right leg I then tied a large bag, into which was packed a Sten gun, together with an oblong-shaped walkie-talkie radio, and a small entrenching tool; a quick release catch allowed this bag to be lowered in mid-air so that it would dangle below on a thin cord and hit the ground before I did ... [w]e were loaded like pack donkeys – one of the drawbacks of being taken into battle by air with so few vehicles available to carry kit. If we were to eat, drink, dig and fight with some hope of success against the heavily equipped German troops who were waiting for us, we would need everything we were carrying.

The glider troops did not have to bear the burden of a parachute and harness, but were similarly weighed down by their kit. It made the wait to emplane for glider troops and parachutists alike a long and uncom-fortable one. The men passed the time by chatting, playing cards, writing letters and reading – anything that did not require much move-ment. When the units were eventually directed to move to the aircraft, there was considerable relief, but to many it was tinged with renewed and acute anxiety. Albert Blockwell of 7/KOSB recollects:

we were marched over the field to the waiting planes and gliders. There they stood on the runway, two rows of black, ugly gliders down the centre and each appropriate tug plane on the outside of each glider. The very sight of those black, ugly gliders made me feel sick inside, and this morning was no exception.

Standing on the runway by the Horsa's door Blockwell continues:

we shook hands with our pilots and had a few cheery words . . .
We all climbed aboard, we didn't say much . . . There were no
cheers, no heroics, we just had a final look around, shoved a bullet
up the 'spout' of the rifle and then closed the door.

The parachutists, meanwhile, were so overloaded that they struggled to
climb the steps of their C-47 transporters and had to be assisted by a
couple of other men who gave them a push up. Once in the aircraft,
the men immediately sat down and prepared themselves for the flight.
'Even at this late stage', remembers Len Wright, 'many of us half
expected to be told that the operation was cancelled; but with every
passing minute the prospect of getting into action increased.' Donald
Burgett says:

We were all in bucket-seats with seatbelts fastened . . . The men
with the machine guns, mortars and other heavy or cumbersome
gear sat closest to the exit door so they could go out first . . . This
was the time I didn't like about a jump. The cabin became warm,
smelled heavily of gas and oil fumes, and seemed to close in on
us from all sides. We wanted to get started, to become airborne
so we could get some fresh air inside. But we just sat there in
silence.

The silence that Burgett experienced was extremely common for, as
John Frost explains:

The time waiting for the aircraft to take off is, for the parachutist,
the transition from peace to war. For him there is no gradual,
growing consciousness of battle that other Arms must feel. There
are no enemy positions to study with binoculars. No preliminary

bombardment to wait for, no careful moving up in the dark or wet with fingers crossed against the enemy's defensive fire . . . There came a roar from the engines as we started to move, and now my thoughts turned to the pilot, the navigator, the men in the plane, the escort, the glider pilots and the troops on the ground in Holland moving inward to conform with our landing. Our lives and our future lay in their hands and we had nothing to do but trust in their gumption.

Then, at last, the troops began to hear the first aircraft take off and, before long, they too began to move. Burgett recalls the moment:

Then it was our turn. The pilot throttled up and the C-47 shuddered and began moving . . . Our plane made the left turn, lined up with the runway, and the pilot fire walled the throttles. We gathered speed, bouncing and jouncing faster and faster – no turning back now. No one spoke; all eyes were looking forward toward the closed bulkhead door behind the cockpit, visualizing the pilot and crew doing their job. Our wheels left the ground, we climbed a little, levelled off somewhat to gain airspeed, and then we climbed out to follow the others into the sky, circling to form a vast air armada.

Blockwell experienced something very similar whilst in his glider:

[We sat down and] tightened our safety-belts and then listened to the roaring of the engines, waiting for the signal to go. We heard some engines 'open up' louder and louder, and then as they moved off down the runway the roar faded off again to a steady drone . . . We were next! Our 'tug' moved in front of us, moved forward slowly until the rope was tight, and then the engines opened out into a terrific roar of noise and wind. Then the glider gave a sudden jerk and we were away.

By the late morning of 17 September, over 3,000 aircraft were airborne and heading for the coast in two streams: one on a northern route to deliver the 82nd and the 1st British; the other on a southern route to insert the 101st. It was a scene the like of which had never been witnessed before. The columns were five miles wide and took an hour to fly over the towns and villages of southern England. Jane Mayhew was preparing Sunday lunch when she heard the deep hum of aircraft engines:

> I put the crockery on the kitchen table and went out into the front garden to take a look. My neighbours were already gathered in groups looking up at the sky. We had seen such aircraft before, but never in such numbers. They just kept on coming. It was quite eerie ... By the time I went back inside, the glasses and plates were buzzing on the table. They were being shaken by the noise of the aircraft engines.

A 14-year-old Jim Russell watched the air armada from his bedroom window in Essex and ticked off the different aircraft that he could see on a wall chart: 'C-47, Short Stirling, Horsa, Hamilcar – it was the most wonderful sight I had ever seen; a never-ending stream of planes and gliders. I remember thinking that Jerry was going to get a real pasting. In fact we all thought "That's it. This lot will win us the war!"' Sitting in his transporter *en route* to Holland, John Frost would have agreed, for he thought that Market Garden had great potential and later wrote: 'This was the genuine airborne thrust that we had been awaiting and we felt that if things went according to plan, we should be truly instrumental in bringing the war to an end in 1944.'

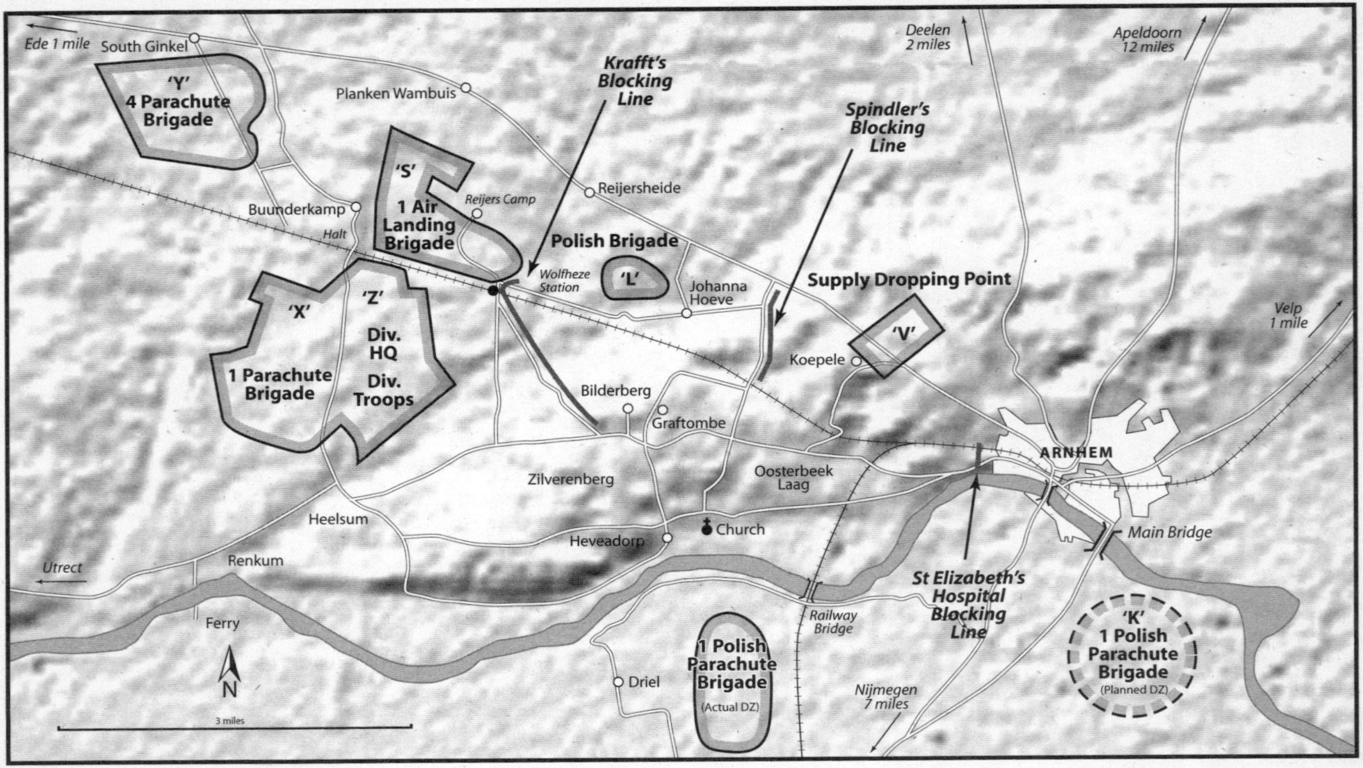
Ede 1 mile
South Ginkel
'Y'
4 Parachute Brigade
Planken Wambuis
Deelen 2 miles
Apeldoorn 12 miles
Krafft's Blocking Line
Spindler's Blocking Line
'S'
1 Air Landing Brigade
Reijers Camp
Reijersheide
Buunderkamp
Halt
Polish Brigade
'L'
Wolfheze Station
Johanna Hoeve
Supply Dropping Point
'V'
Velp 1 mile
'X'
'Z'
Div. HQ
Div. Troops
1 Parachute Brigade
Koepele
Bilderberg
Graftombe
ARNHEM
Zilverenberg
Oosterbeek Laag
Heelsum
Church
Heveadorp
Main Bridge
Utrect
Renkum
St Elizabeth's Hospital Blocking Line
Railway Bridge
Ferry
1 Polish Parachute Brigade
(Actual DZ)
'K'
1 Polish Parachute Brigade
(Planned DZ)
N
Driel
Nijmegen 7 miles
3 miles

Map 3: Arnhem

Jumping the Rhine (I)

(Operation Market Garden: 17–18 September 1944)

The pilot of the C-47 held a steady course, despite the snaking tracer rounds and bursts of flak. Sitting in the rear of the aircraft, Captain John Phillips of 505 PIR craned his neck to look out of a port-hole and glimpsed the fighter escort darting around the armada's fringes like small birds on the wing looking for prey. It was nearly three hours since they had taken off, but now he and his men were approaching the crisis as they flew at around 180 mph. A signal from the cockpit and Phillips gave the command his men had been waiting for: 'Stand up and hook up!' They wrenched themselves to their feet and attached their static lines to the anchor cable which ran the length of the fuselage and the jump-door was removed. The paratroopers were then ordered to 'Check equipment!', which saw them establish that their parachutes and harnesses were in good order and their static lines secure. Then, on the order 'Sound off for equipment check', they bellowed out their numbers and slapped the shoulder of the man in front: 'Sixteen OK!', 'Fifteen OK!' and ending with Phillips nearest the door, 'One OK!'

Moments later an explosion by the port wing rocked the aircraft violently and forced the braced paratroopers to strengthen their grip on the anchor cable. The wait that followed seemed interminable, but it was just a matter of seconds before Phillips shouted: 'Red on! Close up and stand to the door!' On the command, the stick shuffled forward, and Phillips himself moved towards the exit void. Holding the door jamb tightly, he placed his left foot on the very edge of the sill. Seconds later the pilot pulled back the throttle to achieve jump speed and the green light flicked on. Phillips commanded, 'Go! Go!' and flung himself out of the aircraft followed by his men at the rate of one every second. They jumped into a sky already full of parachutes, whilst those that had landed scrambled to deflate their parachutes, remove their harnesses and retrieve equipment. 82 US Airborne Division had arrived in Holland; the battle for a Rhine crossing had begun.

The Germans facing XXX Corps continued their defensive works on the morning of 17th in the warm weather. An Allied attack was expected as reports had been filed over the previous two nights noting 'continuous enemy motorized movement' and 'heavy enemy supply traffic with headlights at full beam': the Irish Guards Group were moving into their jumping-off positions for Operation Garden. RAF bomber raids on airfields throughout Holland had also been noted, and that Sunday morning they were intensified with fighter and bomber attacks against Dutch coastal defences, barracks and munition dumps. Known anti-aircraft batteries were also targeted, but in some areas the flak remained heavy. Sergeant Arthur Parker of the 101 Airborne's artillery saw a C-47 hit and crash right in front of him just after he had landed:

[I] entered the plane but it was empty except for the pilot and co-pilot, both dead. We tried to get the bodies out, but gas fumes forced us out of the plane. I will never forget that co-pilot. He had the bluest eyes and flaming red hair. Even though he was dead, his eyes seemed to follow our every move as we tried to get him out. I still see his face from time to time.

Flight Officer Thornton G. Schofield was flying a Waco. He watched his tow aircraft hit by flak as it approached the Son bridge:

I was beginning to relax a little when my glider took a hell of a whack and I saw the left wing of another glider sweep over the top of mine. The other pilot must have been dead or dying when he slammed into the tail of my glider from the rear. We collided at about 150 feet and my glider shuddered violently and then nosed down and dived towards the ground at an angle of about 75 degrees.

First there was a terrifying crunch as we hit the ground and then an incredible shock when the jeep we were carrying slammed down on me. I suffered a dislocated pelvis and left ankle, a broken leg, and assorted other injuries. When I regained consciousness, I realized that my head and left arm had punched a hole in the Plexiglas windscreen. It took a bunch of airborne troopers, working with axes and crowbars, about seven hours to free me from the wreck.

Yet despite losses, the flak caused just a small fraction of the 40 per cent casualties predicted by the air force, and by 1400 hours, 16,200 parachutists and 3,200 glider troops had landed in a remarkably successful first lift.

That morning, Brian Horrocks had climbed on to a factory roof on the south bank of the Meuse–Escaut Canal to survey the front line prior to XXX Corps' attack. He later wrote:

It was a lovely Sunday morning, completely peaceful except for the occasional chatter of machine gun fire in the distance. It was rather a terrible thought that on my word of command 'all hell' would be let loose ... I knew that this would be a tough battle; especially so, owing to the nature of the country, with its numerous water obstacles and the single main road available for thousands of vehicles; but failure never entered my head.

The sight and sound of 101 US Airborne Division flying over his positions a couple of hours later was, according to Horrocks, 'inspiring' and shocked the waiting Germans. Its psychological impact was strengthened by the hour-long low-level RAF attack on the German positions that followed, and then the 35-minute bombardment by 350 guns. With the ground preparation completed, the Guards Armoured Division broke out of their bridgehead. In the lead were the Irish Guards, whose historian relates:

At 1435 hours Lieutenant Keith Heathcote, in the leading tank, shouted 'Driver – Advance!' No. 3 Squadron drove straight up the main road, keeping close to the barrage ... The gunners were firing a narrow rolling barrage into the woods along the roadside 'where Jerry ought to be', and the tanks advanced in the hope that the Germans would run away or surrender. The Typhoons were circling overhead in a 'cab rank', waiting to be whistled up by their link to the ground. The clouds of dust made it difficult to see the actual shell-bursts, so that several times Lieutenant Heathcote got involved in the barrage ... For ten minutes all went well.

Yet despite the weight of munitions that fell on the German troops, enough survived to open fire with their anti-tank guns and panzerfausts as the British advanced up the road towards them. Nine tanks were knocked out in just two minutes, which sent those following scurrying for cover, whilst the infantry took to the ditches. Sergeant Bill

Prentice was in one of the first Shermans to be hit; he wrote later to his officer from hospital:

> Willis [the driver] has some shrapnel in both forearms, and Weedall [operator] several pieces in his leg and side ... We were hit three times, I think, and one of the shots must have come through the front and glanced off my leg, as my right leg is broken (fibula) in about three places, just above the ankle ... We had a hectic time after we baled out. I jumped into a ditch with a couple of Jerries, but poor Willis had about six in his trench. Weedall went in another direction and also met some of our friends, but by shamming being badly wounded they left him, then he was joined by Sgt. Smith ... At that moment another Jerry appeared on the scene [and] Sgt Smith put two shots in him, but before Jerry died he put five shots in Smith's leg.

The British had expected tough opposition around the bridgehead, but Student's men were stronger than expected, boasting ten battalions along with anti-tank weapons, artillery and some self-propelled tank-destroyers on the road to Valkenswaard. The Germans had developed a killing-zone and it took 230 sorties by the Typhoons before the infantry could clear the area. The Irish Guards History recalls:

> The Typhoons came cutting in from every angle at zero feet, bombarding with rockets the enemy positions within a hundred yards of the road. It was frightening enough for the battalions, and how much more so for the Germans who took the rockets. The din was appalling – tanks, trucks, planes, shell and rockets, machine guns all roaring and blazing. Colonel 'Joe' Vandeleur [the Irish Guards CO] seemed to enjoy it.

An officer later reported: 'I have never seen Guardsmen so angry, nor officers. The Krauts got rough treatment that day.' Some 250 prisoners were taken during this period, of which a large number were wounded. Guardsman Jim Hetherington remembers:

> I saw a young German soldier staggering along the road, grey in the face, obviously in a bad way. He collapsed near our tank, and I could see the back of his tunic was bloodstained . . . I got down from the tank and dragged and guided the German lad to the grass verge. I hadn't a word of German, or he of English, but we tried to talk, although he was obviously dying. I stayed with him until one of our First Aid men came along and said, 'God help him. He's gone.' It has occurred to me since that he might have been glad of my company.

Although the enemy in and around the bridgehead had been overcome, the Germans had successfully delayed XXX Corps. Brian Horrocks could only hope that it had been merely a defensive 'crust'.

As the Irish Guards lurched forward, 1 British Airborne Division's first lift had arrived accurately and on time: the gliders of Pip Hicks' 1 Airlanding Brigade, followed by Gerald Lathbury's 1 Parachute Brigade. Few Germans fought hard on the DZs and LZs, with most either running away or surrendering quickly. James Sims has noted:

> Dressed in their best Sunday uniforms, they were, at that moment, probably the most embarrassed soldiers in the German Army. They had been caught in the fields where we had landed, snogging their Dutch girl friends, and their faces went redder and redder by the minute as they caught the drift of what some of the grinning paratroopers flung at them.

Having organized themselves, the parachute battalions set off for their objectives in Arnhem, whilst the air landing troops prepared their defences in anticipation of the subsequent lifts. Lieutenant-Colonel David Dobie led 1 Para along the Amsterdamseweg to the high ground around the north of Arnhem which was to be defended against German counterattacks. Just a little to Dobie's south, 3 Para, commanded by Lieutenant-Colonel John Fitch, advanced along the Utrechtseweg to seize the main Arnhem road bridge and occupy east Arnhem. Lieutenant-Colonel John Frost's 2 Para, meanwhile, pushed down the road which ran close to the northern bank of the Lower Rhine – followed by 1 Parachute Brigade headquarters – to take a railway and pontoon crossing over the river, occupy the western part of the town and help take and defend the Arnhem road bridge. Dividing the brigade into three was a risk, but the ground was so close with woods and buildings that there was little option unless Lathbury's men were to be strung out in a useless and vulnerable column.

Yet that same terrain made lateral movement problematic if the Germans managed to block any of the routes – a real possibility considering the distance of the DZ from the objectives. However, to mitigate against the risk of the brigade not being able to seize the main bridge quickly, Major Freddie Gough's Reconnaissance Squadron – consisting of 275 men in four troops of jeeps and motorcycles – was to act as a *coup de main* force, despite landing several miles from the bridge. The initiative did not work: shortly after setting off for Arnhem on the northern route, Gough's men slammed into the northern end of a German blocking position. Sepp Krafft had deduced that the British aim was 'an advance on Arnhem [to] occupy the town and take the Rhine bridges, thus forming a bridgehead for the Allied land forces now advancing through Belgium and Nijmegen'. He immediately established a line with his SS Panzer Grenadier battalion to cut off 1 Para's route, and touch 3 Para's at its southern extremity. Just like the men in the Neerpelt bridgehead, Krafft had deftly exploited a critical weakness in the British plan and successfully slowed them down.

The fate of the Reconnaissance Squadron was indicative of an underestimation of the German ability to move swiftly in reaction to Operation Market Garden. Although initially believing that he might be the target of an airborne raid, Model fled the Tafelberg Hotel and headed for II SS Panzer Corps headquarters in order to coordinate a response. Assisted by the tight daylight insertion of the Allied airborne troops, the corralled XXX Corps advance and the acquisition of a copy of the entire Allied operational plan found on the body of a dead 101st Airborne officer in a crashed glider, Model and his subordinates came up with a coordinated riposte. Immediately recognizing the weaknesses of the Market Garden plan the Germans harnessed the collective power of their disparate formations and threw them at the Allies to isolate the airborne divisions, whilst slowing down XXX Corps. To help achieve this, Willi Bittrich's 9 SS Panzer Division was sent to deal with the British in and around Arnhem, whilst 10 SS Panzer Division was directed to sweep south and defend the crossing over the Waal at Nijmegen. It took some time for these dispersed formations to assemble and move off, but as they did so Harzer's Reconnaissance Battalion reconnoitred into Nijmegen in an attempt to forestall any early American attempt to seize the bridges there. Such structured movements dovetailed well with local initiatives to provide a comprehensive answer to the potentially overwhelming Allied attack. Krafft, for example, noted in his battalion's war diary:

We must delay them at all costs, even that of self-sacrifice. We must give the High Command time to put into effect efficient counter-measures to beat the enemy back and relieve pressure on the Bn and prevent its otherwise certain annihilation.

As a result, 1 Parachute Brigade struggled to break into Arnhem as its men ran into Krafft's men and then followed this with a failed attempt to outflank them to the south. Meanwhile 3 Para, although managing to skirt under the SS troops, advanced cautiously through a built-up area. Slowed down by well-meaning locals who had come out onto the streets to greet their liberators and by occasional riflemen taking pot-shots, at one point the lead platoon, commanded by Lieutenant Jimmy Cleminson, ambushed the Arnhem Town Commandant's car after it had left Krafft's headquarters. Corporal Tom Hoare describes the scene:

As we reached the crossroads from Wolfheze, some of the leading platoon were past the crossing when a German staff car came racing down the road from the village of Wolfheze. The driver realized his mistake too late, and while he was skidding to a stop, our boys opened up from both sides of the road. The car and driver were both riddled with bullets. [Major-General Friedrich Kussin] the front-seat passenger, along with two others were shot as they tried to leave the car. We left the bodies where they lay and kept going: we had to make the most of what daylight was left.

By dusk, the sluggish 3 Para was still making its way through Oosterbeek. Hearing fighting to the north and unsure what lurked in front of them, they decided not to try to enter Arnhem that night. Unfortunately, in spite of the proximity of his tactical headquarters, near Wolfheze, to the fighting, Urquhart was unable to influence the developing situation because his communications had failed. Using 22 sets to communicate with the brigade and Browning's corps headquarters 15 miles away, these radios could be relied on to transmit and receive within a diameter of three to five miles, but were tempera-mental in and around woods and built-up areas. This meant that during the push to the bridge, it was extremely unlikely that the division would be able to talk to 1 Parachute Brigade. Major Anthony Deane-Drummond, the 27-year-old second-in-command of the division's signals, had raised concerns about this with his Commanding Officer when he heard the details of the plan on 15 September. However, with time short and the plan set, he concedes that 'like almost everyone else, I was swept along with the prevailing attitude: "Don't be negative and, for God's sake, don't rock the boat – let's get on with the attack".'

Because of the communication difficulties, Urquhart decided to go forward to find out what was happening. Having failed to find Pip Hicks at his headquarters, he dashed off to find Lathbury on the southern route. As he caught up with the tail of 2 Para, he became concerned:

> They were moving in single file staggered along each side of the road, and moving very slowly. Further on, others had halted. Frost was not at his HQ; he had gone ahead because some of his leading elements had run into trouble. I tried to impart a sense of urgency, which I hoped would be conveyed to Frost . . .

The momentum of the battalion's advance was, like 3 Para's, being sapped by locals on the street and by clutches of enemy. James Sims and his Mortar Platoon, for example, were targeted by a German machine gun which hit three men:

> It was a terrifying experience, as we were lying on top of the road and there was no ditch to crawl into. Our only hope was that with Jerry firing blind we might escape. All we could hear was the fiendish whine of the bullets and the sobbing moans of our wounded comrades.

Lieutenant Reginald Woods, Sims' 25-year-old platoon commander, scrambled over to a house and provided covering fire for his men whilst they got off the road. Sims says: 'The firing ceased as the German machine gun crew departed, having achieved what they set out to do – hold us up.' The advance continued, and one of the companies slipped off the road to seize the railway bridge across the Lower Rhine just to the south of Oosterbeek, but it was blown up as they approached it. When the battalion found a little later that the pontoon bridge had also been dismantled, the plan to get men onto the south bank to take the main Arnhem bridge from both ends was in tatters. There was a chain-ferry linking Heveadorp – just south of Oosterbeek – to the south bank near Driel, but its value had been overlooked during planning and in any case a local man had put it out of action, fearing that the Germans might make use of it.

Meanwhile, Urquhart headed north in his jeep, where he found Lathbury on the cobbled Utrechtseweg with a stalled 3 Para. The situation was the antithesis of what the General had hoped to find, and he later wrote:

> I could now hear the plop and whine of mortars, and some of these bombs were falling with unsettling accuracy on the crossroads and in the woodland where many 3rd Battalion men were under cover . . . Medical orderlies were busy, and the shouts from the wood indicated that men were being hit and wounded by tree bursts.

The battalion was struggling to attain any forward momentum – not helped by mapping which lacked adequate detail – and as darkness fell had only managed to reach the Hotel Hartenstein in central Oosterbeek. An anxious Urquhart tried to find out what was happening. He spent some time with Lathbury discussing enemy blocking positions, and walking on back to his Jeep, witnessed it being struck by a mortar, which damaged his radio and wounded his driver. Tactically impotent in his current situation as his plan unravelled, Urquhart began to feel immediately frustrated. Yet whilst wanting to return to his headquarters, his route back was very possibly in enemy hands and so he had little option but to remain with 3 Para until daylight and brood on his problems. In such a position, he had no idea that 2 Para had reached the Arnhem road bridge at dusk. Frost and his men had achieved something of a coup, for finding that its northern end was lightly defended, 25 buildings were immediately occupied by the battalion and 1 Parachute Brigade headquarters established. A defensive perimeter was set up: 250 yards wide at its base, 375 yards across at its widest point and about 270 yards from top to bottom. Frost found a suitable house for his battalion headquarters, but on entering it the owner tried to argue that the Germans had gone. 'When I convinced him', Frost says, 'that the Germans were still very much there and furthermore that we didn't merely want billets, but proposed to fortify the house in readiness for a battle, he retired to the cellar quite horrified, leaving us to our own devices.' That evening, preparations for battle were made: buildings prepared; slit trenches dug; mines laid; and weapons positioned to achieve the best field of fire – including machine guns, two 3-inch mortars and six 6-pounder anti-tank guns. Only when this task was completed did Frost feel ready to order a series of attempts to cross the southern side of the bridge: but on each occasion they were thwarted by primed German defences.

During the evening, a trickle of British troops were welcomed into the Arnhem bridge perimeter and given a role. They included a group of Royal Engineers, a platoon of the Royal Army Service Corps, a few men from 3 Para's C Company – including Lieutenant Len Wright – which had managed to seep through the Germans in Oosterbeek, and Freddie Gough and a small part of his Reconnaissance Squadron. Thus by the early hours of Monday 18 September, some 750 of the planned 2,000 men had arrived at Arnhem Bridge. But at this isolated British outpost, supplies of all necessities were extremely limited and there was no radio communication with any other headquarters, although the Forward Observation Officer (FOO) of 1 Light Regiment Royal Artillery at the bridge was able to contact the 75mm guns in support near Oosterbeek church with a 22 set. As he anxiously awaited a German reaction to the airborne presence in Arnhem, Frost recognized that both the guns and the radio were critical lifelines for his small and vulnerable perimeter.

With the weaknesses of the British plan at Arnhem having been immediately exposed by the Germans, it was important that the two American airborne divisions achieved their objectives so that the Guards Armoured Division could advance swiftly. Jim Gavin's 82 US Airborne Division landed with just one transporter having been shot down and against very little resistance. Having rendezvoused close to their western DZ, Colonel Reuben H. Tucker's 504 PIR quickly set out for their objectives. The 2nd Battalion was to take the vital bridge over the River Maas at Grave and Company I's Captain T. Moffatt Burriss remembers that the Germans defending the bridge soon panicked. 'As soon as my men fired the first shot at them', he recalls, 'one of them took off his white undershirt and waved it. It was a smart move.' Captain Carl W. Kappel of Company H had a similar experience, noting in a report that 'many empty uniforms were found at positions, indicating the local defence forces were intent on escaping by mingling with the civilian population'. To Tucker's delight, the bridge was taken quickly whilst the rest of his regiment secured an important sector of the road leading from Grave to Nijmegen, and although other bridges over the Maas–Waal Canal were destroyed, another at Heumen was captured intact. With the bridge over the canal on the shortest route to Nijmegen at Honinghutje still to be taken, the Heumen crossing-point could yet be vital.

Colonel William E. Ekman's 505 PIR landing in the east of the divisional area had provided some troops who endeavoured to take the Maas–Waal crossing with the 504th, but his men were more successful in taking the village of Groesbeek, some nearby high ground, and patrolling the silent Reichswald. 'The forest was as quiet as a grave', says Private Don Shanks, 'and twice as frightening. It was eerie and played tricks on us. We had been told to expect the enemy, and in that dark, dense place we saw things that weren't there. It was exhausting work, but we ended the day without having clamped eyes on the enemy.' Also landing near Groesbeek was Jim Gavin's divisional headquarters, including Len Lebenson who helped establish the command post (CP) in 'a wooded area near some railroad tracks' on a road leading into Nijmegen. Lebenson continues:

> We dug our individual holes on either side of the dirt road from the CP and did so with particular vigour after we began to be bombarded by heavy artillery each afternoon and evening ... I dug an L-shaped hole for myself about 2 feet wide and 4 feet deep, with enough length to accommodate my body without extending into the bottom of the 'L'. I cut down some small trees with a borrowed axe and crossed the open top of the hole with small logs, covering them with dirt from the hole which was placed in plastic gas-protective bags and then repeated the process, making a very secure den. Over the course of time, I cut a couple of shelves into the dirt and constructed a step coming into the L from the outside. It was fairly homey.

On the way to the CP late that afternoon, Gavin was the second Allied airborne general to nearly become a casualty that afternoon when he came under direct machine gun fire along with his Dutch liaison officer, Captain Arie Bestebreurtje. As bullets whipped around them, the two men dived into some cover. Recognizing the danger of their predicament, Gavin took the initiative by crawling to the top of a high embankment to see what he could learn, and found himself just ten yards from the German MG-42. As the general took the direct route, Bestebreurtje moved around the flank and recalls that when he saw the machine gunner move his head, 'I raised my carbine and fired. My shot hit him right in the centre of the forehead.'

Colonel Roy E. Lindquist's 508 PIR, meanwhile, landed on the DZ closest to Nijmegen. Its battalions had to grapple with some dispersed objectives, but this was not a problem initially as enemy reaction was limited to a few localized counterattacks. Consequently, the regiment successfully achieved its objectives, which included a 3½-mile sector of high ground from the outskirts of the city south-east to Berg en Dal and the establishment of a defensive position in southern Nijmegen. Company F moved into the outskirts of the city that evening, with Communications Sergeant Dwayne T. Burns later writing:

We sent scouts and moved within Nijmegen's borders, meeting no enemy resistance. We didn't drop our guard, even though the streets seemed still and silent on what became a dark, moonless night … Suddenly a German machine gun opened up right in front of us. Our scouts had walked right past it in the dark. The captain and I were at the head of the company and I saw the muzzle blast flashing right before us with its aim a bit to the left. Tracer shots went right down the middle of the street, the shots looking like a long finger of light you could reach out and touch. We scattered and hit the ground, trying to find some kind of cover from which to return fire, but there was none. One trooper did a quick draw with his rifle and started laying down a round of cover fire. A grenade suddenly erupted. Then all went deathly quiet.

As Gavin's men moved towards their objectives, a rethink allowed for one unit to push towards the River Waal. In a late revision to the 82nd's plan, it had been decided that the 1st Battalion, commanded by Lieutenant-Colonel Shields Warren Junior, would endeavour to capture the Nijmegen bridges soon after landing. Having landed, Warren's first move was to send a reconnaissance patrol into the city with orders to signal back intelligence that would assist the battalion. However, their party was also hampered by radio failure and so Warren's men had to move off towards the bridges at dusk, not knowing what lay ahead of them. It was extremely fortunate, therefore, that a local man offered to guide Companies A and B through a maze of streets to bring them within striking distance of the road bridge over the Waal. It was here that the battalion ran into their first German defenders, the outposts of the 9SS Panzer Division Reconnaissance Battalion, which had slipped over the Arnhem bridge to Nijmegen before Frost's men had blocked the way. Corporal James Blue of Company A was startled by the ferocity of this initial encounter:

A German MG-42 opened up; you could hear the tracers rico-cheting off the cobblestone street. The first burst got the lieu-tenant in the leg. We ran and pulled him along the iron picket fence ... a BAR opened up, up front [Private] Dikoon came running back and reported he had knocked out the machine gun crew. Then Lieutenant-Colonel Shields Warren came ... to see what the situation was. Colonel Warren said, 'Good work men, keep the ball rolling.'

There followed a tremendous and confused confrontation as Warren's two companies tried to push through a strong and well-organized opposition. Blue was in the vanguard of the fighting in a forward position, and as men were being scythed down around him, he dived into a large German foxhole:

Here within two hours, two of my basic training comrades had been killed. 'Mac' [Corporal MacMillan] and myself were in a hell of a position in this hole and something had to be done. The Germans had spotted us and were throwing grenades trying to hit the hole and they were coming close ... I pushed Johnson's body aside, reached for a phosphorous grenade, pulled the pin, and threw it in the direction of the MG position ... I could hear the machine gun crew breaking down the gun and going out of action.

Mortars, machine guns, rifles, grenades, bayonets and trench knives were all used in this nasty, intense little battle which eventually ran into stalemate. The drastically under-resourced paratrooper *coup de main* had failed in its important task, but that night Gavin consoled himself with reports from all three regiments that 'they had the situation well in hand'. Even so, with three bridges still to be taken – two of which were over the mighty Waal – and with enemy resistance likely to increase during the second day, Gavin remained under no illusions as to the difficulty of his task. He therefore hoped that the 101st Airborne to his south would grant XXX Corps a clear and expeditious run to his area of operations.

The role of the 101 US Airborne Division was to secure the highway and its bridges which linked Eindhoven to Nijmegen. Dropping on a DZ approximately one mile north-west of Son, Colonel Robert Sink's 506 PIR was to take the bridge in that village over the Wilhelmina Canal and then push into Eindhoven. To achieve this, 1st battalion attacked the Son bridge from the west, having approached through the Zonsche Forest, but ran into three 88mm guns on the north bank of the canal. In Company A's log, First Lieutenant William C. Kennedy described what happened next:

At this point the group was about 200 yards from the bridge and the objective. The 2nd Platoon was leading the attack. A German 88 gun opened up, firing into the trees above . . . our troops. Sgt Joe Powers of 2nd Platoon was hit by shrapnel at this time and was believed to be the first casualty. Captain Davis urged the company forward. The enemy fire from the 88 gun increased in intensity and was joined by enemy mortars. In those 15 minutes five men were killed and eight wounded.

In that group was Don Burgett, who says:

Suddenly, without warning, explosions ripped through the trees. Men were instantly killed and wounded as dust, bark, tree limbs, and shell fragments filled the air. There was mass confusion among the troops . . . Instinctively we charged forward into the mêlée. We had to get the enemy gunners and kill them in order to stop the shelling. More shells slammed into the forest around us . . . I choked on the dust and dirt as I hit the ground . . . Off to my right rear, Captain Davis, our company commander, lay bleeding from multiple wounds. Lieutenant Retan was dead, and Lieutenant Couch, First Sergeant Sizemore, and Sgt Joe Powers were wounded.

Desperate for suppressive fire, the paratroopers brought up a machine gun and targeted the 88mm gun that was firing at them. Its crew retaliated by firing a shell at the machine gun which killed two men and wounded two others. It was a bloody exchange which led to casualties lying in heaps and just three officers managing to escape being wounded. In this situation the leadership of the NCOs came to the fore, and another attempt was made to silence the German gun. Burgett was in the leading group:

The bloodied remnants of A Company poured from the woods and charged madly toward the guns that had been killing us. I pulled my bayonet from its scabbard and affixed it to my rifle, charging forward as hard as I could. I saw the 88's muzzle, a burst of orange fire belching out that seemed to cover the entire scene in front of me . . . We had to get past the muzzle quick . . . We kept running forward. Suddenly we were on them . . . A shot was fired; one of the German soldiers on the far side of the gun-pit fell dead. A German soldier on my side threw his hands up over his head, turned to face me, and fell back against the sandbags. He was crying, sobbing like a young child . . . I swung my rifle round with the bayonet aimed at his midsection. My intent was to kill him and he knew it. Somehow I stopped. I don't know how or why, but I did . . . Two troopers grasped his arms and hauled his body up over the sandbags to the ground.

Corporal Charles Shoemaker remembers arriving on the scene:

A very young German soldier was lying at the bottom of the gun-pit. His belly had been ripped open from side to side. Another one was standing there wringing his hands. He told one of our people who spoke German that they had grown up together in the same village and were very close. Neither one of them was over 16 years of age. He begged one of our men to put his friend out of his misery. Of course, nobody would do that. Then he begged someone to give him a gun so that he could do it. Nobody offered him a gun. I don't know what happened from there on, as we kept moving.

A second 88mm gun was overrun in a similar fashion whilst 2nd Battalion, which had advanced straight down the road from the DZ into the village of Son, silenced another with a bazooka, killing one German in the process, whilst another six fleeing the scene were felled by a machine gunner. But the gun teams had done a fine job delaying the paratroopers, for they had provided the time to prepare the crossing for destruction. Sergeant Hugh Pritchard recalls:

We were closing in on the bridge and were 200 feet from it when there was an explosion. We immediately took cover around some buildings as large pieces of wood, masonry and other debris fell on us. We were about 200 feet from the bridge when the Germans . . . We had missed our opportunity to take the bridge intact.

With the Germans having now withdrawn, the airborne soldiers improvised a footbridge across the canal from some locally sourced wood, which included a couple of barn doors. It took the 2,000 men of the regiment several hours to cross the canal, and so, with dusk falling, it was decided that the advance on Eindhoven would have to wait until the following morning.

Meanwhile, Colonel John H. Michaelis's 502 PIR attempted to capture their own bridges. For example, 3rd Battalion's Company H sought to seize the Best bridge to offer as an alternative crossing over the Wilhemina Canal, but was parried by German outposts and forced back to the edge of the Zonsche Forest. From here the Company Commander, Captain Robert E. Jones, ordered his 2nd and 3rd platoons to use the cover offered by the trees to get as close to the bridge as they could. Lieutenant Ed Wierzbowski and PFC Joe E. Mann of 2nd Platoon were extremely close when they were spotted by the enemy who immediately reacted by lobbing grenades at the American paratroopers. The two men only just escaped to dig in on the edges of the wood with the rest of the platoon in the drizzle, hoping for reinforcement. By this time 1st battalion had seized the bridge over the Dommel at St Odedenrode after P-51s had cleared the way with excellent supporting work. The resulting carnage that the advancing unit passed on the way to the town was remarkable, with one noting in his journal: 'we passed the charred remains of the dead in grotesque poses. The smell of burning flesh, mixed with gas and oil is disgusting. It has impregnated my clothes.' Elsewhere, T/5 Carl F. Kelley noticed: 'two German tanks, one had been following the other. Both were knocked out. The lead tank's engine was still running ... There was a dead German up in the hatch.' The strike by the American aircraft had had the desired effect: it incapacitated around a dozen German vehicles and prepared the ground for the battalion to move quickly towards its objective. There were a few sharp engagements in St Odedenrode, but the superior quality of the American paratroopers soon told, and the streets were cleared, buildings were secured and the two highway bridges were quickly taken.

The most northerly objectives for the 101st were assigned to Colonel Howard R. Johnson's 501 PIR and included road and rail crossings over the Zuid Willems Canal at Veghel. The majority of the regiment landed as scheduled on a DZ to the south-east of the town, but it was planned for 1st battalion, commanded by Lieutenant-Colonel Harry W.O. Kinnard, to drop on the other side of the town to take the road and rail crossings over the Aa. In the event, the battalion was dropped five miles too far north-west, which necessitated a long march into town, whilst Captain David Kingston, the medical officer who landed in a tree, treated jump casualties in a nearby castle (where the Catholic chaplain had landed in the moat). In the meantime, the main part of the regiment took the village of Eerde near the DZ, blocked the road to St Odedenrode and then, with Kinnard's men arriving to play their part, took all four bridges intact before clearing Veghel. Second Lieutenant Robert P. O'Connell says of his first combat experience:

> We seized Veghel quite quickly with minimum opposition. In working along a street fight in Veghel, we killed three Krauts . . . we moved up the street, I jumped over their bodies and thought – 30 seconds ago they were alive! The reality of the war came to me then.

However, O'Connell had been trained to expect rapid German counterattacks and immediately set his men to dig in. As the regiment was reorganizing itself, Kinnard received word that his battalion's castle outpost was under attack by 50 Germans with mortars. A platoon was sent to assist, but Johnson's refusal to send more men was sound, for a little later 2nd Battalion in the north-west of Veghel came under attack from 300 German paratroopers who had edged forward under cover of the dark and a dank mist. It was a confusing situation, as PFC Samuel L. Raborn recalls: 'I don't know where the other companies were. It was rough. We lost half of my platoon and were pushed back to the railroad and bridge and there made another stand.' Suffering 40 casualties in the process, Company E fought hard throughout the night, as did Company D on its left. The Germans were driven off, but had learned a considerable amount about the Americans' defences, and Johnson was sure that they would be back. Veghel, with its four bridges, the regiment's commander had always maintained, would be considered by the enemy as a critical point on the highway. That night, at a conference in his headquarters, Johnson reiterated this belief to his battalion commanders, saying: 'if I were a German commander, I would target this town. You know my feelings on the matter. We are central to this operation. The 501st will succeed. We will hold Veghel to the bitter end.' Immediately after ending the meeting, Johnson got on the radio to division to enquire after XXX Corps' latest progress.

The Guards Armoured Division advance resumed on the afternoon of the 17th, just as soon as the tank wrecks had been cleared away, the rolling barrage retrieved and the Typhoons recalled. It remained a sluggish affair: the leading tanks eventually arrived in the outskirts of Valkenswaard and, supported by the infantry with FOOs directing artillery on to areas of resistance, reached the centre of town at 1930 hours. It had taken the Guards around five hours to advance just eight miles, and they were still six miles short of the scheduled overnight stop in Eindhoven. Although severely tempted to strike on again, hearing that 506 PIR had not reached the city and concerned about the vulnerability of his armour in the dark, Adair decided to use the night to rest, rearm, refuel and reorganize his division. Even at this early stage, there were some cautious hands on the reins of XXX Corps.

At the Wolfsschanze that afternoon, an agitated Adolf Hitler had been receiving reports about events in Holland. Although OKW had been expecting a new Allied attack, both its location and form had been a surprise. In the mid-afternoon, the Führer complained of feeling ill and, according to Dr Morell, was suffering from stomach spasms, pressure around the right eye and 'dizziness, throbbing head, and the return of the tremor to his legs, particularly the left, and hands'. Morell noted that these maladies had developed quickly and 'after great agitation'. At a Situation Report Conference that evening, a sour Hitler closely examined the developing situation in Holland, and asked what formations were moving in to counter the Allied thrust. He was given details about the German forces in the vicinity, and Lieutenant-Colonel Heinz Waizenegger of the Operations Staff announced:

> The First Parachute Army is pulling all available forces together in order to destroy the airborne enemy . . . Summary: the impression we have so far is that the enemy will try, together with the assault group from the [Neerpelt] bridgehead . . . to reach the Ijssel-Meer.

The Germans had quickly deduced Market Garden's ambition, and OKH, OB West and the subordinate commands in Holland all recognized the need to slow XXX Corps, deny the Allies the bridges and, when the time came, destroy the airborne forces. The following day promised the arrival of more airborne troops in Holland, and another punch by XXX Corps, desperate for some momentum, but the success of both depended on the speed, strength and organization of the German riposte. The race was on.

As dawn broke in Holland on the 18th after a night punctuated by fighting along the Operation Market Garden corridor, the three airborne divisions prepared themselves for German counterattacks. At Arnhem bridge several German trucks pulled up outside the buildings occupied by the men of 2 Para – obviously unaware that the area was in enemy hands – and a fire fight ensued. Joined by infantry and tanks which began to probe the perimeter from the east, the engagement escalated and lasted for much of the morning. Len Wright's 3 Para platoon, Major R.P.C. Lewis's C Company headquarters and sappers of 1 Para Squadron Royal Engineers, commanded by Captain Eric Mackay, had occupied a schoolhouse adjacent to the ramp on the east side of the bridge. They were immobile in their building, and the Germans focused on the group and tried to destroy them. Wright's diary simply states: '18/0200–0900hrs MMG, infantry, and grenade attacks from buildings to N and E, repulsed.' Sims also felt the effect of this attack from the east in his slit trench dug into a large traffic island on the other side of the bridge:

> the Germans put down a sustained artillery and mortar bombardment . . . The barrage lifted as suddenly as it had begun, and a column of light tanks and armoured cars manned by the SS approached from the east along the road which led underneath the bridge and ran between our island and the White House [a warehouse on the opposite side of the road manned by riflemen and sappers]. They attacked with great spirit, but we were lucky enough to have two 6-pounder anti-tank guns manned by the airborne artillery . . . these gunners manhandled their guns to meet the new threat and with their first shot brought the leading enemy tank to a flaming halt. It slewed half round and came to a stop directly under the bridge, thus completely blocking the way for the following armour. The German AFVs were knocked out one after another as they tried desperately to disengage or negotiate the flaming metal coffins.

Later that morning, a number of German armoured cars from 9 SS Panzer Division's Reconnaissance Squadron returning from Nijmegen attempted to cross the bridge from the southern end. Catching Frost's defences by surprise, the first four vehicles reached safety, but those following were stopped by a combination of PIATs, anti-tank guns and some of Eric Mackay's sappers dropping grenades from buildings into the open-topped half-tracks. Indeed, sapper Lieutenant D.J. Simpson noted in a report: 'a couple of our fellows excelled themselves with Sten and MG. They fired into the top of the half-tracks knocking out 6 right in front of the houses; the remaining half-tracks were knocked out by the rest of the bn.'

Some 20 vehicles were eventually destroyed, but there followed some strong localized German counterattacks which dominated the afternoon and spilled over into the evening. Having assessed the strength of the British positions by this stage, Frost recognized that his enemy would not relent.

The small airborne force in Arnhem bridge was a major hindrance to the commanders of 10 SS Panzer Division, as it blocked the shortest route to Nijmegen where Harmel had been tasked with defending the Waal crossings. Although some of the lighter elements of the division had managed to get to Nijmegen on the morning of the 18th – thus relieving the 9th Reconnaissance Battalion which allowed it to return to Arnhem – Harmel's trucks and armoured vehicles required a strong bridge to cross the Lower Rhine. As there was no such bridge in the vicinity, one was built by engineers at Pannerden, six miles to the southeast of Arnhem.

While this bridge was being constructed, 9 SS Panzer Division's Kampfgruppe Brinkmann – actually from 10 SS Panzer Division, but given to the 9th in compensation for its reconnaissance battalion being sent to Nijmegen – organized more attacks against the northern end of the Arnhem bridge, whilst Kampfgruppe Spindler began moving into blocking positions in Oosterbeek. Meanwhile, pushing towards the town from the opposite side and offering the western jaw of the German vice, was Kampfgruppe von Tettau, a new organization made up of assets from northern Holland. Urquhart's formation was being surrounded, but Harzer wanted the Arnhem bridge reopened before moving in to destroy the rest of the airborne division. Thus, on the afternoon of the 18th, the battle against Frost's men intensified, with mortars, infantry, armoured cars, SP guns and tanks crashing into the perimeter, but the airborne force, assisted by the 75mm guns which shattered attacks, remained unmoved. With casualties mounting and resources already strained, 'the odds against an outcome in our favour were', said Frost, 'heavy indeed'.

Ideally, 1 Parachute Brigade headquarters would have received word that XXX Corps was making rapid progress towards Arnhem, or that reinforcement from the rest of the division was about to arrive, but this was not the case. However, whilst the Guards prepared themselves in Valkenswaard, 1 and 3 Para were trying to bludgeon their way through Spindler's defences, which were set in a bottlenecked, built-up area in the west of the town by the St Elizabeth Hospital. In the thick of the action was 3 Para's Corporal Tom Hoare, who was in charge of the company's PIAT. The PIAT was a rather lame and cumbersome spring-loaded anti-tank weapon which lobbed a warhead capable of penetrating four inches of armour from around 50 yards. Yet despite its many deficiencies, the PIAT remained a crucial weapon in the airborne arsenal, as Hoare recalls:

My section's first encounter with the enemy armour was when we heard a tracked vehicle coming down a side street, its tracks clattering on the cobblestones. We took cover behind some gas pumps in front of a garage, and the vehicle proved to be a self-propelled gun. We fired a bomb from the PIAT, scoring a direct hit, and it withdrew back behind the buildings, but not before we had taken care of some of the crew with small-arms fire.

The fighting became bloody and confused, with heavy losses in officers and NCOs. Anthony Deane-Drummond, moving forward to the battalions to alert them about a change in radio frequency, found a company whose commander had just been killed: 'To take over seemed to be the only thing to do', he said:

Street fighting is always a pretty bloody business and this was no exception . . . I gave orders to capture [a group of houses] whilst the rest of the battalion caught up with us on our left. While we were advancing under cover of the river bank, we were under a certain amount of small-arms fire and at one point three Germans threw some stick grenades at us. These did no damage and they soon stopped when we threw back some of our own. By the time we reached our objective, only 20 men were left out of the whole Company.

By dusk on 18 September, 3 Para had shrunk to the size of a single company. Still accompanying this shattered unit were Roy Urquhart and Gerald Lathbury, who were hemmed into some terraced housing. A small party, including the two senior officers, decided to try to make a break for it. They launched themselves from a house, as Urquhart describes: 'I came out of the back door and was striking over the fence, with Lathbury alongside, when his Sten went off. The shot narrowly missed my right foot . . . it would have been too ironic for words to be laid low by a bullet fired by one of my own brigadiers.' Having scaled a 10ft brick wall, the group found itself in a narrow arched passageway and a narrow cobbled street. Here Lathbury was hit by a burst of machine gun fire, which forced Urquhart and two young officers – Lieutenant James Cleminson and Lathbury's intelligence officer, Captain Willie Taylor – into a house around the corner. The General later wrote:

We laid Lathbury on the floor and a quick examination revealed that he was not dangerously wounded; he had been partially paralysed by a bullet which had snicked his spine. He was bleeding but still conscious. All of us knew he could travel no further. The Germans knew roughly where we were and it would be senseless to try to take them on. As if he knew what we were thinking,

Lathbury urged: 'You must leave me. It's no use staying. You'll only get cut off.' I turned to the two officers, one of whom was Jimmy Cleminson . . . at that moment I spotted a German soldier as he appeared at the window. I had an automatic in my hand and fired point-blank at a range of a few feet; the window shattered and the German dropped outside.

Leaving Lathbury in the care of the couple who owned the house, the men slipped out the back door into a maze of tiny fenced gardens which they crossed before entering another house. The area was swarming with the enemy, so the three officers took refuge in the attic where, expecting the Germans to burst into the house at any moment, they settled down to wait and started to eat some of the General's sweets. Urquhart found himself staring at Cleminson's moustache: 'This enormity in hirsute handlebars had earlier been lost on me, but now there was little else to look at. On such a slightly built man they looked weird.'

Deane-Drummond's situation had also taken a turn for the worse for Germans were trying to enter the building in which he and his few remaining men were holed up. 'We all dived into a lavatory on the ground floor and locked the door on the inside', he remembers:

Eventually they broke [into the house led by an officer]. To our dismay a section of ten soldiers followed him in and on upstairs. From the sounds of tile-removing and furniture-shifting the house was being converted into a strongpoint in the German defensive position. We sat in turns on that lavatory seat for the following three nights and three days.

All over the battlefield, the British airborne troops were in tight spots, but those that witnessed the arrival of the second lift that afternoon found their optimism strengthened. Although delayed by low cloud in England, its arrival in Holland was extremely successful, and bore the remaining 4,000 men of 1 Airlanding Brigade and 10, 11 and 156 Para of Brigadier Shan Hackett's 4 Parachute Brigade. As they landed on the DZ at Ginkel Heath, the glider infantry and Pathfinders were seeking to hold the enemy back. H.L. Davey, 10 Para's CQMS, recalls:

> Two minutes after landing I suddenly realized I was still standing on the same spot on the DZ with mortar and MMG fire going on around. I was spellbound by the wonderful sight above me of hundreds of parachutes dropping from the sky. I quickly made tracks for the surrounding woods and joined up with HQ.

It had been 4 Parachute Brigade's plan to strike out for Arnhem down the Amsterdamseweg to support its sister parachute brigade as soon as it was able, but events had made that impossible. With only a small part of 1 Parachute Brigade at its objective, Hackett's men were needed as a battering-ram to break through to the bridge – hardly an ideal airborne role. Nevertheless, Brigadier Pip Hicks, the 49-year-old commander of 1 Airlanding Brigade who had been commanding the division in Urquhart's absence from the Hartenstein Hotel in Oosterbeek, sought to facilitate this. His decision was immediately to detach 11 Para from Hackett's brigade to support 1 and 3 Para along with part of 2/South Staffordshire that was fighting in west Arnhem. Whilst this took place, Hackett – angered that one of the battalions he had forged was being taken away from his brigade – sought to press through the woods to the north of Oosterbeek and a railway leading into Arnhem. Whilst 10 Para was providing cover for 133 Field Ambulance treating the jump casualties, Lieutenant-Colonel Sir Richard de Voeux's 156 Para advanced at 1700 hours. The battalion had not got far when it crunched into the forward positions of Kampfgruppe Spindler.

The entire situation was muddled, and with impeded units littering

Oosterbeek and the Arnhem approaches, Hackett went to confront Hicks to complain about what he believed was 'an untidy situation'. Already angry at the detachment of 11 Para, his disquiet was given added piquancy as he was Hicks' military senior and had not been informed of Urquhart's wish that Hicks should take command should the GOC and Lathbury become incapacitated. The meeting soon degenerated into an argument in the failing light before both men, recognizing the futility of such an outburst and their responsibilities, hatched a new plan: just before dawn, 11 Para would advance down the river road to link up with 1 and 3 Para, whilst 10 and 156 Para – along with the 7/KOSB, which replaced Hackett's 'lost' battalion – would take the high ground of Koepel just north of Oosterbeek. If successful, 4 Parachute Brigade would turn Spindler's flank, link up with 1 Parachute Brigade and make a push into Arnhem. In an intense, curious and disjointed battle, this was an attempt to take the initiative and reassert order.

As Arnhem bubbled and boiled on the 18th, 82 US Airborne Division continued the struggle to protect its newly won gains, and take those bridges that were still in German hands. At 0730 hours Shields Warren's 1st Battalion of the 508th PIR renewed its attack towards the road bridge over the Waal in Nijmegen, but once again found the German defences too strong in the area of Hunner Park and a medieval observation tower called the Belvedere at the southern end of the bridge, and from guns on the opposite bank of the river. Nevertheless, although outnumbered and outgunned, the parachutists recognized the objective as crucial and forged on. 'Every time we tried to move forward, we were blasted back – literally', said one NCO in Company A. 'You can only achieve so much with a battalion, particularly one that is taking heavy hits. I began to think that if I was still alive by the time we got to the bridge, I'd be the only man left standing.' The isolated battalion managed to claw its way to a roundabout approximately 200 yards from the crossing, but could go no further. Had there been more men available to reinforce Warren they might have forced the issue, but the 82nd was being stretched to its limits fending off the Germans. Instead, Gavin suspended the Nijmegen attack and redeployed those troops in defence of his most northerly DZ. Across the sector the German pressure was incessant and, had the second lift arrived as scheduled that morning, it would surely have been caught up in a maelstrom. As it was, the situation had eased by the afternoon, but anti-aircraft fire had not been eliminated and casualties continued to mount. Captain Elgin D. Andross landed his Waco as battles raged around the fringes of the LZ, and the medical team that he was carrying was immediately pressed into action. 'I talked to one glider pilot who had been brought in', Andross says, 'and he had a bad wound in the upper left chest that was covered with a bloody bandage. He lifted the bandage and I was able to look straight through him'. Even so, an extremely valuable 1,800 men, eight AT guns, 36 howitzers, 200 jeeps and 120 trailers successfully landed, which allowed for another attempt to be made on the Nijmegen road bridge.

As preparations for a new attack were made, the remainder of the division attempted to shore up its operational area. A battalion of the 508th, for example, secured Beek which was located on some high ground just to the east of Nijmegen. From here a platoon spotted several hundred German troops, led by a staff car with an officer sitting in the back, marching towards the town. Sergeant Dwayne T. Burns writes:

> Hollywood could not have created a better scene ... I looked over at [Polette, the platoon commander] ... With a quick double shift of his eyebrows he said, 'Let's go get 'em' ... Without another moment's hesitation, and even though we were greatly outnumbered, he took off down the hill. I was still trying to ready my own weapon and join the run when Lieutenant Polette started firing his first shots ... Slamming down the hill, firing from the

hip and screaming at the top of our lungs, we acted like crazy Indians on the warpath . . . The Jerrys broke and ran like whipped puppies . . . [We] ran after them until we got to the road. There Polette called a halt. He shouted his orders, 'This is as far as we go! Pick your targets.' He dropped down on one knee for better aim, and his Thompson jumped every time he cut loose. I took a place at the roadway's edge and picked a target. Down on the flats the Germans were running for their lives. There was no cover. All they could do was try and get out of our range . . . [W]e finally stopped firing and sat down to watch them finish their way across the flats. Between the two sides, one could see scattered pieces of equipment and dead or writhing Krauts for a thousand yards.

Elsewhere, elements of 504 PIR established defences to protect the western approaches to Nijmegen against a German assault, and linked up with men from the 508th to take Honinghutje bridge over the Maas–Waal Canal. There was little sign of the enemy, but as the American paratroopers approached the bridge there was an explosion which rendered it impassable to heavy traffic. The taking of Heumen bridge the previous day, despite being on a more circuitous route to Nijmegen, had been prescient.

By the evening of the 18th, although Gavin had devised a plan to take the Nijmegen road bridge, the attack was postponed as another wave of German pressure spread across the division's front. Yet although the Guards Armoured Division was due in Nijmegen that evening, the formation again found advancing up the single narrow road a difficult business. First it was held up by four 88mm guns and infantry covering the bridge over the Dommel just south of Eindhoven, and then at dusk the Irish Guards were forced to crawl through Nijmegen's streets, which teemed with locals and men of 506 PIR. Sink's men had approached their objective cautiously that morning, with scouts moving ahead of the lead platoons – watching and listening. Leading the way on the extreme left flank was Lieutenant Bob Brewer. Standing over six feet tall with a map-case hanging round his neck, stopping at regular intervals to peer through his binoculars, he could be immediately identified as an officer. A single shot rang out, and Brewer fell, shot in the throat. He later wrote:

> A round entered my right jaw and exited my left neck. Both holes, just below the third molar from the back, spouted blood immediately and blood flowed from my mouth like a fountain. I knew I was going into shock. While the above was going on, I heard one of my men yell, 'Lieutenant Brewer's dead! Get going into those trees ahead!' and I remember feeling good about that order. Someone was taking over.

The advance continued with several more similar incidents occurring across the regiment's front. With no time to waste on complicated methods to neutralize the snipers, some units resorted to methods not found in any of the training manuals, as First Lieutenant Alex Andros describes:

> I do remember trying to flush out snipers by getting them to fire at us. Stupid as we were – we'd run across the road and have someone watch to see if we were fired on and pick out the spot where the shots came from and have one of our men pick them off. Fortunately, none of us got hit.

Once in Eindhoven the regiment ran into several German strong-points. Captain Lloyd E. Willis says: 'The advance continued for approximately the distance of five city blocks, where it was stopped cold by intense fire from enemy machine guns and dual purpose 88mm guns from positions in buildings and street intersections.' In this situation, textbook company attacks were used; the positions were outflanked and 'approximately 300 enemy were killed or captured by the regiment ... [T]he battalions commenced to mop-up and by 1700 hours the first Dutch city was in Allied hands.' For the people of Eindhoven, the event was the cause of great celebration. Pauel Velay was 13 years old in 1944, and remembers his first sight of the paratroopers:

> My parents had been told that the Americans were on the way and I cannot remember seeing them so excited before. My mother changed her clothes, and my father found some long hidden wine ... I first caught sight of the paratroopers in the early afternoon. At first they did not look at us, but kept to the side of the road looking all the time up at the windows, but later on we spoke to them. They gave me some candy, and I gave them some apples. Then the British tanks arrived.

The Irish Guards were not clear of Eindhoven until after 1900 hours, the time when they should have been approaching Nijmegen. The armour immediately pressed on to Son, which was reached at dusk. Here the XXX Corps engineers immediately set about constructing a Bailey bridge across the Wilhelmina Canal, whilst just to the west the battle at Best continued to rage.

The two battalions of 502 PIR at Best were put under debilitating artillery, mortar, small-arms and 20mm anti-aircraft gun-fire from the town throughout the night and it intensified at dawn on the 18th. That morning, German counterattacks designed to disrupt the American push to the bridge were repulsed, but with heavy losses. During one of them, men of second battalion's 2nd platoon which was closest to the bridge watched in mute frustration as the Germans destroyed the crossing. News of this did not reach battalion or regiment, however, because Lieutenant Ed Wierzbowski's radio was not working. During the afternoon, the fighting became relentless, as T/5 John Fitzgerald remembers:

September 18th was one of the darkest days for the third Battalion. The battalion had unknowingly come across a very large group of enemy . . . Fire was so intense that the trees began to burn. Casualties were mounting all around us. [The CO Lieutenant-Colonel Robert] Cole decided that the only option left to him was to call for air support . . . When our P-47 fighters arrived, all hell broke loose as they started to strafe the area.

Although an after-action report details an enemy advance 'to within one hundred yards of our battalion lines' and Cole – a holder of the Congressional Medal of Honor – was killed, the 502nd's line held. But the Germans had partially achieved their aim at Best, for they had skilfully pinned down John Michaelis's regiment which, in turn, stretched General Maxwell's division. Consequently, the late arrival of the second lift caused considerable anxiety, and although the delivery of a further 2,500 men together with more guns and jeeps eased the division's predicament, the loss to the Germans of a significant portion of a later resupply drop was keenly felt. The appearance of the Household Cavalry followed by the Guards' armour at Son, was therefore, a major boon as it immediately offered the prospect of valuable fire support.

Even so, XXX Corps was considerably behind schedule, and as Browning, Horrocks, Gavin and Adair were all very aware, it was unlikely to be able to pick up speed in the foreseeable future. With the Nijmegen bridges still in enemy hands and German units continuing to converge on the highway, Allied momentum to Arnhem was being severely diminished. By the evening of 18 September, Operation Market Garden's health was not all that it might have been. Lewis Brereton, as if rather surprised by what was happening, noted in his diary: 'The reaction of the enemy made it clear that he was going to fight bitterly to defeat the corridor into Germany.'

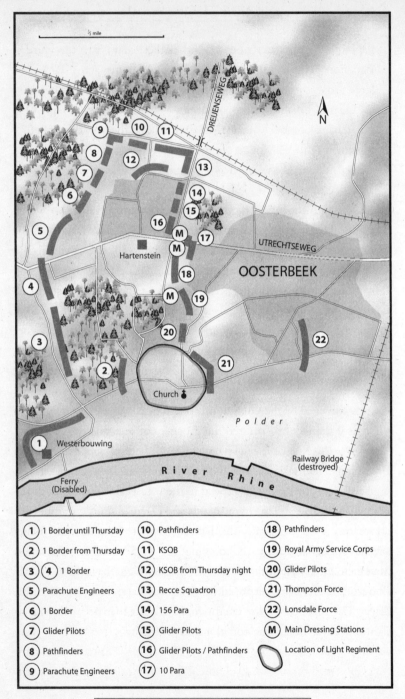

Map 4: The Oosterbeek Perimeter

CHAPTER 6

Perimeters

(Operation Market Garden: 19–21 September 1944)

The battle was draining: physical exertion, fear and concentration all taking their toll. There was also the constant assault on a soldier's senses. The noise was relentless: the shouting, the screams of the wounded, the yelling of commands, the rip of machine guns, the snap of rifles, the boom of exploding bombs and shells. And the smell was inescapable: from burning buildings, damp rubble dust, cordite, the odour of colleagues, the very different odour of the enemy, and from the smoke which drifted and swirled through the streets, seeping into rooms and permeating clothing. The Germans also suffered, but it was worse for the British at Arnhem bridge as they were besieged with their movement restricted within a tiny perimeter. Moving from room to room, and particularly from building to building, was fraught with danger. Having picked his way through destroyed bedrooms, offices and classrooms by carefully side-stepping piles of masonry and bodies – alive and dead – as he went, the defender got into position to make a dash to a neighbouring edifice. Steeling himself for the ordeal, he then launched himself from a doorway hoping to avoid the attentions of the snipers, the machine guns and the indiscriminate mortars.

The atmosphere at the bridge had become increasingly claustrophobic throughout the day and there was an increasing feeling of isolation which was heightened by a lack of information, dwindling supplies of ammunition, empty stomachs and tiredness. Lieutenant Len Wright spent Monday evening touring his platoon position ensuring weapons were correctly sighted, encouraging and talking to his men whilst checking provisions. His gaunt face and thin moustache did not make the young officer look particularly friendly, but he was approachable, well liked and respected by his men. Joining 3 Para after it had returned from its Mediterranean adventures had left Wright feeling severely disadvantaged as he lacked combat experience, but he had worked hard since the spring to forge a close-knit outfit that reflected his personality: feisty, lean, tenacious and professional. From what he had seen of his men in action over the previous two days, he had succeeded. There had been nothing that his platoon had not been willing and able to do, and it had fought skilfully through to the bridge in a manner that revealed considerable initiative and guile. Now, in the early hours of the 19th, they listened for the enemy in between heavy stonks of enemy artillery and mortaring, which brought their world down around their ears. The dark provided new opportunities for the Germans to attack. They used it to cloak their movements, forcing the British to strain to pick up on the slightest sound that might give those movements away. Then a silence suddenly descended. The German infantry crept cautiously forward towards the platoon's shared position. An order was quickly whispered through the building, directing the airborne troops to hold their fire, allowing the structure to be surrounded. The Germans believed that the occupants were dead, but on the word of command the defenders opened fire in one simultaneous blaze. A cacophony of noise accompanied by explosive flashes forced the Germans to flee, leaving 30 dead behind. Then silence descended once more, punctuated only by the whimpering of the wounded and Major Lewis running from room to room laughingly declaring that he had not enjoyed himself so much since he last went hunting.

Tuesday 19 September was the first day that XXX Corps could have realistically linked up with 1 British Airborne Division, and John Frost's men knew it. Relief could not arrive fast enough for the tired defenders in their burning buildings at the bridge after a night of German infiltration and destruction. The fighting was unremitting and the situation for the British was serious, but it might have been catastrophic had the Germans concentrated their resources for a single decisive punch to shatter the perimeter. Instead they merely nibbled away at the edges. Frost's men had inflicted such casualties on SS troops that Brinkmann had decided on a conservative approach to dislodging the airborne troops, which included using his firepower systematically to destroy their buildings. It was a tactic that, although far from efficient, certainly undermined the defenders' ability to hold out. Sims says that 'the separate explosions now merged into one almost continuous rolling detonation and the earth shook as if it was alive ... I kept repeating to myself over and over again, "Hold on ... hold on ... you must hold on".' Exacerbating the situation was German armour which began to roam the street outside brigade and battalion headquarters. He continues:

The German SP crashed out and a second shell hit the White House. We watched in horrified silence as the walls appeared to breathe out before the whole structure collapsed. The roof and the floors fell inside and a towering column of flame shot into the sky. A cut-off scream marked the end of many gallant riflemen and engineers. The sudden collapse of such a solid-looking edifice was a terrific shock to our morale ...

Sims was wounded shortly after: 'A blast of hot air hit me in the back and at the same time a burst of shrapnel tore into my left leg ... My leg suddenly went numb and my head seemed swollen to twice its normal size ...' He was taken to the cellar of the headquarters building and placed next to an officer riddled with machine gun bullet wounds who 'mumbled, reliving his last patrol, then talking to his wife and children'. The two doctors and few medical orderlies did what they could for the men, but with the Germans pressing in, the building on fire and basic supplies running short, conditions deteriorated rapidly.

Attempts to try and reach the beleaguered force at the bridge on the morning of the 19th were wholehearted, but ultimately doomed to failure. At 0400 hours the South Staffordshires with 1 and 11 Para attacked towards 3 Para at St Elizabeth's hospital, but crumbled against the German defensive wall. After two bloody hours the attack was halted after it failed to pierce the enemy's line, but in that time it did inadvertently release Urquhart, Cleminson and Taylor from their attic confinement. Immediately racing to the Hartenstein in a jeep to be greeted by astonished staff officers, the general was quickly appraised of the current situation – it was not prosperous: there would be no success on the Utrechtseweg, 1 Airlanding Brigade was being attacked fiercely to the north-west and west, whilst 4 Parachute Brigade's attack was failing north of Oosterbeek. This push by 10 and 156 Para supported by the KOSB was suffering so badly that it was decided to stop the attack and pull the battalions to the south, lest they become isolated from the rest of the division. This simple direction, however, was fraught with danger and the possibility of chaos, for while most of 156 Para could scramble over the steep railway embankment separating the brigade from Oosterbeek, 10 Para was sent back to use the Wolfheze crossroads and many brigade vehicles had to use a tunnel between the two. CSM Bob Grainger of D Company describes the deteriorating situation as 10 Para disengaged:

LC Horton was wounded in the kneecap and as I was applying the first field dressing he was wounded again, this time in the thigh. He was in great pain. The general situation then became untenable and we had to clear. It was decided to leave Horton. But not liking to leave him to the mercy of the Germans, Capt. Henry and I carried him over to the glider LZ. We had to proceed very slowly and we had only travelled approximately 50 yards when we were all three shot. Capt. Henry was knocked about 15 yards, Horton fell where he was and I went about seven yards and – when I found I was not killed – I went to Captain Henry. I saw that he was in a very bad state. Horton had been wounded for the third time and was in a very bad way too.

As the battalion began to cross the LZ, gliders of the Polish third lift began to land and events degenerated into farce. Working hard to unload the aircraft as quickly as they could, the Poles came under sustained fire which, in the confusion, some returned towards friendly forces as well as the enemy. Sosabowski's men suffered substantial casualties, but they would have been even worse had bad weather in England not forced the postponement of the drop of his three parachute battalions on DZs south of Arnhem bridge, which were still in enemy hands.

The 25 Polish gliders were not the only aircraft to get through to Arnhem that afternoon, however. A resupply lift also arrived. Despite heavy anti-aircraft fire, the bravery of the aircrews was remarkable, as they remained focused on the need to deliver their cargoes accurately to the division. Sergeant H.W. Rose, a navigator on a Dakota, recalls that his aircraft dropped its panniers from just 800ft. It was met by heavy fire:

We went in straight and level, speed right back, tail well up, and as the dropping bell started its penetrating and incessant clamour, our first bank of panniers went out in five seconds flat, to the accompaniment of a deafening roar from the metal runners. [The next bank] the RASC [Royal Army Service Corps] despatchers ... succeeded in despatching in eight seconds. A frantic signal to the pilot sent us into a diving turn away, and then up, the engines snarling at full boost, literally clawing us into the dubious safety of the thin clouds a short distance away. A last look back at the shambles revealed the solitary Dakota, its final drop accomplished, now shrouded in flames from nose to tail, falling to the ground in a gentle, gliding turn.

This was an aircraft piloted by 30-year-old Flight Lieutenant David Lord, who was awarded a posthumous Victoria Cross for his selflessness, having remained at the controls of his burning aircraft while his crew baled out. Of the 165 aircraft that were despatched to resupply the division, 13 were lost, 5 dropped their panniers on the incorrect DZ, and of the 390 tons of ammunition, food and medical supplies that arrived, most was collected by the Germans after attempts to redirect the delivery failed. It was a sad episode, as Urquhart lamented:

From foxholes and slit trenches and from the restricted spaces to which we were trying to attract the pilots; from blasted buildings and ditches and emplacements of rubble and earth, the eyes of hundreds and possibly thousands of careworn soldiers gazed upwards and through the battle haze. We were spellbound and speechless, and I daresay there is not a survivor in Arnhem who will ever forget, or want to forget, the courage we were privileged to witness in those terrible eight minutes.

As the vital resupply fell into enemy hands, the remnants of the group that had failed to break through to the bridge near St Elizabeth's hospital began to further disintegrate. During that afternoon and lacking resources and leadership, the shattered units began to withdraw back towards Oosterbeek along the river road. They were met a few hundred yards before the old Oosterbeek church by Lieutenant-Colonel 'Sheriff'

Thompson, commander of the Light Regiment Royal Artillery, who formed around 400 men into a defensive position to protect his guns and block any German attempt to undermine the division by advancing along the road. 'Thompson Force', as it became known, withstood an early battering from the enemy as it followed up the withdrawal with strikes down the road. The fighting was frenetic, improvised and at close quarters, but the line held. All over the battlefield the predatory Germans, sensing weakness, began to close in. They gave 4 Parachute Brigade little respite that afternoon, and after dark continued to harass its battalions. That night both 10 Para and 156 Para – a mere 250 officers and 176 men – completed their move south of the railway embankment. There had been many acts of bravery to achieve this, including that by Captain Lionel Queripel who, with the remnants of his A Company, gallantly defended a strip of woodland near Wolfheze to protect the retreat. After organizing his split force by crossing and recrossing fire-torn ground, carrying a wounded man to the Regimental Aid Post, receiving a wound to his face, killing the crews of two machine guns and capturing an anti-tank gun, he sent his men away when it looked liked the position was going to be overwhelmed and was last seen fighting with pistol and hand grenades. He was awarded a posthumous Victoria Cross. Although the two battalions successfully rendezvoused, they still had to enter the defensive area that was forming around the Hartenstein Hotel. This thumb-shaped perimeter consisted of men from all four brigades – including the Poles and the glider pilots – with Thompson Force anchoring it to the banks of the Lower Rhine in the east, near Oosterbeek church, and the Border Regiment doing the same in the west, on the high ground of Westerbouwing. Approximately three-quarters of a mile wide, and a mile long – the northern extremity stretching several hundred yards north of the Hartenstein Hotel – the perimeter increased in strength as units, small groups and individuals fell back to it. Its development meant that the Germans had managed to squeeze the British into two pockets –

one at Arnhem bridge and the other in Oosterbeek – and from the evening of the 19th they proceeded to try and destroy them. Krafft and Spindler pressed towards the Hartenstein perimeter from the north and east, whilst von Tettau lent in from the west. The Germans were strangling 1 British Airborne Division and a saviour was not yet in sight.

At 0630 hours on the morning of the 19th the Household Cavalry led the Grenadier Guards over the newly completed Bailey bridge at Son and XXX Corps set off for Arnhem once more. It took the first vehicles just half an hour to reach Veghel, and a link-up with the 82nd Airborne at Grave was achieved in just an hour and 20 minutes after that. In the column, Major H.F. Stanley of 1 (Motor)/Grenadier Guards remembers: 'They fairly brought the whip out that morning; the speed we were travelling at the back end of the column was terrific – just full throttle the whole way. All went splendidly.' It was a wonderfully successful morning's work, with the Irish Guards history proclaiming: 'All the way the battalions were greeted by cheering crowds and Americans, who were as glad to see them as they were to see the Americans.' But although good progress had been made that morning, the corps was still a day and a half behind schedule when its vanguard reached the outskirts of Nijmegen at noon. This meant that although armour and manpower could now be lent to attempts to take the bridges, there was precious little time to plan an attack. Moreover, it was not a task that Allan Adair had spent much time pondering, for as he later wrote: 'My orders had said that the Nijmegen bridge would be in airborne hands by the time we reached it, and we would simply sweep on through.' Nevertheless, a plan was hatched for tank-infantry attacks on both road and rail bridges using the Grenadier Guards Group and 2nd Battalion of 505 PIR.

The attacks did not start until 1500 hours due to the time it took the Guards Armoured Division to get to the city via Heumen bridge. The first push was little more than an information-gathering exercise to assess the German defences. Waiting for them were men largely drawn from the 10 SS Panzer Division who, despite their difficulties crossing the Lower

Rhine, were well set. Consequently, although the second push towards the railway bridge got to within 500 yards of the structure, and the attack on the road bridge closer still, both were repelled. Major Stanley noted: 'The Battle Group heading for the main bridge drew 88mm fire and small-arms fire from the area of the roundabout . . . John Holler's tank of the 2nd Battalion brewed up and John was killed. Thereupon, a slogging match ensued . . . Fighting continued until dark'. A third attack here also failed, leaving a desolate scene of abandoned tanks and armoured cars, flaming buildings and scores of corpses. Adair comments: 'We were opposed by really tough troops who had covered all the roads, fortified every square, and set fire to every fifth house in a defensive perimeter round both bridges.' Allied casualties were substantial – there were already 600 American wounded in the city hospital and another 150 missing or dead – and yet still no crossing had been taken and time was passing. Indeed, with more German troops crossing the Waal that night, Willi Bittrich's men retained such a stronghold on the bridges that the situation threatened to completely derail the entire operation.

Gavin and Adair had to think again. They could not afford to be drawn into a slogging match that suited the German aim of slowing XXX Corps to a halt. The result was a new plan. The following morning the western suburbs of Nijmegen would be cleared, and there would be a new attempt to take the bridges. Meanwhile, 3rd Battalion 504 PIR would cross the Waal in 33 small boats one mile west of the railway bridge, whilst supporting fire was provided by the Irish Guards. With the German defences turned and with paratroopers on the north bank, it was believed that the southern end of the bridges would fall to Grenadiers just as the northern end fell to the men of the 504th. Speed was essential to success, but both commanders knew that the Germans had had ample time to wire the bridges for demolition, and they could well be destroyed as soon as the Allies set foot on them.

A signal was sent back down the XXX Corps convoy to bring forward its flimsy canvas assault craft for the Waal crossing. The 101st Airborne continued its sterling work of ensuring the highway remained open to Allied traffic. At Best, after the titanic struggle of the previous day, the Germans struck out against the new Son bridge, with the 502nd's 2nd and 3rd Battalions trying to stop them. Corporal Pete Santini, who was exhausted after almost non-stop action since landing, describes the attack:

> It went all quiet for a moment and then it seemed like all 'Hell broke loose'. Mortars, 88mm, 20mm, machine pistols, rifles, and our own mortars, machine guns, tommy guns, rifles, carbines, shots from all directions, a bedlam of noise which was impossible to describe. This went on all morning.

Close to the destroyed Best bridge, Lieutenant Ed Wierzbowski's isolated platoon fought for its survival. The end came for four-times-wounded PFC Joe Mann when an enemy grenade landed in his shell hole and, shouting 'Grenade!', he threw himself on it to save his comrades. He was awarded a posthumous Congressional Medal of Honor. It was a desperate situation and the surviving members of the platoon were running out of ammunition and eventually had no option but to surrender as the Germans surged over them. Even so, the situation was far from lost, for waiting to strike back were 2nd and 3rd Battalions supported by some units of 327 Glider Infantry Regiment and British armour from the 15th/19th Hussars. This armour made an immediate impact, as PFC Richard Ladd describes:

> Around noon we became conscious of a sound of armour approaching from the DZ. Enemy fire abruptly slackened. A lone British major with a scarlet cloth cap on his head and a white lanyard running to his sidearm, strode into the woods and inquired loudly as to the location of the regimental CO . . . A brief conference with Colonel John Michaelis was followed by a throaty roar as six Churchills and one Challenger tank advanced along the road

parallel to the wood's line. At the first crack of 76mm fire from the Churchills and the flame-thrower from the Challenger, the men of 2nd and 3rd Battalions began to move forward . . . over 1,100 prisoners [were] escorted back to the DZ that afternoon.

At the end of a ruthless battle the 502nd had, at last, wrecked the German ability to mount any further sustained offensive action in the area.

This was an important success, for with the Best bridge destroyed, the Son crossing had to be protected at all costs. Consequently, a similar buffer zone to the east was sought and 1st and 2nd Battalions of 506 PIR were sent to clear the area. With his men riding into the village of Helmond on a squadron of Hussars' Cromwell tanks, 2nd Battalion's Easy Company ran into 50 armoured vehicles of the 107 Panzer Brigade pushing towards the main highway. It was, says the company's commander, Dick Winters, 'more than we had ever seen at one time'. The meeting led to a confrontation that ended in 15 Easy Company casualties. Some of the German armour managed to get within range of the Son bridge and threatened to demolish it, but a well-aimed 57mm anti-tank round destroyed one of the tanks, while a bazooka halted another and initiated the enemy's withdrawal.

On such fine margins hung the fate of the entire operation. Once again it seemed that had the Germans been more determined, they could have made a difficult situation much worse for the Allies and the action around Son was just one of many German attempts to retake the bridges and cut the road that day. Like Gavin's division, the severely overextended 101st was seriously undermined by the non-arrival of nearly half of its third lift gliders. Although a significant proportion of 327th Glider Infantry landed safely, nearly half of Maxwell Taylor's artillery pieces did not, and this was a potentially devastating setback as increasing numbers of German tanks were homing in on the long and exposed Allied corridor. Had XII and VIII Corps swept up the flanks as the plan demanded many of these difficulties could have been overcome, but in reality these formations just could not keep pace with the attack. Their stilted operation has several causes, but chief amongst them is the conservatism shown by the commanders, who were understandably concerned about over-extending their divisions and rendering them vulnerable to counterattack. Other factors include a lack of adequate resources for the task; difficult cross-country terrain; and a late start. VIII Corps, for example, only managed to cross the start line on 19 September. In such circumstances, it is hardly surprising that the Germans on either side of the corridor enjoyed a freedom of movement that the lack of flanking forces and restricted Allied air support gave them. As Kurt Student, a serious student of airborne warfare, later commented: 'We had liberty to attack the Allies whenever and wherever we pleased. It was not a situation that we had recently enjoyed. This important factor was invaluable to us for we used it effectively to cut the highway artery to Arnhem, and watched as the operation gradually lost its strength.'

Thus, by the end of 19 September 1 British Airborne Division had lost its offensive initiative and adopted a defensive posture, while just 10 miles away the Guards Armoured Division sought to capture the elusive Waal crossing. Both 82 and 101 US Airborne Divisions, meanwhile, remained under tremendous pressure as a myriad German units sought to cut the main highway and retake key bridges. Even so, although having suffered trauma, Operation Market Garden was not dead. If the Nijmegen road bridge could be quickly taken and Frost's men could hold on in Arnhem, then XXX Corps could still be across the Lower Rhine by the end of the following day. The prize the Allies desired was still attainable, and both they and the Germans remained motivated by the notion. As Len Wright has said of this phase of the fighting in Holland: 'Both sides had hope and so the race continued – in fact, the intensity picked up. Who would end up winning this race was not clear – the fog of war is often dense and it was never denser than when it smothered Operation Market Garden.'

This feeling of impending doom had not yet gripped the British at Arnhem bridge; nevertheless they grew weaker every hour. By dawn on

Wednesday 20 September, John Frost's men were close to exhaustion: the bearded, grimy, red-eyed troops found it difficult to concentrate for extended periods and lacked much of what they needed to continue their fight. Although the first radio communication with divisional headquarters was made that morning, the news was not good: the rest of the division had been blocked and Nijmegen bridge remained in German hands. Aware that his men needed reassuring as well as cajoling in such circumstances, Lieutenant Len Wright spent much of his time visiting his positions and motivating his men: 'We found it difficult to do anything with precision as we were so tired and the men began to jump at shadows, seeing things that were not there. I tried to be cheerful and positive, but it was not easy.'

The Germans continued to try and dislodge the 1st Airborne troops through a mixture of infiltration and destruction, but as the last link in the Allied chain across the Lower Rhine, Frost's men did not need to be reminded of the need to remain resolute. In fact, being surrounded, outnumbered and outgunned was an airborne speciality. They would stand firm until they could fight no more or were relieved. Sensing this, the Germans stepped up the intensity of their attacks during the day, with both Bittrich and Brinkmann focused on opening the bridge to facilitate the speedy reinforcement of Nijmegen to deny the Allies a Waal crossing. This escalation had the effect of angering the British troops rather than cowering them, and resulted in some tenacious displays of bravery. The 2 Para's 26-year-old Lieutenant John Grayburn, for example, led an attack against an enemy party that was setting charges under the bridge's ramp as a contingency against a British armoured breakthrough. The A Company platoon commander had already been shot through the shoulder leading an abortive attack across the bridge during the first evening, and was wounded for a second time as his men temporarily drove the Germans off. The Royal Engineers had time to remove the explosives' fuses, but when the Germans replaced the fuses, Grayburn, his arm in a sling and his head bandaged, immediately rallied his men and struck back. This time, however, the enemy were stronger, as Sapper commander Lieutenant Donald Hindley describes:

The enemy had by now moved up a tank to cover the work. We were quickly mown down. Lieutenant Grayburn was killed – riddled with machine gun fire. I escaped with flesh wounds to my shoulder and face.

For three days of outstanding leadership and remarkable courage, John Grayburn was awarded a posthumous Victoria Cross.

By this stage the defence of the bridge perimeter was shrinking and was manned by just 140 men. There was nowhere to find a moment's sanctuary as the fighting was incessant as well as brutal, bloody and sometimes hand-to-hand. Among the casualties that day was Len Wright, who had grappled with a German SS trooper before being wounded and left unconscious by a shell that hit the roof. 'My world swirled and blurred', he says, 'and I can remember falling to the dusty floor, and then coming to in the cellar.' John Frost, meanwhile, languished in the basement of a building on the other side of the bridge after mortar splinters had ripped into his legs: 'There was a sudden savage crash . . . I was thrown several feet and I found myself lying face downwards on the ground with pain in both legs.' He was taken to the Regimental Aid Post, where he tried to fortify himself with a slug of whiskey from his hip flask, but it made him feel like vomiting. Having been carried downstairs, Frost tried to command but eventually found it impossible:

I was quite affected by the blast as well as being wounded and I wasn't really able to control things. Freddie [Gough] came along, and I told him to carry on – not that there were any orders much to give by then. That was the very worst time, the most miserable of my life. It was a pretty desperate thing to see your battalion gradually carved to bits around you.

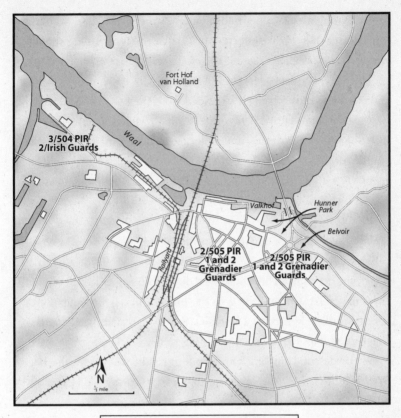

Map 5: The Waal Crossing
Nijmegen 20 September 1944

Freddie Gough had been a midshipman in the First World War and a commander of a Provost section at Dunkirk before joining the paratroopers. He was an excellent leader. One of his first actions that afternoon was to negotiate a temporary ceasefire with the Germans in order to remove the most seriously wounded from the battlefield. Thus, with a ferocious battle between two elite forces reaching its crescendo, the SS troops helped to move their bloodied enemy out of harm's way. John Frost, who was drifting in and out of consciousness, has a clear memory of a German NCO asking that they leave the building as soon as possible:

> With the help of one of the bomb-happy cases he dragged me up the stairs to the door. We had to move quickly outside to avoid burning debris from the house. I sat down among the stretcher-cases on the embankment leading to the bridge. All our buildings were burning fiercely and, as I watched, the old battalion headquarters collapsed into a heap of smouldering rubble ... The SS men were very polite and complimentary about the battle we had fought, but the bitterness I felt was unassuaged. No living enemy had beaten us.

This rather incongruous event was not without military benefit for both, however, for while the British took a deep breath and undertook a little reorganization, the Germans had a good look at the airborne defences and crept forward. The two sides had the measure of each other, and neither believed that the battle would last many hours more. By dusk another 60 British soldiers had become casualties.

As the struggle at the bridge moved into its final phase, the rest of Roy Urquhart's division was beginning to cement its position in Oosterbeek. 4 Parachute Brigade moved into the perimeter developing around the Hartenstein, having collected in a position to the south of the railway line the previous night. Moving off at 0615 hours, 10 Para followed 156 Para towards the Utrechtseweg, but soon ran into the enemy in some woods.

Trying to outflank them, the force suffered a number of casualties and the battalions split up: 10 Para made good progress as they moved away, but 156 Para and Shan Hackett's attached brigade headquarters were targeted by self-propelled guns and tanks which brought them to a dead halt. All but one of Hackett's brigade staff were wounded in the ensuing engagement, and both the CO of 156 Para Lieutenant-Colonel Sir Richard de Voeux, and his second-in-command, were killed. Swift and bold action was required if the survivors were not to be surrounded and annihilated, and Hackett, never one to shun a challenge, ordered a company to attack and clear a hollow alongside a road just short of the Hartenstein perimeter. Major Geoffrey Powell led the charge:

No one hesitated. The men rose to their feet the moment I stepped out into the open from behind the shelter of a tree. Major Michael Page's solid bulk running parallel with me, half a dozen of his men following . . . Corporal Rosenberg broke into a scream of rage, harsh and furious. The yell spread down the line . . . Now I was careless of everything. We did not stand a chance, but this was the right way to go. This was the proper way to finish it all. Nearly hysterical now with rage and excitement, I heard my own voice join in the screaming.

The stunned Germans opened fire as the paratroopers stormed towards them from a distance of 50 yards. Powell continues:

I brought my Sten down to hip-level to press the trigger; it flashed through my mind that this was the first time I had fired the weapon since the battle started. My forefinger squeezed the metal. Northing happened. It had jammed . . . There were figures moving among the trees. First a couple, then half-a-dozen dark-shapes were outlined against the green background, men sprinting away, men disappearing through the trees. The Boche were running away. We had done it! We had driven the enemy out at the point of the bayonet! This was the ultimate in war!

A group of 150 men fought from the shallow depression for the rest of the day, repelling enemy advances but doing little to improve their vulnerable position. Thus at around 1700 hours and having suffered a further 60 casualties, Hackett personally led another charge which aimed to break into Urquhart's perimeter. Surprised and not a little frightened by the sight and sound of this cluster of outraged airborne soldiers attacking them for the second time that day, the German response was limp and only a couple of paratroopers were wounded. Hackett entered the divisional area via the slit trenches occupied by the Border Regiment, and was soon informed that 10 Para had arrived earlier that afternoon barely 70 men strong. 4 Parachute Brigade had suffered heavy losses and was extremely tired, but even so, with every single rifle-bearing soldier so valuable to the division, Hackett's men were immediately deployed in the defences.

During the day the Oosterbeek perimeter had seen a marked increase in the number of attacks, as increasing numbers of German troops, tanks, self-propelled guns, armoured car and other weapons began probing the airborne positions to assess their strength and positions. The Germans were easily thwarted, but as Roy Urquhart and his ADC Captain Graham Roberts found out, the situation was extremely dangerous. Visiting the defences in a jeep to get a picture of the front, the general – not for the first time since arriving in Holland – very nearly became a casualty:

On one of my trips, I went to see Boy Wilson and his Independent Company [Pathfinders] who held a number of houses in a heavily wooded district . . . We were given directions by some troops which led along a wooded ride. Suddenly we found ourselves in the middle of a vigorous dispute between the Independent Company and a number of SS men. From slit trenches on the roadside, faces appeared and men shouted and gesticulated. I braked hard, and, with Roberts, made an undignified dive into a ditch.

Meanwhile, just to the east of Oosterbeek church, Thompson Force was under the cosh as the enemy endeavoured to dislodge the division's anchor on the Lower Rhine. Hemmed in by a boggy flood plain on their left and housing on their right, the Germans were largely canalized down the road, when they ran into a 6-pounder anti-tank gun commanded by 21-year-old former butcher Lance-Sergeant John Baskeyfield of the South Staffordshires. The six-man crew allowed the German armour to close to within a hundred yards before opening fire, and in this way managed to destroy two tanks and a self-propelled gun, but they all became casualties. Baskeyfield received a severe leg wound, but continued to work the weapon under heavy fire while shouting encouragement to his comrades until it was knocked out. Undeterred, the NCO then crawled across fire-strewn ground to another 6-pounder, which he used to engage a second self-propelled gun, stopping it with two rounds. He was killed, however, preparing to fire a third. Baskeyfield's body was never found, but he was awarded a posthumous Victoria Cross in recognition of the key role he had played in maintaining the cohesion of Thompson force and, therefore, the Oosterbeek perimeter.

During the attritional battle that was gradually grinding 1st Airborne into Oosterbeek's sandy soil, it was inevitable that British casualties would be high. They were treated by medical teams operating out of a variety of locations: 16 Field Ambulance had taken over St Elizabeth's hospital on 17 September and, although it had subsequently fallen to the enemy, its surgical teams continued their work and were joined by German doctors, with whom they cooperated extremely well. 181 and 133 Field Ambulances, meanwhile, occupied two hotels at a road junction in Oosterbeek just to the east of the Hartenstein – a place that became known as MDS (Medical Dressing Station) Crossroads – and also at the nearby Tafelberg Hotel. The walking wounded made their own way to these dressing stations, but those who could not walk were picked up by jeeps. Lieutenant Derrick Randall, a medical officer at the Schoonord Hotel, remembers:

> Non-surgical casualties were virtually non-existent . . . [and] I had no psychiatric casualties. Only later in the battle did we have a few cases of true 'battle exhaustion' and all recovered when allowed 12 hours or more continuous sleep . . . The situation often appeared to be fluid and one day my corporal set out with some casualties when he was unexpectedly stopped by a very smart SS lieutenant and asked in excellent English where he was going. The corporal replied he was taking casualties to the dressing station and hoped that he would be allowed to proceed. The SS officer replied 'If I do I suppose you will give away my position.' The corporal replied 'Yes, sir.' After a pause the officer told him to 'carry on'.

By 20 September MDS Crossroads, formerly a relatively peaceful spot, was in the front line on the eastern side of the perimeter and life there became barely tolerable. Indeed, during the afternoon the Germans overran the area for the first time, forcing various other buildings into service, including the Hartenstein, as Randall explains:

> By this time General Urquhart and his staff had to move to the basement and as everywhere filled with casualties, work at HQ became very difficult! Though they were very tolerant, as the congestion increased it became even more important to find somewhere else for the casualties. We managed to 'evacuate' them to various houses nearby where they were looked after first by my corporal, then the odd stretcher-bearer, but mostly by the magnificent local inhabitants.

The siege of Oosterbeek had began.

As the men of 1st Airborne dug in, ten miles away 82nd US Airborne and Guards Armoured Divisions fought to deliver Urquhart's men from their purgatory as quickly as they could. Detailed plans for an assault crossing of the Waal by the 504th had been drawn up overnight, and by noon Major Julian Cook's 3rd Battalion were waiting for boats one mile to the west of the railway bridge. Tension amongst the paratroopers on the riverbank was palpable. They knew that they would have to cross a broad river with strong currents and against waiting defenders. Over the hours that they waited, the reluctant sailors turned the unit's unenviable situation over in their minds – and it did not get any less troublesome. Meanwhile, the boats made their way through a XXX Corps traffic jam that stretched back beyond the Meuse–Escaut Canal. The crafts' progress had been impeded the previous night by a heavy German air raid on Eindhoven, which could have made casualties of Lewis Brereton and Matthew Ridgway, who were travelling through the city in a jeep. The FAAA commander wrote of the incident in his diary:

Our path was blocked by bombs and we turned up a road which was a dead end. There we ditched the vehicles and ducked into a city park, remaining flat on our stomachs for almost an hour while approximately 120 Stukas and Ju-88s bombed Eindhoven. Considerable damage was done to the city and ammunition and supply trains . . . we decided to make a run for the open country. A bomb landed about 15 feet from us, between us and another jeep . . . That would certainly have been the end of some of us had not the bomb been a dud. The city was in flames and the roads were blocked. Estimated civilian casualties were 250 killed, 3,000 wounded.

The Germans also tried to undermine the Allies' ability to move freely up the main highway by putting intense pressure on Jim Gavin's five under-resourced battalions that were defending a 12-mile sector of front to the south-east of the city. Threatening not only Nijmegen but also the Groesbeek Heights and the Mass–Waal Canal, II Parachute Corps and Corps Feldt fell heavily on the 82nds flank. As part of Feldt's formation, 406 Landesschützen Division attacked towards Beek with Lieutenant Thomas Abt's platoon in the van:

> We were told that British armour had reached Nijmegen and we needed to make it difficult for the airborne troops to keep the main road open to the city. It was simple, we were to be a nuisance and push against the edges of the American's ground . . . It was not long before we ran into their outposts. My platoon was part of the leading company with a panzer in support. The tank was soon ripped apart by an anti-tank round and we scattered before working our way into the American positions . . . The fighting was a bloody business. I used grenades and the butt of a rifle on several occasions. We took 50 per cent casualties.

Both Beek and Wyler in the northern part of the sector were taken by the Germans, while in the south the village of Mook was temporarily lost. This put the critical bridge at Heumen under great strain. Yet although they lost ground in certain areas, the 82nd did not lose any that immediately undermined the operation, and this meant that XXX Corps traffic continued to flow and Julian Cook's delivery finally arrived.

As the men of the 3rd Battalion put their disturbingly flimsy canvas boats together, the enemy's positions on the northern bank were attacked by ranks of Typhoons, the guns of two squadrons of Irish Guards tanks and approximately 100 artillery pieces. Then at 1500 hours, after a smoke screen had been laid, the paratroopers slipped and slid down towards the water, as Moffatt Burriss explains:

> It was like a Laurel and Hardy movie, only with real lives at stake – hundreds of lives . . . I looked to the right and left. Everyone was prepared to move. I didn't see fear in anyone's eyes – only grim

determination. Then the tanks stopped firing. Each crew grabbed a boat loaded with weapons, ammunition, and equipment and charged [forward] . . . The wind had already blown away the smoke, and our position was completely exposed . . . The air strike fifteen minutes earlier had hit few, if any, enemy gun positions. As we plunged into the dark, swirling water, we could see that the Kraut guns were intact and trained in our direction.

The first wave took to the water – five or six men in dangerously over-loaded vessels:

As soon as we launched the first boats, mine among them, chaos reigned . . . Several boats were swept downstream before everyone could scramble on board . . . Two or three boats capsized and dumped ammunition, equipment, and men into the river . . . German shells began landing nearby.

Using their rifles as paddles, the men moved slowly across the 300-yard stretch of water as they fought the Waal's eight-knot current:

A few shells tore into the water around us, but so far no one had been hit. When we were a third of the way across, the river suddenly exploded. As the Krauts unleashed their full firepower, the surface of the water looked like it was in the middle of a sudden rainstorm, the sky actually hailing bullets . . . Men began to slump forward in their boats. Some screamed, but most went silently . . . I was sitting on the stern of our boat next to the [British] engineer. Suddenly, I noticed his wrist turn red. 'Captain', he said, 'take the rudder. I've been hit.' Just as I reached for the rudder, he leaned forward and caught a 20mm high-explosive shell through his head – a round that was meant for me.

Burriss caught some of the shell fragments in his side but was not badly wounded. Having pushed the body of the engineer overboard, he shouted instructions to his men as they landed on the north bank. Disembarking as quickly as they could under heavy fire from German mortars and machine guns 900 yards away across a flat plain, Burriss ordered his men to attack:

> Without hesitation, every single man, including several who were wounded, jumped from the embankment and started running forward and firing furiously at the machine guns ... Men began to drop on both sides of me, some grabbing their legs or shoulders and others falling like sacks of sand.

The feverish Americans covered the ground quickly, and showed no mercy to the machine gun crews that latterly tired to surrender. They wiped them out with bullets and hand grenades. As the terrible clearance unfolded, the boats returned to the south bank to pick up the remainder of 3rd Battalion and the 1st Battalion follow-on force. In order to turn the tactical foothold into an operationally significant success, the 504th then had to take the north end of the bridges as a potent mix of paratroopers and armour took the other.

With a fire still burning fiercely in their bellies, Cook's men carved into the stunned Germans who stood in their way, causing them to flee across the bridge where they were gunned down by airborne troops and guardsmen finishing their successful southern attack. The 504th then headed off to deal with the road bridge, as the Grenadiers and men from the 505th surged forward in Nijmegen. Here the battle had been as unrelenting as it had been savage, with heavy casualties taken on both sides. SS-Sturmann Urs Ebersbach, who was taken prisoner at this time, confesses:

> I surrendered along with several others. I was in a slit trench on the radio at the time and looked up to see a young American para-

trooper standing over me – his whole body shaking, his finger twitching on the trigger of his tommy-gun held at his shoulder. I immediately raised my hands and in English said, 'Do not shoot!' He didn't, I don't know why, in a similar situation I would have pulled the trigger without a second thought.

At 1900 hours two Grenadier Guards tanks began crossing the bridge under heavy fire, and for a handful of minutes observers watched to see if the bridge would be destroyed. It remained intact and the tanks linked up with the relieved 504th's paratroopers. The reason why remains a mystery, for Heinz Harmel had decided to detonate the charges which remained in place. Whether his failure to do so came about as the result of human or mechanical error, the work of the Dutch resistance, or fast-working British sappers is not known. But the crossing of the Nijmegen road bridge kept Operation Market Garden alive, and knowing this, General Horrocks sent forward several cases of champagne by way of celebration.

With such a great obstacle cleared, and knowing that the British airborne division was struggling, it was with considerable disgust that Gavin's troops watched as the Guards Armoured Division, rather than pushing on, settled down for the night. Yet however irrational that decision may have seemed at the time, Allan Adair believed that it was the correct one: 'General Horrocks', he later wrote, 'knew that only infantry could operate in the country beyond Nijmegen, which was low, a mass of dykes, waterlogged and entirely unsuitable for tanks.' The XXX Corps commander was a great advocate of the armoured night attack, but he believed that it would have been suicidal for the Guards to have pushed up an unreconnoitred road in the dark against a cohesive German defence that was known to include anti-tank guns. Instead, Major-General Ivor Thomas' 43 (Wessex) Division had been called forward, and would take the lead on arrival, leaving the Guards Armoured Division to help the American airborne troops keep the highway open to the south. Such support was desperately needed, for that day the Germans had launched another attack by 107 Panzer Brigade against Son. The 101st Airborne defeated this and at the same time had taken the opportunity to expand its defensive buffer zone around Veghel. Although well aware that the corridor remained vulnerable, and that Urquhart was in distress, Horrocks believed that Wednesday 20 September had been a successful day. 'I went to bed a happy man', the general wrote, but he also noted that it was 'almost the last time that I was to do so in this battle. So far fortune had favoured us, but the sky was darkening.'

By Thursday 21 September the Germans had fully recovered from the psychological shock proffered by Market Garden and had stabilized their front. Thus XXX Corps probes that morning into 'The Island' (as the area south of Arnhem was aptly known) soon ran into a strong defensive screen south of the village of Elst composed of infantry, armour, anti-aircraft and anti-tank guns. The unseen guns knocked out the three leading Irish Guards tanks very quickly. Following in a Sherman behind this lead troop was Guardsman Jim Hetherington:

> I was seated alongside Claude [Kettleborough] in the driving compartment where there was little to do except fire bursts on the machine gun ... Eventually we were ordered to carry on forward, and we knew that our tank would be hit before long, and it was. The noise was what I imagine it would be like to be inside Big Ben when it struck, the tank immediately went on fire ... Claude and I hopped out quickly, and saw flames roaring out of the turret. Rocky [Steers, the troop sergeant] was on the ground, and appeared to be badly wounded, the gunner and the operator had obviously not got out and must have been killed instantly.

The infantry dismounted and deployed in the polder on either side of the road, where they themselves came under German small arms, mortar and field gun fire. With their own artillery support severely limited by a lack of ammunition, and communications with RAF Typhoons having broken down, no further progress towards Arnhem was made that day. Yet, even if the Guards had broken through to Arnhem bridge on the 21st, they would have found its northern end in German hands. After a night that had seen their positions fatally undermined by further enemy infiltration, the 200 exhausted airborne soldiers still fighting in the bridge perimeter at dawn were staring at their last rounds of ammunition and pulling on their final ounces of stamina. In their final moments, however, the defenders did what they could to prolong the airborne's resistance, as Urquhart has described:

> In the grey morning light, the Germans began to winkle out the gallant fugitives. From cellars in opposite sides of the one ruined street, the crews of light automatics, one British, the other German, had been fighting it out. As their ammunition ran down, the British held their fire for longer spells. Then came a final burst and the awed Germans saw two very young paratroopers emerge from the cellar. While the leading man attempted to draw the German crew's fire, the other followed up with a knife.

The two men were wounded before they could do any damage, but the Germans were impressed by the act and many others like it for, as one SS officer later said, 'it was not spontaneous but obviously thought out'. Once the Germans were satisfied that they had cleared the shattered buildings that had housed Frost's men, they began to bring out the wounded. James Sims could not believe the devastation that greeted him that morning, nor the civility of his captors:

> A tough-looking SS soldier with a silk scarf round his neck sauntered up and said, 'Good fight, Tommy', as if we had been playing football rather than trying to kill each other. We were to be shifted further back into the town. Two other wounded paratroopers

hung their arms round my neck as we struggled under the northern end of the bridge, and then along a road to the left. We were amazed to see the large numbers of German dead in the streets ... We turned into a street with trees down each side, and under these, parked nose to tail, was a long line of Mark IV tanks. A young German soldier shouted out, 'Yes, Tommy, these were for you in the morning if you had not surrendered.'

The force, which had amounted to little more than a battalion initially, had held out for three days and four nights against a series of sustained attacks in which 81 of them had lost their lives. The perimeter at the bridge had proved a major hindrance to the German ability to move as they would have wished in response to the Allied offensive. As soon as it had been removed, SS troops flooded across the bridge to strengthen the Island's defences, whilst others applied themselves to the destruction of the remainder of Roy Urquhart's division.

There had been a lull in the fighting around the Oosterbeek perimeter through the night of 20/21 September, as the Germans drew breath. The British took full advantage by distributing what limited supplies of food, water and ammunition they had and organizing their 3,000-man defence. It was a short respite, however, for as soon as the force at Arnhem bridge had been mopped up, Harzer unleashed a series of attacks around the perimeter (or 'Der Kessel' – 'the Cauldron' – as the Germans called it). Indeed, near Oosterbeek church the Germans pushed so hard against Thompson Force that the hard-pressed airborne troops were forced to give a little ground. Sheriff Thompson was wounded by a mortar during the attack, and he passed the reins over to Major Dickie Lonsdale, the second-in-command of 11 Para. That afternoon Major Robert Cain of the South Staffordshire Regiment fought tirelessly to stop his position from being overrun by armour using a PIAT, but his last bomb exploded prematurely just after he had fired it. 'It blew me over backwards' Cain says, 'and I was blind. I was shouting like a hooligan. I shouted to somebody to get onto the PIAT, because there was another tank behind. I blubbered and yelled and used some very bad language. They dragged me off to the Aid Post.' Patched up, he returned to the front line to continue his work and later received the only Victoria Cross of the battle that was not awarded posthumously. As the Cain and Lonsdale force grappled with the German armoured attack, the KOSB in the northern part of the perimeter endeavoured to fend off swarms of infantry. Captain Jim Livingstone explains that defence in such situations required considerable nerve:

> They came across – running and shouting – to within about 20 yards of us before I opened fire. I killed an awful lot of Germans then, with my Sten. There was a big tree in front of me, and there was one German who was on his knees, wounded, but still preparing to fire. I remember David Clayhills, the Adjutant . . . shouting 'Kill the bastard!', and I did so. I'm a bit ashamed of it now, but I was bloody angry at the time.

On the opposite side of the perimeter that morning the crucial area of Westerbouwing and its hotel were lost, which gave the Germans the advantages bestowed by significantly higher ground overlooking the river and the southern part of the British perimeter. Lance-Corporal Ginger Wilson of 1/Border Regiment, who defended the area, faced both armour and infantry:

> As soon as it was daylight, we heard tanks coming. They turned off the road and headed straight for the hotel. There seemed to be hundreds of Germans like a football crowd. We opened up with everything . . . As the Germans overran the top of Westerbouwing, I saw to my left in the trees Lieutenant John Wellbeloved, a Canadian officer in command of 22 Platoon,

standing up firing his sten gun and shouting, 'Come on you Heiny bastards'; then he too was overrun and killed.

Despite attacks around the perimeter, however, the Germans failed to make a breakthrough, partly because of the stoic airborne defence, but largely because Bittrich and Harzer did not concentrate their increasing strength at critical points. The II SS Panzer Corps commander later said that his aim was to exploit what he believed to be a 'lack of initiative of British junior commanders and NCOs'. By forcing them into a series of situations that would gradually lead to their loss of cohesion, Bittrich was convinced that 1 British Airborne Division could be 'nibbled to death'. Moreover, the terrain lent itself to piecemeal attacks and time was on the Germans' side around Oosterbeek. The Germans were also well aware of the destructive impact of the British Second Army's artillery, which had proved so potent in destroying concentrated attacks in the past. Thus, just as soon as Urquhart had been told communication had been made with Miles Dempsey's 64 Medium Regiment, whose guns were in range of the perimeter, he asked them to assit. The support that they were to provide was critical to the division's survival, for the regiment not only dismantled innumerable German attacks, but also raised morale. Roy Urquhart later explained in his memoirs:

> Thus started one of the most exciting and remarkable artillery shoots I have ever experienced. From a range of about eleven miles, these gunners proceeded to answer our calls with a series of shoots on targets . . . some of which were not more than one hundred yards from our perimeter line . . . [I]n the afternoon the shelling had a quite noticeable effect on the Germans. Hearing the whine and the tremendous blast of these medium shells – there is surely no more terrifying noise in war – we felt glad the 64th were on our side. And now, supported by a battery of heavies, these gunners broke up several attacks supported by self-propelled guns in the eastern flank.

The British were also buoyed up by the arrival of the Polish Parachute Brigade's paratroopers late that afternoon on a DZ south of the river near the village of Driel. What with the lift having been postponed twice due to bad weather, the glider force having landed in the middle of a pitched battle on the 19th, and the brigade's mission having been changed from reinforcing the British at Arnhem bridge to reinforcing the Oosterbeek pocket, all of Stanislaw Sosabowski's worst fears seemed to have been realized. But many other disappointments were waiting in the wings: 41 of his 114 Dakotas were forced to return to England due to bad weather, the aircraft remaining were met by a hail of anti-aircraft fire and the 1,033 Polish paratroopers had to jump into a cloud of crossfire laid down by the enemy on the Westerbouwing Heights and the Island. German commanders had been told that the transporters were on the way by a network of observers, and the message was received by many German units in the Arnhem area.

But even those in the field, for whom their arrival was a surprise, used their initiative and instinct to good effect, as SS-Corporal Rudolf Trapp reveals:

> When we saw fresh paratroopers landing we lined up along the Rhine's edge and shot for all we were worth. I set up my machine gun and fired long protracted bursts because there is so little time before they all get to the ground. This was a shock – a second front!

Up in the air, Lieutenant Kaczmarek reported that he was aware of 'so much noise and tracer' that he thought 'every gun was aimed directly at me', while Lance-Corporal Bazyli Borowik says: 'We were under fire from machine guns whilst we were in the air, and then mortared on the ground.' The Poles, however, wasted no time establishing a defensive position in the village of Driel. But having done so, Sosabowski's plans were crippled by news that Urquhart could not be raised on the radio and that the Heveadorp ferry – his one hope of getting men across the Lower Rhine – was unusable. He also became aware that the Germans were busy establishing a defensive line to protect their eastern flank south of Arnhem against the possibility of a Polish attack. Moreover, probes by these rapidly deployed forces towards Driel that evening led to several intense engagements. It was with relief, therefore, that contact was eventually made with Urquhart through Captain Ludwik Zwolanski – the Polish liaison officer at 1st Airborne headquarters – who had swum the river to inform Sosabowski that the division would endeavour to find some boats and get them to the Poles. With Driel taking fire from the German screening forces, a nonplussed Sosabowski was left wondering not only where the beleaguered airborne troops were going to conjure adequate boats from, but also whether his parachutists were being asked to reinforce defeat.

The Poles' difficulties were merely the symptom of a wider breakdown in the 1 British Airborne Division plan, which in turn necessitated an operational review by Horrocks. The loss of the north end of Arnhem bridge and of the formation of the Oosterbeek perimeter left the XXX Corps commander with a dilemma on the evening of 21 September, for although the clear aim of Operation Market Garden was to take the road bridge at Arnhem, circumstances also necessitated the relief of Urquhart's division in the perimeter. There were two ways of reaching troops in Oosterbeek, but as the most obvious route over Arnhem bridge was blocked and likely to take days to open, Horrocks decided to send the Household Cavalry, followed by a brigade of 43 (Wessex) Division (which was due to arrive the following day) to outflank the German defences and head cross-country towards Driel, from where they would cross the Lower Rhine in XXX Corps boats. General Horrocks later wrote: 'I hoped that this fresh infantry division would succeed in joining up with the Poles, and that together they would be able to bring succour to the hard-pressed 1st Airborne.'

Like the original Operation Market Garden scheme, this new plan was fine in principle, but its prospects depended on many unknowns.

Would enough boats arrive in time for a large-scale crossing? How would the Germans overlooking the river react to this reinforcement? And was it likely that a reinforced Urquhart would be able to break out and retake the northern end of Arnhem bridge, as Horrocks hoped he would? Perhaps the reality of the situation was somewhat different when Horrocks had taken stock of the myriad difficulties on both sides of the Lower Rhine and the corridor to the south. Although it had been a relatively quiet day along the highway, reports from the airborne divisions and the Dutch Resistance pointed to the Germans regrouping in preparation for strong counterattacks which might be launched at any moment. Whilst Model ordered that II SS Panzer Corps and II Parachute Corps dealt with the British in the Arnhem area and the Americans around Nijmegen, Student was to concentrate on cutting the highway to the south. To this end, First Parachute Army's LXXXVIII Corps' War Diary states: 'Field Marshal Model has ordered that the enemy columns marching on Nijmegen are to be attacked at the Veghel bottleneck on 22 September from the west and east.' From Model down, the Germans had recognized that the progress of the head of the XXX Corps attack could be severely hampered if its lines of communication were broken through attacks on the vulnerable highway and bridges. The British, it could be argued, had reached their culminating point and the Germans were ready to exploit that. In such circumstances, perhaps the XXX Corps commander had already consulted with his superiors and decided that the foundations needed to be built for an evacuation from Oosterbeek, that Operation Market Garden was terminally ill and needed to be eased to a dignified end.

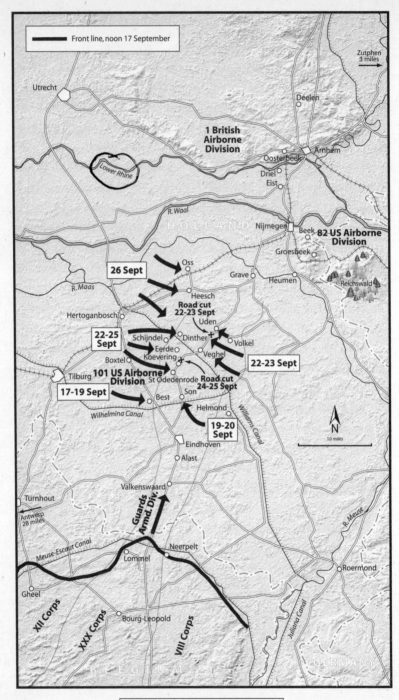

Map 6: Market Garden
German Counterattacks

CHAPTER 7

Touching the Rhine

(Operation Market Garden: 21–26 September 1944)

Sergeant Karl Krahl had expected to find himself in action soon, but found himself threatened even before he reached the front. The 24-year-old infantryman had been heaved into a truck along with 15 other men who were recovering from a variety of wounds received in Normandy. Krahl, a tall, muscular man, had been wounded by shell fragments during an Allied artillery bombardment on 20 July. Seven pieces of jagged metal were subsequently extracted from his right shoulder and neck by a surgeon working out of a farm dairy. Krahl was a lucky man, for one penny-sized fragment had been found to be pressing against his carotid artery. He was informed that he required several months of rest and rehabilitation before returning to the front. Even so, on the morning of 17 September he was sent south in a five-truck convoy 'to bolster the defences behind the lines'. Feeling weak and tired, having just shaken off yet another fever, the young soldier was in a fatalistic mood and remained unshaken when the vehicles were temporarily caught up in an Allied air raid on Arnhem. However, having crossed the Waal, Krahl heard the distinctive rumble of scores of low-flying aircraft and tensed up when the driver yelled, 'Paratroopers!' The truck sped on, its occupants trying to catch a glimpse of an airborne division dropping just a few miles to the east. 'It was a frightening sight', recalls Krahl, 'a thick mass of aircraft and parachutists already on the ground. There we were, unarmed cripples in the middle of a great airborne offensive.'

The convoy continued in a southerly direction before coming to a halt in the village of Best, which was a frenzy of activity: 'A harassed officer pointed us towards a barn which was acting as an armoury and we were handed weapons', says Krahl. 'I was given a rifle, 20 rounds, two hand grenades and attached to a company. That day was a blur of preparation, digging in and patrolling, but here we fought for the next two days and I was wounded again during an air raid.' It was only when he was having his damaged hand attended to at an aid post that Krahl learned he had become a member of a replacement battalion in 59 Division.

I had little idea where I was or what was going on, but on the afternoon of the 20th I was given command of a platoon in a company under an officer whom I had met only briefly, which formed part of a *Kampfgruppe* commanded by a man whose name I didn't know. My men were convalescents and boys so I tried to make it simple: we had to retain our discipline, hold our nerve and fight. On the following day we attacked an American position and a 17-year-old was shot clean through the head by my side.

Returning to his lines, Krahl made his report and was told to prepare for an attack on Veghel. There was no time for a reconnaissance, and there was not much of a plan, but he briefed his men and cleaned the submachine gun that he had taken from a dead man the day before. 'I hoped that I would have a chance to use it', Krahl explains, 'as most of us believed that we were being sent on a suicide mission.'

General Horrocks' plan was put in motion before dawn on Friday 22 September, when two troops of the Household Cavalry set off down minor roads to the west of the main highway towards Driel. Using early morning mist to cover their advance, they successfully navigated the narrow country lanes to join with the Poles. XXX Corps had, at last, reached the Lower Rhine and linked up with a unit from the British Airborne Division, but in the circumstances there was no fanfare, no self-congratulation and no champagne from Horrocks. The light armour was immediately despatched to assist in the protection of the village from continued German attacks, but the command vehicle remained at Sosabowski's headquarters so that he could use its radio to talk with Horrocks and Browning. Outlining what he knew of Urquhart's situation to each of them in turn, and emphasizing his need for boats, the conversation ended with Browning telling the irascible Pole, 'Everything that can be done, is being done.' Nevertheless, Sosabowski remained unconvinced.

Following the Household Cavalry's route, 43 (Wessex) Division's 214 Brigade headed to Driel later that morning led by 7/Somerset Light Infantry, whilst 129 Brigade attacked the main German defences on the highway. But the Somersets soon ran into enemy armour at the village of Oosterhout, which immediately stalled them. Straight-jacketed by the tight terrain and boggy ground, the battalion struggled to make any further progress until artillery support succeeded in loosening the German hold. The 43 (Wessex) Division history reports:

Stunned by this determined blow, the enemy surrendered in considerable numbers. Two enemy tanks were knocked out at the entrance to the village; another was captured undamaged along with an 88mm gun; over 130 sullen troops from an SS division gave themselves up. By 4.30 p.m. the battalion had completed the occupation of the smoking ruins of the village and thus brutally and effectively opened the way.

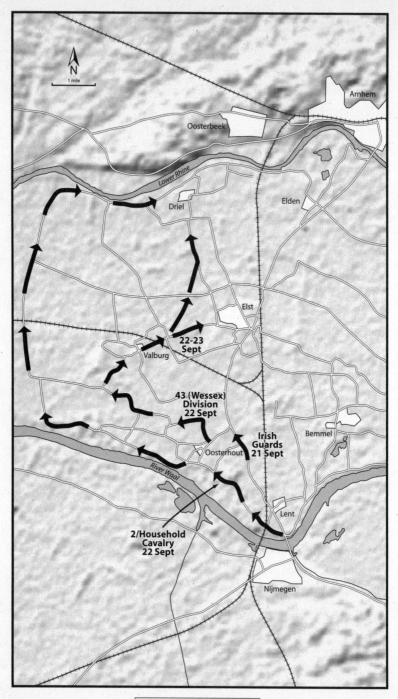

Map 7 : The Island

To exploit this success, and to add some impetus to the flagging attack, 5/Duke of Cornwall's Light Infantry (DCLI) moved through to complete the 10 miles to Driel. The CO, Lieutenant-Colonel George Taylor, reported:

> I had been told that, as soon as the Somersets had cleared Oosterhout, my battalion was to break through and move with all speed up to the Rhine. The Airborne Division was in a desperate situation and we must link up with them that night, taking supplies on DUKWs [large amphibious vehicles]. It was already late afternoon ... Light was fading as we reached Driel, where the leading tank was blown up on a mine laid by the Poles ... Contact was made with the Household Cavalry and the Polish Brigade HQ.

Also arriving on the south bank of the Lower Rhine were Lieutenant-Colonel Charles Mackenzie, Roy Urquhart's Chief of Staff, and Lieutenant-Colonel Eddie Myers, the division's Chief Engineer. The two officers had rowed across so that Myers might help organize future river crossings and Mackenzie could ensure that the two corps commanders fully understood the difficult circumstances in which the airborne division found itself. Mackenzie lost no time in using the Household Cavalry's radio to contact Horrocks at his headquarters in Nijmegen and give him an outline of the 1 Airborne's situation. He then agreed to a meeting the following day for a detailed discussion. In the meantime, temporary relief would be provided in the form of a resupply operation that was to be undertaken across the river starting at 2100 hours that night. The problem, however, was that the only boats in Driel to facilitate this were four rubber dinghies. Nevertheless, it was optimistically believed that they could transport 200 Poles into the perimeter whilst the DUKWs delivered ammunition, food and medical supplies.

Those supplies were desperately needed by the men in the perimeter, as the 22nd saw continued German efforts to fragment and destroy the airborne division. Indeed, it was Urquhart's growing concern at the developing situation that had led him to despatch Charles Mackenzie to Driel, asking the taciturn colonel 'Above all, do try and make them realise over there what a fix we're in': one report that particularly alarmed the general outlined mounting casualties. German shells and mortaring accounted for most, which led to the airborne troops making sure that their positions included as much fortification as possible. REME Craftsman Joe Roberts had dug himself a slit trench but, he explains, it offered limited protection:

> You had to be careful when you put your head out of a trench because you built them to protect you from shell burst. Once I was standing in my trench observing the scene when a shell landed near by – I didn't hear it coming: the explosion crushed my chest, it took my breath away and I spent days spitting up blood.

Snipers were also prevalent within the perimeter and were much hated, as Urquhart recognized:

> The snipers were more numerous inside our lines, and the ambitious character with his sights on the rear door of Divisional HQ was again provoking strong language among those whose dignity he ruffled. I was standing close to this door talking to Iain Murray [Lieutenant-Colonel, Glider Pilot Regiment] when bullets from this familiar foe started pinging into the walls. I had earlier heard of his prowess, some of which went so far as to claim that he had put several shots in one door and out of another.

A patrol was sent out to try to 'remove' this sniper. But he was soon replaced. 'Sniper-hunting patrols' were called upon whenever these marksmen began to menace a position, and they went about their business with a blithe ruthlessness. Glider Pilot Staff-Sergeant George Milburn was part of one such team:

> One of our pilots ... had a Bren and thought he saw a sniper high in a tree. He changed his magazine for a full one, took careful aim and fired off the whole magazine of at least 28 rounds. The sniper fell straight down and hit the ground like a sack of coal. Then we heard the chap on the Bren say, 'Watch him; he might not be dead.' That was the macabre Londoner's humour. The German must have had several bullets in him and fallen at least 60 feet. There were a few laughs at that.

Self-propelled guns and tanks also became a menace, with their mobile firepower destroying buildings for fun. They were targeted by 17-pounder anti-tank guns when available, as Gunner George Hurdman describes:

> We heard the tank several times but had to lie low until it came into view. It eventually appeared about 400–500 yards away, coming out of the woods on to the avenue. We were ready and I don't think it moved far before we opened fire ... It burst into flames. Nobby [Sergeant Nobby Gee] said, 'Give them another bugger, just to make sure' ... [Later] you could see where our armour-piercing shell had gone through the front. Inside there were only ashes; it had completely burnt out, including the crew of course.

However, their light weapons and a lack of ammunition severely undermined what the airborne division could achieve against determined German attacks, particularly if they contained armour. It was a weakness that was common to all airborne troops, and whilst the British locked horns with their enemy around Oosterbeek, their American cousins encountered similar difficulties to the south, as they confronted Model's troops attacking the corridor with considerable venom.

In choosing to attack Uden and Veghel in the 101st Airborne sector, the Germans targeted an area that was weakly held and had the potential to cause enormous disruption to the Allied convoy if it was overrun. The attempt was conducted by the First Parachute Army's Kampfgruppe Huber in the west – a regiment from the 59 Division supplemented with some Panther tanks and guns – and Kampfgruppe Walther to the east – 107 Panzer Brigade with some additional infantry and artillery. Maxwell Taylor had long recognized that the Uden–Veghel area was likely to become the subject of strong German counterattacks. Information supplied by the Dutch Resistance reported that units were concentrating in the vicinity, and this served to reinforce his belief. Up to this point in the battle the general had found it impossible to spare any troops to reinforce the area, but on the morning of the 22nd, as the two British flanking corps were at last threatening the German forces around the Wilhelmina Canal, Taylor felt able to redeploy the 506th from Son to Uden. Rushing north in a mixture of vehicles to meet any early enemy moves, an advance party under Lieutenant-Colonel Charles Chase, consisting of 150 men, reached the village at 1100 hours, just as Kampfgruppe Walther struck. On his arrival as part of this group, Captain Richard Winters climbed the church steeple in order to spot any enemy movement. He spent a few minutes scanning the countryside with his binoculars and then scampering down the steps to announce to the waiting Easy Company platoon: 'Men, there is nothing to get excited about. The situation is normal; we are surrounded.' Outnumbered and outgunned, the paratroopers did what they could to slow the German advance, but found it increasingly difficult to hold them. Nevertheless, their exemplary defence left scores of Germans dead, and it was the attackers that wilted first. Chase later said: 'Had the Germans realized that my force consisted only of Regimental Headquarter Company and a platoon from the 2nd Battalion, the Germans might have overwhelmed us.' However, such was the superb organization of the highly motivated airborne force that when they combined first-class marksmanship with changing of positions, the Germans became confused and more tentative. The division's historian states: 'It was touch and go all the time, but Colonel Chase made masterful use of his meagre forces, rushing them back and forth across town, firing, creating an impression of strength. And the Germans never went all-out against them.'

An hour later, Walther launched his second attack, a more powerful effort directed on Veghel. This village had already been wrecked by a series of previous assaults, and was described by one airborne trooper as having a 'haunting air':

The village looked like a Kerr Eby lithograph of First World War ruins. Many of the houses had been shelled and gutted. Mortars had blown the tiles and lathing off many roofs and 88s had punched holes in the walls. The trees were torn, the windows smashed, telephone wires dangling from their post.

A battalion of the 501st *in situ* in Veghel managed to repel Walther's initial advances, but they were too thinly stretched to stop a subsidiary advance by armour just to the north, which succeeded in cutting the road. It was a success that should not be underestimated, as the men of the 101st were well aware:

Men who were there don't need to be told that the enemy's cutting the road did not mean simply his walking across a piece of asphalt. That road was loaded with British transport vehicles of every type. Cutting the road meant fire and destruction for the vehicles that were caught. It meant clogging the road for its entire length with vehicles that suddenly had nowhere to go. For the men at Nijmegen and Arnhem, cutting the road was like severing an artery. The stuff of life – food, ammunition, medical supplies – no longer came north.

The Germans continued to develop their attack on Veghel as the main body of the 506th arrived in the village *en route* to Uden. These men were deployed quickly, and along with men from the 327 Glider Infantry Regiment, who were following on, were rallied by the division's artillery commander, Brigadier General Anthony C. McAuliffe, who implored them to 'hang tough, and give the Krauts a beating'. Even so, the German artillery targeted the American positions remorselessly and pummelled the village throughout the day until it became a living hell. The shelling was the heaviest that the men of the 506th had experienced thus far in the war. Private David Webster remembered:

Our slit trench – for we never dug one-man foxholes – was two feet wide, six feet long, and four and a half feet deep. And none too soon. BzzYOObzzYOO . . . BAMBAMBAM! . . . The shells had landed on the cobblestone road . . . Sitting in an inch of water, I closed my eyes, gritted my teeth, held my breath, and clutched my elbows with my arms around my knees . . . I felt as if a giant with exploding fingers were looking for me, tearing up the ground as he came. I wanted to strike at him, to kill him, to stop him before he ripped me, but I could do nothing. Sit and take it, sit and take it.

The defenders' anti-tank weapons provided vital firepower, and were brought into action when two Mark IV tanks appeared on the main road with supporting infantry. Sergeant James C. Weatherford commanded the three guns that had been positioned there for just such an occurrence. He later reported:

> The tanks were firing point-blank at us with 88mm guns and machine guns. Our guns fired several rounds and set one tank on fire. The ammunition in the tank started exploding, and the Germans evacuated it. With a light machine gun I opened fire on the Germans and killed one. Meanwhile, the gun in the road engaged the second tank . . . [and hit it] causing it to turn and start back toward its own lines.

The offensive initiative remained with the Germans, however, for the next major test of Maxwell Taylor's men came when Kampfgruppe Huber attacked Veghel at 1400 hours from the west. This battle group was supposed to have launched its attack concurrently with Walther, a prospect that might well have seen them overrun the village, but two battalions of the 501st had engaged the *Kampfgruppe* as it approached from the west and held it up. By the time Huber moved into a position to begin his attempt on the bridge over the Willems Canal, a squadron of British tanks and a company of the 506th were in position to stop him. The *Kampfgruppe* then tried to cut the road south of Veghel, but they ran into two battalions of 327 Glider Infantry Regiment. It was during this push that Sergeant Karl Krahl was wounded for the second time in Holland and the third time since the summer:

> The attack began with a heavy mortar bombardment and then some armoured vehicles advanced down a narrow lane leading to the main highway. It should be remembered that tanks need to keep to roads where the ground is soft, and that makes them

excellent targets. My platoon followed a Mark IV, keeping a little behind as we expected the vehicle to draw fire. Then – THUMP! – the tank exploded before our eyes and the air was alive with bullets, bombs and shells. The fields to our left and right erupted, throwing dark soil skywards and we threw ourselves to the ground and crawled towards the ditches ... Above our heads, bullets buzzed and zipped by. We needed to move for to stay in that position meant certain death. I stood up to show the way, and was immediately hit by two American bullets: one in my shoulder, and another in my thigh ... I was removed from the field of battle and later heard that the platoon – 28 men strong at the start of the day – ended it with just 12. For the second time in just a few months, I was lucky to survive and within the week had been evacuated back to Germany.

The Germans were denied once more, but although the 101st Airborne managed to parry a flurry of punches on the 22nd, it was a tense and difficult day. By nightfall the road between Veghel and Uden remained cut off, but the two villages stayed in American hands, like anchors in a turbulent sea, pinning Maxwell Taylor's men to the highway. The day's events were a serious setback for Operation Market Garden, but to stop it from becoming a disaster Horrocks released 32 Guards Brigade – consisting of Grenadier and Coldstream Guards Groups – to help retrieve the situation. Fortunately for the Allies, this armoured support was not required by Jim Gavin's 82nd Airborne, as it enjoyed a relatively quiet day while the storm raged around it.

The Germans had once again deftly undermined the Allied offensive, pinpointing a weakness in the plan and then exploiting it. Had it not been for the supreme quality of the airborne troops defending what they called 'Hell's Highway', the situation could have been far worse. Just 48 hours earlier the Waal had been crossed, the northern end of Arnhem bridge was still in British hands and there was still hope that Market Garden could succeed. Now the operational picture had changed dramatically, with Brian Horrocks later calling that Friday the 'black 22nd', adding, 'it was a worrying day for me':

Looking back I am certain that this was the blackest moment of my life. I began to find it difficult to sleep. In fact I had to be very firm with myself in order to banish from my mind, during those midnight hours when everything seems at its worst, the picture of the airborne troops fighting their desperate battle on the other side of the river in front. I had sufficient experience of war to know that any commander who finds it difficult to sleep will soon be unfit to be responsible for other men's lives. And here I was going that way myself – an unpleasant thought.

Operation Market Garden was in serious trouble. It was being strangled. The Germans had cut off the highway, the route to Arnhem was blocked, XXX Corps had no momentum, the American airborne divisions were being stretched and 1 British Airborne Division was being systematically destroyed. The Allies struggled on, making it difficult for the Germans to apply the *coup de grâce*, but they could only do so whilst they had strength, and that strength was ebbing away.

The attempt to provide 1 British Airborne Division with some sustenance by ferrying men and supplies across the Lower Rhine that night was not a great success. Staff-Sergeant Juhas rowed the first tiny dinghy through the river's swift current using a shovel as a paddle. With only 400 metres of British-held bank to aim for, and the Germans watching for any activity, the crossing was tricky and dangerous. Leading the way, Juhas successfully managed to negotiate the challenge before the Germans realized what was happening, but the following Lieutenant Smaczny ran into a curtain of fire. Observers had spotted movement and the Germans sent up flares to illuminate the river; they swept the water with machine gun fire and peppered it with mortar and artillery rounds. Smaczny says that the water 'was alive with water spouts and explosions', and he expected to be hit at any moment. He paddled 'like a man possessed', pushing against the current, ignoring the pain in his shoulders, and trying not to think about the metal that scudded past his soft body. It was, therefore, with great relief that he landed on a British-held sector of the north bank in one piece, but to his utter dismay was then engaged by the British, who were unaware that a Polish crossing was taking place. Smaczny threw himself to the ground shouting, 'Don't shoot, you bloody fools! We're Polish!', and only then did the firing stop. By dawn a mere 50 Polish paratroopers had managed to scramble into Urquhart's perimeter. The heavy DUKWs which contained valuable supplies had found it impossible to find an appropriate crossing point on the saturated ground, and had slipped off a road leading to the riverbank and ditched. 'It was', says engineer Sergeant 'Jimmy' Riddle, 'bloody typical. What did anyone expect? These vehicles were so ungainly, totally unstable. We'd had problems like this before and we shouldn't have been surprised when they failed to make it into the water. Putting heavily loaded DUKWs onto mud was like putting elephants on ice-skates.' The failure proved a painful body blow to Urquhart, virtually ending the division's attacking potential (such as it was). As a result it shifted opinion as to what Operation Market Garden was still capable of achieving.

Attempts to retrieve the situation began during the morning of Saturday 23 September with the vital task of reopening the main road to XXX Corps traffic. 32 Guards Brigade approached Uden from the north, as the Grenadier Guards historian describes:

The Group's journey to Uden was eventful only by reason of the little clusters of Dutch people who congregated in the villages to watch the tanks go by, obviously believing that the liberation had come to an untimely end . . . Uden was a strange sight. American paratroopers had set up headquarters in the school, and a small Stars and Stripes fluttered from the window.

The Grenadiers pushed into the village whilst the Coldstreamers advanced towards Volkel, a small village south-east of Uden, to create a buffer zone to assist the removal of the German blockage. As the Grenadiers continued south towards the critical area, Lieutenant-Colonel Frederick von der Heydte's 6 Parachute Regiment renewed the German offensive on Veghel. This regiment had replaced Huber's ravaged battle group overnight, but it too was weak, consisting of tired and inexperienced infantry in a mere two battalions, which were, in Heydte's words, 'inadequate to meet the requirements of such an attack'. Nevertheless, an assault was put in on the 501st's 2nd Battalion, supported by heavy mortar fire. The advance over open ground saw the blighted units cut down without sympathy.

A renewed attempt in the afternoon with increased numbers of infantry supported by assault guns met the same end when devastatingly accurate artillery fire shredded the regiment. A similar fate was awaiting Kampfgruppe Walther when that formation renewed its attack against Veghel during the morning. Aware of 32 Guards Brigade's presence to their north, and the closing VIII Corps to their south, the weary battle group was not minded to fully commit itself to the task, and by noon it was withdrawing.

Seizing the opportunity presented to him to reopen the road to Uden, Anthony McAuliffe reacted swiftly and at 1330 hours ordered two battalions of the 506th to link up with the Grenadier Guards, with support provided by Shermans of B Troop of the 44 Royal Tank Regiment (RTR), a unit which had helped repel the attacks on Uden the previous day. The 506th was pleased to be in a position to take the offensive again, but for 3rd Platoon of Company F, tasked with taking the lead, the decision was not so well received. Sergeant Russell Schwenk remembers:

Our platoon leader [Lieutenant Schmitz] was visibly shaken and practically shell-shocked. What we got from him we got by questioning. 3rd Platoon was to lead the attack – right smack into the Germans and their tanks. These orders, as everyone knew . . . were Schmitz's [death] warrant. The road on which we were to move was strewn with wreckage from a British convoy, which the Jerries had smashed the day before. The trucks were still burning.

The platoon moved off nervously down the road, smoke billowing from several vehicles, an acrid residue biting the back of the men's throats, their weapons primed. Schwenk continues:

We started the attack. 3rd Platoon on the road to Uden or until we were stopped . . . After moving only one hundred yards, a big BANG!, totally unexpected. One of the burning trucks had exploded . . . Lt Schmitz and radioman Pvt. Carl Pein, both dead . . . [Then] I couldn't believe my eyes. Three Panther tanks came rolling down the road towards us – all guns blazing. 75-mm shells exploding on the road. Smaller turret guns swinging and firing continuously. This was not a good place to be. We had some cover, as the roadside ditches were about two feet deep . . . The tank was almost between us. I could count the bolts on its tread. There was a .57-mm anti-tank gun back aways . . . just then the gun fired and nailed the tank, spinning him to the left. The disabled tank turned into a field and began to burn. The men who tried to crawl out of the turret were easy for our guys. I noticed the other two tanks had turned back – they had no infantry with them.

As the attack began, armour from 107 Panzer Brigade mounted a last-ditch attempt to keep the road closed, but it ran into the airborne anti-tank guns and 44RTR. Tank commander Sergeant Taylor says of this engagement:

We went straight up the highway . . . and took a road to the right
and moved along a ditch through an orchard area. There we
spotted a German half-track several hundred yards away. We were
going around in the hope of cutting that dude off and . . . all of
a sudden an enemy officer raised up in front of me . . . He was
hollering '*Kamerad, Kamerad, Kamerad!*'

As 44RTR and the 506th pinched the Germans from the south, the
Grenadier Guards squeezed from the north and the Coldstream
Guards secured Volkel, having incurred heavy casualties. The
Germans gradually began to melt away, the Allied pincers met and
traffic began to flow along the main highway once more. It was an
important achievement, for supplies were desperately needed for the
XXX Corps' attempt to crack the Germans at Elst and to strengthen
its presence on the Lower Rhine. Meanwhile, the 101st was relieved
to receive its artillery and the balance of 327 Glider Infantry whilst
Gavin's formation was reinforced by the arrival of 325 Glider
Infantry Regiment. These American divisions received Horrocks'
full admiration:

What impressed me so much about them was their quickness to
action; they were great individualists. They were also commanded
by two outstanding men . . . Both were as unlike the popular
cartoon conception of the loud-voiced, boastful, cigar-chewing
American as it would be possible to imagine. They were quiet,
sensitive-looking men of great charm, with an almost British
passion for understatement . . . Whenever I rang up Jim Gavin to
find out what was going on he gave me the same answer: 'We're
just having a bit of a patrol.' I usually discovered that this 'bit of
a patrol' had consisted of at least one hundred US paratroopers
carrying out a large-scale raid on the German positions.

The Americans said of the Guards:

> At almost our darkest hour the Guards Armoured Division, gallantly led by General Adair, came across the Maas to join us . . . I must say that in all my years in the war, I've never met such courage and gallantry and cooperation on the part of Allied troops as the Guards Armoured Division.

But events of the 23rd revealed not only that XXX Corps and the airborne troops retained some residual strength, but also that the Germans were struggling to maintain the scope and intensity of their operations. Although retaining their flexibility and desire, the energy levels of Model's troops were waning. Having endured so much recent turmoil, the regeneration of German forces in Holland had been remarkable, but they were not sufficiently well placed to unhinge Market Garden with finesse. They were, however, capable of turning the confrontation into a slogging match. It was a situation which concerned Horrocks and Browning, but they hoped that the German resistance would fade away or suddenly break. In so doing they allowed hope to cloud the reality of the situation that faced them.

On 23 September the attrition directed against 1st Airborne in the Oosterbeek perimeter was stepped up. Albert Blockwell of the KOSB came directly under the enemy's heavy metal cudgel that day and recalls:

> We were beginning to give up hope of being relieved, I guess . . . The hours wore on, mortars still blasting the houses and ground all around, surely they would run short of bombs soon, but why should they when the RAF had dropped them enough weapons and bombs to blast us for a month . . . Once more I expected to die . . . With every dawn I expected it to be my last, and yet

somehow at the back of my mind I had a sort of feeling or sense I would get back home again.

The day began with a 'morning hate' that consisted of a ferocious bombardment. Blockwell explains: 'The same routine started, watching and waiting for Jerry to attack, mortar bombs dropping, 88mm shells "*shzipping*" over, and the never-ending *snap* of the snipers.' The intense opening to the day's hostilities gave way to a series of German attempts to infiltrate through the gaps that their guns had prepared, sometimes with armour and infantry, but often with unsupported infantry. Faced with such fierce onslaughts, the airborne forces were sometimes forced to withdraw, but with such little depth to their positions, counterattacks had to follow in order to restore the fragile perimeter. It was an energy-sapping business, and having consumed their iron rations long ago, empty stomachs became a major issue for Geoffrey Powell and his 50 men: 'Food was now the dominant problem', he says, 'the only thing to do was forage among the houses, although the chances of finding much were slim indeed after four years of war and rationing.' Sending out a party to see what they could find, they returned within an hour 'bearing a variegated collection of provisions, but enough when added to the Compo [British rations] to make a reasonable meal for everyone'. With ration pallets falling to the Germans and stores failing to cross the Lower Rhine, the '1st Airborne Division Scavengers' set to work. The ability of soldiers to sniff out food is legendary, but one company commander was amazed when his headquarters was presented with a live chicken, a bottle of wine and some chocolate 'with the compliments of No. 2 Platoon'.

Simple pleasures such as eating a meal or settling down to a 'brew' were denied Urquhart's force. This was not only due to a lack of the requisite comestibles but also because of Bittrich's desire for 'unrelenting violence'. Consequently, certain parts of the perimeter were attacked time and time again. One such place was an area on the eastern side defended by some glider pilots, the KOSB and a mixture of 156 Para, Reconnaissance Squadron and 21 Independent Parachute Company. Albert Blockwell remembers that the action reached new heights that afternoon:

The firing across the gardens was getting heavier now. Jerry was closing in and bringing in more men. Every so often I could hear the Germans shouting to each other and making screams ... I must admit it didn't do the nerves any good to hear them and be unable to see them in the woods and undergrowth ... We lay there with fingers on triggers and mumbling something like 'Come out, you blasted, bloody square-heads!'

German tactics became predictable but deadly: a short preliminary bombardment followed by infantry utilizing fire and manoeuvre to try and get into the British lines, where they would begin throwing grenades. It was a frustrating business, as Powell describes:

About noon the Germans attacked once again, their assault preceded by another hellish mortar and artillery concentration. We all knew now what such a bombardment signified and as soon as the guns and mortars lifted, our heads were up and ready for the camouflaged figures sliding around the corners of the houses towards our trenches ... After a few minutes some Germans were spotted in the upper room of the smashed house at the end of our garden. Then a spandau started to fire from the back of the room, spraying bullets all around us, but after a long burst from Lance-Corporal Williams's Bren it was silent. Another Boche with a grenade in his hand started down the garden path towards us, but he got no further than five yards from the back door before he fell ... Something must be done. The enemy must not be allowed to collect in that house, so very close to us.

Powell ordered Colour Sergeant Bower forward with his PIAT:

A professional, he took his time, dwelling carefully on the aim and squeezing the trigger slowly and firmly. The bomb flew true, straight through the window, to explode on the wall behind. The sheet of flame and smoke gushing back into the garden coincided, which eddied from the depths of the room. Then there was silence.

There was also heavy fighting around the MDS crossroads, which by this stage in the battle was coated in an ugly debris consisting of tree branches, burnt-out vehicles, masonry, shell fragments and cartridge cases. This was an area that attracted considerable German attention, for the Utrechtsweg led to the heart of the perimeter and the Hartenstein, but the location of the two dressing stations at the junction meant that the German attacks there were stymied. To try and overcome this difficulty a German officer appeared under a Red Cross flag on the evening of the 23rd to give Shan Hackett an ultimatum: withdraw 400 yards or the wounded would suffer the consequences. This demand was refused out of hand, but even though the Germans did not deliberately shell the hospitals, it was inevitable that rogue shells, bombs and rounds clattered into them.

It was a situation that has led Captain Stuart Mawson, the medical officer with 11 Para, to say that the exhausted field ambulances were in an 'appalling situation'. Working out of the Schoonoord Hotel, Mawson found it increasingly difficult to provide the care that he would have wished. The hospital was, he says,

a crumbling ruin and yet, confined within its battered, shell-torn walls, were some four hundred wounded men in the direst need of food and fresh dressings, as well as the specialized medical and surgical attention their conditions demanded. We who looked

after them not only lacked the means, but in some cases the physical strength to administer these necessities.

The Germans continued to plug away at the MDS crossroads, but with
little success. Yet they spurned an opportunity to launch an attack from
the dominating Westerbouwing Heights. Had such a push been coordinated with a similar move towards Oosterbeek church, then it
might even have succeeded in cutting the airborne soldiers off from
their vital river lifeline.

Roy Urquhart's continued access to the Lower Rhine was essential
to his division's prospects, as it remained both an entrance to and an
exit from the perimeter. In the Hartenstein, ravaged by shell fire,
continually picked at by snipers and the focus of considerable activity
with soldiers coming and going at all hours of the day and night, there
was growing concern. The Poles, who had dropped at Driel in order
to provide reinforcements, were impotent without boats and taking
casualties as the Germans continued to pin them down in the village.
Indeed, when the balance of Sosabowski's paratroopers arrived on the
23rd, they had to be dropped south of Nijmegen and then march up
to the Lower Rhine. The lack of any real dynamism by XXX Corps to
help get the Poles over the river and drive the operation forward was
a vexation that Mackenzie articulated when he met Horrocks and
Browning in the city that morning. The response that he received
from the generals left him unimpressed and disconsolate. Everything
that could be done, was being done. There were no new ideas, no
boldness, no initiative. It was as if the operation's two critical corps
commanders were waiting for something to happen, or had given up
and were waiting for Market Garden to run its course and slip quietly
away. Fearing the worst, Urquhart signalled XXX Corps that evening
with a situation report:

Many attacks during day by small parties inf, SP gns and tanks including flamethrowers. Each attack accompanied by very heavy mortaring and shelling within Div perimeter. After many alarms and excursions the latter remains substantially unchanged. Although thinly held. Physical contact not yet made with those on south bank of river. Resup a flop, small quantities amn only gathered in. Still no food and all ranks extremely dirty owing to shortage of water. Morale still adequate, but continuing heavy mortaring and shelling is having obvious effects. We shall hold but at same time hope for a brighter 24 hours ahead.

It was met with understanding, gratitude for his division's continued effort, but only a limited resolve to put things right. Mackenzie's return late that night did little to allay Urquhart's anxiety for, in the general's words, '[Mackenzie] was certain in his own mind now that no reinforcement of any consequence could possibly arrive in time, but he chose to gloss over this interpretation and to give me the official picture which was rosier.'

Brian Horrocks continued to put his faith in renewed attempts to break through the German defences before Arnhem bridge using 129 and 214 Brigades, while reinforcing Driel with units from 130 Brigade. 1 British Airborne Division, meanwhile, was to expect another river crossing that night. In the event the lack of adequate boats again undermined the attempt and underlined the impact that the German highway block north of Uden was having on the operation. With a mere 12 boats arriving on the south bank for the attempt, Lieutenant-Colonel Eddie Myers was left shaking his head in bemusement at the absurd situation. But he did what he could to get the Poles across the river as efficiently as possible. As it turned out, the operation became a pathetic attempt to resurrect Urquhart's division, although the fault did not lie with Sosaboswki's men, as Myers later argued: 'I can find no fault with the attempts; they did all they could. They had not been trained in river crossings, and the Arnhem plan had not envisaged one, and no one had any proper boats. But the less said about their watermanship the better.' Consequently, only a paltry 153 Poles managed to enter the Oosterbeek perimeter. They were immediately organized to take up defensive positions, and were gratefully received by the stretched division; but their numbers would not allow Sosabowski's men to have a decisive impact on Urquhart's situation.

Although the battle for the perimeter remained savage on Sunday 24 September, the seventh day of Operation Market Garden, there was a notable lack of sustained offensive action by the Germans. This was partly due to a weariness that had been washing over Model's forces over the previous couple of days. It was also due to the damage done by the morale-sapping accuracy of the British guns, which by this time were positioned on the south bank of the Lower Rhine. These guns slammed shells into the German positions, broke up countless attacks and were supplemented, at last, by some close air support from rocket-firing Typhoons. The devastation caused by the mixture of weapons led to some of the heaviest German casualties of the battle for Oosterbeek, many of whom joined their adversaries in British-run hospitals, dressing stations and, increasingly, Dutch homes. Kate ter Horst and her five children played host to scores of wounded in her home nearby Oosterbeek church. Known as the 'Angel of Arnhem' by those she cared for, ter Horst was a considerate and tender nurse who used her linen for dressings and her rooms as wards. Captain Frank King, commander of 11 Para's Support Company, was delivered into her care after being shot in the chest and leg: 'The floor was already packed tightly so my stretcher ended up on two rickety trestles across the width of the French windows. And here I met Kate . . . I noticed how the whole room brightened up at her arrival and how the soldiers hung on her every word.'

It was exhausting, emotional work for ter Horst, whose children remained in the family home just behind the front line. She noted in

Left: General Sir Bernard Montgomery during the summer of 1944: a great British military hero who believed that airborne warfare had great potential.
IWM H 38632

Below: The Supreme Commander (centre) and his Chiefs, 1 February 1944. From left to right: General Omar Bradley; Admiral Sir Bertram Ramsay; Air Chief Marshal Sir Arthur Tedder; General Sir Bernard Montgomery; Air Chief Marshal Sir Trafford Leigh Mallory and Major General Walter Bedell Smith.
IWM CH 12109

Left: Montgomery accompanied by his spearhead commanders near the Meuse–Escaut Canal on 15 September. From left to right: Major General Allan Adair; Monty; Lieutenant General Sir Brian Horrocks and Major General Pip Roberts. IWM B 9973

Field Marshal Walter Model, the commander of Army Group B whom von Rundstedt believed to be little more than a 'good regimental sergeant-major'. IWM MH 12850

Field Marshal Gerd von Rundstedt, the capable 69-year-old commander who replaced Model for his second stint as OB West in early September 1944. IWM MH 10132

Colonel General Kurt Student, commander of First Parachute Army, whose knowledge of airborne warfare allowed the Germans to act swiftly and successfully against Operation Market Garden. IWM 6100

Right: 'Our world was coming to an end': withdrawing Germans head into defensive positions on 6 September. BUNDESARCHIV

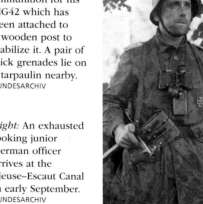

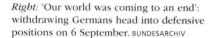

Left: A German trooper grapples with a belt of ammunition for his MG42 which has been attached to a wooden post to stabilize it. A pair of stick grenades lie on a tarpaulin nearby. BUNDESARCHIV

Right: An exhausted looking junior German officer arrives at the Meuse–Escaut Canal in early September. BUNDESARCHIV

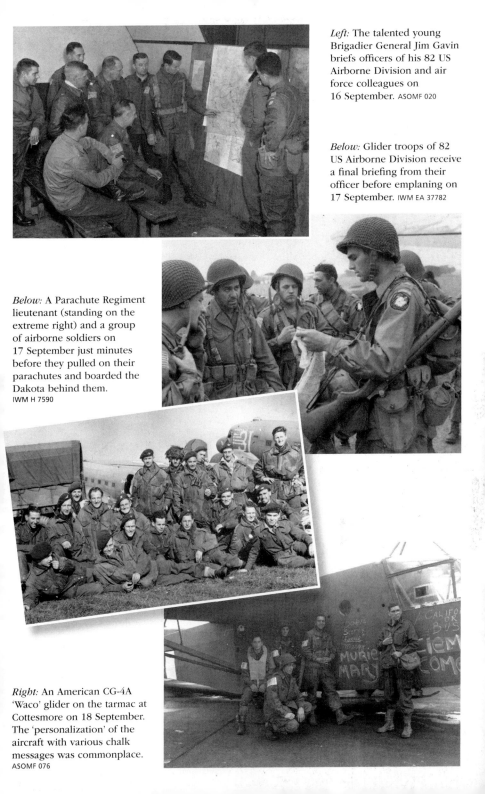

Left: The talented young Brigadier General Jim Gavin briefs officers of his 82 US Airborne Division and air force colleagues on 16 September. ASOMF 020

Below: Glider troops of 82 US Airborne Division receive a final briefing from their officer before emplaning on 17 September. IWM EA 37782

Below: A Parachute Regiment lieutenant (standing on the extreme right) and a group of airborne soldiers on 17 September just minutes before they pulled on their parachutes and boarded the Dakota behind them. IWM H 7590

Right: An American CG-4A 'Waco' glider on the tarmac at Cottesmore on 18 September. The 'personalization' of the aircraft with various chalk messages was commonplace. ASOMF 076

Right: The first wave of the 101 US Airborne Division jumps from their Dakotas on 17 September. ASOMF 041

Below: Men of the 101 US Airborne Division leave their DZ on 17 September to be greeted by smiling Dutch locals. IWM EA 38132

Bottom: The perils of glider insertion. A broken Waco in the sandy soil north of Son is investigated by men of 101 US Airborne Division on 18 September. IWM EA 38134

Above: Watching and waiting. A German soldier in the Neerpelt bridgehead on 16 September 1944.
BUNDESARCHIV

Top right: A young German soldier armed with grenades and Panzerschrek anti-tank rocket launcher in the Neerpelt bridgehead.
BUNDESARCHIV

Above right: Men of 9 SS Panzer Division endeavouring to push towards Oosterbeek along the Utrechtseweg.
BUNDESARCHIV

Middle right: The ecstatic inhabitants of Eindhoven smother a Guards Armoured Division tank soon after it enters the town. 'The greeting we received in the town', recalled one driver, 'brought tears to our eyes.' IWM BU936

Bottom right: An aerial reconnaissance photograph taken in the late morning of 18 September showing the Arnhem road bridge over the Lower Rhine and, in the buildings in the top half of the image, a large part of Lieutenant Colonel John Frost's defensive perimeter.
IWM MH 2061

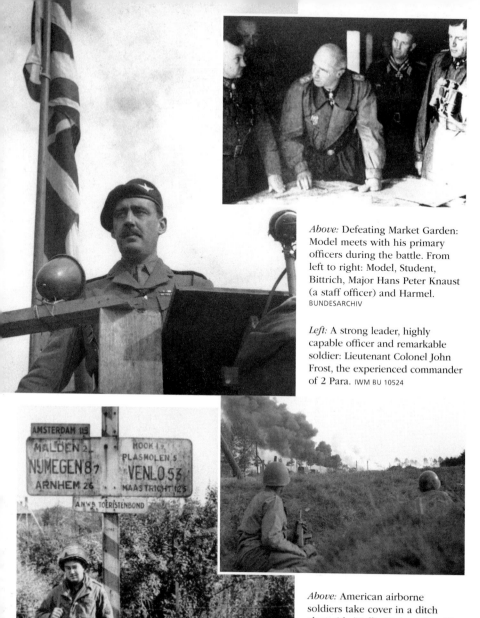

Above: Defeating Market Garden: Model meets with his primary officers during the battle. From left to right: Model, Student, Bittrich, Major Hans Peter Knaust (a staff officer) and Harmel. BUNDESARCHIV

Left: A strong leader, highly capable officer and remarkable soldier: Lieutenant Colonel John Frost, the experienced commander of 2 Para. IWM BU 10524

Above: American airborne soldiers take cover in a ditch alongside 'Hell's Highway' on 20 September after a German artillery bombardment destroyed a British ammunition truck. IWM BU 1062

Left: A trooper of 505 PIR, 82 US Airborne Division, poses for his photograph at Molenhoek, an objective south of Nijmegen on the Maas–Waal Canal. ASOMF 105

Above: The Household Cavalry in AEC armoured cars lead the Guards Armoured Division to Nijmegen having just crossed the Bailey Bridge over the Wilhemina Canal at Son. IWM B 10147A

Left: In spite of his deep reservations about Lieutenant General Frederick Browning – seen here on the left – Brigadier General James Gavin worked hard to develop a good relationship with him. Here the two men are pictured near Groesbeek shortly after XXX Corps had linked up with 82 US Airborne Division. IWM HU 72434

Above: British tanks advance across Nijmegen bridge over the Waal on 22 September. IWM B 10172

Right: Taken as the battle raged around him on 22 September, this photograph shows Major General Roy Urquhart, the 43-year-old commander of 1 British Airborne Division, standing outside his Hartenstein Hotel headquarters in the Oosterbeek perimeter. IWM BU 1136

Left: Engineers of 101 US Airborne Division help to clear a village on 25 September. Moments after this photograph was taken, German artillery rounds began to fall on this road and casualties were suffered. ASOMF 116

Below: German armour moves forward towards the Oosterbeek perimeter on 21 September. BUNDESARCHIV

Above: Defending the objective. Airborne troops from 82 US Airborne Division open fire on the enemy from a fox-hole just outside Nijmegen. ASOMF 117

Left: The morning of 26 September: the exhausted survivors of the Oosterbeek perimeter look relieved having crossed the Lower Rhine to safety. IWM HU 3722

Above: A tense moment. A British airborne soldier prepares to jump from a Dakota during an exercise in April 1944. IWM H 37720

Below: A section briefing of men from 3 Parachute Brigade using an accurate model based on aerial reconnaissance photographs. IWM H 41577

Left: Lieutenant General Lewis Brereton, commander of First Allied Airborne Army, chats with a 6 British Airborne Division soldier during an exercise in November 1944 with his deputy, Lieutenant General Frederick Browning, looking on. IWM H 40771

Left: German troops preparing their defences on the edge of the Diersfordter Wald on 23 March 1945. BUNDESARCHIV

Below left: A 6 British Airborne Division paratrooper checks his Sten gun on 24 March before jumping into Germany. IWM H 41574

Below: British paratroopers check their parachutes on the morning of 25 March with their Dakota in the background. IWM H 41564

Left: 17 US Airborne Division arrives over the Rhine on the morning of 25 March. 'It was the most perfect spring morning', wrote one paratrooper, 'and we had come to kill and destroy.' IWM BU 2571

Below: Winston Churchill and Field Marshal Sir Alan Brooke (with binoculars to his eyes) watch the airborne landings from the west bank of the Rhine on the morning of 25 March. IWM BU 2236

Above: Horsa gliders land outside Hamminkeln. One experienced pilot recalls: 'As if landing a plywood crate filled with men wasn't bad enough, the Germans put enough steel into the air to cut us to ribbons before we hit the ground.'
IWM BU 2285

Right: German prisoners held in a bomb crater amid the ruins of Wesel.
IWM BU 2332

Left: A photograph taken minutes after the crash landing of a Horsa glider containing men of the Royal Irish Rifles. IWM BU 2277

Below: Amongst the first German prisoners taken by the airborne forces on 25 March were these two 'soldiers' who lacked training, weapons, and even uniforms that fit. IWM BU 2419

German armour was positioned near likely LZs and DZs prior to the arrival of the two Allied airborne divisions. IWM BU 2396

Right: British airborne troops during the clearing of Hamminkeln on the afternoon of 25 March. IWM BU 2293

Left: Major General Eric Bols (commander of 6 British Airborne Division) drives Brigadier James Hill (commander of 3 Parachute Brigade) to a meeting with Major General Bud Miley at 17 US Airborne Division headquarters. IWM BU 2395

Left: As the Rhine river crossings continued apace and airborne troops were engaging the enemy during the afternoon of 25 March, the key Operation Plunder Varsity commanders met for a conference. Seen here from left to right are: Major General Matthew B. Ridgway; Lieutenant General Sir Miles Dempsey; Lieutenant General William H. Simpson, and Field Marshal Sir Bernard Montgomery. IWM BU 2232

Right: A trooper from 17 US Airborne Division stands on a British tank on the morning of 26 March. 'Friendly tanks', one paratrooper says, 'are one of the most eagerly awaited arrivals for the airborne soldier.' IWM BU 2738

Left: A British Parachute Regiment soldier raises his binoculars to his eyes to catch sight of an increasingly elusive enemy on 26 March. IWM BU 2547

Left: American troops look on as a line of German prisoners is led down to the River Rhine on 26 March. BUNDESARCHIV

Below left: With the breakout from the Rhine bridgehead underway, Aberdonian Guardsman Angus of the Scots Guards shares a warming fire with two American 17 US Airborne Division paratroopers: PFC Rudy Dzubiel from Newark, New Jersey (on the left) and Sergeant Harry Staughton of Richmond, Virginia. IWM BU 2913

Below: Lieutenant General Sir Brian Horrocks, commander of XXX Corps, holds a conference with the field commanders of 51 (Highland) Division in the ruined town of Rees on 26 March. IWM BU 2411

her diary: 'The hours drag by. The air seems to be growing more and more suffocating round us. The children sleep heavily as if they were drugged . . . At the backdoor I see the padre and two men with shovels, near a large freshly dug hole. The dead had been removed from the path.' A total of 57 men were eventually buried in her garden, their interment overseen by the chaplain to 1 Airlanding Light Regiment, the Revd S. Thorne. The padre, a sensitive, calm and mild-mannered man, also undertook a host of medical duties and provided important reassurance to the young soldiers at a time when they most needed it. He also did what he could to keep the violence as far away from the ter Horst household as possible by bravely confronting any Germans who opened fire on the building. Indeed, on one occasion Thorne dashed out under a Red Cross flag to remonstrate with the crew of an approaching Tiger tank and refused to move away until he had received the commander's word that the house would be spared.

Meanwhile, at the MDS crossroads, medical officer Lieutenant Derrick Randall was incensed when some of the casualties in his care were wounded again whilst in the hospital. He moved as many men as he could to nearby houses, but the problems continued as 'eventually these houses too became overcrowded, and in many cases, untenable, as indeed by this time were most of the remaining medical stations'. In such circumstances, Colonel Graeme Warrack, the division's Senior Medical Officer, sought to organize a ceasefire in order to evacuate some of the most badly wounded of the 1,200 casualties in the perimeter. Roy Urquhart acquiesced to this request, later writing: 'I did not want to encourage the Germans to think that we were ready to throw in our hand, yet it would be inhuman to deny the wounded their only chance of recovery.' Thus, having talked to the local SS commander, Warrack and a Dutch liaison officer, Lieutenant-Commander Arnoldus Wolters, were driven to the St Elizabeth's hospital, where they were met by a German doctor and General Bittrich in order to arrange the details. There followed a highly civilized meeting in which sandwiches and brandy were produced for the filthy British airborne officers, and a truce was quickly agreed. As the two men left, they were invited to fill their pockets with as many morphia capsules as they could carry. The resulting cease-fire came into effect at 1500 hours and lasted for two hours, during which time some 500 casualties – including Shan Hackett, who had been wounded in the leg and stomach – were removed to the safety of St Elizabeth's hospital.

As the battle of Oosterbeek raged on, Horrocks and Sosabowski climbed the church tower in Driel in order to survey the perimeter. They could not see any movement, but the intensity of the fighting under the dense tree canopy was clear from the thick plumes of black smoke and the incessant bang of explosions and clatter of small-arms fire. Horrocks commented on the width of the Lower Rhine and its strong current, as though surprised by the power of the river. The dour Pole standing at his side made no comment until Horrocks looked him in the eye and asked directly what options were available. Sosabowski replied in a clinical tone: 'There are only two options: a major rein-forcement or withdrawal.' Horrocks nodded, and turned back towards the boiling Oosterbeek in silence. Descending into the village again minutes later, the XXX Corps commander immediately informed General Thomas 'that in order to relieve pressure on the bridgehead he was to carry out an assault crossing that night with a minimum of one battalion'. This was not the 'major reinforcement' that Sosabowski indicated was needed in order to provide Urquhart with new offensive vigour. It was, therefore, preparation for an evacuation.

Horrocks' decision was arrived at using the knowledge that Urquhart's perimeter was barely retaining its coherence, and an understanding that the Germans retained a potency rooted in an obstinacy and tenacity that belied their weariness. That morning Lieutenant-Colonel Harry Kinnard's battalion of the 501st fought against another 6 Parachute Regiment attack against the highway at

Eerde and came close to being overrun. Colonel Howard Johnson's timely release of nine Shermans from 44RTR managed to check the Germans, but it was not until the artillery was unleashed that the enemy withdrew. But the Germans did not give up. Moving next against the Allies' southern flank, they made for Koevering to the south of Veghel. When 502nd at St Oedenrode heard about the developing situation, it sent two companies to defend the village, but even though they managed to get to Koevering before the enemy, they could do nothing to stop them from cutting the road just to the north. It was an event that provided yet more evidence that the Germans only needed to apply a little pressure at the right place in order to bring XXX Corps to a grinding halt. Moreover, it also showed how Model's forces could successfully exploit the inability of below-strength, immobile and lightly armed fire-fighting American airborne units to meet and defeat his incessant challenges on the highway. Like 1 British Airborne Division, Operation Market Garden was entering its final days, and this was marked by Frederick Browning receiving permission from Miles Dempsey at Second Army to withdraw Urquhart's men across the Rhine if necessary. An end was in sight.

There was a final attempt to reinforce the Oosterbeek perimeter on the night of 24/25 September, but once again the cut road undermined the attempt. With XXX Corps traffic backed up for 60 miles, only one lorry of boats managed to wend its way through to the river in time for a crossing by 4/Dorsetshire Regiment. Each craft was capable of carrying 2 engineers and 10 infantrymen together with ammunition and supplies for four days, but it would take the small fleet several crossings to get the battalion across. With burning buildings illuminating the river, the Dorsets took to the water at 0100 hours supported by the XXX Corps artillery, but German machine gun and shell fire immediately caused casualties, while the current led to some of the boats being swept downstream. Some 315 men made it across the Lower Rhine, to be scattered in groups across its north bank. Several parties were engaged by the enemy, fighting from atop the Westerbouwing Heights. Lance-Corporal Wally Smith explains:

> We had dug in along the bank and the Germans were raining stick grenades down on us. I was 2i/c on the Bren, and my Bren gunner, Private Harold Wyer, was hit by a sniper and killed ... I estimated that there were about ten of us left in a space of about 200 yards. We used up what ammo we had during the morning and just lay doggo until dark.

Of those who endeavoured to break into the perimeter, only a few succeeded. Some quickly becoming casualties, others – some 200 out of the 315 – were taken prisoner.

During the early morning of Monday 25 September, as Urquhart and the 4/Dorsets counted the cost of the night's activity on the Lower Rhine, the Germans at their Koevering road-block came under attack. Units from 506 PIR were joined by a battalion from the 502nd and another from XXX Corps' 50 Infantry Division, to fight a bloody battle in which no quarter was given and which lasted all day. It ended after the Germans were surrounded on three sides with the help of armoured attacks from the north and south. The road was eventually reopened, but significant damage had been done to the outlook for the sickly Allied offensive. It led to a decision to release 1 British Airborne Division from its incarceration. The Germans had contrived to squeeze the final breath out of Operation Market Garden and Urquhart was caught between being thankful and disappointed. The general had been handed a letter from Ivor Thomas at 0600 hours that morning, and in it he read that Second Army had abandoned plans to cross the Lower Rhine and permission had been given for 1st Airborne to be withdrawn across the river. Urquhart thought about the situation for a couple of hours,

and then signalled the 43 (Wessex) Division headquarters via the
artillery radio net asking for the evacuation to take place that night.
He remembered: 'There were now about 2500 of us left – a quarter
of our original strength. Outnumbered and outgunned for days, men
had fought at close quarters and on empty stomachs. The dressing
stations were again full.' By 1030 hours Urquhart's senior officers
were in a planning meeting.

As a scheme for withdrawal and evacuation was developed in the
Hartenstein, the Germans continued to winkle the British airborne
troops out of their increasingly sparse positions. The attacking
troops, sensing victory, began to encroach on the perimeter, taking
advantage of the fact that the defenders had to conserve their
meagre supplies of ammunition. The officers and senior NCOs
continued to scamper around, ensuring that their men were focused
and awake, for while commanders remained alert by staying busy and
on the move, their men were prone to drop off if they were left
alone and inactive for a protracted period. Geoffrey Powell came
across one of his men fast asleep beside his Bren gun:

> However exhausted the poor devil was to have allowed himself
> to fall asleep, it was a crime impossible to overlook. A salutary
> lesson was needed to stop the same thing happening again.
> Shifting the Bren well to one side, I dropped on top of the lad,
> grasping him around the neck as if to throttle him. With a
> choked gasp of terror, he squirmed for a moment under me
> before he recognized my voice. Then I let go, cursing him for his
> stupidity.

Those that failed to remain alert often paid the price with their lives,
for it was not uncommon for small groups of the enemy to sneak up
on a British slit trench and silently despatch its occupants, or to
launch a surprise attack without any of the usual preliminaries. But

while these limited strikes were highly problematic, it was the belated German attempt to drive a wedge along the river road by attacking towards Oosterbeek church that caused the greatest concern on the 25th. Stopping this attack was crucial if the withdrawing division was to be able to gain the access that it required to the north bank of the Lower Rhine. Barring the way, however, were a mere handful of airborne soldiers fuelled by adrenaline, and some 75mm guns firing over open sights at very short ranges. An unknown officer recalls:

> The enemy established themselves in a wrecked house about fifteen yards from our forward post. While a sort of snowball fight with hand grenades was going on, I got the gunners to put a round into the remains of the house. The range was about seventy yards and it was a lovely sight – showers of sparks and dust and the whole place collapsed. One German was seen to flee; the rest were dead.

It was another close call for the British, but the line held and the river gateway remained open.

With the division fighting for its life, the evacuation could not take place soon enough for Urquhart and his staff. But before darkness fell the enemy delivered another shock. As the perimeter troops received their orders for the night's complex activities, the Germans struck a heavy blow at the northern end of the perimeter, using tanks, self-propelled guns and infantry covered by artillery and mortar fire. The defenders in the area, to their horror, found that their flanks were not secure, and the Germans managed to penetrate to within a couple of hundred yards of the Hartenstein. The situation was retrieved, however, by the Royal Artillery's medium guns – directed by a FOO from the roof of a house in the perimeter – firing from a range of 15,000 yards. As soon as the first rounds plunged into the leading waves of infantry and vehicles the attack was checked, and within a few minutes the Germans were forced into a withdrawal. Following up, the airborne soldiers fought at extremely close quarters to reclaim their lost ground in a confused and brutal mêlée. SS-Sturmmann Otto Egger, who had fought on the Eastern Front and in Normandy, says that 'the engagement hardly rates a mention in the history books, but was the most violent of my experience'. He continues:

> The bombardment suddenly stopped, shell craters, bodies and body parts were scattered all around. Whilst we were reorganising ourselves, British paratroopers appeared out of nowhere screaming like crazy men, firing from the hip, throwing grenades and clutching trench knives. I went down onto one knee to take careful aim, my ears still ringing with the sound of the artillery explosions, and was about to loose off a few rounds when THUD! I was hit in the side of the head by a rifle butt. I fell backwards and saw a wild man standing with his arms raised about to finish me off with his bayonet, but he suddenly went limp and fell on top of me, his blood oozing across my face. I pushed the body away, scrambled to my feet and ran back to our lines. Our attack had been defeated.

As the battle in the perimeter wore on, the finishing touches were put to preparations for the evacuation. Sixteen paddle assault craft and 21 Storm Boats with motors were made ready to be divided between two crossing points, while Thomas arranged for all the firepower he could muster to cover the operation. The British hoped that the Germans would think that another reinforcement bid was being launched, and the 1st Airborne team carefully choreographed the withdrawal. The scheme was based on the knowledge that Urquhart had gained at Staff College about the successful evacuation of troops from Gallipoli during the First World War. He placed great emphasis on secrecy, with the plan relying on troops following taped routes down to the riverside with their positions being gradually thinned so as not to alert the Germans. The enemy were to be kept occupied once the able-bodied and walking wounded had vacated their positions by a façade of resistance mounted by the more seriously wounded and the transmission of false radio traffic. These men, it was agreed, would eventually fall into enemy hands along with some of the chaplains and medical staff who had volunteered to stay behind. Derrick Randall remembers the day well:

> Monday 25th seemed much as usual till early evening, when a staff officer came to inform me of the decision to evacuate across the Rhine that night and, presenting the General's compliments, asked me to stay behind and look after the wounded. I accepted this as necessary . . . Eventually there was a lull in the casualty inflow, presumably because of the evacuation from the area around, so I took the opportunity to lie down on the floor. I must have been so tired that, although the noise was getting louder and nearer until I was expecting it to completely encompass me, I fell fast asleep.

Operation Berlin began at 2100 hours on 25 September and was helpfully masked by a very dark night and heavy rainfall. Brian Horrocks later wrote of this conjunction of events: 'As the exhausted paratroopers swam or were ferried across the river in torrential rain, it seemed that even the gods were weeping at this grievous end to a gallant enterprise.' The withdrawal was carefully planned and controlled. Queues quickly formed on the north bank, and the first boats crossed the river at around 2130 hours. As they did so the artillery and machine guns of 43 (Wessex) Division and the medium guns of XXX Corps opened up and the perimeter burst into flames. The German guns returned the compliment, but it was not until midnight that they seemed to realize what their enemy was really up to.

When they did, their mortaring and shelling increased in intensity with special concentrations on the north bank and the river. Sergeant Peter Quinn of the Reconnaissance Regiment recalls that his move to the riverbank was disrupted by a particularly heavy German barrage:

> A clatter of mortar bombs came down, lighting the woods and road with a queer blue light. The men scattered like demons in a pantomime. I was lifted off my feet with the blast of one bomb, and came to lying against the foot of a tree. A machine gun was firing at us, so we dashed pretty fast across where there was a clearing on the right, until we came, more or less, under cover . . . It was a bit dodgy at times, but we followed a guide tape and eventually we arrived at the end of the queue.

Having made their way to the riverbank, the airborne troops had to wait patiently until it was their turn to cross in one of the small boats crewed by sappers. It was an agonizing wait without cover. Enemy patrols posed a constant threat as they lurked on the fringes trying to disrupt the operation. Sergeant David Christie made his way down to the riverbank and recalls being told by marshals not to tarry, but then in true army fashion was told to wait when he reached his destination:

> After an hour . . . on the riverbank we moved forward approximately twenty yards. Then the officer decided to go up front to see what was happening. He returned in about thirty minutes and said there were only two boats and nearly 400 men in front, all waiting like us. He estimated that we should get across at about two o'clock in the morning. It was then a quarter to twelve.

Roy Urquhart made his crossing just after midnight:

> By the light of the tracer I could see other boats dimly through

the rain. I climbed aboard from the sodden, slippery groyne. It was a tight squeeze and the boat was low in the water. There was an exclamation from the Canadian sapper who was running this ferry . . . We had, in fact, stuck in the mud. Someone slipped over the side to push us off . . . Spandaus covered the river and metal splashed into the water as we seemed to go all too slowly across the two hundred yards towards the south bank. We were about half way over when the engine gave out . . . The boat drifted in the strong current. It was only for a few minutes, but it seemed an absolute age before we were on our way again . . . Suddenly the boat bumped alongside a groyne, veered round and a voice croaked, 'All right. Let's be having you.'

The pace of the withdrawal did not slacken at any point during the night, and at 0230 hours on Tuesday 26 September the last airborne soldiers left their positions in the perimeter to make their way down to the water's edge. It was these men who found themselves stranded on the north bank when a decision was taken at dawn to abandon the evacuation as the Germans enjoyed such good observation over the river and its south bank. Cold, wet, listless and vulnerable, some of the remaining soldiers plunged their exhausted bodies into the Rhine's chilly water, and tried to swim across – many never to be seen again. The majority, however, made their way back into the perimeter to be taken prisoner by the Germans.

And so Operation Market Garden was allowed to slip away. A total of 3,910 officers and men managed to cross the Lower Rhine during the evacuation. Of the 11,920 British airborne soldiers flown into the battle, 1,485 were killed (or died later of wounds) and 6,525 – including wounded – were taken prisoner. Some 450 residents of Arnhem/Oosterbeek also died during the battle. Elsewhere, 82 US Airborne Division lost 1,432 men and the 101st 2,118, which made a total of around 11,000 casualties, the near equivalent of one airborne division. Of the three British corps involved in Operation Market Garden, XXX Corps suffered 1,480 casualties while XII and VIII Corps had 3,784 between them. It was a large and ponderous tally for what on the face of it looked like nothing more than the creation of a large and vulnerable salient. In spite of the outstanding efforts of the Allied forces involved, Field Marshal Bernard Montgomery's impudent scheme had failed to provide him with the springboard he so desired for further offensive action, and Eisenhower was denied the Rhine crossing that he craved. Those who had sought to learn what FAAA could achieve had plenty of evidence to ponder. Its commanders had many lessons to learn before their next operation – if airborne forces were to be given another opportunity before Germany was defeated. Just how the Western Allies were going to manoeuvre themselves into a position to finish off their enemy now that it was clear that the war in Europe would continue into 1945 had still to be decided. The important business of breaking into Germany, however, seemed to demand three clear phases: a move up to the border, the cracking of the Siegfried Line and the seizing of that elusive Rhine crossing. However these phases were tackled, and no matter what form the continued Allied offensive took, the Allied commanders had to bear in mind the obvious fact that Operation Market Garden had accentuated: the Germans were not finished yet.

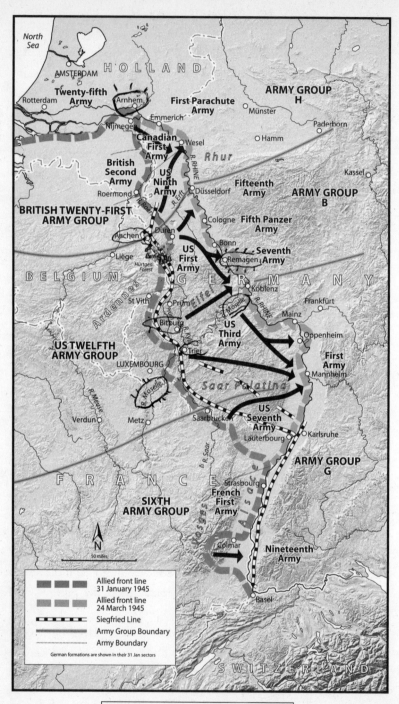

Map 8 : Advance to the Rhine

CHAPTER 8

Riposte

(The Ardennes and Advance to the Rhine:
October 1944–March 1945)

Field Marshal Bernard Montgomery, dapper and visibly preening, strode into the cold hall in the depressing Belgian village of Zonhoven. His audience fell silent. Despite his uniform, he looked like a schoolmaster making his way to the front of his class. He clutched his notes and spectacles in one hand, while with the other he smoothed down a brand-new maroon airborne beret worn with two badges – the Monty way. The men of the British and American press had been kept waiting long enough to become restless, but they remained eager to hear what the chirpy little commander had to say about the battle of the Ardennes. Anticipating a few words of wisdom about the conduct of the fighting, and perhaps a message of conciliation to calm the recent stormy waters of the Anglo-American relationship, the press instead received something very different.

Taking his seat behind a low desk, Montgomery placed his spectacles on the bridge of his long nose and immediately dipped his head to peer over them in a haughty manner. Beginning the lesson with a small cough, he proceeded to read from a script in a voice that was, by common consent, squeaky and irritating. During the short speech, the Field Marshal went to considerable lengths to emphasize the importance of 'the good fighting qualities of the American soldier and the team-work of the Allies' in the eventual defeat of the German offensive, but other passages saw the correspondents shift uneasily in their seats. An unnatural quiet came over the room as soon as Monty began to describe his role in affairs, for he was sanctimonious and hyperbolic in equal proportions. Recognizing the gravity of what was being said, the audience dared not breathe for fear of missing one excruciating word. They learned that when 'the situation began to deteriorate' Monty had moved decisively to 'head off' the enemy in order to 'see him off' and then 'write off' the threat. In other words, the great man had gone to the aid of the Americans and saved the day.

If the aim of the press conference had been self-promotion without fear of the consequences, then Montgomery had given a brilliant performance. But in contriving to exaggerate his own importance to events at the expense of all US personnel except Dwight Eisenhower, he managed to hurt the Americans at a time when they were feeling particularly sensitive and vulnerable. Indeed, Eisenhower later confessed that Monty's words on 7 January 1945 caused him 'more distress and worry' than anything else in the entire war. In just ten minutes Montgomery had managed to poison the very relationship that he had sought to imbue with a vigour that it had recently lacked. At the end of the conference, the amazed war correspondent Alan Moorehead buttonholed Brigadier Bill Williams, Monty's Chief of Intelligence, and said: 'Why didn't you stop him? . . . It was so awful.' Williams replied that he couldn't. He was right, Monty couldn't be stopped, and he could not stop himself: he possessed a self-righteousness which at times bordered on personal infallibility.

Montgomery was not a man to allow operational setbacks to undermine his ambitions, and the failure to achieve a crossing over the

Lower Rhine at Arnhem in September was a case in point. Whilst many officers sought to ensure that the correct lessons were learned from Operation Market Garden and 1st Airborne received the plaudits, Monty got on with fighting the war and moved on to the next challenge. That challenge not only included the immediate military situation facing Twenty-First Army Group but also the strategy to which Dwight Eisenhower clung, and the British role in it. Monty remained adamant that the Supreme Commander's approach to the defeat of the German armed forces was all wrong; a view that was strengthened by his belief that Ike was poorly equipped and positioned to be Land Forces Commander. Consequently, the Field Marshal wished for the 'inefficient and ineffective' broad front to be replaced by a narrow front conducted by his army group, and for land operations to be overseen by himself. Never one to stand on ceremony when an opportunity to express his opinion homed into view, Monty outlined his concerns to General George Marshall when the two men met on 8 October:

> I told him that since Eisenhower had taken personal command of the land battle, being also Supreme Commander of all the forces – land, sea and air – the armies had become separated nationally and not geographically. There was a lack of grip and operational direction and control was lacking. Our operations had, in fact, become ragged and disjointed and we had now got ourselves in a real mess. Marshall listened but said little. It was clear that he entirely disagreed.

The American probably felt like pulling the little man limb from limb, but remained calm, deciding that it was Eisenhower's job to put the 'snivelling runt' in his place. After the war Marshall recalled:

> Montgomery was criticizing the fact that he had been relieved

from command, from active command as he called it ... and I was under a terrific urge to whittle him down ... I did not think that there was any logic in what he said, but overwhelming egotism.

With plenty of 'top cover', Eisenhower felt that he could pursue his conservative, politically adroit, but controversial broad front with confidence. But there was one crumb of comfort that he offered his subordinate: his belief that the northern advance towards the Ruhr remained potentially the most profitable for the Allies. However, the Australian war correspondent Chester Wilmot opined that the reasons that Montgomery's army group did not receive even more backing were multifaceted:

The political difficulty of restraining Patton, the universal optimism of the American High Command, and the desire to form a united front from Switzerland to the North Sea, a front broad enough for the ultimate employment of the 30 divisions still waiting in the United States were, it seems, the real factors behind Eisenhower's reluctance to provide Montgomery with sufficient resources to capture the Ruhr.

Add to this list the strong anti-Montgomery feelings – particularly in the wake of Market Garden – and it was hardly surprising that the British were not strengthened on prime cuts of meat and then unleashed. But Ike had no reason to regret indulging Montgomery with Operation Market Garden, for he always calculated that even if it failed the thrust would very likely wear down the German forces and gain some territory. General Omar Bradley, on the other hand, was growing increasingly tired of Britain's 'unconscionable strategic demands' and was determined to ensure that his Twelfth Army Group was not used as mere 'military ballast'. He was perhaps being thin-skinned, but

Montgomery had begun to irk him, and he refused to stand by whilst 'that self-important SOB was allowed to win the war on his own'. Thus, in late September, whilst all eyes were turned towards the flamboyant scheme unravelling in Holland, Bradley worked to ensure that his advance towards Germany was not allowed to wither on the vine, despite the chronic supply problems. Nevertheless, as the days grew shorter and weather closed in around US First Army's advance towards Aachen and US Third Army's advance towards Metz, he found – just like Monty – that enemy resistance was stiffening.

By mid-October Ike's force had signally failed to exploit the outstanding opportunity that had been offered to it by the chaos that followed the Battle of Normandy. In spite of the quantitative superiority that they had in men, aircraft, tanks and guns, as well as the weakness and disarray of the German armed forces, the Allies had lost their momentum. More than this, the failure of Montgomery and Bradley to break into Germany and through the Siegfried Line – the minimum expected by the many optimists at SHAEF during the late summer – had given Field Marshal Gerd von Rundstedt's hard-pressed forces the chance to catch their breath, reorganize and strengthen their defences. These were disappointments that were used by Montgomery to support his anti-broad front stance, but at a strategic planning conference in Brussels on 18 October, Ike remained steadfast. Here the Supreme Commander, Tedder, Bradley and Montgomery agreed on the next phase of operations. Within this the British would concentrate on securing the vulnerable salient that Market Garden had created pointing towards the Lower Rhine, continue their clearing of the Channel coast and open the port of Antwerp. Thus, with Patton continuing his attack towards the Saar – a task which was thought by the British to offer 'limited strategic prospect' – it was Hodges' US First Army, with the US Ninth Army on his left flank, that would conduct the main ground-taking offensive towards Cologne on the Rhine as the first stage of the encirclement of the Ruhr. On hearing this decision, Alan

Brooke in London was despondent. Unchanged in his opinion that Eisenhower was not up to the job and that his strategy sought to make an unwarranted virtue of dilution, he noted in his diary: 'I do not like the layout of the coming offensive, and doubt whether we [will] even reach the Rhine, it is highly improbable that we should cross over before the end of the year.'

Twenty-First Army Group's task of opening the port of Antwerp to shipping was central to the Allies' unfolding strategy. Operation Market Garden had been pushed through despite calls for the logistic difficulties that were crippling front-line formations to be solved by clearing the Scheldt. Deputy Supreme Commander, Air Chief Marshal Sir Arthur Tedder, later wrote: 'I was never able to convince myself that at any stage until we held Antwerp, Montgomery really believed that we could march a sizeable army to Berlin with our existing resources of supply and maintenance.' Alan Brooke agreed: 'I feel that Monty's strategy for once is at fault. Instead of carrying out the advance on Arnhem he ought to have made certain of Antwerp in the first place.' But both Ike and Monty had sought to prosper whilst the Germans reeled, although both now saw the absolute need to solidify the logistic base, as Eisenhower wrote to the Field Marshal: 'All operations will come to a standstill unless Antwerp is producing by the middle of November. I must emphasise that I consider Antwerp of first importance of all our endeavours on entire front from Switzerland to the Channel.'

The First Canadian Army began operations to clear the Scheldt on 3 October, and four weeks of hard fighting in poor weather followed. Les Wagar of the Queen's Own Rifles of Canada has clear memories of the struggle:

All I remember is the mud and the lack of cover. Companies did not go into battle here; this was section-job fighting, done by platoon-sized groups acting alone, with widely variable mortar and artillery support, bounding and crawling from one set of farmhouses to the next, yard by yard, dike, by dike, over polders with little or no cover.

Although eventually successful, the operation cost some 18,000 Allied casualties, and even then shipping could not dock until the Royal Navy had cleared 267 mines from the estuary. It was not until 28 November – 85 days after the docks had been so dramatically captured by Pip Roberts' men – that the first Allied ship was unloaded in the port. It was an event which was to prove a watershed in the ability to sustain Allied offensive action as its spearheads approached the German border, but its impact was not immediately felt in the front line. It took some eight weeks before supplies were able to leave the port quickly, due in part to V1 and V2 raids on Antwerp, but largely because of the time that it took to build a new road and rail infrastructure. In the meantime, Allied operations continued to be undermined for want of adequate resources, even though it was often the case that those resources were neatly stacked in the port's warehouses. Sergeant Brian Milburn of the Royal Army Ordnance Corps complains:

We would load the wagons up with ammunition, send them on their way, and then hear that they were held up just a few miles outside Antwerp. It was so frustrating as we knew that the loads were desperately needed by troops in the front line, but there was nothing that we could do about it . . . One day I went out with a Royal Military Police unit to witness the traffic jams for myself. They had to be seen to be believed.

Elsewhere, the British and American troops continued their defence of the Market Garden salient in northern Holland, a miserable experience which led to 82 and 101 US Airborne Divisions doubling the number of casualties that they had suffered during September. Babe Heffron of

506 PIR retains a bitterness about the episode, saying simply: 'We took a beating in Holland. It was awful. Montgomery did an awful job . . .' Meanwhile, Miles Dempsey's British Second Army attacked east of Eindhoven to move up to the River Maas, the last important water obstacle before the Rhine, on a 30-mile front. The fighting was tough, laborious and unglamorous, but essential if the front was to be strengthened, as well as offering considerable offensive potential for the future. Nevertheless, such actions left Montgomery's Chief of Staff, Freddie de Guingand, 'rather depressed at the state of the war in the West'. He argued that although 'the SHAEF plan had achieved nothing beyond killing and capturing a lot of Germans . . . we were no nearer to knocking out Germany'.

Yet whilst the British attempt to take a step closer to the Rhine was undoubtedly trying, Hodges' experience was horrendous. Endeavouring to clear some wooded hills defended by some second-rate German troops just to the south-east of Aachen – a city which had taken three weeks to fall – the US First Army became embroiled in a clash that had cost them heavy casualties before success in early December. The battle of Hürtgen Forest was badly handled, and whilst certain divisions signally failed to enhance their reputations, both. Bradley and Hodges also emerged with little credit. The fighting which took place was highly reminiscent of 1916's battle of Verdun, as this account of an attack by 110 US Division from the US official history illustrates:

No sooner had they risen from their foxholes than a rain of machine gun and mortar fire brought them to earth. After several hours of costly infiltration, one battalion reached the triple concertina wire surrounding the bunker, but the enemy gave no sign of weakening. Platoons got lost. Direct shell hits blew up satchel charges and killed men who were carrying them. All communications failed. The chatter of machine guns and the crash of artillery kept frightened, forest-bound infantrymen close

to the earth. In the late afternoon the depleted units slid back to
the line of departure.

Although US First Army did finally manage to break through to the
River Roer and link up with US Ninth Army on its left flank, it was a
bruising episode which left them winded and fragile. Some 24,000 of
Hodges' men became casualties during the battle, whilst trench-foot,
frostbite and exhaustion accounted for a further 9,000. More substantial progress was made by US Third Army when it attacked across a 60-
mile front on 8 November. Linked to an advance by Sixth Army Group
on its south flank, Patton's troops managed to cross the River Moselle
and press forward to Metz. By the time the city fell, some five weeks
later, the Siegfried Line had been breached from Strasbourg to the Saar,
but no further penetration was possible after torturous fighting over
muddy and mine-strewn ground. Omar Bradley summed up the situation when he wrote:

> To put it candidly my plan to smash through to the Rhine and
> encircle the Ruhr had failed . . . Between our front and the Rhine,
> a determined enemy held every foot of ground and would not
> yield. Each day the weather grew colder, our troops more miser-
> able. We were mired in a ghastly war of attrition.

Such limited and difficult progress by the Allied ground forces made
Monty despair, and led to him complaining in a letter to the Supreme
Commander on 30 November:

> We have definitely failed to implement the plan contained in the
> SHAEF directive of 28 October, as amended on later dates. That
> directive ordered the main effort to be made in the north, to
> defeat decisively the enemy west of the Rhine, to gain bridge-
> heads over the Rhine and Ijssel rivers and deploy in strength east

of the Rhine preparatory to seizing the Ruhr. We have achieved none of this and have no hope of doing so, we have suffered a major strategic reverse.

There was no denying the truth of these words, even though by mid-December Eisenhower's troops were on or very close to the German border. After three months of some of the hardest fighting that the Allied troops had experienced since Normandy, SHAEF was left contemplating some disturbingly high casualty figures for such relatively small territorial gains: US Ninth Army: 10,056; US First Army 47,000; US Third Army 53,183. However, as Eisenhower was keen to point out, the campaign was not just about the taking of ground, it was attritional, and because German losses were at least three or four times higher than those suffered by his own troops, the recent operations had to be considered a success.

That 'success' would have meant little to the troops at the sharp end. Although it directly affected them, they were not concerned with strategy, the petty squabbles in the High Command, personality clashes and politics. As Charles B. MacDonald, one of the US official historians and an infantry officer in north-west Europe during 1944–45, argues:

What did it matter to an American GI in a foxhole, fighting for his life in the harsh cold and snow who commanded him at the top? Who was this Montgomery? Who was Bradley? A front-line soldier was immensely well informed if he knew the name of his Company Commander.

Fulfilling the basic needs of a soldier in the front line became increasingly difficult during the early winter of 1944. Some of the problems were caused by the continued logistical difficulties, but the weather and grinding nature of fighting were also to blame, with some officers reporting that low morale and motivation in their units was beginning to affect fighting effectiveness. The continual bad weather, characterized by persistent rain, driving wind, ubiquitous mud and (increasingly) freezing temperatures, only served to heighten the anguish surrounding the fighting. With conditions contriving to weaken both body and mind, US Twelfth Army Group suffered a total of 113,742 non-battle casualties over the period 1 September – 16 December 1944. Everything became a strain, with even the simplest tasks taking far longer in the filthy conditions. Those out in the open for protracted periods lived in a permanently damp world where their equipment was mired, their weapons rusted and their personal effects grew mould. The unfortunate were then ordered onto their weary feet and marched into battle, where they were shelled and shot at, witnessing all kinds of horrors. Private Alan Hudson, a rifleman in 50 British Division, remembers:

It was not a pleasant time. The weather seemed miserable for weeks on end, the sky was always cloudy and a good day was when it was just grey and cold. Most of the time it seemed to rain, and with every day it got colder ... The rain got everywhere, soaked our uniforms, our skin, our kit. The equipment just wasn't up to much. It was basic; it got wet and stayed wet ... Living out of foxholes was a nightmare whether we were static or on the move. If we were static they became difficult to maintain, and if we were mobile then we had to dig them every time we stopped.

American Company Clerk, Staff-Sergeant Donald Kennedy of 28 US Division, has similar memories:

No matter how hard we tried to keep dry, we just couldn't. It was a running battle to keep equipment in working order. Radios, weapons, vehicles, all suffered. Anything that got damp just didn't

work as well or didn't work at all – and that includes the infantry
... It became difficult to do our jobs and to feel good about
things. Our buddies helped a lot, but it was a difficult time.

War correspondent Alexander Clifford wrote home from the German
border:

Here it is all damp and bleak and dreary, and my blood runs cold
at the thought of the winter ... I confess I feel horribly stale.
Thank God winter clothing arrangements seem pretty good. I
have got a leather waistcoat and a very fine pair of gloves ...
[and] the most superb pair of top boots in which I can plod about
in the mud ... unscathed.

Officers and NCOs did what they could to ensure that the needs of
their men were catered for so that morale did not suffer too badly.
Every soldier's needs were different, but few would have turned down
the chance of a refreshing sleep, dry clothes, a full stomach and a
competent officer. Captain Charlie Harris of 7 British Armoured
Division worked tirelessly to try to make his men as comfortable as
possible:

We tried to make sure that the men had the basics: food, ciga-
rettes, post, dry billets – whenever possible. I remember once
after a particularly difficult couple of days when we had been the
lead platoon of an attack and had lost five men. The men were
really down. It was raining, miserable, and difficult to see an end
to it all. But then I heard that some showers had been brought
forward, and so we made sure that the men got to them. A warm
shower, a clean set of clothes and hot meal and everybody brightened up. It wasn't anything big, but we had to be grateful for small
mercies, as they say.

When possible the troops were given a rest from the stresses and strains of combat. Again, 'small mercies' could make a difference. To men who had endured days of shelling whilst cowering in a slit trench, a short time in reserve could prove a restorative, but time away from the front and leave were much coveted. However, because there were too few new men taking the place of casualties, there was scant opportunity for rest.

The British tried not to keep men in the front line for more than a couple of weeks before giving them a couple of days' rest, but for the US troops it was often four or five weeks, and sometimes double that. The Americans tried to establish a rotation programme to improve this, but it still only led to one man per company being pulled out of the line every month. Home leave was virtually unknown, and men tended to rely on the war ending rather than pinning their delicate hopes on the chance of getting to see loved ones.

In such circumstances it was not uncommon for soldiers to feel demotivated. Whilst few continued to go about their business driven by esoteric concepts such as patriotism or political causes, most would have understood notions of duty, comradeship, pride and honour. But with every passing day more men felt that they had 'done their bit' and, recognizing that the war was unlikely to last much longer, did not want to become one of its last casualties. Private Tommy Hobson of 3 British Division had landed in France on 6 June 1944, and concedes that:

I had had enough by Christmas. Too much fighting, too many mates that had died, too much marching and bad food. I prayed for the day when it would all be over and I could go home. We all did I suppose, but the fighting was just something you had to get through and it was best to be fatalistic: get on with the job, and allow events to take care of the future. In that way, I found that I could cope with things. If my chums could do it then so could I. We were in it together. We looked out for each other.

The Germans, of course, suffered in the same conditions but in a distinctly uncomfortable strategic predicament, often with fewer resources and very little attention to their morale. By October, Gefreiter Richard Ritterbecks of 246 Division expected his war to end any day in capture, wounding or death:

It was bad for us. Poor conditions and losing battle after battle, slowly being pushed back home. But would we ever see home? Most of us did not think so. We had seen and heard the Allied war machine: the troops, trucks, tanks, guns, planes, and we did not expect to survive.

But whilst the Germans may have lacked morale, most remained motivated, for they were fighting for their lives and their homeland, as Obergefreiter Herbert Piplak, an anti-aircraft gunner, explains:

Having fought in Normandy and all the way back to the German border I had seen a great deal of death and my unit had suffered many setbacks. Fighting then withdrawing, fighting then withdrawing was an unhappy experience. Any attempts to exhort us to fight for Hitler and the Reich would not have been well received: we fought for our family, our friends, our country, ourselves – but certainly not for Hitler.

Omar Bradley's aide, Major Chester Hansen, believed that the Allies had made a mistake demanding the unconditional surrender of Germany as it gave its people no option but to carry on fighting. Writing on 11 December, Hansen opined:

I believe we have committed a smug and profound psychological error in announcing a program for unconditional surrender, since the German is obviously making capital of this in his effort to fan the fanaticism of the German defence ... Our demands do nothing to persuade him to realise the folly of his fight. They give him nothing to quit for.

A British intelligence officer who had sifted through scores of reports about enemy motivation and fighting spirit declared:

Few thought that Germany had any hope of final victory; most had had their fill of fighting and recognised the futility of continuing the struggle. Nevertheless, they all fought hard. The deduction would seem to be that no matter how poor the morale of the German soldier may be, he will fight hard as long as he has leaders to give him orders and see that they are obeyed.

Some, however, just wanted it all to end and to surrender at the first opportunity. Private Erich Hinrichs of 275 Division says:

I had decided that I would fight on to the last, to die in combat like a man. However, the Americans put in a tremendous artillery bombardment which shook me and the whole company and as soon as we saw the first of their infantry we stuck our hands up ... We were disarmed, searched and sent back behind the lines. We were treated well and ended up being guarded by a man who spoke reasonable German. He said that his company had taken over 1,000 prisoners during the previous few days and that the war was over for Germany. I agreed and said that was why I had surrendered. He laughed and gave me a cigarette.

Montgomery went to great lengths to look after the troops under his command, but when questioned as to the single most important thing he was doing to reinforce his troops' morale, he replied: 'I am conducting operations which will lead to the destruction of the German forces and which will bring the war to an end.' Thus, he entered the Strategic Planning Conference in Maastricht with Eisenhower, Tedder and Bradley on 7 December determined not to be browbeaten by the Americans. He argued that his northern thrust should be reinvigorated with at least ten divisions of a US Army under his command. Whilst Hodges continued his advance around the southern Ruhr, Montgomery wanted to cross the Rhine between Nijmegen and Wesel, and to be given the opportunity to complete the encirclement of Germany's Ruhr. In arguing for this, he was prodding at an open American wound, which so infuriated Bradley that he wrote:

> When you analyse how difficult it would have been for the British to accomplish anything, even in the beachhead or coming across France, except where we were pulling them along, why would he [Montgomery] think the British would step out and win the war while the Americans stood still? He wanted to take a bunch of Americans to do it with.

Yet to the Twelfth Army Group commander's chagrin, Eisenhower still saw merit in developing the northern attack, and he agreed to support a British push towards the Rhine with Lieutenant-General William Simpson's US Ninth Army on his right. Hodges, meanwhile, would continue his advance towards Cologne, whilst Patton and US Seventh Army would crack the Siegfried Line and press on to the Rhine and Frankfurt. Montgomery had won a small victory, but he was far from satisfied with Ike's continued dispersal of the Allied resources, and after the conference broke up wrote to P.J. Grigg, the Secretary of State for War, in London: 'I hope the American public will realize that, owing to the handling of the campaign in western Europe from 1 Sept. onwards, the German war will now go on during 1945. And they should realize very clearly that the handling of the campaign is entirely in American hands.' Montgomery began his meticulous preparations for an offensive which he hoped would see his forces on the River Rhine before the end of the winter. Yet before any of Eisenhower's commanders completed their detailed planning, the Germans launched a massive and unexpected counterattack through the Ardennes.

Hitler's health had continued to decline along with his strategic prospects. With the Soviets destroying all before them in the East, the rest of the Allies pressing in from the West, and aircraft bombing Germany in between, the outlook was bleak. The Führer had lost more weight over the autumn, and looked weak and utterly exhausted. After meeting Hitler on 11 December, General Hasso von Manteuffel, the commander of Fifth Panzer Army, wrote in his diary:

A stooped figure with a pale and puffy face, hunched in his chair, his hands trembling, his left arm subject to a violent twitching which he did his best to conceal, a sick man apparently borne down by the burden of responsibility. When he walked he dragged one leg behind him . . . he talked in a low and hesitant voice.

As the news from the fighting fronts became consistently negative, Hitler became increasingly irrational and lost what little residual understanding he had of the capabilities of his armed forces. Yet he continued to nurture the hope that a great counterattack in the West would reverse his fortunes. Having conceived of a plan in the heat of August, Hitler announced his intentions to his operations staff at the Wolfsschanze on 16 September. In the 'night, fog and snow' of the coming Ardennes winter, armoured forces would push 60 miles to seize Antwerp and in so doing, divide the Americans from the British and Canadians and so exacerbate the friction that existed within the Allied High Command. Such an attack, he was further convinced, would not only provide the time that was needed to pool resources for a strike back at the Soviets, but also give the V-weapons an opportunity to undermine Allied resolve. It was a remarkably bold concept, the generals argued, but it was totally impractical: there were not the resources for such an attack, the weather and terrain would prevent it, the flanks would remain vulnerable and the Americans would counter-attack. Thus when Walter Model heard of the scheme he immediately complained: 'This plan hasn't got a damned leg to stand on.' He then picked up the telephone and when put through to OKW said without preamble: 'You can tell your Führer from me, that Model won't have any part of it.' Gerd von Rundstedt was of a similar mind, and later recalled: 'When I received this plan in November I was staggered . . . It was obvious to me that the available forces were far too small for such an extremely ambitious plan.' Colonel General Sepp Dietrich, commanding Sixth SS Panzer Army, the formation charged with making the thrust, complained that the offensive lacked the one prerequisite for any such operation − achievable objectives: 'I had merely to cross a river, capture Brussels, and then go on and take the port of Antwerp, and all this in the worst months of the year, through the Ardennes where snow was waist-deep and there wasn't room to deploy four tanks abreast.' Nevertheless, Hitler swept all concerns aside arguing that 'such pessimism had already led to numerous missed opportunities', whilst theorizing that as the task was so challenging, Eisenhower would not be expecting it.

When the attack began on 16 December the German offensive did manage to catch the thinly spread Americans cold and totally unpre-pared. Omar Bradley was so bemused by the sudden appearance of enemy armour thrusting between his First and Third Armies that he did not at first think that it was anything more that a local counter-attack. When he eventually became convinced that what was developing equated to a major German action he was left asking: 'Where the hell has this sonofabitch gotten all his strength?' The remarkable surprise achieved by the assault initially allowed for some of the panzers to plunge 20 miles into the American lines, causing alarm and widespread confusion. Watching from the sidelines at this stage, Montgomery could not help gloating:

> It looks as if we may now have to pay the price for the policy of drift and lack of proper control of operations which had been a marked feature of the last three months ... The present American tendency is to throw in reserves piecemeal as they arrive, and I have suggested a warning against this. I have myself had no orders or requests of any kind. My own opinion is that the general situation is ugly, as the American forces have been cut clean in half, and the Germans can reach the Meuse at Namur without any opposition.

Even so, as the difficulties that the German generals had highlighted when the concept was first mooted began to bite, the Americans recovered their poise. Ike called on FAAA's assistance which led to 82 US, 101 US, 17 US and 6 British Airborne Divisions being rushed to the area and into action, whilst Monty took command of US First and Ninth Armies on the northern flank. Through improvisation, cooperation and some outstanding defensive actions, the crisis passed, the front was stabilized and a counterattack was launched. With Hodges moving in from the north, Montgomery from the north-west and Patton from the south, on 7 January 1945 Hitler ordered the withdrawal of his overstretched and helpless force.

The Americans were justly proud of the way in which they had handled the 'Battle of the Bulge', but it was tinged with embarrassment that their forces had been surprised in the first place. Montgomery's stunningly impolitic press conference, therefore, quickly led to several US heavyweights falling on him. Marshall, Eisenhower, Bradley, Hodges and Patton were all furious, the British felt humiliated, and in a war that had severely tested and strained the 'Special Relationship',

Anglo-American relations reached a nadir. Winston Churchill, who recognized the need not to antagonize the Americans more than was absolutely necessary (and not at all if the chances of success were virtually nil), felt the need to write to Theodore Roosevelt in the wake of Monty's *faux pas*:

> I hope you understand that, in case any troubles should arise in the press, His Majesty's Government have complete confidence in General Eisenhower and feel acutely any attacks made on him. He and Montgomery are very closely knit and also Bradley and Patton, and it would be a disaster which broke up this combination which has, in nineteen forty-four, yielded us results beyond the dreams of military avarice . . . I have a feeling this is a time for an intense new impulse, both of friendship and exertion, to be drawn from our bosoms and to the last scrap of our resources.

Nevertheless, the situation had not been mended by the end of January and the British and Americans had a series of unseemly arguments about Monty, Ike and the efficacy of the broad front at the Combined Chiefs of Staff meetings held in Malta. At one point George Marshall threatened to resign if the British did not fall into line, and it took Roosevelt's influence in support of Eisenhower's strategy before Churchill asked Brooke to return his gunboats to port, recognize defeat and ensure that Montgomery did the same.

Between the middle of December 1944 and the end of January 1945, the strategic situation in northern Europe changed considerably. The fighting in the Ardennes had been a setback for the western Allies and led to 41,000 American casualties between 16 December and 2 January, but it was not a disaster. The drive to restore their position had by early February cost a further 40,000 men, but such losses, although causing some tactical and operational difficulties, were not strategically damaging. The German losses of between 80,000 and 100,000 men, along with most of the tanks and aircraft that had committed to battle, however, were devastating for von Rundstedt, and made him virtually impotent against the next phase of Allied offensive action that he knew must come. Only those still closing their minds and averting their eyes to the reality of Germany's situation could have thought that the destiny of the war was in any doubt, particularly after the Soviets had undertaken a devastating offensive from the Vistula to the Oder which ended with their troops just 50 miles from Berlin, but Hitler demanded that his forces fight on. Thus, with numerous military and political objectives before them, a place in history beckoning and the lives of their men on the line, Eisenhower expected the struggle for priority between Monty and Bradley would continue. But he was in no mood for audacity at this stage. Having been stung by the Germans in late December, the Supreme Commander retreated into a super-conservative mindset, which left nothing to chance. Explaining his reasons to Monty, he said:

We must make certain that [the enemy] is not free behind strong defensive lines, to organize sudden powerful thrusts into our lines of communication. As I see it, we simply cannot afford the large defensive forces that would be necessary if we allow the German to hold great bastions sticking into our lines at the same time that we try to invade his country.

Thus when Ike met with his army group commanders on 31 January to agree offensive moves for the spring, the discussion centred on the premise that no move would leave any force vulnerable. Exactly what Ike's forces were likely to have been rendered vulnerable by after the destruction of von Rundstedt's armoured threat was never made clear – but the broad front would grind on. The Allied spring offensive, therefore, sought to advance Eisenhower's force up to the River Rhine on a 250-mile front. But whilst the Supreme Commander was in no mood for another Market Garden type operation, he did reaffirm the decision that he had taken in early December to support Montgomery's attack by putting US Ninth Army under his command. As a result Montgomery was capable of undertaking two interconnected operations to move up the Rhine around Wesel: Operation Veritable, which would be fought by First Canadian Army and required an attack east from Nijmegen through the forest of the Reichswald; and Operation Grenade, in which US Ninth Army would cross the River Roer and push north-east to link up with the British near Wesel. Twelfth Army, meanwhile, was to use its US First Army to clear the approaches of the Rhine from Cologne to Koblenz in Operation Lumberjack, whilst US Third Army moved up the Rhine from Mainz to Mannerheim as Sixth Army Group's US Seventh Army headed for the river north of Strasbourg. The aim, Eisenenhower stressed, was to achieve a crossing in Montgomery's area to facilitate the capture of the Ruhr and, whilst the Supreme Commander would not dissuade Bradley and Devers from taking any bridges over the Rhine that presented themselves, any exploitation was to be undertaken only with the aim of diverting German resources away from the main effort. Bradley felt slighted and raged at Eisenhower that if he was forced to cede US Ninth Army to Monty, then he would ask to be sent home. Ike replied: 'I thought you were the one person I would count on for doing anything I asked you to.' 'You can, Ike', said Bradley. 'I've enjoyed every bit of my service with you. But this is one thing I cannot take.' The Supreme Commander managed to talk him round, but the confrontation was more robust than any he had had with Monty. Eisenhower later reflected that trying to keep his subordinates contented was like 'trying to arrange the blankets smoothly over several prima donnas in the same bed'.

Montgomery built up a powerful force for Operation Veritable which he was determined would crack the German defences wide open. The attack was the responsibility of General Henry Crerar's Canadian First Army which, incorporating British XXX Corps, totalled

300,000 men, 35,000 vehicles and 1,000 tanks. After Monty's eschewing of his usual operational fastidiousness with Operation Market Garden, Veritable was a return to type. Indeed, Alexander McKee wrote of the attack on 30 January: 'It's a typical Monty set-up. Bags of guns crammed into a narrow front, all your force at one point and bash in. Unsubtle but usually successful. Jerry knows you're coming, but he can't do very much.'

The planning was a meticulous and exhausting business, as II Canadian Corps Staff Officer Lieutenant-Colonel Baker lamented in his diary: '3–5 February 1945: We have all reached the state where we are completely pooped and have had to resort to the use of Benzedrine tablets and black coffee to try and stay awake.' Nothing was left to chance, for it was not in Montgomery's nature to leave things to chance, and he was not a general who was willing to take risks with men's lives unless it was for a critical military imperative. Thus, although the Field Marshal and Crerar knew that the German force before them amounted to little more than 12,000 men from Lieutenant-General Alfred Schlemm's First Parachute Army, they were respectful of the likely strength of their defences, not least because Schlemm was a capable commander who had gained considerable experience of defensive operations and fighting withdrawals during the Italian campaign. The Allies therefore expected Schlemm to make a stand, and that was exactly what he was planning: a 'rigorous and determined defence' which sought to slow the attacking force down, and then grind them to a halt. To facilitate this, Schlemm would use the three belts of the Siegfried Line in his sector which fully integrated various strong-points that were to be found in the surrounding woods, towns, villages and the close, hilly terrain of the Reichswald. Schlemm was under no illusion that his task was anything other than fantastically difficult, but he was stoic whilst lamenting the loss of the flexibility and initiative which German army officers had so recently enjoyed:

My orders were that under no circumstances was any land between the Maas and the Rhine to be given up without permission of the Commander-in-Chief West, von Rundstedt, who in turn had to ask Hitler. For every withdrawal that I was forced to make due to an Allied attack, I had to send back a detailed explanation.

The Führer demanded that there would be no withdrawal behind the Rhine to superior defensive positions, and was determined that the nation's last great defensive barrier in the West would be defended to the last round.

Allied heavy bombers delivered a destructive preamble to Operation Veritable on the night of 7/8 February, when key towns within the German defences were targeted in an attempt to dislocate Schlemm's command and control. Corporal Heinz Kempa was burying a telephone line just outside Xanten when the aircraft struck:

> The weather had been so bad recently that there had not been much bombing, but that night we really caught it. The landscape was suddenly full of disorientating flashes. It was difficult to judge where the bombs were landing.
>
> I was caught between wanting to watch the drama unfold, and getting into safety. I was eventually dragged into the cellar of a nearby farmhouse and we could hear the booming, rumble of the explosions. The fires burned for days. The devastation was immense.

At dawn another parcel of devastation was delivered by 1,050 artillery pieces which sought to destroy the enemy's defences and then their guns. Sergeant Mick White of the Royal Artillery was relieved to be underway: 'We had spent weeks preparing for this attack. Digging gun positions, piling up the ammunition, studying maps and aerial reconnaissance photographs, making plans, checking plans, co-ordinating plans. When we loosed off the first shells, it was a wonderful feeling.' A.E. Baker, a wireless operator with the Royal Dragoon Guards, was impressed with this great show of force:

> At one minute to five that morning everything was peaceful. It was still dark and there was a slight mist. At five o'clock all hell broke loose! It was as bright as day, and the noise was like nothing on earth ... At 5.30, as arranged, the tanks began to fire ... The row was absolutely beyond belief, and long before it finished I had a splitting headache. It wasn't only the concussion of the bigger guns, but the ceaseless sharp hammering of the Vickers just beside our tank.

At 1030 hours, those tanks advanced on a 7½-mile front with mine-exploding flail tanks leading the way. Whilst the armour worked to break in to the enemy's defensive positions, the infantry following moved in to clear them and mop up. The attack started well, but then some of the tanks became bogged down in the heavy mud, and losing their support, the infantry became more vulnerable. There was some fierce fighting within the first belt of the Siegfried Line and up to the edge of the Reichswald, but although managing to destroy six of the seven German battalions found there, the tempo of the attack began to slow down. The Reichswald proved a very difficult place to clear, and despite the Allied expectation of scything through it in a day or two, the wood eventually took a week to capture. Thus by 11 February, the date by which the operation should have been completed, a mixture of tenacious German defence, saturated ground and blocked towns had slowed the Allied advance down to a crawl. One of those choking-points was the critical communication town of Cleve, entered by men from 43 (Wessex) Division. An infantryman from the 4/Wiltshires Regiment says:

There were craters and fallen trees everywhere, bomb craters packed so tight that the debris from one was piled against the rim of the next in a pathetic heap of rubble, roofs and radiators. There was not an undamaged house anywhere, piles of smashed furniture, clothing, children's books and toys, everything was spilled in hopeless confusion amidst the bombed skeleton of the town.

The ruined town caused the British convoys considerable problems because they relied on its roads whilst the surrounding countryside was waterlogged. Moreover, the subsequent traffic-jams promoted a sluggish attack which provided the Germans with an excellent opportunity to reinforce its stretched defenders. The speed with which Schlemm exploited this situation can be seen in the report made by Brian Horrocks on 14 February, in which he stated that he was being opposed by one panzer, one panzergrenadier, four parachute and three infantry divisions. In good weather these formations might not have been able to move on to the battlefield, as Allied aircraft would undoubtedly have stopped them, whilst also providing some much-needed support to the ground units, but the weather remained shockingly wet. As a consequence, the town of Goch in the second defensive line was not taken until 22 February, but the following day an optimistic message was sent by Horrocks to his troops:

> You have now accomplished the first part of your task. You have taken approximately 12,000 prisoners and killed large numbers of Germans . . . A strong US offensive was launched over the Roer at 0330 hours this morning against positions, which thanks to your efforts, are lightly held by the Germans.

That US offensive was Operation Grenade, the attack which should have begun shortly after Crerar's attack but had to be postponed due to the German flooding of the Roer valley. By the time that the water had subsided enough for US Ninth Army to begin its move, the Germans opposing it had been heavily diluted in order to frustrate Operation Grenade. After a highly successful assault crossing of the River Roer on the 23rd, supported by a 1,500-gun bombardment, Simpson's men made rapid progress towards their objectives. Consequently, by 26 February Schlemm's First Parachute Army had started to be squeezed between the two Allied pincers and forced into a bridgehead 20 miles deep and ten wide. 'It was a terrible situation', says Heinz Kempa, 'we were staring annihilation in the face. I looked at a map upon which my officer had drawn a red line to represent the limits of our perimeter. Every time I looked – and sometimes that was every hour or so – the area was smaller.' The Germans were being overrun, assisted by the clearing skies which not only allowed for some aerial support but also helped to dry the ground. On 3 March, Veritable's 53 (Welsh) Division linked up with Grenade's 35 US Division at Geldern. As Crerar and Simpson turned to face the Rhine and Wesel, it would have made sound military sense for Schlemm's beleaguered German force to have withdrawn to the east bank of the Rhine in an attempt to live to fight another day, but that was not allowed. Hitler had issued strict orders that the bridges under the general's command were to be kept open for as long as possible, and none prepared for demolition until the enemy was within 12 miles of them. In a conversation about Schlemm's situation with von Rundstedt, the Führer said: 'I want him to hang on to the West Wall as long as is humanly possible, since withdrawal would merely mean moving the catastrophe from one place to another.' Any officer who surrendered a bridge to the enemy faced execution. With several bridges in his sector, it was perhaps not surprising that Schlemm said later, 'I could see my hopes of a long life rapidly dwindling.'

As the German bridgehead shrank, Schlemm destroyed the bridges that would otherwise have fallen into enemy hands. By 6 March his bridgehead was a mere ten miles wide and eight miles deep. Desperate to withdraw, he telephoned von Rundstedt and said:

> If you have a map before you, you will take in the situation at a glance. My divisions are surrounded with the Ruhr at their back, Under these conditions I cannot do anything against the enemy's superior forces. I am asking for authorization to withdraw to the east bank of the Rhine.

Having contacted OKW to obtain the permission that he required to allow Schlemm to withdraw, von Rundstedt was informed that a staff officer would be despatched to Wesel immediately in order to adjudicate on the urgency of the situation. Arriving at Schlemm's bridgehead headquarters in a shining staff car and wearing a pristine uniform during a heavy exchange of fire on 7 March, the General asked the Lieutenant-Colonel whether he would like a tour of the bridgehead to help inform his decision. Turning a little pale and making his excuses, the staff officer left as quickly as he could, but by the end of the day Schlemm had received his authorization to withdraw. Over the course of the next two days, troops around the perimeter, in a situation not dissimilar to that faced by 1 British Airborne Division at Oosterbeek, fought to maintain their positions whilst an evacuation took place behind them. Schlemm remained in the front line, directing operations until the very end, which came at 0700 hours on 10 March, when he ordered the bridge to be destroyed. Several hours later, as the final defenders of the redundant bridgehead were being mopped up, other Allied units moved into positions which allowed them to overlook the Rhine's east bank. After a hard-fought battle which cost Crearar and Simpson a total of 22,000 casualties, Montgomery had won the right to begin his detailed preparations for a great set-piece battle to cross the Rhine.

Montgomery, however, was not destined to be the first Allied commander to move his troops across the river. Whilst Operations Veritable and Grenade closed towards the mighty obstacle, Omar Bradley and Jacob Devers successfully advanced their armies to the Rhine against negligible opposition. As they sped towards their objectives, the Germans withdrew over numerous bridges and then destroyed them, but the spearhead of First US Army's 9 Armored Division came across the damaged but intact Ludendorff railway bridge at Remagen on 7 March. When Bradley was informed that men from Company A of 27 Armored Infantry Battalion had used the bridge to cross the river, he could hardly contain his delight. He had beaten Montgomery across the Rhine using speed and guile and without incurring a single casualty. Nevertheless, a conversation with SHAEF about developing a bridgehead and exploitation quickly brought the American commander back down to earth. They knew that there was difficult terrain beyond the bridge and so asked Bradley, 'Where are you going to go from Remagen?' Ike's headquarters recognized that the seizing of the Remagen bridge was a great psychological blow to the Germans and a great boost to the Allies, but they also reflected their bosses,' view that the best place to exploit a Rhine crossing was in the north with Montgomery. Grudgingly accepting that he was not going to win this argument, and frustrated that the British were still developing a massive attack to attain a crossing more than two weeks after Hodges' troops had first stood on the east bank, he needed a fillip. He received one when an elated Patton called him the day before Monty was due to launch his crossing attempt, to say that some of his men had crossed the Rhine at Oppenheim by rowing across in some assault boats. Patton said with undisguised scorn at Monty: 'I can outfight that little fart anytime.' Directing his words squarely at the Field Marshal's elaborate preparations further north, Bradley penned a cutting communiqué to announce Patton's success:

'Without the benefit of aerial bombardments, ground smoke, artillery preparation and airborne assistance, the Third Army at 22:00 hours Thursday evening, 22nd March, crossed the Rhine river.'

Montgomery had lost the race to cross the Rhine, but he had shown no sign of competing in a race and was certainly unaware of its rules. Whilst it would be naïve to suggest that an individual as competitive as Monty would not have gained a great deal of satisfaction from pushing British troops across the river before Bradley, it would be equally naïve to say that his ambition had not moved on. The reason why Bradley and Patton were so delighted by their crossing coups was because they had been forced to look on whilst Monty undertook a one-man extravaganza. This show was the prelude to Twenty-First Army Group striking out for military and political objectives that were of far more strategic significance than the half-hearted crossing of a water obstacle. Bradley may have crossed the Rhine first, but if the Twenty-First Army Group's projected crossing were successful, it would be Monty and not Brad who would be remembered as the commander who played the greater role in knocking Germany out of the war.

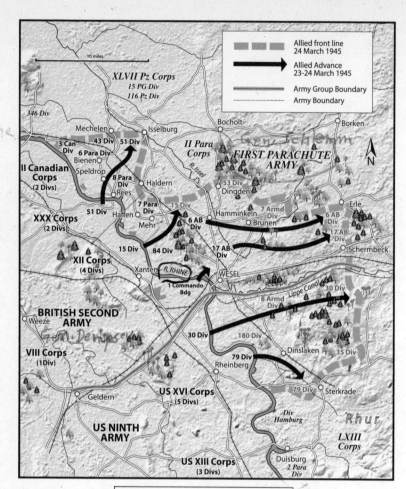

Map 9: Plunder Varsity Plan

CHAPTER 9

The Deluge

(Planning and Launching Plunder Varsity:
10–24 March 1945)

Winifred Steets tried not to expect his letters any more. Sometimes she received two or three a week, then none for weeks until a large bundle of envelopes arrived. Like so many of Germany's formerly reliable services, the postal system just could not cope with the challenges posed by the war. Her husband, Hans-Dieter, wrote to her often even when in the midst of battle. The couple's correspondence was crucial to their relationship as they had not seen each other for over a year. It brought them together despite their physical separation which, in the middle of March 1945, found Winifred in Magdeburg, 100 miles closer to the Red Army than she was to her husband at Wesel on the Rhine. Not that she knew where Hans-Dieter was: his letters gave no indication, and he rarely mentioned the war. The young infantryman tried not to worry her and so preferred to write about trivial events and his friends, and she did the same. He did not want to give his wife an inkling of what life was like fighting in the front line, whilst Winifred did not want to let him know how difficult life had become for her: the six 12-hour shifts a week, the lack of food and fuel, the air raids. She had mentioned to him that her friend had died in January, but had not said that she had died in an Allied bombing raid on Magdeburg. In so doing, the letters provided a distorted version of reality, were peppered with half-truths, and evoked memories of how things used to be – and they both knew it.

During the afternoon of 23 March, Gefrieter Hans-Dieter Steets of 1051 Grenadier Regiment, 84 Infantry Division, a veteran of the fighting against American airborne troops and British armour in Holland, was maintaining his machine gun in a wrecked house in Wesel. The building had no roof, had lost its back wall, but it had a reassuringly deep cellar and a good view of a road junction. He was feeling anxious because three days earlier the division had been put on high alert and there were rumours that the long-awaited British attack across the Rhine was going to be launched that night. Having mulled his situation over, and packed away his oily rags, Hans-Dieter did what he always did when he was feeling low, he picked up pen and paper and wrote to Winifred, his best friend, his childhood sweetheart, the one he missed so very much. He was just finishing his letter when the first Allied shells smashed into a neighbouring ruin.

By the middle of March all three of Dwight Eisenhower's army groups were either on the west bank of the Rhine, or completing their moves up to the river on a 250-mile front. The Allies had finally attained a position from which they could launch a major operation to cross the obstacle, and Bernard Montgomery was busy preparing it. On 10 March, the day on which his men had removed the enemy's Wesel bridgehead, he wrote to his son David: 'I am busy getting ready for the next battle. The Rhine is *some* river, but we shall get over it.' As Monty's words suggest, the broad, fast-flowing Rhine was not just any river – it was Germany's last natural obstacle in the West and a psychological crutch upon which the nation's people had always leant. For centuries the great river had been a dependable defensive barrier against foreign aggression, and there was the belief – or perhaps hope – that it would continue to be so in the coming days and weeks. The fact that the Americans had already managed to cross it at Remagen was cause for concern, for there was general agreement that a massive breach would spell the end for Germany. Sophie Becker had lived on the banks of the river at Hamminkein all her life, and aged 83 wrote in her diary on 16 March:

> The fighting gets closer. A number of families are leaving the town as they fear the worst. Where they are going, I do not know, but I intend to stay. We are not defeated. Germany still has the Rhine and it has always protected us. I pray to God that it protects us now in our hour of need. Perhaps the Americans [*sic*] will fail?

The question with which Frau Becker concludes her entry suggests that she was not entirely convinced that the Rhine would prove as impenetrable a barrier as it needed to be in the circumstances. She was quite right to be sceptical, for her countrymen were in no position to back the river's natural defences with bullets and bravery, and Montgomery was preparing a massive offensive to sweep all before him. His plans to cross the Rhine were based on the power of Lieutenant-General Sir Miles Dempsey's Second Army which with Lieutenant-General Matthew Ridgway's XVIII US Airborne Corps under command, amounted to a powerful and flexible force. Standing Canute-like with the invidious task of repelling the incoming Allied tide was Lieutenant-General Alfred Schlemm and his ravaged First Parachute Army. Ordered to 'stand firm' by General Johannes von Blaskowitz at Army Group H, Schlemm took a deep breath, gathered his troops and tried to anticipate the form of the coming attack. 'The most difficult thing for our commanders to do', says one of Schlemm's men, Major Klaus Beich, was to try to cover all the options with so very little. Where would the enemy choose to fight? When would they strike? How would they strike? These were all important questions which needed to be asked if our resources were to be used efficiently. Similar questions were posed by the troops waiting to receive the attack and the waiting and not knowing was difficult for all of us.

Undermining German prospects of successfully defending against an Allied offensive was Hitler's constant interference in his generals' work. Many – including Field Marshal Gerd von Rundstedt – thought that Hitler should have tried to achieve a negotiated peace months ago, but as this was never likely he had worked to ensure that defeat would not come at the cost of the complete destruction of the German armed forces. He recognized, therefore, that it was often militarily necessary to trade territory for stronger defensive positions, but withdrawals were something that Hitler would not countenance and heavy casualties resulted. Von Rundstedt had been desperate to withdraw his force to the east bank of the Rhine during February, but instead the Allies were allowed to carve into them during the battle of the Rhineland.

It was ironic, therefore, that the arrival of the Allies on the Rhine cost von Rundstedt his job; he was replaced as OB West by Field Marshal Albert Kesselring. 'Smiling Albert' had been the *bête noire* of the Allies in Italy, as he used the terrain brilliantly in a series of rear-guard actions which slowed their advance northwards to a crawl. Such talents were in great demand in Germany during March 1945, but although the job had little to recommend it, the new man immediately applied himself to the task by asking for a situation report as soon as he arrived at his headquarters. Lieutenant-Colonel Wilhelm Hagemann, an operations staff officer, says:

The Field Marshal was immediately told the worst – he appreciated plain speaking – and he stood impassively as he was told the latest . . . We lacked manpower, ammunition, trucks and fuel. We had very few tanks, the Luftwaffe was virtually non-existent . . . Morale was poor, but the troops were still fighting well. He was informed of the details about the American crossing [at Remagen], and that Montgomery was preparing to launch an attack in the north . . . When the briefing had finished, the Field Marshal asked, 'Is there any good news at all?' The staff officers looked at each other and shrugged. There was silence.

The German armed forces in the West were punch-drunk after a catalogue of reverses that had begun in Normandy the previous summer and contrived to drive them back to within their own national boundary. The battle of the Ardennes had destroyed their offensive capability, and the defence of the west bank of the Rhine – in which the army had lost approximately one-third of its manpower in the West – had severely limited their ability to provide a competent and coherent defensive force. Corporal Heinz Kempa described the general situation with regard to his own:

If the German Army was anything like my unit, there were four key retrograde steps: in Normandy we were strong, at Arnhem we were weakening, in the Ardennes we struggled and on the Rhine we relied on hope. We were not bad soldiers all of a sudden, but we lacked what we needed to do the job. I was a radio expert by March 1945, but I hadn't used one since November 1944 – we just couldn't get hold of radios.

The Allies, however, seemed to have solved the logistical difficulties that had been plaguing them since the previous summer. As a consequence, Eisenhower's 73 divisions (drawing on nearly four million

Allied troops on the Continent) were well supplied, whilst Kesselring's 26 divisions were severely undermanned and under-resourced.

The German ability to resist was slowly but surely crumbling, but although Wilhelm Hagemann recognized this, he thought that the fight could go on if the correct mental approach was adopted: 'The fighting needed to be passionate, frenzied even, to make up for deficiencies in other areas. Every soldier knew what was expected of him, each man saw that the future of his homeland depended on a collective stoicism.' In saying this, however, Hagemann seems to have neglected the potential for the troops' fighting prowess to be diluted by their presence on home soil. 'It was demoralizing', says Obergefreiter Herbert Piplak, 'to have to fight through our devastated communities. There were many times when I thought that the act of surrendering would bring the war one step closer to an end and stop Germany from being destroyed.' In deciding to defend a town or village, an officer was in effect inviting its destruction. Wesel, for example, was bombed three times on 16 February alone. Derek S. Zumbro has written of the horror and confusion:

The explosions were so concentrated that the steel doors of air raid shelters blew inward and were torn from their fittings. Women collapsed as their nerves broke under the strain, and children screamed and cried as they clung to anyone within reach. A policeman shot his daughter, his wife, and then himself as they cowered under the hail of bombs.

For the German troops forced to file through Wesel's rubble-strewn streets, it was a difficult experience. On the morning of 17 March, medic Peter Kress found himself providing assistance to civilians, in spite of the desperate need for his services in the line:

I should not have been there, I was needed at Xanten, but after some business in a nearby village which was acting as a dressing station, I felt drawn into Wesel to help. It was awful. Rescue teams were searching the rubble for survivors. Row after row of corpses lined the roads. I had seen plenty of death since 1942, but what I saw in Wesel really affected me because it involved civilians. Whole families were wiped out. Old lay next to young, men next to women, the mutilated next to those without a scratch on them. These were German people, my people, and I wept for them. And the children – the poor, dead children in their little shoes – their lifeless eyes seemed to be asking me a shattering question: 'Why?'

Wesel was destroyed, but it was bombed time and time again over the following weeks, until its streets looked like a mouthful of rotten teeth and some areas had been reduced to brick-dust.

Whilst air raids had blighted Germany for years, the arrival of the fighting front to its streets brought with it a new raft of horrors and privations which caused acute distress. Nowhere seemed safe, and those who fled their homes in the west knew that a rampaging Soviet Army bent on revenge was pushing in from the east. Hitler continued to neglect the impact that the war was having on the home front because he had no answers to it other than to say: 'The fate of the German people is inextricably linked to the fate of our fighting forces. Sacrifices will be justified with success on the battlefield.' He callously directed that the nation's food and infrastructure was destroyed, as ground was lost, to prevent their use by the Allies. It was a situation which led to Albert Speer, the Minister of Production, driving around the country imploring generals not to carry out the order – and most agreed not to, despite their oath of loyalty to Hitler. Speer was taking his life in his hands doing this, but courted further personal danger in trying to awaken Hitler to the reality of Germany's situation. On 18 March, for example, he sent Hitler a report which predicted the next stage of the breakdown of Germany: 'In four to eight weeks', he wrote, 'the final collapse of the German economy is certain ... after that the war cannot be continued.' Speer was not the only one trying to influence the Führer for Major-General Siegfried Westphal, Kesselring's Chief of Staff, also tried to tackle Hitler on the subject of the difficulties faced by the German people. He explains:

> Hitler became particularly uncomfortable when I mentioned the sufferings of the civilian population, who were beginning, in their desperation, to cease to regard our own troops as protectors but as ones whose presence threatened to bring about the loss of that little which still remained to them. Hitler deliberately avoided discussing this point, even though I answered one of his reproaches by saying that a 'behind-the-lines existence' was no longer possible in the cities of the West because of the misery reigning there. Only those who are acquainted with the atmosphere in which it was uttered appreciate that remark to the full.

The German armed forces had become unwilling accomplices in the destruction of their homeland and at every turn faced violence and suffering. In such difficult circumstances they had little option but to concentrate on their own problems, and for those digging in opposite Second Army, it was time well spent.

Montgomery had overseen provisional plans for the crossing of the Rhine – Operation Plunder – as early as the previous autumn, but the detailed planning began only as his troops embarked on their final approach to its west bank. He held his first full Plunder conference on 9 March at which Crerar, Dempsey and Simpson – the three army commanders concerned – gave presentations of their respective plans. Having been present at the meeting, Major-General Frank Simpson, a staff officer reporting to Brooke, wrote:

Each of the generals had his own very clear plans which, subject to one or two quite minor amendments made by Monty, were completely accepted. The whole conference could have taken no longer than two hours.

This really was to my mind an ideal way of arranging what was clearly going to be a most complex operation because in addition to the Rhine being historically symbolic as an obstacle, it was a very wide river indeed, and on some parts of the British front it was 500 yards wide, which meant that the crossing operations and the eventual bridging operations were very considerable.

I went back to London on March 10 with a very clear picture in my own mind as to what everyone was going to do and was able to put the CIGS fully in the picture.

With the general scheme agreed, Monty issued his orders and left his subordinate formations to begin their detailed planning and preparation. Operation Plunder was to begin on the evening of 23 March and would use XXX Corps and XII Corps of British Second Army to attack on the left with 51 (Highland) Division, 15 (Scottish) Division and 1 Commando Brigade, whilst XVI Corps of US Ninth Army struck on the right with 30 and 79 US Divisions. Two divisions of XVIII US Airborne Corps – 6 British and 17 US Airborne Divisions – were to provide support in Operation Varsity. The initial aim of Operation Plunder Varsity was to seize Wesel and create a bridgehead, the depth of which 'was to be sufficient to provide room to form up major forces for the drive to the east and north-east'. The general objective was 'to secure a bridgehead prior to developing operations to isolate the Ruhr and thrust to the heart of Germany'. It was to be an attack of 'such drive and strength' that the enemy would be swiftly overwhelmed and it would thus lead 'quickly to final victory in the campaign'.

Waiting on the east bank, totally unaware of what Monty was

planning, were Schlemm's men: General Eugen Meindl's II Parachute Corps, consisting of 12,000 men in 6, 7 and 8 Parachute Divisions, and the 8,000 men of 84 and 180 Divisions in General Erich Straube's LXXXVI Corps. Supplementing this meagre but capable force was the equivalent of another three weak divisions found in local training units and depots, whilst the Volkssturm – a national militia which conscripted males between the ages of 16 and 60 who were not already serving – and other quasi-military organizations provided another 30,000 untrained men lacking equipment. There was also a local armoured reserve which, owing to the German inability to pinpoint exactly where the Allied strike on the Rhine would fall, was held 15 miles to the north-east of Emmerich. General Heinrich von Lüttwitz's XLVII Panzer Corps consisted of 116 Panzer Division with 70 tanks and 15 Panzer Grenadier Division, which boasted 15 tanks and some 20–30 assault guns. It was in the hope that Blaskowitz at Army Group H and his corps commander might withhold the armoured reserve if they were kept guessing about the true extent of the offensive, and where its centre of gravity lay, that the planners decided to stagger the river crossings: the first division was to attack at 2100 hours and the last six hours later. Up until the armoured reserve was released, the defenders on the east bank would be heavily reliant on their artillery, which was extremely limited. For example, 84 Division was supported by a mere 50 medium and field guns. Schlemm therefore placed considerable faith in the Rhine itself initially slowing the Allied assault enough for him to concentrate his forces. He hoped that if the Allies did manage to make a lodgement, it could be contained and destroyed later when the armoured reserve pushed them back into the Rhine. Whilst driving around his sector to organize his local commanders, Schlemm was confident and encouraging, but privately he harboured many fears:

> Our intelligence was very poor – it is very difficult for an army in
> reverse to look forward – and we only had a vague idea of what

was facing us. Travelling around our positions it was clear that we were very stretched and morale was shaky ... My subordinates tried hard and did a good job with what little they had, but there was no doubt in my mind that anything other than a probe by Montgomery would defeat us. We might cause some local upsets with our characteristic counterattacks, but not much more.

Considering the weakness of the German forces on the east bank of the Rhine, Operation Plunder Varsity might be considered an extravagant and unnecessary luxury. The Allies had a very clear picture of their enemy's strengths and weaknesses because their sophisticated intelligence machine was producing huge amounts of information. Aerial reconnaissance photographs in particular revealed valuable details about Schlemm's defensive positions which could be turned into detailed targeting information for the many thousands of guns that were being massed for the operation. It may, therefore, have been tempting for Montgomery to regard the German forces defending the Rhine as little more than a speed-bump on his road to the German heartland. But he didn't, believing after Arnhem that they still deserved respect. Hürtgen and the Ardennes had shown their remarkable recuperative powers after seemingly devastating military reverses. Moreover, the Field Marshal did not accept that the strategic situation warranted the sort of risk-taking that he felt appropriate for Operation Market Garden. There were also practical fighting issues to consider, such as the difficulty of making a successful assault crossing of a wide river against prepared enemy positions. In such circumstances, the British reasoned, the attack needed to be large and extremely powerful, which led to it being complicated. The Americans in particular were dismissive of what Bradley called 'an unnecessarily overblown British contribution', pointing to their success at Remagen as an example of what could be attained with boldness, flair and a willingness to seize opportunities. But Montgomery remained unabashed, knowing that the great American luck surrounding their crossing had come about as a result of the Germans massing in the north to defend against the British. Indeed, Albert Kesselring was later extremely complimentary about Twenty-First Army Group's concept of operations:

> Montgomery had the most difficult of assignments; his armies, which had suffered great losses in the preceding battle west of the Rhine, were confronted by a most formidable obstacle, defended by divisions with a recognized combat tradition ... The technical preparations for this manoeuvre were exemplary, however, and the massing of forces was commensurate with the undertaking and the Allies' resources.

Operation Plunder Varsity might also be considered a conservative plan, particularly in the way in which the airborne forces were used. Whilst Operation Market dropped widely dispersed airborne forces up to 60 miles behind enemy lines and in front of the ground forces, Operation Varsity sought to insert its divisions side by side and just a couple of miles beyond the enemy. In fact, they were to land so close to the river that they needed to be dropped the morning after the river crossing if they were not to be bombarded by British guns supporting the assault. Once on the ground the airborne force was to help secure the bridgehead by taking key ground along with bridges over the River Issel, which would not only be important for the subsequent breakout but also be crucial for defending the bridgehead against German armoured counterattacks. It was a plan similar to that followed in Normandy and allowed the divisions to fight well within their capabilities.

The reasons for this distinctly unadventurous airborne scheme included intelligence reports which suggested that the Germans expected a parachute and glider operation in the Wesel area. Kesselring, Blaskowitz and Schlemm all agreed that with FAAA available and the flat, open ground behind the river providing perfect LZs and DZs, the temptation for Allied commanders to use airborne troops would be too great. First Parachute Army tried to develop some anti-airborne defences by deploying some armour in the woods by the open fields to provide mobile firepower support, and positioned 712 light and 114 heavy flak guns in the Emmerich–Bocholt–Wesel triangle. As Monty said, when aerial reconnaissance photographs revealed heavy concentrations of flak: 'From their location it seemed clear that the enemy anticipated the use of airborne forces in our crossing operation.' Other reasons for the lack of imagination centred around a caution in the approach to utilizing airborne forces in the wake of Operation Market Garden, which derived from the lessons learned from that Dutch experience. Specifically, Market Garden had highlighted the need for the following: intelligence-based planning; greater respect for the German ability to react to airborne operations; caution when intelligence identified enemy armour in or near the area of operations; the insertion of divisions in a single lift; DZs and LZs close to objectives; the use of gliders for *coup de main* tasks; the need to take bridges from both ends; the relief of airborne forces by ground forces within 48 hours; the ability to call on supporting artillery fire from the ground forces, and close air support. These lessons were so pervasive that none of the Allied airborne formations were left untouched by them. It was therefore disingenuous of Lieutenant-Colonel Clifford Norbury, who was on the 6 British Airborne staff, to say:

In 6th Airborne we reckoned we had nothing to learn from 1st Airborne Division, as we were better at planning our operations and always considered it essential to jump or land as close to our objectives as possible. After Normandy we also appreciated that on a night drop a high percentage of kit and troops went astray – hence the daylight drop on the Rhine . . . and fortunately, we had enough aircraft for us all to go in one lift.

The lessons percolated through FAAA down to the planning teams. Brigadier James Hill, commander of 3 Parachute Brigade, says:

> I was left in no doubt that my plan was to be scrutinized for elements that were inconsistent with the conclusions of the several papers that were written in the wake of Market Garden. I have to say that although it was of course sensible to learn from previous experiences, there was a temptation to be overly protective of troops which, if they are devoid of surprise and audacity, lack a reason for being.

With the frailties of airborne warfare having been so cruelly exposed by the Germans during Operation Market Garden, Montgomery and XVIII US Airborne Corps (which was responsible for the Varsity plan) were keen to show its strengths and deliver success. The two divisions chosen for Varsity provided an excellent blend of experience and zeal. Whilst Major-General Eric Bols' 6 British Airborne Division had performed excellently in Normandy the previous year, Major-General William 'Bud' Miley's 17 US Airborne Division was yet to make its first combat jump. To rectify this the 82nd Airborne's 507 PIR was transferred to Miley on its return from the Continent to give the 17th some instant experience.

Yet, even whilst the regiment was bedding-in during the winter, both Varsity divisions were rushed to Belgium to help restore the situation in the Ardennes. By the time that the formations returned to their bases in February 1945 – 6th Airborne in England and the 17th Airborne in France – they were battle-hardened but needed to reorganize and recuperate quickly before the Rhine crossings. By early March, both formations were deeply involved in their preparations, which led to a flurry of activity with the divisions and brigades producing their plans. James Hill visited 9 Para at its camp in Netheravon to outline his 3 Parachute Brigade scheme to its CO,

Lieutenant-Colonel Napier Crookenden, and his officers. Listening intently to the charismatic young brigadier as he pointed to maps, aerial photographs and three-dimensional models, Crookenden and his team were impressed:

> As he went on to describe the task and the plan of the Brigade, the dozen or so people present pressed a little closer to the model, breathed a little more quietly and gave the concentrated silent attention to the one man speaking, characteristic of all briefings for a battle.

Hill was keen to impress on his audience the fact that the divisional plan had gone to great lengths to mitigate the many risks that are inherent in all airborne operations. He ended by saying:

> Gentlemen, the artillery and air support is fantastic. And if you are worried about the kind of reception you'll get, just put your-self in the place of the enemy. Beaten and demoralized, pounded by our artillery and bombers, what would you think, gentlemen, if you saw a horde of ferocious, bloodthirsty paratroopers bristling with weapons, cascading down upon you from the skies?

Having heard Hill's presentation, Crookenden felt that his battalion was well placed to undertake the role that the brigadier asked of it, but admits that 'the presentation of such a plan in practice produced a queer but well-known feeling in the stomach'.

As the airborne plans were completed in the units, preparations for the ground offensive reached their climax. In the days following 10 March, the British and Americans took up positions overlooking the Germans on the east bank of the Rhine, and there began a game of cat-and-mouse which continued until D-Day. The Germans were desperate to deny the Allies observation of their defensive positions, and Schlemm's divisions immediately tested their gunners by asking them to destroy potential observation points. Gunner Heinrich Balck remembers:

> We received orders to take down a church spire on the opposite side of the river. We were given the coordinates, made the necessary calculations, adjusted the gun and fired six shots. The first two and the fifth missed, but the other three managed to do the job ... We were just in the process of congratulating ourselves, when we ourselves came under artillery fire. The first round dropped about 20 metres short and we threw ourselves to the ground. Before we had managed to dive into our slit trenches, a second round screamed down and was very close. The third did the job. A direct hit – our gun was destroyed. The enemy had spotted us when we fired on the church. We thought a little more carefully before firing our gun after that.

Meanwhile, any movement on the east bank was either noted by an observer with his binoculars, photographed by an airman or targeted by the guns. Allied aircraft also attacked, with a series of strikes across the front on enemy defensive positions, communications centres, gun batteries and other targets. For the first couple of days, the Germans tried to build and develop their positions during daylight hours, but the deadly attention that they attracted soon made them nocturnal. Although safer, working in the dark did cause some problems, as Corporal Heinz Kempa describes:

> I had been asked to provide a telephone link between some flak positions in and around the Diersfordter Wald. The job took two or three times as long as it ought to because we couldn't see what we were doing. No light was allowed whatsoever. Everyone was extremely conscious that we were being watched, and we paid a

great deal of attention to camouflaging our work and concealing any new gun or vehicle that came into our sector. It was a time-consuming business, but absolutely vital.

The Allies also took precautions, the first of which was to remove all civilians from the area where they were building up their attacking forces for fear that they might pass on important information to the enemy. In the end, some 24,000 people were removed from the vicinity and into the town of Bedburg 45 miles away. The British and American formations also observed very strict radio protocol, with no unnecessary communication being made and telephones being used whenever possible. Other security measures included a rule that reconnaissance parties were not allowed closer than 1,000 yards from the west bank when observing the enemy lines.

The British also used artificial fog to mask their preparations from the enemy's view. Portable generators pumped out a thick toxic blanket during the day which left a greasy residue on anything it touched. Captain Michael Williams, a British medical officer, found that a large number of the troops reacted badly to the fog and his workload suddenly increased:

We received the usual complaints: coughs, cuts, sprains and other soft-tissue injuries. But we also saw a great influx of men with rashes, puffy, weeping eyes, respiratory difficulties and nausea with the fog . . . One man who came to see me could hardly breathe and was in a desperate state. His treatment was simple, however: he was sent ten miles behind the lines and here recovered his health quickly. He made a point of returning to his battalion for the attack and I doubt that he ever suffered from the condition again.

The fog was loathed by the troops as it coated their skin, permeated their uniforms and tainted their food. Indeed, one Twenty-First Army report noted: 'Our soldiers would prefer that the Germans could see them.'

The cover provided by the fog allowed Dempsey to bring forward the necessaries for his assault across the Rhine 24 hours a day with impunity. The remarkable build-up included: 250,000 men, 5,500 artillery pieces, 256,000 tons of supplies and 32,000 vehicles including nearly 700 tanks, and scores of assault craft, storm boats and amphibious vehicles. It required a tremendous effort to keep this operation secret, organize its movement and distribute it correctly. As Dempsey later said:

It was this sort of unglamorous work that is at the heart of any military success. There are many unsung heroes in any operation and Plunder had more than many. We had just a few days to get everything that we needed, where it had to be. The potential for chaos was great, but it all went extremely well.

Time was also built into the programme for units to conduct full briefings. For example, 314 Regiment of 79 US Division had its intelligence team set up a hall that was full of important information about the formation's objectives:

A sand table, 8ft by 6ft, was prepared covering the actual crossing of the Rhine. Each house, road and railroad track was represented by pieces of wood and the river and woods by coloured dyes. Each grid square on the 1/25,000 map was blown up one foot by one foot. Upon completion each battalion was allotted sufficient time so that their platoon leaders could be present at the table for orientation. Each company was allotted two hours each for its officer.

Units also trained for specific tricky tasks and 79 US Division went to great lengths to find places behind the line that were similar to those being attacked by its troops. A stretch of the River Maas, for example, was used to represent the Rhine and hosted a number of mock assaults. Here the troops practised lifting their boats over a 25ft dyke before launching them into the water. Private Ralph Albert and his group found this particularly difficult: 'Although we practised over and over again, every damn time one or other of us would trip, slip or drop the boat as we raced up the slippery slope in the dark. After several days it was no longer a joke and we dreaded the real thing.' Nevertheless, they persevered until they got it right. Units also mastered the art of embarking and disembarking from craft in a variety of situations; taking control of boats and amphibious craft in case their crews became casualties; storming riverbank trenches; climbing the steep dykes in heavy equipment; unloading landing craft – there was plenty to learn. To provide added value, the division always tried to involve the specialists from other arms that would be supporting their troops: the engineers; tank crews; boat crews; FOOs; headquarters groups and the like. In this way an understanding was developed which led to close cooperation and allowed for some last-minute fine-tuning of the plans. There was also an opportunity to fine-tune various pieces of essential equipment: some of the Buffaloes, for example, rather disconcertingly failed to work when they took to the water, and Storm Boat engines often failed until it was found that they preferred a certain kind of synthetic oil.

Having conducted its assault-crossing training, units of 153 Brigade of 51 (Highland) Division practised taking certain key objectives. Sergeant Rick Andrews explains:

We were told that there was a potentially tricky German strong-point covering a road junction just in front of our company objective. A week before the off we were taken into a barn where a model of the position had been made by battalion headquarters, and we were shown aerial reconnaissance photographs of the position. It was remarkable, all for a strong-point. We'd cleared scores of these in our time . . . But I was flabbergasted when we were taken by truck to a similar road junction behind our lines where a mock strong-point had been established and manned by men from another regiment. We practised on it for two days . . . That training made us feel strong and when it came to the attack, we took the strong-point in about five minutes – it was empty!

Although there was not the time to conduct training in all of the special skills required for the Rhine crossing, nor to prepare for every eventuality, troops believed that the instruction that they received was extremely helpful. Major David Moores of 15 (Scottish) Division head-quarters contends:

The time spent before a set-piece attack is usually so rushed that you hardly have the time for reconnaissance and orders, or so protracted that you become lax and unfocused. Idle soldiers are a dangerous bunch because they get bored, idle officers are a dangerous bunch because they tinker. But prior to Operation Plunder there was none of this, we had time to rest, but we also had the space and resources to prepare for our missions thoroughly. It gave the men so much confidence and, importantly, filled their minds with useful information rather than allowing them to fill themselves with images of what might be.

The date of the offensive was kept from the troops until the morning of 23 March – D-Day. The men of 1 Commando Brigade were informed by Lieutenant-General Sir Neil Ritchie, the commander of XII Corps, when he gathered them together in the factory where they were billeted to make a speech. After days of waiting the time had finally come – they were going to cross the River Rhine. Ritchie's words made them feel proud to be part of such an important undertaking: 'I think, although my knowledge of military history is a little rusty', he said, 'that you will be the first British troops ever to cross this river. Not even Marlborough attempted it.' Such words made the enormity of what they were about to undertake sink in. They gave Trooper Bob Nunn of 46 Royal Marine Commando 'a sinking feeling' which, he says, was made all the worse because it was such a beautiful morning. The corps commander stepped down from the wooden pallet that was acting as a podium to be replaced by the popular and inspirational brigade commander, Brigadier Derek Mill-Roberts. He spoke softly and slowly at first, but his pace and volume increased as the minutes passed and he gave a passionate performance. Mill-Roberts ended with a parody of Winston Churchill's famous speech: 'Never in the history of human warfare have so many guns supported so few men. When you go in tonight, cut *hell* out of them.' He stepped down amidst a crescendo of clapping and cheering. Having been dismissed, the men of 1 Commando Brigade had the rest of the day to themselves, but as Bob Nunn says:

> We were too enthused, too excited and could talk about nothing but the operation. We just lay on our bunks or gathered in small groups to talk while checking weapons and ammunition yet again. I remember I couldn't even eat, and one of my mates, who did get his dinner, went sick with nerves not long after.

Within the attacking formations along the Rhine, there was considerable anxiety that afternoon. In the headquarters, staff officers hoped that everything that could be done, had been done, desperate not to let their units down. David Moores worked in Operations (G3) and was exhausted by the planning and preparation process:

> It was not so much the time that we spent on getting our part of

the operation right – although that was considerable – it was the intensity and the mental strain. Things needed to be turned around quickly and so there were bursts of action, and then my mind would have to turn to something else. I had to think on my feet and try to keep up the highest standard of work because I knew that lives depended on the accuracy of what I was doing. That responsibility can wear a chap down, and in the days before the operation I slept poorly – I'm not sure whether that was because my head was spinning, or because I kept thinking about the men of the division having to cross that blasted river in the teeth of the enemy's defences.

Meanwhile, as the sun began to drop behind the Allied lines, the officers and men of the attacking units made their final preparations. Most had spent some time that day quietly thinking about their role, ensuring that their equipment was in perfect working order and that their men were ready and organized. The critical importance of the Rhine to the Germans had been talked about for so long that few of them believed a crossing would be anything other than an extremely tough assignment. Nothing they had recently seen persuaded them otherwise. Why else would such a huge operation be taking place? Why else had so many senior officers been seen so close to the front? 'Everything pointed towards this being the big one', says Sapper Bill Potts, 'and it made many of us nervous. Fear? Yes, I was afraid – who wasn't?' These soldiers feared being killed or maimed, but they also feared failure. Failure to perform to the high standards expected, and failure to achieve objectives. But above all else, they did not want to let their mates down. Sergeant Rick Andrews describes the waiting:

I tried not to think about things too deeply, but as the hours ticked by, I could not help it. It was clear that everyone in the platoon was going through the same torture, and so someone began to sing to take our minds off things. It was as though we were as one. We had been through so much together and I would not let them down.

Few of the waiting troops had a clear idea of what sort of enemy reaction awaited them on the opposite bank. Those with vivid imaginations suffered the worst. 'The most debilitating aspect of being a replacement without experience is that you have nothing to use as a benchmark for reality', explains Private Nobby Clarke, 'I had only been with the [Highlanders] a couple of weeks and had never been under fire and my imagination ran wild. Fear of the unknown was a dangerous thing.' On the afternoon of the 23rd, whilst some were 'enthused' others were understandably concerned about the attack. As a consequence some tried to confront death for the first time. Scottish infantryman Corporal Alistair Trewin made a simple entry in his diary next to the date 23 March: 'Today I will die. I have no doubt about this and am ready for it. Please God, make it quick.' (He survived.) American 154 Infantry Regiment soldier John Bird, meanwhile, just wanted to get the whole thing over with:

If I was going to die, fine, just don't keep me waiting. That last afternoon there was a great deal of false bravado going around and I wanted none of it. I wrote home, tried to get some sleep and check my rifle – three times. It was the longest afternoon of my life. I just wanted to get it over with.

At 1500 hours Montgomery sent a message to the men of Twenty-First Army Group:

The enemy possibly thinks he is safe behind this great river obstacle. We all agree that it is a great obstacle; but we will show the enemy that he is far from safe behind it. This great Allied fighting machine, composed of integrated land air force, will deal with the problem in no uncertain manner. And having crossed the R. Rhine, we will crack about in the plains of Northern Germany, chasing the enemy from pillar to post ... Over the R. Rhine then, let us go. And good hunting to you all on the other side.

An hour later, he signalled the code words from his headquarters – 'Two If By Sea' – and in so doing launched the largest combined amphibious and airborne operation since 6 June 1944. There followed a 5,500-gun preliminary bombardment. 'The noise was ferocious', says Private Brian MacDonald of the Highlanders, 'and I nearly felt sorry for the poor sods on the other side – nearly!' Across the choppy water, Germany seemed to be aflame, exploding violently until it glowed red. The shells hammered some 1,000 pre-identified targets across the river: artillery positions, troop concentrations, headquarters, road junctions, strong-points, supply depots and the like. The aim was to make the enemy tactically deaf, dumb and blind and so unable to react to the Allied attack when it came. The high explosive shells seared into the German positions, destroying whatever they touched, ripping up the ground and clawing at buildings. Then the guns shifted their attention to the German front line along the east bank. The aim was the destruction of the German front-line positions and their occupants' will to fight. Explosion fell on explosion, and the bank began to splutter and boil. 'We were certain that nothing could have survived that', continues MacDonald, 'but then we had thought that before and I remembered that there was a week of bombardment before the battle of the Somme – and that didn't go so well.'

At 1900 hours the assault troops began their move to their jump-off positions. Dave Morris of the Commandos says: 'We had all blackened our faces and were loaded down with equipment. The quartermaster issued each of us with rum and biscuits and just after that there was a final mail delivery.' John Buckingham recalls that 45 (Royal Marine) Commando were assisted in their attempt to get to the riverbank by the gunners: 'Finding our way was easy because the Royal Artillery had a pair of Bofors guns firing two lines of red tracers to mark our route. We marched under the tracer and thousands of shells screamed over our heads and hit the enemy positions on the far bank.'

As 1 Commando Brigade organized themselves in preparation for their attack, 51 (Highland) Division began the first Plunder assault at 2100 hours. Two and a half minutes after their Buffaloes carrying the two lead battalions of 154 Brigade entered the cold swirling water of the Rhine, they landed on the east bank near Rees. The crossing had been far less traumatic than many of the troops had expected. The British, at last, had crossed the Rhine. Other formations followed along the front at intervals throughout the night. At 2200 hours, 1 Commando Brigade began its attack. Bob Nunn and 27 comrades climbed into their amphibious vehicle and headed towards the Rhine:

Our Buffalo skidded on the top of the dyke and seemed to slide down sideways. We entered the water with a huge splash that drenched most of the men inside. But the Buffalo ran quite smoothly, although low down, which seemed safer as the enemy shells which were pitching into the river appeared less dangerous. This was a fallacy we realized soon after when shrapnel and bullets began to hit us.

It took around four minutes to cross towards Wesel and they were met by Germans who fought hard for a while with small arms before being overwhelmed. One of them later complained: 'We couldn't see anything properly. The noise was terrible and we were blinded by the flashes. We thought they had landed tanks and couldn't understand where the men had come from.' Subsequent waves of Commandos also landed successfully and moved forward to join the lead elements just outside Wesel. Here they waited for a programmed RAF bombing raid on the town. This began at 2230 hours when 200 bombers dropped more than 1,100 tons of explosives. Royal Engineer Corporal Ramsey watched the scene unfold from the west bank:

It was like fireworks. First a rain of golden sparks as the leading aircraft dropped markers right over an enormous fire that already lit the town like a beacon. Then we heard the main force. It was a terrific sight. All colours of sparks flying off everywhere: red, green, yellow, and the fantastic concussion as the bombs went down. On our side of the river the ground shook and we could see waves of light shooting up into the smoke. It was like stoking a fire, the dull glow burst into flames and it was like daylight.

Canadian BBC correspondent Stewart MacPherson later wrote:

Bomber command delivered a crushing blow on the enemy in Wesel, while the commandos lay doddo over there, a bare thousand yards from the bomber target, and waited. Smack on time, Arthur Harris & Company, House Removers, as they were called by the commandos, arrived and delivered a nerve shaking blow on the former Wesel stronghold. Back at headquarters, minutes ticked by. Officers waited anxiously for word from the commandos across the river. Suddenly there was a signal, and a voice literally purred over the wireless: 'Noisy blighters, aren't they?'

The waiting Commandos were picked up and thrown down by the explosions, the breath was snatched from their gasping bodies and it felt as though their heads would be split open by the pressure. Getting to their feet once the 'removal men' had left for home, the soldiers were stunned and temporarily deafened. Nevertheless, they pushed quickly on to Wesel which they found ablaze. Some weak defences in the rubble manned by men of the 180 Division and some paratroopers were overcome, but then the attackers were confronted by another obstacle: their maps were useless. John Buckingham explains:

> The RAF had devastated the town: whole streets lay in ruins; the railway was a twisted lattice-work against the night sky; fires were raging out of control, and the Germans came out fighting . . . All our study of maps and photos was not much use amid such a shambles, and we scrambled around bomb-craters and over rubble, following the man in front, hoping someone remembered the way.

Stumbling forwards, some officers using a compass to keep their bearings, the brigade slowly penetrated the smoking ruins. There were occasional fire-fights, but resistance was pushed aside. By 0100 hours the entire brigade had managed to fight its way through to the centre of the town and began digging in. During the rest of the night, pockets of Germans were reduced, lines of communication were secured, counterattacks were repelled and the town fell, although it would take another 24 hours before it was completely free of the enemy. Scores of prisoners were taken in Wesel that night including a young machine gunner from Magdeburg: Gefrieter Hans-Dieter Steets. As soon as the bombing began, he and three colleagues had taken refugee in the cellar of the house at the front of his company's position. Several bombs had landed close, but there were no direct hits on the building, although the cellar steps were blocked by rubble. By the time the three dusty figures had managed to free themselves from their incarceration, the Commandos were waiting for them. Steets later wrote to his wife:

The cellar ceiling had fallen in and it took some time to remove the masonry around the door. We exited into a world that I did not recognize. None of the buildings that had been standing were more than shells, fires burned brightly and the streets were full of enemy troops. We raised our hands as soon as we saw them – and I was relieved. One of the Tommies smiled at me and nodded towards a line of prisoners that was forming nearby.

It was the first time Hans-Dieter had ever written to Winifred about his war, but by the time he penned this, he was safely ensconced in a prisoner of war camp in England. His war was over.

Monty's Rhine crossings continued through the night, and each was successful. Attacks by 15 (Scottish) Division and 30 US Division at 0200 hours encountered limited opposition, and by the time that 79 US Division took to the water an hour later, even that opposition had melted away. All three divisions quickly established themselves on the east bank and began to create their own bridgehead areas. In common with the earlier crossings, the formations benefited greatly from a stretched and under-resourced German defence which had been unhinged by the ferocious preliminary bombardment. However, by the time of the later attacks, a considerable number of defending troops had deserted their positions rather than wait to be attacked. From the scraps of information that Kesselring, Blaskowitz and Schlemm received from the front, the situation was discouraging, but they implored their troops to counterattack, whilst hoping that the fog of war would eventually clear. Conversely, by dawn, the Allies knew exactly what was going on and retained a firm hold on the initiative. Montgomery, Dempsey and Simpson reviewed the situation with pleasure. Allied troops, equipment, supplies and vehicles continued to cross the Rhine to help develop a burgeoning bridgehead. A firm lodgement had been made on the east bank of the Rhine; the forward German defences had largely been vanquished, seen off or contained; and casualties had been relatively light. 'Plunder began more successfully than any of us dared hope,' Dempsey later wrote. 'We had crossed the Rhine and so all the hard work had paid off.'

The Allies had gained a firm foothold on the German side of the River Rhine, and Montgomery had achieved an ambition that he had held since he had first discussed key objectives for north-west Europe with Dwight Eisenhower in early 1944. It had been completed after months of hard fighting which had seen the German armed forces systematically eroded to the point where, in spite of the river's natural defensive features, they no longer posed a serious threat to Allied offensive operations. Thus it could be argued that when Monty finally came to undertake an offensive to cross the River Rhine on 23 March 1945, his Operation Plunder was ponderous and over-resourced rather than dynamic and powerful. The truth was that the British commander was content to use a mixture of overwhelming superiority and meticulous preparation to make certain that his forces were successful. He did not see any need to rush the operation, believing that it was important at this stage in the war to preserve life and ensure that the Germans were not given a chance to strike back unexpectedly. Thus, on the morning of 24 March with a large integrated bridgehead still to be created and German counterattacks still a possibility, the battle had reached the point where the two Allied airborne divisions could be unleashed: Operation Varsity was about to fall on the Germans.

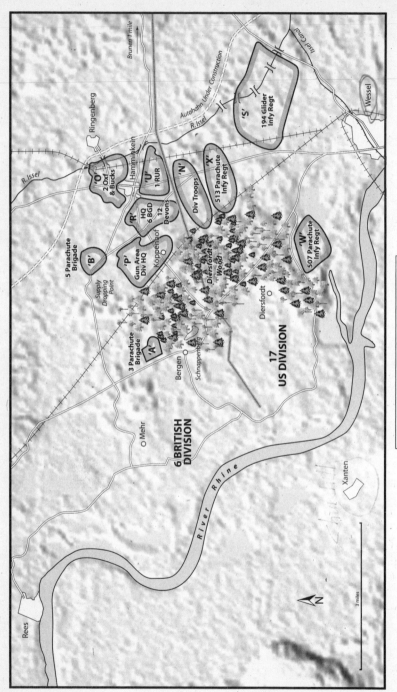

Map 10 : Operation Varsity

CHAPTER 10

Jumping the Rhine (II)

(Operation Varsity: 24–28 March 1945)

On the morning of 24 March 1945, Winston Churchill stood waiting at an Observation Post overlooking the River Rhine near Xanten. One enemy shell could have had disastrous consequences for the British war effort, as accompanying him were Field Marshals Alan Brooke and Bernard Montgomery as well as General Henry Crerar. The Prime Minister, dressed in an army uniform with a peaked service cap, stood puffing a trademark Romeo y Julieta cigar surveying the scene. They had finished a breakfast hamper, provided by Monty's Tac headquarters an hour before, and were now chatting, their conversations frequently interrupted by the booming guns which covered the hill. Churchill was happy, giddy even, for he never felt more alive than when he was at the front. It annoyed his hosts, who were responsible for the Prime Minister's safety, and Monty in particular did not enjoy the politician's self-indulgent visits as they took the soldier away from his work. The Field Marshal had managed to keep the frustrated general from observing the Normandy landings the previous summer, but he had recently found it more difficult to dissuade Churchill from popping over. Just three weeks ago, he and Alan Brooke had been invited by the Prime Minister to join him in urinating on the Siegfried Line. 'I shall never forget the childish grin of intense satisfaction that spread all over his face', Brooke noted, 'as he looked down at the critical moment!' Churchill had insisted on seeing the Rhine crossing as he perceived the event as a turning-point in the war: 'Like plunging a cold knife into Germany's ribs'.

At 0950 hours came the moment for which the Prime Minister had been waiting. Dakotas carrying the two Allied airborne divisions came rumbling low overhead, their open fuselage doors framing parachutists standing ready to jump. Churchill grinned and hopped from foot to foot shouting, 'They're here! They're here!' whilst pointing skywards, glancing over to his more staid colleagues for a reaction. The air armada flew straight over the Rhine and into a haze which hung over the east bank. However, just minutes later, the Prime Minister's demeanour changed as aircraft returned smoking, in flames and out of control. A Dakota crashed in a ball of flames just behind the party. The mighty Allied force was being shot out of the sky.

The airborne divisions had enjoyed a good flight from their airfields in south-eastern England and northern France. The weather was cool, the sky was clear and there was little wind. As the two streams of aircraft merged near Brussels, an immense air armada was formed – the largest ever – in which 21,680 paratroopers and glider troops were conveyed in 1,696 transport aircraft and 1,348 gliders, whilst nearly 900 fighters provided an escort. There had been a proposal for Operation Varsity to involve a third division to join 6 British and 17 US Airborne Divisions, but it was rejected because it would have required a second airlift. Keenly aware of the legacy of Operation Market Garden, Ridgway rejected the extra power that the formation would have provided for the advantages of a single lift. Moreover, the US XVIII Airborne Corps commander was convinced that two divisions were adequate for the task, particularly as the Germans had suffered so grievously in the battle of the Rhineland:

An airborne division is a single entity and if carved into separate parts it becomes vulnerable ... In any case, two divisions were more than capable of achieving the aims that had been' agreed. The Germans had been dealt a blow defending the Rhine, and were considerably weaker than they had been just four weeks earlier.

The decision to insert the corps over just an hour, whilst ensuring that its battalions were landed close to their objectives, was an important one. The plan was for the two divisions to help develop the Operation Plunder bridgehead, and as the requirements of the airborne forces were met, Ridgway was convinced that the German defences would be unhinged and a rapid breakout would be possible. The wily soldier also reckoned that the mere arrival of such a force over the heads of the enemy would have a disadvantageous psychological impact on their ability to conduct coherent defensive operations: 'The Krauts will pee themselves', he advised Bud Miley.

That morning, the awesome sight of the two divisions in the air at the same time certainly drew the attention of everybody that they flew over. Lieutenant-Colonel Peter Harris, watching from just outside Brussels, admits that he had a tear in his eye as he saw the aircraft surge towards the Rhine: 'In that moment I knew that we had won the war. I was watching history unfold. For me, it was a defining moment of the war.'

Lance-Sergeant Ronnie Joyce, a British gunner, was also impressed and made his first diary entry in three weeks:

24 March: Weather fine and clear. At 9 o'clock an air fleet flying towards Germany came overhead. At first we thought that they were bombers, but then saw they were airborne transporters. They were in what seemed like endless lines. This has got to mean that the war will end soon.

Few people could have failed to be mesmerized by the massed aircraft and the potential for those pods of violence to crush the enemy: a physical representation of the Allies' military superiority which acted as a reminder of what was in store for the Fatherland. It was enough to make German prisoners glad that they were safe. Paul Gerber, 19 years old, had been one of the first prisoners taken by British troops during Operation Plunder. He was astounded by what he saw:

> We were ferried across the Rhine in an amphibious vehicle during the night, and held until dawn near the riverbank. During the morning we were marched to the rear through huge numbers of British troops, tanks and vehicles and stores. We were amazed at what we saw . . .
>
> And then the aircraft arrived. Thousands of them. It made me shudder. Didn't the generals realize what we were facing, that we could not win the war? The Rhine had been crossed and, by the look of things, the British were in a position to carry on to Berlin! I already knew that we would lose the war, but now I knew that we would lose the war very soon.

Flying a couple of thousand feet above their awe-struck audience, a numbing tension suddenly gripped the airborne soldiers as the German border approached. Over the previous couple of days, these men had felt a complicated mixture of apprehension and excitement at the prospect of going into action: apprehension because of the vicissitudes of airborne warfare and a concern at what would be waiting for them in Germany, and excitement at taking part in such a massive offensive. They were told (as they always were) that the operation would hasten the end of the war. As a consequence, the atmosphere at the airfields that morning had been intense, as the adjutant of 507 PIR describes:

The air was pregnant with tense expectancy. Strained jokes were cracked, they were greeted with brittle laughter and wisecrack banter. This was it – D-Day – the biggest D-Day, the day for which countless hours of sweaty toil had been shaping us. The 507th was this day to take part in a jump into the Fatherland itself. The apex of every paratrooper's dream was becoming a reality.

The task that the XVIII US Airborne Corps had been asked to fulfil was tactical rather than strategic. Ridgway's men were not to seize an objective that was of immediate strategic significance, but to create the conditions in which major objectives could be taken. Thus, although the tasks that the divisions were asked to carry out fell well within the classic airborne repertoire, Operation Varsity was a very different type of operation to Market Garden and much more akin to that undertaken in Normandy. The formations were to take key ground objectives and bridges, secure their area against German counterattack, and link up with the advancing ground forces. Eric Bols' division was to dominate the ground, produce a firm front and seize bridges over the River Issel in the northern part of the corps' area, whilst Bud Miley's division was to do the same in the south. As Ridgway said: 'our priority is to protect the developing ground-force lodgement on the east bank of the Rhine, our second [aim] is to provide the means for a breakout to win the war'.

All of 6 British Airborne Division's units had fought in Normandy, although some of the replacements that had joined the formation when it returned to England had not made a combat jump before. In 17 US Airborne Division, however, only Colonel Edson Raff's 507 PIR had previously jumped into action and he hoped that Varsity would prove a less exacting experience than that of the previous summer. 'I was more nervous on the Rhine operation than I had been before Normandy because that was just so horrible', says Private Teddy Smith of 1st Battalion, 'there I jumped out of a burning plane, was wounded whilst in the air, nearly drowned in a swamp and then had to attack a gun. And that was just the first ten minutes.' But whether experienced or not, pre-insertion nerves were just something airborne troops had to expect and indeed cope with. Lieutenant-Colonel Napier Crookenden, the commanding officer of 9 Para, found that after his battalion's extremely testing time during Normandy, one man had decided not to accompany the battalion to Germany:

I was getting into my jeep for a final tour of the battalion's aircraft, lined up around the perimeter track, when I heard the sound of a shot. Driving down the line I found one of my sergeants lying on the ground, looking ruefully at the ugly mess of his right foot. He was whisked away in a jeep and subsequently faced a court martial for a self-inflicted wound. I later discovered he had done it because his wife threatened to leave him if he ever jumped again.

It was an incident that shook the sergeant's platoon at a time when they were exposed, and their flight into battle was all the more nerve-racking because of it. In other aircraft, however, the soldiers' banter quickly diminished as on entering the fuselage they became more focused and thoughtful. The journeys were long and boring, and so any incident that brought some light relief was welcomed, as 6th Airborne's Ernest Rooke-Matthews explains:

Most of the lads settled down for a kip. The urine bucket was passed around, and used ... To watch a paratrooper with full gear, bag strapped to his leg, strapped into a parachute harness, with about five layers of clothing, trying to perform in an aircraft that is not exactly flying stable like a modern-day airliner, is a sight worthy of the music hall and guaranteed to assist the relaxation [of the watchers]. The sick-bucket was also christened.

Meanwhile, the glider troops tried to forget that they were in what some referred to as 'army-sanctioned death-traps', but inevitably their thoughts turned to equally gloomy subjects. Private Denis Edwards of the OBLI, for example, harboured deep concerns fighting in the enemy's homeland 'where the Germans could be relied upon to fight with more determination than ever'. His views were shared by a platoon sergeant of his acquaintance who, Edwards explains had a premonition while waiting to emplane that his aircraft was fated and doomed:

> He ran off, only to be later detained, tried, stripped of his rank and sentenced to military detention. He might well have received a more severe sentence than a few months' detention had it not been for the fact that premonition was justified. The glider in which he would have travelled took a direct hit and was destroyed with no survivors.

The first aircraft to arrive over the Rhine were those carrying the parachute formations: the British on the left and the Americans on the right. There was no need for Pathfinders as it was a daylight drop with many obvious landmarks: the Rivers Rhine and Issel, Hamminkeln, the Diersfordter Wald and the ruined Wesel. The soldiers tried to catch a glimpse of the Rhine as they passed, the mother of their current predicament, the infamous watercourse upon which hung so much strategic import.

Private Doug Jilks of 3 Parachute Brigade recalls:

> I could see columns of transport below. I was wondering what they were thinking about down below; it must certainly have been an impressive sight ... We were told to hook up. I began to perspire now, and I could feel a sudden coldness in my stomach. It was only a matter of minutes now, I thought. One of the

fellows shouted, 'Look, there's the Rhine!' I looked out of the little window behind me to take a look at this river which we had journeyed so far to cross; it was just like a ribbon of silver as the sun shone on it. Flak was beginning to creep up at us now. Everyone was tensed.

In crossing the river, the airborne soldiers recognized that they were but minutes away from landing on German soil and braced themselves for the flak barrage. It began with a few desultory puffs, but soon became dangerous and, as Winston Churchill and his party saw, some of the aircraft were hit. With every passing minute, the Germans got more guns into action and they coughed their fury into the sky. The Allied artillery had fired a preliminary bombardment on known enemy defensive positions that morning, and then spent another half-hour specifically targeting known anti-aircraft guns, but many remained active whilst others now revealed themselves for the first time. As soon as the Allied bombardment ceased with the arrival of the transporters over the Rhine, the shaken German gunners dragged themselves out of their cellars, slit trenches and bunkers to prepare their guns for action. Lieutenant Otto Leitner had spent the previous two days ensuring that his four 20mm anti-aircraft guns were properly sited and defended. He had been ordered to the area because 'of the very real possibility of an airborne attack in the area of the Diersfordter Wald'. He was at his billet-cum-headquarters, a small farmhouse near the woods, when he first heard – and then saw – the approaching Allied aircraft:

I jumped up and ran outside as our guns started to open fire. It took a moment before they latched on to one of the transporters, but quickly winged one. They were so low and slow. It kept on its course: it was hit in the fuselage, lurched dramatically to the left and plunged earthwards. A couple of its parachutists tried to jump clear, but they hit the ground without their parachutes opening just as their aircraft crumpled into the ground.

The German aim was to try to destroy the attack before it could get started by targeting the airborne troops whilst they were at their weakest and most vulnerable. The Germans were trained to provide a remorseless wall of anti-aircraft and machine-gun fire against the airborne troops when in their aircraft, floating to earth, exiting their gliders, recovering their equipment or rallying. The Dakota carrying Lieutenant Peter Elliot Forbes of 9 Para was hit by light ack-ack:

> The red 'stand-by' light was on, and we were waiting for the green 'Go!' when the port engine, only yards away from the door, burst into orange flames and black smoke – either hit by flak or over-stressed. The jump-master screamed for us to get back from the door and ran up to the cockpit; fortunately the 'green' did not come on. This was accompanied by a violent lurch back to the left which almost chucked us out of the door and through the flames ... The pilot did an excellent job, flying the machine on one engine, the flames were put out, we scrambled back to our seats and I consumed what was left of my whisky. We landed an hour later in Louvain.

Leitner explains that 'with so many aircraft it was difficult not to hit something. I ordered my men to keep firing in the hope that by filling the sky with metal, some of it would do some damage.' As a result of this unscientific but extremely successful tactic, the Dakotas were peppered by pieces of shell and small-arms fire. A number of men were wounded whilst waiting to jump, and as a result most exits were extremely fast – one launched himself into the sunlight shouting 'Here we come, you square-headed bastards!' – but once in the air he was then at the mercy of sharpshooters as he dangled beneath his parachute. Ken Williams of 8 Para says that a number of his comrades in arms were wounded or killed before they hit the ground, but the closest he came to disaster was when 'one piece of metal tore a hole through my parachute making me so worried that I didn't notice the ground coming up fast and hit with a hell of a wallop which completely winded me'. Each unit of XVIII Airborne Corps was affected by the anti-aircraft barrage as they tried to land on their DZs and LZs, and for some, it accounted for the largest portion of the casualties during Operation Varsity. It meant that as soon as they landed, the men of 6th and 7th Airborne were fighting for their lives. But if they survived long enough to form up for an attack, the German defenders were well aware that they would be fighting for their lives as well.

Brigadier James Hill's 3 Parachute Brigade arrived just to the north of the Diersforter Wald into a curtain of German small-arms fire. Lieutenant-Colonel George Hewetson's 8 Para, for example, was tasked with securing the DZ and the elimination of German positions located on the edge of the adjacent forest. These positions, in common with many others like them across the corps' area of operations, had been specifically developed to counter an airborne drop. This meant that they were secreted in the fringes of woods overlooking the open spaces that were likely DZs and LZs, and consisted not only of anti-aircraft batteries but also a sprinkling of armour and infantry armed with rifles, sub-machine guns, machine guns and mortars. During the Allies' preliminary bombardment these teams took sanctuary in cellars, trenches and fox-holes, but as soon as the shells stopped they immediately manned their defences. Panzer Grenadier Rolf Siegel was in a position covering 8 Para's DZ with five others:

We had dug a slit trench on the fringes of the wood – it was hard work digging through the roots – but it was deep and secure. I was the trigger man on an MG-42, an excellent weapon, and with this we were confident that we could do some damage if airborne troops landed. During the artillery barrage, we pressed ourselves into our trenches – they didn't seem quite deep enough then – only to re-emerge as the first aircraft arrived. By the time that we had set up the gun, parachutists were in the air. Within a few minutes there were hundreds of them, and many were collecting together at various places. I am sure that we must have drawn attention to ourselves, because one group fell on us quickly.

During the landings, Siegel claims to have accounted for perhaps 20 British paratroopers, but suggests that it may have been fewer as those landing were caught in the crossfire of several machine guns. The fearsome ripping sound that was made by the rapid-firing MG-42s has never been forgotten by Ken Williams, and he says that plans were immediately made to silence them: 'The Jerries were firing at us but nobody seemed to pay them much attention, they were too busy getting ready to attack them.' Such dynamism would have been applauded by Brigadier Hill, who had stated clearly in his operational orders that 'Speed and initiative is the order of the day. Risks will be taken. The enemy will be attacked and destroyed wherever he is found.' Thus Siegel became the object of considerable British ire:

As soon as the paratroopers began to attack us, that was the time to pack up and go – as were our instructions. We were to do as much damage to the landings as possible, and then withdraw to a prearranged place in the woods. However, we were too slow, and found that the artillery had done considerable damage around us and so we struggled to find our way out. One of my colleagues was shot between the shoulders as he left the trench, and I was wounded by a grenade soon after. I was lucky to have been knocked unconscious, because when I came to, the rest of the team were dead.

In a series of small actions such as this, 8 Para cleared the Germans from woods and secured the DZ. Some lightly manned positions were overrun quickly, but certain strong-points fought hard and required several attempts to overcome them. A platoon-strength force from B Company, for example, tackled twice their number in the south-eastern corner of the DZ, but was beaten off, leaving a subaltern and the company commander dead. The position was eventually taken by another platoon using a barrage of mortars and some successful fire and manoeuvre, but they suffered casualties in doing so. The Germans were being overcome, but not without a struggle and sacrifice.

Arriving on the DZ immediately behind 8 Para was Brigadier Hill and his headquarters, followed by 1 Canadian Para. This battalion was to clear the south-eastern corner of the DZ and then move into Diersfordter Wald to occupy its western side along with a section of the main road that runs from Wesel to Emmerich. However, the old military dictum that plans do not survive first contact with the enemy could have been conceived with the Canadians in mind, as events conspired against the battalion from the start. Lieutenant-Colonel Jeff Nicklin, the commanding officer, failed to arrive at the RV and Major John Hanson, the commander of C Company, broke his collar-bone on landing. To make a distressing situation even worse, one of the platoons reported that the battalion's chaplain, Captain Kenny, had been killed during his landing. Nevertheless, drawing on training which prepared each man to take over the job of another at least one rank higher than his own, Major Fraser Eadie – the battalion second-in-command – stepped into the breach and sent the companies off to their objectives. These were achieved quickly and efficiently, but not without A Company becoming involved in a nasty little battle to clear some buildings designated for use by battalion headquarters. An initial attack having been repelled, CSM George Green organized some covering fire, stormed a house and fought to clear it at close quarters. Moving on to take the other houses by similar method, Green was later awarded the Distinguished Conduct Medal for his 'contempt of danger' and for being an 'inspiration to the men'.

Elsewhere, patrols continued to search for the commanding officer. Nicklin was eventually found 36 hours later, his dead body riddled with bullets and still in its harness, having landed in a tree above a German position. The news was received by the battalion with shock and great sadness for although he had been a stern disciplinarian, he was highly respected and, according to Sergeant Anderson, 'seemed indestructible'. But Nicklin's luck ran out that day when he decided not to jump in the middle of the stick, as was the drill (so as to ensure that his headquarters was around him on landing), but to lead his men into battle by jumping first. Nicklin would have been proud of his battalion's performance that day. Using guile and brute force in equal measure, the men that he had trained so hard and with such dedication did everything that was asked of them – and often much more. But whilst there were many acts of gallantry displayed by both sides during Operation Varsity, one stands out. It was extremely difficult for medical teams to recover the wounded from the DZs, for being open spaces any treatment had to be conducted in full view of the enemy. In one instance two members of 224 Parachute Field Ambulance were killed trying to rescue a wounded man. Seeing what had happened, 27-year-old Corporal Frederick Topham, a medical orderly in 1 Canadian Para, ran across to the casualty under heavy fire, and proceeded to administer first aid to him. As Topham was applying a dressing, he was shot through the nose, but although in great pain and bleeding profusely, he continued to care for his patient. He then carried the man to safety by running the gauntlet across a fire-strewn DZ. Subsequently Topham returned to the field several more times to recover other casualties to the RAP. He had already shown outstanding bravery that day, but when Topham then went to find his company, he came across a Bren carrier which had received a direct hit. Although the area was under heavy mortar fire and the burning vehicle was filled with ammunition, Topham ignored orders not to approach it. He rescued three wounded crew and carried them to safety. Topham was not only extremely courageous – for which he was awarded the Victoria Cross – but also extremely modest. When asked why he put himself in such danger he replied: 'I only did what every last man in my outfit would do', and when questioned about his apparent lack of concern for German bullets and mortar bombs he gave an embarrassed smile and retorted: 'I didn't have time to think about it. I was too busy.'

The last battalion of James Hill's brigade to land in Germany was 9 Para which was tasked with clearing the northern and eastern sides of the DZ and securing the Schnappenberg feature in the Diersfordter Wald. This time, unlike its disastrous insertion in Normandy, the unit arrived in good order and the companies took their objectives without difficulty. However, as Lieutenant-Colonel Napier Crookenden explains, their job was only half done:

By 1330 hrs we were dug-in on our final positions: a picnic compared to Normandy. The next excitement was a counterattack by a German assault gun and a few brave infantry, who came straight up the road through B Company's position; the gun reached B Company's HQ. Everyone dived into their slits or the ditch, but the company clerk, Tillotson, jumped up as it passed and banged a Gammon bomb on the engine covers. The gun stopped, a German put his head out of the hatch, Tillotson shot him and the rest surrendered. The SP gun was still a runner, so two ex-RTR men in the battalion took it over and it rumbled along with us for a week or so as we marched into Germany.

German counterattacks were something that each unit in the two divisions had to be prepared for, but lacking firepower the units had to rely on Gammon bombs, PIATs and their 6-pounder anti-tank guns. With reports of several minor armoured incursions having been successfully repelled during the day, Hill was delighted that evening that the enemy had not been able to infiltrate the British positions whilst they were still organizing. He was also confident that with the arrival of the division's guns along with increasingly settled defensive positions, his formation was well placed to face the Germans over the next 24 hours. With the corps' north-west flank having been successfully anchored, Hill was further reassured that the plan was working well when he received word that at 1530 hours, an advance by 8/Royal Scots from 15 (Scottish) Division had managed to break through to link up with the brigade. Hill's formation therefore not only had support on its southern flank but also a means of sustaining itself from the west bank of the Rhine. It had been an excellent day.

Meanwhile, landing on a DZ north-west of Hamminkeln, Brigadier Nigel Poett's 5 Parachute Brigade arrived to defensive fire that was even more intense than that experienced by Hill's brigade. His battalions suffered considerable casualties not only in the Dakotas but also when the guns began to fire airburst at the descending parachutes. Nevertheless, 7 Para landed and moved slickly into action. The battalion's commanding officer, Lieutenant-Colonel Geoffrey Pine Coffin, later explained:

My battalion was ordered to establish itself at the end of the DZ and to take on all opposition which might interfere with the other two battalions which were to capture the brigade objective. In short, 7th Battalion came down looking for a fight, which is not a bad role for any battalion.

They set about the enemy viciously and one would have been forgiven for thinking that 7 Para's reputation had gone before it, for when A Company landed in a small wood containing a battery of 88mm guns, their crews ran away. The German commander ran after his men shouting oaths, threats and orders, but to no avail. As the rather startled company mopped up the position, Lieutenant-Colonel Ken Darling's 12 Para fought to take up a position astride the Hamminkeln road. Some of his men had landed a short distance from their intended DZ after their Dakota pilots had taken evasive action when some 88mm guns opened up on them. Sergeant Bob Pratt landed in the woods:

I saw this big tree coming up to hit me and I landed some 40 feet up in its branches. My thoughts were immediately to get out of that tree as soon as I could. I remembered what had happened to some paras who had landed in trees in Normandy. They were not given a chance, and were shot hanging from their harnesses. I unclipped my harness and dropped 40 feet to the ground. I wounded myself, and hurt my back, but that was certainly the lesser of two evils.

By the time that Pratt had linked up with the rest of the battalion, it was moving towards the Hamminkeln road, taking an 88mm gun and clearing farmhouses as it went. Lieutenant-Colonel Peter Luard's 13 Para, meanwhile, landed and pushed out to the east to take up a position that would assist that held by 3 Parachute Brigade. The battalion made simple work of its task. Private George Butler neatly summarizes the course of events: 'Immediately on landing we swapped our helmets for our red berets, rallied to the officers blowing "tally ho" on their hunting horns, took our objectives and secured the left flank in just two hours.'

With both 3 and 5 Parachute Brigades having safely landed and taken their objectives by the early afternoon – and in so doing providing a 'hard top' to the divisional area – it was up to 6 Airlanding Brigade to complete the division's mission when it started to land at 1030 hours. Brigadier Hugh Bellamy's formation was to secure the critical north-eastern corner of the corps' position by taking the town of Hamminkeln, and bridges over the River Issel. This was not only required to ensure the safety of the two airborne divisions against strong German counterattacks but also for the eventual breakout from the bridgehead. The bridgade had planned for a series of *coup de main* parties to land next to their objectives in order to facilitate surprise – a tactic that had worked so well at Pegasus and Horsa bridges in Normandy – but its ability to achieve this was immediately hampered by smoke and dust created by the artillery's preliminary bombardment, which largely obscured the LZs. With the addition of a heavy dose of anti-aircraft fire, chaos could very easily have descended on the operation, but the fact that it did not is testament to the flying skills of the glider pilots and the leadership of the brigade's officers and NCOs. It was a chastening experience for all concerned as the German gunners targeted the large, slow gliders. When a glider took a direct hit from an 88mm gun it was likely to break up in mid-air, leading to the horrifying sight of men falling to their deaths on the LZ. Most gliders, however, did not suffer catastrophic damage, but were hit by bullets and shell fragments which merely splintered and tore the craft with a dreadful sound that resembled a very loud whip crack. Private Denis Edwards, a veteran of the successful landing at the bridge over the Caen Canal on 6 June 1944, recalls:

> Bullets zipped through one side of the flimsy plywood fuselage and out the other as we approached our landing zone, and as we came in to land part of one wing, an aileron, and the tail section were shot to pieces by shell fire. Listening to the bullets ripping through woodwork around us was none too pleasant, but amazingly none of us was hit by them.

The gliders were very easy to damage, and it was not uncommon for the pilots to find that some part of the aircraft's vital mechanism had been rendered inoperable by enemy fire. Staff-Sergeant Joe Kitchener's Horsa, for example, was damaged by light anti-aircraft fire at an altitude of around 2,000 feet:

> There was an almighty 'Bang!' and the instrument panel disintegrated. The air bottle was also hit, so the flaps came down, increasing my angle of descent. I then saw a row of trees with a large field beyond. In the row of trees was a small tree with larger trees either side of it. So I aimed to go over the small tree, hoping would take my wings off, the larger trees which they did. The fuselage slid along the ground.

The first of the brigade's units to land was 2/OBLI. Its task was to seize the road and rail bridges over the River Issel between Hamminkeln and Ringenberg. On the approach to the LZ the glider carrying the battalion's CO, Lieutenant-Colonel Mark Darell-Brown, came under fire from a 20mm anti-aircraft battery and was hit. The aircraft was put into a steep dive by the pilot, Squadron Leader V.H. Reynolds, who further explains: 'I ordered my second pilot to open up with the Sten through the front clear vision panel, when we came within range, and landed alongside the AA position, between it and the railway station.' This remarkable piece of flying against the odds meant that with the infantry having exited the glider exceptionally quickly, the flabbergasted German gun crew were overrun in a matter of minutes. A haze of smoke smothered a plethora of small-unit actions across the LZ to the sound of exploding ammunition in the blazing gliders which punctuated the incessant pop and crack of small-arms fire. Some of the fighting was at extremely close quarters, particularly when gliders crashed into German positions and the infantry carved into the defenders. Nevertheless, a systematic clearance of the enemy's defences was undertaken, and this eventually led to the battalion storming its objectives. The action cost the unit 226 men.

As Darell-Brown's men slugged it out to the north, Lieutenant-Colonel Jack Carson's 1/RUR landed on the other side of Hamminkeln on the division's southern boundary. Its objective was the bridge over the Issel on the road to Brunen, a task that was carried out with great panache by Major Tony Dyball's company after it landed within 50 yards of the crossing. Nevertheless, the Germans quickly recovered from the surprise attack and began to launch a series of counterattacks against RUR positions with a mixture of infantry, armoured cars and some self-propelled guns. Rifleman Paddy Devlin was sheltering by a glider, harassing a group of Germans with bursts from his Bren gun, when he heard the words that every airborne solder fears – 'tanks'.

There was a shout that two German tanks were coming up the road . . . about 70 yards or so away. I repositioned my gun so that I could fire at them as they came up opposite the glider. I would only have fired if the tank commander had his head exposed from the turret. In the event they weren't tanks but armoured personnel half-tracks. The Germans were standing up in the first one, shoulder to shoulder. They had obviously packed it as much as possible . . . As they came opposite me I let them have a burst and they all collapsed behind the armoured sides. I couldn't have hit them all but there was a lot of shouting and screaming.

Devlin had no chance of stopping them, but two 6-pounder anti-tank guns covering the road did the job. At the bridge, meanwhile, Dyball's company successfully deployed its PIAT to fend off an armoured attack – an event that was repeated in several other places around the LZ. Although the PIAT rounds rarely destroyed armoured vehicles, their crews were immediately discouraged from pressing home the advantage that their protection and firepower gave them. It was a feature of German counterattacks during Operation Varsity that gave the airborne forces of both divisions the time and space that they required to strengthen their positions and make it much more difficult for the enemy to dislodge them later.

Lieutenant-Colonel Paul Gleadell's 12/Devons landed on Carson's left flank. They had the job of taking and holding the small town of Hamminkeln, the local communications hub. Whilst his battalion was still in the process of gathering together, Fraser Edwards, a member of 319 Airborne Security Section who was a German speaker, slipped into the town 'to warn the inhabitants to keep indoors until further notice. Anyone found outside would be shot'. Expecting to see panicked locals dashing around in the wake of the airborne offensive, Edwards was surprised to find that the streets were deserted. He eventually found Hamminkeln's inhabitants huddled in the crypt of the church with the minister. Whilst Fraser explained to the clergyman what he needed to do to ensure the safety of the civilians, the battalion moved to seal off the town by blocking the roads leading into it. Then, at 1135 hours, the Devons moved in. There was a skirmish with a small party from 7 Parachute Division, but Hamminkeln fell to the airborne troops in just 25 minutes. With the passing of the town into British hands, the brigade had secured all of its objectives as well as establishing a firm right flank which contained the vital bridges.

Brigadier Bellamy was delighted at his brigades' work, and proudly reported the news of his success to Eric Bols and his team. The establishment of the 6th Airborne's headquarters in a farmhouse at Köpenhof in the centre of the divisional area was important to operational success. Bols was happily ensconced in the building within minutes of landing after his glider touched down just yards from the front door, and shortly afterwards he had communications. Bols' signaller, Lieutenant P.E.M. Bradley, knew how important it was to the general to have working signals: 'Immediate contact was made with 3 and 5 Para Brigades, who reported all well. The commander was there at the time and I don't know which of us was the more excited and pleased.' With communications established to 6 Airlanding Brigade and the Royal Artillery soon after, and then corps' headquarters west of the Rhine and 17 US Airborne Division by the evening, Bols was well placed to benefit from a full tactical and operational picture. The successful arrival of the divisional troops, his guns and some Locust Light Tanks further strengthened his hand. The guns were often called upon that afternoon to lend valuable fire support to battalions under counterattack, although only five of the tanks were capable of lending their weight to the division's defence. Of the three that did not make it: one was destroyed on the DZ by a Panther's 88mm gun; another ended up on its turret after its Hamilcar glider crashed; and a third, according to Flight Lieutenant Patrick Edmonds, was lost when its glider 'disintegrated without obvious cause', sending its crew 'falling like puppets to their death'.

The 17 US Airborne Division landed concurrently with the British formation and to its south. This fact provided the Germans with a major headache for as the formations landed together in such a tight area, their defences were stretched and their ability to counterattack effectively weakened within an hour or so by the presence of the corps on the ground. It was a massive psychological blow to the Germans who were left gasping 'Where are the enemy's weaknesses?' Leading this exercise in disorientation for Bud Miley's division was 507 PIR, his most experienced formation, commanded by the effervescent Colonel Edson Raff. A navigational error led to Raff and 1st Battalion being dropped a mile too far to the west, which led them to secure the flank along the crescent-shaped western Diersfordter Wald, whilst the other two battalions secured the planned DZ. Raff's first move was to clear the forest fringes and in so doing succeeded in taking five machine guns, several hidden field guns and five 105mm guns. His group then headed south to look for the rest of the regiment and disabled two Panzer Vs along the way. By this time it had become clear that the Diersfordter Castle – which was being used as an important LXXXVI Corps headquarters containing corps staff and senior officers from 84

Division – was a main centre of resistance, and an attack was quickly planned to occupy it. The attack was eventually carried out by 3rd Battalion which had being pushing westwards, whilst the other two battalions cleared the southern part of the forest. Leading the assault on the castle was Sergeant Ricky Richards:

> The enemy was firing from positions inside and on the walls. We were directed towards a sort of back door, a big affair flanked by stone pillars. It had already been blown open and we dived through to fan out into the courtyard. It was only minutes before the battalion had gotten into the building itself and we were soon shooting it out through corridors and huge rooms.

The battalion swarmed into the building, their weapons, uniforms and demeanour incongruous in such civilized and decorous surroundings. The fighting was fierce and bloody. Bullets ricocheted off the stone pillars and embedded themselves in the wooden panelling. Doors were kicked off their hinges as antique furniture was blasted aside. Three corpses leaked blood onto the wooden floor at the bottom of a spiral staircase where a German soldier had his face smashed in by a rifle butt. A hand grenade blew the windows out of a bedroom. The clatter of boots and shouted orders merged with grenade blasts and screaming to produce a hideous echo which reverberated through the galleries. The Americans eventually began to make their numbers tell:

> The German position was pretty hopeless and it wasn't long before they were surrendering. But not all gave up easily. I remember a couple of Germans who drove our guys off a stone stairway with Schmeisser fire, dodging from behind columns to let rip as we tried to get up to them. Someone threw a grenade but it bounced off the stone balustrade and came hopping down stair by damn stair – I dived into a small ante room but a couple

of fellers were hurt. The next grenade didn't miss and one German suddenly catapulted over the banisters; the other one gave up.

The Americans gradually overran the castle room by room, until the only place still in German hands was a turret. The occupying group was eventually removed from that bolt-hole by a couple of well-aimed rounds from the 75mm pack howitzers of 466 Parachute Artillery Battalion. The castle took two hours to clear and 300 prisoners were taken, including some senior officers from General Straube's staff and from 84 Division. By nightfall, 507 PIR had consolidated its landings and taken up positions along the edge of the woods having made contact with both 15 (Scottish) Division and 1 Commando Brigade. It had been a challenging, but ultimately successful day.

Colonel James Coutts' 513 PIR landed to the north-west of Raff's men, just to the east of the Diersfordter Wald. The 1st and 2nd Battalions were to secure the area of the DZ and push out towards the 507th, whilst 3rd Battalion was to move towards the River Issel and prevent the enemy crossing the river. Most of the regiment was transported in the larger and faster C-46s which were being used in an operation the first time. These were supposedly to be superior to the C-47, but the Varsity experience exposed a deadly design flaw when it became clear that the wing-tanks leaked fuel into main body of the aircraft when they were punctured by shrapnel. When this occurred, it took just one tracer or incendiary to create a fireball. A total of 19 C-46s were shot down during the insertion of the 513th – many of them being ripped apart in mid-air by massive explosions – and a further 38 were badly damaged. Coutts' regiment suffered from the anti-aircraft fire as much as any other formation that day, and produced some unforgettable memories for the 513 PIR Executive Officer, Lieutenant-Colonel Ward Ryan:

The C-46 was burning when we hooked up and shoved for the door. [The pilot] and the rest of the carrier's crew never said a word. They stayed in there and kept us level and we went over the side into a weird sky of bursting flak, lazy tracers and coloured silk. Flak hit the man in the air and he blew up. Troopers touched the ground and started fighting, but some of them died in their shroud lines. Col. Jim Coutts slipped out of his harness, walked through the burp-gun fire and began to attack before he had a battalion.

The regiment was badly scattered, with many men landing on the southernmost British LZs some two miles too far north. According to Flying Officer Gordon Procter, when he arrived at Eric Bols' headquarters that evening, there were 'American paratroopers hanging dead from the trees. They had obviously dropped in the wrong landing zone and been shot to pieces. We tried to climb the trees to cut them down, but sniper fire came immediately, and it was two days before we got them all down.' There was confusion at first as the field was raked by fire and nobody seemed to know where they were, with Coutts later explaining: 'I started looking for terrain features that I had memorized, but I couldn't find them.' But whilst Coutts worked to identify his location, his men fought *in situ* and engagements of various sizes broke out across the DZ.

A stalemate developed, however, in the southern section, where rifles, machine guns and four field guns pinned down a platoon of 2nd Battalion's Company E. Finding it impossible to return fire, Private Stuart Stryker rallied the platoon and, armed with a carbine, ran to the head of the unit. With bullets buzzing furiously past his ears and striking the ground around him, Stryker led a charge. He was killed 25 yards from his objective, but his comrades followed through and overran the position taking 200 prisoners. He was awarded a posthumous Medal of Honor. As was so often the case in such situations, it took the courage of one man to alter the course of a battle. Meanwhile, with the 513th still unsure exactly where it was, British gliders started to land around its units. It was only after a brief discussion with the glider men that Coutts managed to pinpoint where he was. Pushing south, the colonel arrived at his designated DZ, where he was pleased to find 466 Parachute Artillery already firmly established. The regiment eventually captured its objectives, with the help of men from the 507th in the area, at 1530 hours. The day had been a frustrating one for Coutts and his men, but by dusk they had not only successfully weakened the enemy south of Hamminkeln, they had also secured the corps' southern flank.

Colonel James R. Pierce's 194 Glider Infantry began landing at 1030 hours. The divisional troops touched down south of Hamminkeln and the glider infantry north of Wesel. This later force was to seize several bridges over River Issel and the Issel Canal north-east of Wesel, as well as securing the south-east flank of the corps' position. Pierce's gliders were subjected to a weight of anti-aircraft fire that was similar to that being experienced by the British at the same time. The smoke and dust troubled many of the glider pilots as they scoured the busily veiled landscape for landmarks. Glider pilot Roger Krey, for example, did so whilst attracting the attention of a machine gun concealed in some trees which sent some red tracers arching skywards. Whilst battling to keep his glider level and on course, his passengers began to sing, 'Hail, Hail, the Gang's All Here'. They had hardly finished the first line when a 20mm anti-aircraft round smacked into the glider's nose. Krey was sprayed with shell fragments around his head and upper torso but, cuffing blood away from his eyes, he first managed to miss some power-lines and then carried out a safe landing. The LZ quickly became littered with crashed and broken gliders, whilst those still trying to land had to miss not only the carcasses of the shattered aircraft but also platoons of men, piles of equipment and concentrated enemy gun fire. A number seemed to spontaneously combust as they began their run in, but it was in fact the devilish work of incendiary rounds and tracer bullets which, assisted, by the wind quickly consumed the wooden structures. As one observer later wrote: 'Several gliders were set on fire and streamed across the sky like a comet, to crash with all occupants none of whom wore parachutes.' Private Tony Cancelli still has nightmares of his experience of being trapped in a burning Waco and forced to listen to the screams of his friends being burned alive. He had a very lucky escape: he was thrown clear of the inferno when the glider crumpled into the ground and broke in two.

The survivors of this extraordinary American landing exited their aircraft as quickly as they could, rendezvoused and pushed out to the bridges. Some of the approaches were opposed, but this was largely pushed aside without difficulty although later armoured counterattacks were rebuffed with less ease. A Panther tank engaged 2nd Battalion's Company F as it approached the river. The tank opened fire, but Bazooka gunner Private Weber hit it at a range of about 500 yards and the tank exploded. Once again this single shot was enough to concern other German armour to withhold their attacks, which gave the Americans time to install themselves in stronger defensive positions. The regiment eventually took ten bridges along the canal and river, linked up with the British Commandos in Wesel, and in doing so secured XVIII US Airborne Corps' eastern flank.

Whilst the airborne units were still in the midst of capturing their objectives, a programmed resupply mission was flown in at 1300 hours carrying necessities such as ammunition, food and weapons. Each division was allocated 120 Liberator bombers from US Eighth Air Force, but flying slow at an altitude of just 500 ft, they were perfect targets for the German gunners who damaged 100 of them and caused another 15 either to crash or make an emergency landing. Of the thousands of supply canisters that were dropped, each with a different coloured parachute for easy recognition of its contents, most were widely scattered and only one-third were retrieved by the corps. Nevertheless, this was a low-point which, anti-aircraft fire aside, had been a marvellously successful day for the two airborne divisions. The attack had clearly surprised the Germans, and although some heavy casualties were taken during the insertion, the enemy had been unable to stop units from taking their objectives. Moreover, the first German counterattack had been seen off with some aplomb, with the enemy not showing much appetite for the fight in some of his attempts to recapture vital pieces of ground and bridges. Assisted by good communications which linked Bols' headquarters with Miley's in Flüren and both up to corps and down to their subordinate formations, the two generals could oversee developments and retain the initiative. Ridgway crossed the Rhine in the mid-afternoon from his headquarters in Xanten, and visited both men to see the situation for himself. He left the them feeling confident that everything was in hand and the corps' prospects looked good. His own, however, were nearly ended when his party ran into a German patrol. During the brief skirmish that ensued, Ridgway was hit in the shoulder by a shell fragment after a German grenade exploded under his jeep.

The German commanders had been stunned by the airborne attack that morning. Although they had expected one to precede the river crossing, when it failed to materialize both Kesselring and Blaskowitz believed that Eisenhower must be keeping an airborne operation in reserve. 'After all', said the Field Marshal later, 'our Rhine defences were not very strong and so it was not completely ridiculous to think that a river crossing might be attempted without the use of such a valuable force.' However, the launching of Operation Varsity that morning had achieved a level of surprise which forced the Germans to change their plans. Rather than using the armoured reserve solely against the ground forces, part of it would now also have to be deployed against the airborne troops. Thus, soon after the airborne insertions had begun, Blaskowitz ordered von Lüttwitz's XLVII Corps to send units of Major-General Siegfried von Waldenburg's 116 Panzer Division to the bridges over the Issel without delay and to 'hold them at all costs'. The commander had already despatched 15 Panzer Grenadier Division to counterattack the British left flank at Rees, and some elements of 116 Panzer Division towards the Americans on the right flank. The stretched force was now endeavouring to thrust into an airborne corps to link up with some scattered units that had been secreted in the Diersfordter Wald days before. During the course of the day, that armour was picked off by the Allied airborne soldiers with their AT guns, whilst others tried to make a bid for freedom and break out of the enveloping airborne mass.

The feeling of impending doom that must have spread through the German forces during 24 March was fully justified. After the overnight success of Operation Plunder, the Allies had deftly provided British Second and US Ninth Armies with excellent protection against a German counterattack, further diluted enemy forces in the area and provided the means for a breakout over the Issel. That day had seen the river-crossing forces expand their initial lodgements, with the only pressure-point occurring on the Allied left flank, where 51 (Highland) Division's northern progress was hampered by 15 Panzer Grenadier Division. Nevertheless, all along the attacking front, room had been made behind the assault divisions for new formations to be brought across the river to strengthen the Allied presence. That night, however, von Waldenburg's armour endeavoured to retake the bridges over the River Issel, as ordered. The first tentative probes had been swept away by a mixture of fighter-bomber support, artillery and anti-tank weapons, but at midnight a more serious attack was mounted against the bridge east of Hamminkeln, when German infantry, supported by tanks, attacked 16 platoon of B Company 2/OBLI. The company's anti-tank detachments scored several hits with their 6-pounder anti-tank guns, but they made no difference to the heavy armour, and this time the Germans were not dissuaded from developing their thrust. The fighting continued in the dark, and one of the company's positions at the eastern end of the bridge was overrun.

However, it was then retaken in a counterattack, as Lieutenant Hugh Clark describes:

> I ordered my platoon to fix bayonets, and as soon as we were in line, gave the order to charge. We moved forward at the trot, shouting and firing from the hip as we went. We had only gone about 150 yards to the riverbank, and about halfway there, when a corporal beside me said, 'Hold it a minute, sir, we are on our own.'

The rest of the platoon had fallen back and so Clark retrieved them. The small unit remounted the attack and found to his surprise that the enemy had withdrawn back across the river. There was no time for complacency, however, for a new threat was developing:

> It was not long before we heard and then saw the outline of two heavy tanks moving forward towards the bridge and no more than 75 yards from our position. I called for the PIAT, our platoon anti-tank weapon, and asked the man with the PIAT if he could guarantee to hit the tank first shot, as I was sure once we had fired, they would direct their gun on to our position. He replied that he was not sure that he could, so in a moment of bravado, I told him to give the weapon to me. I loaded it and took aim, not easy in the dark, and scored a hit with the first shot. Fortunately, the tanks did not reply, and I think that we must have put that gun out of action. We heard the infantry scatter when the round hit. I continued firing and scored four more hits.

The tanks pulled back, but then lunged forward again with such success that it looked as though B Company would be overrun. In the circumstances, Hugh Bellamy ordered that the bridge be destroyed, fearful that great carnage would be wrought in the divisional area if the

German tanks got across. The bridge was blown at 0235 hours, and with it von Waldenburg's best chance to make a tactical breakthrough. Hugh Clark was awarded the Military Cross for his leadership during the action.

With the renewed German attempt to undermine XVIII US Airborne Corps' position by 116 Panzer Division having been parried, and resources extremely limited, Blakowitz had quickly to review how he was going to utilize his armoured assets most effectively. As the airborne divisions seemed to be static, he seized the opportunity to counter the threat emerging further south in the Ninth US Army sector. Thus he directed 116 Panzer Division to block any further advances by 30 US Division, and in so doing released the pressure on the airborne corps. In the meantime, the Allies continued to build their strength on the east bank, whilst Bols and Miley defended their hard-won gains. Yet the German counterattacks that day were feeble, uncoordinated, poorly resourced and easily broken up by fighter-bombers, artillery and anti-tank weapons. Small parties of German infantry did try to infiltrate through the airborne lines to create mischief, and there were all manner of probes around the corps' boundary, but nothing that the airborne divisions could not swat away with contempt. What the Germans needed was a strong, concentrated armoured attack against Ridgway's corps, but Blaskowitz did not have the resources to do it. As Flying Officer Gordon Procter astutely observes:

Most of us anticipated a German counterattack, but I suppose, on reflection, the whole airborne landing was so substantial that we and the Americans had virtually destroyed all German resistance, thereby achieving our objective of establishing a bridgehead over which the main British and American forces could proceed into Germany.

By sending his armoured reserve to engage the Allies,' flanks, more-over, the German commander had left himself wide open to a break-through attempt across the Issel. Montgomery, Dempsey, Simpson and Ridgway were already aware of this, and the generals agreed that after a couple more days' preparation, the time would be right to break out. Thus, during the night of 25/26 March, as the bridgehead continued to swell with an expectant exploitation force, 6 British Airborne Division was joined by the Churchill tanks of 3/Scots Guards from 6 Independent Guards Brigade. The arrival of this vanguard into the divisional area was greeted with delight by the airborne troops. Gunner Jim Purser, who was attached to 8 Para as part of a Royal Artillery team, recalls: 'At about 8 o'clock on the Sunday morning there was the rumble of tanks, and lining the track we cheered as Second Army tanks came up to us from the Rhine.'

The arrival of the armour marked the beginning of a new opera-tional phase for the two divisions, for having been the *pièce de résistance* of one of the greatest Western Allied operations of the war, 28/29 March saw the corps clamber aboard 6 Independent Guards Brigade tanks and journey east to help encircle the Ruhr. Operation Varsity had been an outrageous success and had achieved everything that Montgomery had hoped it would. It brought the end of the war in Europe one step closer and provided the airborne forces with a fillip in the wake of Market Garden. Yet although it was a conservative oper-ation, conducted against a terminally weak enemy, its triumph was not a foregone conclusion. Making an opposed crossing of the River Rhine was a great military examination, and Montgomery passed it.

Winston Churchill certainly did not underestimate the importance of Montgomery's achievement, as witnessed by his entry in the Field Marshal's autograph book at his Tac HQ:

> The Rhine and all its fortress lines lie behind. Once again they have been the hinge on which massive gates revolved. Once again

they have proved that physical barriers are vain without the means and spirit to hold them. A beaten army, not long ago the master of Europe, retreats before its pursuers. The goal is not long to be denied to those who have come so far and fought so well under proud and faithful leaderships.

Conclusion

Operation Market Garden was a risk worth taking, whilst Operation Plunder Varsity was justifiably cautious. These two attempts to cross the Rhine during the last months of the Second World War in Europe were strategically and operationally sound. But many commentators would disagree, for debate continues to reverberate around their conception, conduct and achievements. Much of the controversy centres around the role of airborne aspects of the schemes. Both were inherently risky, complicated and reliant upon vast resources from both the army and air force. Market Garden, moreover, has been vilified for being too bold and therefore unconscionable in its ambitions. Plunder Varsity, conversely, has been criticized for being conservative and lacking drive. Both operations, therefore, beg the question: should they have been undertaken? What is easy to forget is that both were products of their strategic environment and were conceived by Field Marshal Bernard Montgomery to fulfil what he considered to be a necessary purpose. They were not creations in search of an objective, but carefully considered schemes developed to achieve critical goals. And they were not unaffected by the petulant strategic arguments that centred around a disagreement in approach between Eisenhower and Montgomery, and which eventually dragged in Omar Bradley.

Both operations took place within the Supreme Commander's conservative, methodical and politically appeasing broad-front design for the advance from Normandy into Germany. However, Montgomery argued that his Twenty-First Army Group should conduct the exploitation at the expense of a thrust by the other two *American* army groups. He believed that such a narrow front would provide a far more efficient, effective and speedy means of defeating the Germans. But with an American Supreme Commander, and the United States providing the bulk of the resources for the campaign, it is understandable that such an argument fell foul of the likes of Marshall, Bradley, Patton and others. The fact that neither Montgomery nor Alan Brooke thought that Eisenhower was the best man to command the land forces added further spice to the situation. In the end, Market Garden was the usually cautious Monty's attempt to exploit German disorganization in the wake of the battle of Normandy by creating a launch-pad for his narrow-front attempt and, thereby allowing the British to punch above their strategic weight, enhancing his own reputation. The fact that FAAA was available to him and ready and raring to go, that there was pressure being applied by Washington to get it into action and a desire by London to see Holland cleared quickly to deal with the V2 threat, made the operation seductive to SHAEF. However, most important in Eisenhower's accession to the operation was its intention to deliver the Rhine crossing that his advance required. Thus, far from Market Garden being developed in a strategic vacuum, it was devised in a heady atmosphere of competing theories and uncompromising patriotism.

The result, as we have seen, was the launching of an operation that has attained the unenviable reputation of being one of the most flawed in history. Tom Hoare, who fought with 3 Para at Arnhem, may be said to reflect a commonly held perception of Operation Market Garden (or 'Field Marshal Montgomery's fiasco', as he calls it) when he writes:

> It is my opinion that Montgomery was a great soldier, but he had an even greater ego. When victory was in sight for the Allies, he degenerated into nothing more than a glory seeker. With little regard for the welfare or indeed the lives of the men of the British 1st Airborne Division, he threw the division away in an insane attempt to go down in history as the greatest military leader of the Second World War.

Hoare speaks from a British airborne perspective, but his American colleagues think similarly. Brad Wiley, of 82nd US Airborne Division, comments: 'Market Garden was a gamble, a risk that shouldn't have been taken. The airborne were asked to achieve too much in screwed-up plan. Montgomery may have been a fine general, but when he came up with this idea he must have been having a very bad day.' There is no doubt that the operation's inability to pass British Second Army over the Lower Rhine was rooted in a plan too flawed to be a success. Its critical weakness, however, lay in the air plan. The three lifts, which were eventually spread over five days, led to a dilution of the airborne division's greatest assets: its surprise arrival and initial attacking strength. It also compromised the ability of the air forces to provide close support to the formations, and led to the British having to arrive on DZs and LZs that were too far from the objectives. Further fundamental difficulties were caused by the single, narrow, vulnerable road that XXX Corps had to progress along and the German ability to react to and undermine the operation. It would seem that I British Airborne Corps severely underestimated the enemy's potential and were far too optimistic about the plan's ability to overwhelm Field Marshal Model's men. Indeed, Brigadier Shan Hackett later opined that his superiors 'used to make a beautiful airborne plan and then add the fighting-the-Germans bit afterwards'.

Yet although the Market Garden plan did contain fundamental weaknesses, the risk was offset by the strategically advantageous objectives that a successful operation would have procured. Moreover, the hazards presented by the scheme were largely to fall on first-class troops whose commanders were willing to accept them. Jim Gavin, for example, later reflected: 'We knew that the risks were great, but we believed that the battle we were about to fight would lead to the battle that would bring the war to an end.' Churchill concurred, and in the immediate aftermath of the operation wrote: 'The battle was a decided victory . . . I have not been afflicted by any feelings of disappointment over this and am glad our commanders are capable of running this kind of risk.'

But was the operation 'a decided victory'? Montgomery later argued that Market Garden was '90 per cent successful' since critical river crossings had been taken, a salient had been driven into northern Holland, the Germans sustained 8,000 casualties and von Rundstedt's troops had been forced to react to the British offensive making them unavailable to strengthen the West Wall. Furthermore, those German forces not destroyed in the push to Arnhem – including an important part of II SS Panzer Corps – had to be defeated at some point, and had it not occurred in Holland, it would almost certainly have needed to have been done in Germany. In this way the operation achieved what Eisenhower's broad front required: it pushed the British Second Army forward whilst wearing down the enemy forces. In this light, Market Garden looks more like a success and the British Official History astutely contends: 'Operation Market Garden accomplished much of what it had been designed to accomplish. Nevertheless, by the merciless logic of war, Market Garden was a failure.'

It very nearly worked and with a little more luck could have succeeded. Freddie de Guingand, Montgomery's Chief of Staff, was not an advocate of the plan, but even so later conceded that 'we might have held our bridgehead over the Neder Rijn if we had experienced really good weather'. But the Rhine was not crossed, and the fundamental objective of the operation was not attained. Therefore, Market Garden cannot be termed 'a victory'. Nevertheless, the risk-taking inherent in launching Market Garden was appropriate, as September 1944 was just the time for a daring operation to shorten the war. In Bradley's words, it was 'one of the most imaginative [plans] of the war'.

The failure of Montgomery's scheme was a decided setback for his narrow-front argument, but it did at least create the conditions in which Operation Veritable could succeed six months later. By clearing the way to the Rhine opposite Wesel, Montgomery provided himself with a second opportunity to cross the river. Operation Plunder Varsity was workmanlike, methodical and restrained. Montgomery has been pilloried for this, despite the operation's success. But here, too, the strategic context affected the method and the plan of attack. The Plunder Varsity plan was a supreme example of risk management, because by this stage in the war the Germans were as good as beaten, great political objectives such as the taking of Berlin had been ceded to the Soviets, and there was a distinct lack of British manpower. Monty, as was his wont, wished to preserve life whenever possible. Faced with the crossing of a tricky obstacle that he anticipated would be keenly defended, he decided that a bold operation was not required. He chose instead an unambitious airborne design which drew heavily on lessons learned from Market Garden. It was a wise decision in the light of his desire to ensure the success of a crossing with very limited early ambition.

Plunder Varsity was anathema to Bradley. His commanders had got over the Rhine 'on the run' by the time Monty launched his attempt. But although the Twelfth Army Group commander later argued that the Germans had diverted all of their forces to his

Remagen bridgehead, thus leaving weak forces around Wesel, this is disingenuous since the strength of the defences against the British Second Army and US Ninth Army Monty increased in the two weeks prior to Plunder being launched. However, there is some truth in the US Army's official account of Varsity that, considering the weakness of the German forces, 'some overbearing need of the special capability of airborne divisions would be required to justify their use', and that need just did not exist. There is little doubt that in the event the ground forces could have taken the objectives, but Monty did not want to take the chance that they would not, and he was keen to give XVIII US Airborne Corps an opportunity to restore some faith in airborne operations – albeit in a non-essential role. Perhaps the same – and maybe more – could have been achieved had Montgomery undertaken an earlier crossing attempt utilizing fewer resources and taking more risks, but by March 1945 the object was not to win a race or to be an exercise in frugality, it was to get east of the Rhine in good order, with few casualties, and to create a position for a rapid break-out. This was all successfully achieved by Operation Plunder Varsity. Of course, after the battle the airborne commanders waxed lyrical about the operation, with Ridgway calling it 'a remarkable success ... one of the most important of the war'. Brereton declared the attack 'a breathtaking attack without which the ground forces' task would have been many times more difficult'. Operation Varsity was the most successful Allied airborne operation of the war, and one of the few wholly successful airborne operations by any nation during the conflict: but it came perhaps at the expense of boldness, imagination and flair.

Market Garden and Plunder Varsity, although very different operations in the scale of their ambitions and eventual outcome, were both firmly rooted in strategic considerations for their conception and design. Such issues, of course, did not trouble the airborne troops that were involved in them, they just sought to do their job to the best of their ability and achieve their objectives. They were a remarkable group of men carrying out a difficult and dangerous job in trying conditions. Such soldiers were trained to fight for their lives as soon as they reached the ground and recognized that being surrounded by an enemy that outnumbered and outgunned them was a normal state of affairs. Their courage, resourcefulness and professionalism was not diminished, whatever the outcome of their operation. As Tom Hoare says of his airborne colleagues: 'the men with whom I served were of the highest calibre, and their training, discipline, and expertise in weaponry was of the highest quality; we could hardly be described as "heroes" or "brave": far from it. Let's just say we did what we had to do, in order to survive.'

US Airborne song 'Gory, Gory'

(Sung to the tune of the 'Battle Hymn of the Republic')

He was just a rookie trooper and he surely shook with fright
As he checked all his equipment and made sure his pack was tight;
He had to sit and listen to those awful engines roar,
  'You ain't gonna jump no more!'

Chorus:
Gory, Gory, what a helluva way to die!
Gory, Gory, what a helluva way to die!
Gory, Gory, what a helluva way to die!
  And he ain't gonna jump no more!

'Is everybody happy?' cried the sergeant, looking up.
Our hero feebly answered, 'Yes', and then they stood him up;
He jumped into an icy blast, his static line unhooked,
  And he ain't gonna jump no more!

He counted long, he counted loud, he waited for the shock,
He felt the wind, he felt the cold, he felt the awful drop;
He pulled the reserve, the silk spilled out and wrapped around his
  sock.
  And he ain't gonna jump no more!

The days he'd lived and loved and laughed kept running through
  his mind,
He thought about the girl back home, the one he'd left behind,
He thought about the medics and wondered what they'd find,
  And he ain't gonna jump no more!

The lines were twisted round his neck, the connectors broke his
    dome,
The risers tied themselves in knots around each skinny bone;
The canopy became his shroud as he hurtled to the ground.
    And he ain't gonna jump no more!

He hit the ground, the sound was 'splatt', the blood it spurted
    high.
His comrades, they were heard to say: 'What a pretty way to die!'
He lay there rolling in the welter of his gore.
    And he ain't gonna jump no more!

There was blood upon the risers, there was brains upon the
    'chute,
Intestines were a-danglin' from his paratrooper suit;
They picked him up still in his 'chute and poured him from his
    boots.
    And he ain't gonna jump no more!

They operated all night through but it was in despair,
For every bone that he possessed was ruined beyond repair;
And so he was buried then, his silken 'chute his shroud,
    And he ain't gonna jump no more!

They say he went to heaven and arriving there I'm told
He got a pair of silver boots and a parachute of gold;
He may be very happy there but I'll stick here below,
    'Cause he ain't gonna jump no more!

Epilogue

The famous bridge is bathed in early autumn sunshine. Hundreds of people wait expectantly at its northern end. A hum of conversation battles with the noise of jeeps, trucks, motor cycles and other vehicles painted olive-drab and waiting by the Lower Rhine. Maroon berets predominate but there are other hues: black, dark blue, red, brown. Their owners take salutes from small boys with a snappy arm lift and a smile. One buffs the window of his reconditioned vehicle with his sleeve. The atmosphere is friendly; the crowd diverse. Along with the re-enactors and children are men and women of all ages, and, it seems, several nationalities. British accents dominate, but there are a large number of Dutch families, some Americans and one or two Germans. On my left sitting on the grassy bank chatting and laughing are the young men of 2 and 4 Para, a dense cluster of maroon above their mottled uniforms. They are serving soldiers in the British Army and are my patient audience.

It has been a long day: the journey to the airfield, the donning of equipment, the flight, the jump-up at Ginkel Heath in front of many thousands of spectators. Scanning the eager young faces of these paratroopers, I am reminded of photographs that I have of their grinning forebears before the battle, laughing and joshing like this group now. Those soldiers are now old soldiers, and some of them are here. Most are wearing blazers adorned with medals and the ubiquitous airborne berets atop their heads. Some fought just yards away from where we are now, on the western boundary of the perimeter. That modern office replaced the ruined building occupied by the men of No. 1 Platoon, 2 Para. Bring some maps, photographs and your imagination and we can try to recreate the scene. Here was where James Sims had his slit trench, and over there is where the German tank blasted the warehouse. This is the site of John Frost's headquarters, and here where John Grayburn was killed. It's a small area isn't it?

A major gives me a nod: the signal that I have half an hour before the ceremony begins to talk to my paras about the fighting here. It is an event that I have been reading about since I was 9 years old. Being here is a career highlight, a massive honour, addressing members of the Parachute Regiment at Arnhem bridge. It is the last stand of the 60th Anniversary Battlefield Tour. I ask an NCO to prepare the group quietly, so as not to attract the attention of those standing around us; – he barks an order that could be heard in Nijmegen and the assembled masses are suddenly silent. A thousand pairs of eyes are trained on me. As I begin my talk, I go into lecturer mode and can hear my voice bouncing off the buildings. I suddenly feel a weight of expectation on me. Time stands still for a second or two, but then I get into my stride with a story that is difficult to make dull. I begin to feel a warmth from those listening to me, bound together by the one thing that we have in common – Arnhem.

Without the battle of Arnhem, I doubt that I would have become a military historian – it drew me in as no other battle has ever done. I would not have travelled around the world to give talks about it, nor enjoyed the friendship of so many people connected with it: academics, soldiers, local Dutch people and, of course, the veterans. I knew Lieutenant Len Wright; I don't recall how we first met, but I asked him to come down to Sandhurst to talk to the Officer Cadets. He was captivating, a wonderful man. I remember him now as I crib his talk, in which he describes his battle in the school by the ramp: the surprise attack by the Germans who surrounded the building; the squalid conditions as the days went by; how he was knocked unconscious; his reaction to being taken prisoner. As I talk, I notice that some of the veterans seem to have lost interest. I carry on, rather perplexed. Out of the corner of my eye I see that a man in a blazer has taken a couple of steps away and is staring down the river. My stomach lurches. What have I said to create such ire? I didn't expect to have veterans in the audience, and this is their battle, not mine.

As I finish, there is a ripple of applause, but the old soldiers look troubled. I want the ground to swallow me up, the Lower Rhine to burst its banks and carry me away. Then a white-haired gentleman approaches, his jacket pocket resplendent with a pair of wings stitched in silver with the Roman numeral 'II' beneath. He puts a gnarled hand on my shoulder. 'Well done, son', he says. 'Spot on, well done.' It seems that I mistook reflection for displeasure. My talk had evoked painful memories and I will endeavour to be more sensitive next time. But for now I am delighted and humbled to be paid a compliment by a man who fought at Arnhem.

Notes

Introduction

p. xv 'In every century great armies have fought ...' Goronwy Rees *The Rhine* Weidenfeld & Nicolson 1967, p. 13

p. xvi 'reasons of their own for anxiety when they realized ...' *Commentaries on the War in Gaul by Julius Caesar* trans. Anne and Peter Wiseman www.livius.org/caa-can/caesar/caesar-t27.html

p. xviii 'From war-room strategy to gritty trench combat ...' Microsoft's *Close Combat: A Bridge Too Far*

p. xviii 'a British disaster where naked courage ...' quoted in Norman F. Dixon *On the Psychology of Military Incompetence* Futura 1988, p. 145

Chapter 1: The Strategy of Exploitation

p. 1 'Private Wally Parr broke the tension ...' account written utilizing various sources including: Stephen E. Ambrose *Pegasus Bridge: June 6, 1944* Touchstone New York 1985; John Howard and Penny Bates *The Pegasus Diaries – The Private Papers of Major*

John Howard DSO Pen and Sword Military 2006; James H. Wallwork DFM supplement to *Aeroplane Monthly*, May 1994, along with correspondence and interviews with John Howard, James Wallwork and Wally Parr

p. 3   'The German armies in north-west France ...' quoted in Ronald Gill and John Groves *Club Route in Europe – The History of 30 Corps from D-Day to May 1945* MLRS 2006, p. 45

p. 3   'By the last week in August, the Germans were disintegrating ...' figures from Richard Hargreaves *The Germans in Normandy* Pen and Sword 2006, p. 244

p. 4   'This was the type of warfare I thoroughly enjoyed ...' Lieutenant-General Sir Brian Horrocks *A Full Life* Collins 1960, p. 195

p. 4   'Brian Horrocks was the best war-time commander ...' Major-General Sir Allan Adair *A Guards' General* Hamish Hamilton 1986, p. 150

p. 5   'surrendering *en masse*' and 'greeted our troops like long-lost family members' diary entry for 28 August 1944, Captain Nigel Rose, 11 Armoured Division headquarters, author's archive

p. 5   'Two and a half months of bitter fighting ...' quoted in Bernard Law Montgomery *The Memoirs of Field Marshal The Viscount of Alamein*, K.G. Collins 1958, p. 265

p. 5   'would be like Normandy all over again ...' quoted in Vivian Taylor *The Armoured Micks 1941–45* Regimental Headquarters Irish Guards 1997, p. 82

p. 5   'German rearguard actions were swiftly brushed aside ...' Horrocks, *op. cit.*, p. 195

p. 5   'We had enough maps to reach Moscow ...' Robert Boscawen, *Armoured Guardsmen: A War Diary, June 1944–April 1945* Leo Cooper Barnsley 2001, p. 104

p. 6   'Still we raced on, regardless of bogie-wheels and tracks ...' ibid., p. 106

p. 6   'It took us two hours to cross the Western Front . . .' Taylor *op. cit.*, p. 82

p. 6   'And from behind one of the lorries was led a scowling . . .' Horrocks *op. cit.*, p. 198

p. 7   'A long day of movement . . .' WO171/1257 3/Irish Guards (Armoured) War Diary, National Archives, Kew

p. 7   'As soon as we were well into the town . . .' Boscawen *op. cit.*, p. 109

p. 7   'It was pouring with rain as the Brigadiers and Commanding Officers . . .' quoted in Adair *op. cit.*, p. 154

p. 8   'German machine guns, anti-tank guns and snipers barked . . .' ibid., p. 157

p. 8   'I can remember being kissed endlessly . . .' Captain Michael Bendix 5/Coldstream Guards 32 Guards Brigade, Guards Armoured Division. Extracts from: *Memoirs of Captain Michael Bendix OBE CStJ JP DL FLS FIBr* File 98/3/1, Imperial War Museum

p. 9   'Everybody was having much too good a time to be disturbed . . .' quoted in Major D.J.L. Fitzgerald *History of the Irish Guards in the Second World War* Gale Polden 1949, p. 454

p. 9   'This mad chase is getting crazier by the hour . . .' quoted in Carlo D'Este *Eisenhower – Allied Supreme Commander* Cassell 2004, p. 586

p. 9   'Sweeping northward and eastward at a speed . . .' Drew Middleton in the *New York Times* 30 August 1944, author's archive

p. 10   'There is a feeling of elation, expectancy . . .' John Colville *The Fringes of Power – Downing Street Diaries 1939–1955* Weidenfeld & Nicolson 2004, p. 483

p. 10   'organized resistance under the control of the German high command . . .' quoted in Cornelius Ryan *A Bridge Too Far* Hodder & Stoughton 1974, p. 74

p. 10 '... a Gallup poll taken in the first week of September' figure taken from Hastings *op. cit.*, p. 17

p. 10 'To my mind 4th September was the key date ...' Horrocks *op. cit.*, p. 205

p. 11 'I realise now that it was a serious mistake ...' ibid., p. 204

p. 12 'Up to July 1944 England had a considerable ...' quoted in Hastings *op. cit.*, p. 3

p. 12 'He walked in the company of the great captains ...' Eric Larrabee *Commander In Chief – Franklin Delano Roosevelt. His Lieutenants, and their War* André Deutsch 1987, p. 471

p. 13 'Montgomery was detested because ...' Robin Neillands *The Battle for the Rhine, 1944 – Arnhem and the Ardennes: the Campaign in Europe* Weidenfeld & Nicolson 2005, p. 37

p. 13 'a little fellow of average ability who has had such a build-up ...' quoted in Carlo D'Este *A Genius for War: A Life of General George S. Patton* HarperCollins 1995, p. 494

p. 13 'the importance of your relations with allies ...' quoted in Hamilton *Monty: Master of the Battlefield 1942–1944* Hamish Hamilton 1983, p. 283

p. 13 'The real trouble with the Yanks ...' quoted by Larrabee *op. cit.*, p. 472

p. 14 'I grew to dislike the very name Montgomery ...' Kay Summersby *Eisenhower Was my Boss* Werner Laurie 1949, p. 166

p. 14 'General Montgomery is a very able ...' quoted in Hamilton *Monty: Master of the Battlefield op. cit.*, p. 338

p. 15 'He was, I think, apt to give insufficient weight ...' Francis de Guingand *Generals at War* Hodder & Stoughton 1964, pp. 100–1

p. 15 '[T]he size of our forces and the extent of our front ...' Supreme Commander's Report HMSO 1946, p. 76

p. 16 'would mark the approval of the British people ...' Alex Danchev and Daniel Todman (eds) *War Diaries 1939–1945 Field Marshal Alan Brooke* Weidenfeld & Nicolson 2001, p. 586

p. 16 'This was possibly a suitable place for a Supreme Commander
. . .' Montgomery *Memoirs op. cit.*, p. 271

p. 17 [Eisenhower's] ignorance as to how to run a war . . .' quoted in
D'Este *Eisenhower op. cit.*, p. 596

p. 17 'to add another three to six months on to the war!' Danchev
and Todman (eds) *op. cit.*, p. 585

p. 17 'we had no fundamental plan which treated the theatre . . .'
Montgomery *Memoirs op. cit.*, p. 270

p. 17 'The quickest way to win this war . . .' ibid., pp. 267–8

p. 18 'sought a high military profile for Britain's limited . . .' Stephen
Ashley Hart *Colossal Cracks – Montgomery's 21st Army Group in
Northwest Europe, 1944–45* Stackpole 2007, pp. 176–7

p. 18 'which would be so strong that it need fear nothing'
Montgomery *Memoirs op. cit.*, p. 266

p. 18 'to secure bridgeheads over the Rhine . . .' ibid., p. 266

p. 19 'The best course of the Allies . . .' quoted in B.H. Liddell Hart
The Other Side of the Hill Pan 1978, p. 428

p. 19 'I said that if he adopted a broad front strategy . . .'
Montgomery *Memoirs*, p. 268

p. 20 'It is clear that the fixed determination of the Nazis . . .' quoted
in D'Este *Eisenhower op. cit.*, p. 588

p. 20 'It is at least as likely that Hitler will be fighting . . .' ibid.,
p. 588

p. 21 'the best-rounded combat leader I have yet met in our service'
quoted in Hastings *op. cit.*, p. 73

p. 21 '[The] principal advantage of the American plan . . .' Omar N.
Bradley *A Soldier's Story of the Allied Campaigns from Tunis to the
Elbe* Eyre Spottiswoode 1951, p. 398

p. 21 'to be on the Rhine on 10 September' quoted in Nigel Hamilton
Monty: The Field Marshal 1944–1976 Sceptre 1987, p. 17

p. 21 'Brussels–Antwerp on 6 Sep directed on Wesel and Arnhem
. . .' ibid., p. 22

p. 23 'I consider we have now reached a stage . . .' Montgomery *Memoirs op. cit.*, pp. 271–2

p. 24 'should be started as soon as possible . . .' quoted in Major L.F. Ellis with Lieutenant-Colonel A.E. Warhurst *Victory in the West, Volume II The Defeat of Germany* HMSO 1968, p. 9

p. 24 'mismanagement of the campaign had again . . .' interview with Major Peter Merchant referring to a diary entry made on 9 September 1944, 16 July 2005

p. 25 'While agreeing with your conception . . .' quoted in Montgomery *Memoirs op. cit.*, pp. 272–3

p. 25 '[Eisenhower] keeps saying that he has ordered . . .' quoted in Hamilton *Monty: The Field Marshal op. cit.*, p. 43

p. 26 'So far as I was concerned that settled . . .' Montgomery *Memoirs* p. 274

p. 26 'They're balls, sheer balls, rubbish!' quoted in D'Este *Eisenhower op. cit.*, p. 606

p. 26 'Steady Monty, you can't speak to me like that . . .' quoted in Geoffrey Powell *The Devil's Birthday – The Bridges to Arnhem 1944* Buchan & Enright 1984, p. 24

p. 28 'the leading troops ran straight into a large black . . .' Fitzgerald *op. cit.*, p. 474

p. 28 'Obviously boldness is the thing. We will rush the bridge' ibid., p. 476

p. 28 'When the order came from Sgt Steer . . .' quoted in Taylor *op. cit.*, p. 91

p. 29 'Well done, well done!' quoted in Fitzgerald *op. cit.*, p. 477

p. 29 'the large-scale operations by Second Army . . .' quoted in Montgomery *Memoirs op. cit.*, p. 276

p. 30 'After discussing ways and means of supporting left flank . . .' quoted in Summersby *op. cit.*, p. 155

p. 30 'The Saar thrust is to be stopped . . .' quoted in Hamilton *Monty: The Field Marshal op. cit.*, pp. 57–8

p. 30   'Naturally, these measures are emergency ones . . .' quoted in Ellis *op. cit.*, p. 23

p. 31   'rapid and violent' quoted ibid., p. 27

Chapter 2: Withdrawal

p. 33   'At the door of the wrecked wooden chalet . . .' account written with reference to a large number of sources including: Joachim Fest *Inside Hitler's Bunker – The Last Days of the Third Reich* Pan 2005; Roger Moorehouse *Killing Hitler – The Third Reich and the Plots against the Führer* Jonathan Cape 2006; Ian Kershaw *Hitler 1936–1945: Nemesis* Penguin 2000 and Alan Bullock *Hitler – A Study in Tyranny* Penguin 1962

p. 35   'He sought psychological shock . . .' Richard Overy *Why the Allies Won* Jonathan Cape 1995, p. 153

p. 36   'when he arrived the whole town . . .' Gefreiter Hans Jungbauer WO 208/5537, National Archives, Kew

p. 37   'I pray every morning and every evening . . .' Diary of Michael Hirsch – a copy of which was provided by his son, Steffen – who was taken prisoner by Canadian forces in late July 1944

p. 37   'The whole site is resplendent with luscious greenery . . .' quoted in David Irving *Hitler's War 1942–1945* Macmillan 1977, p. 657

p. 37   'a mixture of cloister and concentration camp . . .' Nuremberg Papers part XV, p. 283

p. 38   'End the war, you fools. What else can you do?' quoted in Ryan *op. cit.*, p. 37

p. 41   'There are you, seriously injured . . .' quoted in Irving *op. cit.*, p. 673

p. 42   'It was a soldier's nightmare of retreat and defeat . . .' Summersby *op. cit.*, pp. 159–60

p. 43   'All approaches to [the river] are hopelessly jammed . . .' quoted in Michael Reynolds *Sons of the Reich – II SS Panzer Corps in*

Normandy, Arnhem, Ardennes and on the Eastern Front Spellmount
Staplehurst 2002, p. 93

p. 43 'The divisions which were taken back from Normandy . . .'
quoted in Matthew Cooper, *The German Army 1933–1945 –
Its Political and Military Failure* Macdonald & Janes 1978
pp. 512–13

p. 44 'The whole west front has collapsed . . .' quoted in Robert
Kershaw *It Never Snows in September – The German View of
MARKET GARDEN and the Battle of Arnhem, September 1944*
Shepperton Ian Allan 1994, p. 19

p. 44 'If necessary we'll fight on the Rhine . . .' quoted in Bullock *op.
cit.*, pp. 755–6

p. 45 'There was no order, no leadership . . .' interview with Julius
Lange, 28 July 2007

p. 46 'A young *Leutnant*, unshaven and with a mad . . .' interview with
Oskar Bieber, 29 July 2007

p. 46 'Our only hope is to be taken prisoner . . .' quoted in Hastings
op. cit., p. 18

p. 47 'We had to scavenge for food . . .' quoted in Hargreaves *op. cit.*,
p. 237

p. 47 'It was the civilians or us and there was no contest . . .' correspondence with Gerhard Keller, 16 September 2004

p. 47 'In May 1940 I first set foot on French soil . . .' quoted in
Hargreaves *op. cit.*, p. 238

p. 47 'a *Leutnant* shot in the head . . .' ibid., p. 237

p. 48 'For stragglers, small groups or single vehicles . . .' quoted in
Richard Hargreaves *The Germans in Normandy* Pen and Sword
2006, p. 237

p. 48 'it was like trying to scoop up water with an open hand' interview with Heinrich Mayer, sometime staff officer in headquarters OB West, 23 May 2007

p. 48 'Hold! Hold!' quoted in Cooper *op. cit.*, p. 515

p. 48   'There could be no question of systematic supplies ...' Siegfried Westphal *The German Army in the West* Cassell 1951, p. 172

p. 49   'good regimental sergeant-major' quoted in Ryan *op. cit.*, p. 43

p. 49   'I am considering disbanding the Luftwaffe ...' quoted in Irving *op. cit.*, p. 703

p. 49   '[The] Führer spoke first: a tirade against the Luftwaffe ...' quoted in Irving *op. cit.*, p. 703

p. 50   'Our own forces are tied up in battle ...' quoted in Cooper *op. cit.*, p. 514

p. 51   'We had been fighting since 8 June without much time ...' interview with Lars Hahn, 16 June 1995

p. 51   'The general opinion ... was that as the war would be over ...' Lieutenant Erich Schneider WO208/5537, National Archives, Kew

p. 52   'The overall situation in the west was serious ...' Westphal *op. cit.*, p. 172

p. 52   'With the enemy's advance and the withdrawal of our front ...' Model Order of the Day dated 3 September 1944, author's archive

p. 53   'Over 16 days, 65,000 men ...' figures from Kershaw *op. cit.*, p. 24

p. 54   'build a new front on the Albert Canal' quoted in Kershaw *op. cit.*, p. 21

p. 54   'the sweepings from Germany ...' interview with Volker Holzman, 16/17 March 2006, with reference to a diary entry dated 8 September 1944. Hauptmann Holzman was a staff officer at Student's headquarters for just five days before being wounded by a strafing Allied aircraft.

p. 55   'Standing alongside young volunteers were old NCOs ...' quoted in James Lucas *Battle Group! German Kampfgruppen Action of World War Two* Cassell 2000, p. 156

p. 56   'Montgomery's waltz through northern Europe' from a letter written by Sergeant Len Wallis, 75th Anti-Tank Regiment Royal Artillery, 11th Armoured Division 13 September 1944

p. 56   'no long tr[ainin]g marches were made ...' Leutnant Lingenhole WO 208/5537, National Archives, Kew

p. 56   'The personnel of the Division suffered ...' Major Geyer WO 208/5537, National Archives, Kew

p. 57   'The combined effects of brave ...' George H. Stein *The Waffen SS – Hitler's Elite Guard at War 1939–1945* Oxford University Press Oxford 1966, p. 224

p. 57   'Our training was indeed hard ...' quoted in Gordon Williamson *Loyalty is my Honor: Personal Accounts from the Waffen SS* Brown 1999, p. 40

p. 58   'while the SS elements as usual fought to annihilation ...' quoted in Stein *op. cit.*, p. 225

p. 59   'a real soldier's soldier, no airs and graces ...' quoted in Williamson *op. cit.*, p. 49

p. 59   'The first company was caught ...' quoted in Kershaw *op. cit.*, p. 16

p. 60   'The situation could change ...' quoted in Kershaw *op. cit.*, p. 16

p. 61   'The highway was overcrowded with fleeing vehicles ...' Wilhelm Tieke *In the Firestorm of the Last Years of the War*, trans. Frederick Steinhardt, J.J. Fedorowicz Winnipeg 1999, p. 218

p. 62   'on its right wing it will concentrate an attack force ...' quoted in Kershaw *op. cit.*, p. 31

Chapter 3: Chasing the Dream

p. 65   'Perched on the edge of the hole ...' account written largely from an interview with Davey Jones, 16 August 2007

p. 66   'We ought to have a corps of at least five thousand ...' Ministry of Information *By Air to Battle – The Official Account of the British First and Sixth Airborne Divisions* HMSO 1945, p. 7

p. 68 'a colourful personality ... all the qualities of superb ...' quoted in Maurice Tugwell *Airborne to Battle – A History of Airborne Warfare 1918–1971* William Kimber 1971, p. 125

p. 69 'I think it would be dull of us to say ...' quoted in Leonard Rapport and Arthur Northwood *Rendezvous with Destiny – A History of the 101st Airborne Division* 101st Airborne Division Association Fort Campbell KY 1948, p. 9

p. 70 'The 101st ... has no history, but it has a rendezvous with destiny ...' Gerard M. Devlin *Paratrooper! The Saga of Parachute and Glider Combat Troops During World War II* Robson 1979, p. 131

p. 71 'solidly built, hawk-visaged, no-nonsense soldier ...' Len Lebenson *Surrounded by Heroes – Six Campaigns with Division Headquarters, 82d Airborne Division, 1942–1945* Casemate (Philadelphia) PA 2007, p. 103

p. 71 'best airborne tradition ... [to rely] on madmen instead of firepower' quoted by Stephen Ambrose *Band of Brothers* Pocket Books 2001, p. 225

p. 71 'Every 82nd Airborne trooper is by the nature ...' quoted in Phil Nordyke, *All American – All the Way – The Combat History of the 82nd Airborne Division in World War II* Zenith Press St Paul MN 2005, p. 1

p. 72 'Be your age. What do you know about parachuting? ...' quoted in Julian James *A Fierce Quality: Life of Alistair Pearson, Para Extraordinaire, DSO and 3 Bars MC* Leo Cooper Barnsley 1989, p. 22

p. 72 'If I had to soldier, I wanted to soldier in an elite unit ...' Spencer F. Wurst and Gayle Wurst *Descending from the Clouds – A Memoir of Combat in the 505 Parachute Infantry Regiment, 82d Airborne Division* Casemate Havertown PA 2004, p. 33

p. 72 'I was going to enlist in the Marines ...' William 'Wild Bill' Guarnere and Edward 'Babe' Heffron with Robyn Prost *Brothers in Battle, Best of Friends – Two WWII Paratroopers from the*

Original Band of Brothers Tell their Story Berkley Caliber, New York 2007, p. 67

p. 73 'common sense and character ...' Ministry of Information *By Air to Battle op. cit.*, p. 14

p. 73 'Among those who came nearly half had no documents ...' Major-General John Frost *A Drop Too Many* Sphere 1983, p. 25

p. 73 'the object was to break all but the fittest ...' Captain W.C. 'Colin' Brown File 97/19/1 IWM

p. 74 'The physical training was organized ...' Ernest J. Rooke-Matthews File 92/37/1 IWM, 'One Third of My Life'

p. 74 '"Why do you hate your mother?" ...' James Sims *Arnhem Spearhead – A Private Soldier's Story* Imperial War Museum 1978, pp. 4–5

p. 74 'Through these portals pass the toughest paratroopers in the world' photograph of Fort Benning Parachute School in 1942, author's collection

p. 74 'took even more verbal abuse ...' Spencer Wurst and Gayle Wurst *op. cit.* p. 36

p. 74 'We were always tired and hungry ...' interview with Fenton Richards, 22 March 2007

p. 75 'Camp Toccoa was only about one thing ...' Guarnere and Heffron *op. cit.*, pp. 18–19

p. 76 'beasting to encouragement' interview with Stanley Livermore 18 November 2007

p. 76 'They made small men feel tall ...' Rooke-Matthews *op. cit.*

p. 76 'The Army and RAF were not exactly bosom buddies ...' quoted in Colin John Bruce, *War on the Ground 1939–1945* Book Club Associates 1995, pp. 195–6

p. 77 '[The] theme was kept up all throughout our schooling ...' Wurst *op. cit.*, p. 39

p. 77 'turn around, go down the steps ...' interview with Ron Reeve, 2 March 2006

p. 77 'The last tower was the best . . .' quoted in Nordyke *Four Stars for Valor op. cit.*, p. 21

p. 78 'Our qualified brother officers were unanimous . . .' Frost *op. cit.*, p. 28

p. 78 'about 10 per cent . . .' Captain W.C. 'Colin' Brown File 97/19/1 IWM

p. 78 'Bring it back and I'll give you another one' quoted in Bruce *op. cit.*, p. 201

p. 78 'I heard all sorts of facts and figures . . .' interview with Stanley Livermore, 18 November 2007

p. 79 'Colonel Flavall was cheerful in almost any circumstance . . .' Frost *op. cit.*, p. 30

p. 79 'no jump thereafter gives the same thrill . . .' Ernest J. Rooke-Matthews *op. cit.*

p. 79 'We were all worried about flinging ourselves . . .' interview with Bob Collins, 6 May 2005

p. 79 'I always had doubts about being successful . . .' Wurst *op. cit.*, p. 39

p. 80 'one of the greatest moments of our lives . . .' Sims *op. cit.*, p. 16

p. 80 'Those wings made you different . . .' Guarnere and Heffron *op. cit.*, p. 28

p. 81 'that once on the ground his future lies . . .' Richard Gale *With the 6th Airborne Division in Normandy* Sampson Low Marston 1948, pp. 2–3

p. 81 'helped us greatly in future operations' Wurst *op. cit.*, pp. 44–5

p. 81 'the training got harder and more complicated, more combat-orientated' Guarnere and Heffron *op. cit.*, p. 28

p. 81 'Through specific small-unit training . . .' interview with Fenton Richards, 22 March 2007

p. 82 'a wonderful aircraft which handled impeccably . . .' quoted in Bruce *op. cit.*, p. 218

p. 83 'The Hamilcar was a remarkable design . . .' interview with Andrew Taylor, 28 October 2006

p. 83 'a dark green blunt-nosed dragonfly' quoted in John L. Lowden *Silent Wings at War – Combat Gliders in World War Two* Smithsonian Institution Press Washington DC 1992, pp. 11–12

p. 83 'scrounged up armoured plate' Lowden *op. cit.*, p. 12

p. 84 'It was felt that those accepted should . . .' quoted in Bruce *op. cit.*, p. 214

p. 84 'The maximum age was thirty-five . . .' Lowden *op. cit.*, pp. 10–11

p. 85 'Well, when he said that I guess anybody . . .' Albert Blockwell (ed. Maggie Clifton) *Diary of a Red Devil – By Glider to Arnhem with the 7th King's Own Scottish Borderers* Helion 2005, pp. 58–9

p. 85 'We didn't choose the gliders . . .' interview with Jimmy Mason, 12 July 2005

p. 86 'A weeding-out process started . . .' quoted in Blockwell *op. cit.*, p. 59

p. 86 'close-order drill, manual of arms . . .' Lebenson *op. cit.*, p. 13

p. 87 'So we climbed in, fastened straps . . .' Blockwell *op. cit.*, p. 74

p. 87 'Vomiting was part of the deal . . .' interview with Corporal Chuck Wilson, 12 July 2006

p. 87 '[I] and 19 volunteers from brigade headquarters . . .' Napier Crookenden *Dropzone Normandy – The Story of the American and British Airborne Assault on D Day 1944* Ian Allan 1976, p. 43

p. 87 'who would like being cooped up . . .' interview with Billy Meyers, 12 December 2006

p. 88 'The trailer snapped its mooring lines . . .' Lowden *op. cit.*, p. 29

p. 89 'Join the glider troops! No flight pay . . .' quoted in Crookenden *op. cit.*, p. 23

p. 89 'I'll tell you straight out . . .' quoted in Lowden *op. cit.*, p. ix

p. 90 'We were 18, 19 years old . . .' Guarnere and Heffron *op. cit.*, p. xx

p. 90 'Many soldiers who could have . . .' Wurst *op. cit.*, p. 112

p. 90 'gained the ability to anticipate . . .' Diary of 2nd Lieutenant Harold Watkins, entry 2 April 1944

p. 91 'we didn't care [about anything] . . .' Blockwell *op. cit.*, p. 70

p. 91 'It was always E Company versus . . .' Guarnere and Heffron *op. cit.*, p. 23

p. 91 'Every man a clone of the CO . . .' quoted in Clay Blair *Ridgway's Paratroopers – The American Airborne in World War II* Naval Institute Press Annapolis MD 2002, p. 51

p. 92 'It was a fair fight, with little serious slugging . . .' Lowden *op. cit.*, p. 24

p. 92 'weren't particular who they fought . . .' Frost *op. cit.*, p. 26

p. 92 'There was this thing they did . . .' quoted in Blair *op. cit.*, p. 53

p. 93 'Gentlemen, despite your excellent training . . .' quoted in Lloyd Clark *The Orne Bridgehead* Sutton Stroud 2004, p. 16

p. 93 'When you first lead your men into the valley . . .' quoted by John Hanlon in Colonel Robert E. Jones *History of the 101st Airborne Division – Screaming Eagles – The First 50 Years* Turner Paducah KY 2005, p. 3

p. 93 'Dozens of planes went down . . .' Lebenson *op. cit.*, p. 60

p. 94 'I do not believe in the airborne division' quoted by Hanlon in Jones (ed.) *op. cit.*, p. 12

p. 94 'at a time when we are scouring the country . . .' WO 219/2860, National Archives, Kew

p. 94 'seriously jeopardized the future of airborne . . .' quoted by Hanlon in Jones (ed.) *op. cit.*, p. 11

p. 95 'Of the 162 [officers and] men . . .' quoted in Nordyke *Four Stars of Valor op. cit.*, p. 221

p. 95 'We ran through training over and over . . .' Guarnere and Heffron *op. cit.*, p. 90

p. 96 'would have as its purpose a maximum . . .' Lewis H. Brereton *The Brereton Diaries – The War in the Air in the Pacific, Middle East and Europe 3 October 1941–8 May 1945* William Morrow New York 1946, pp. 308–9

p. 97   'Not since the days when the Greeks . . .' quoted in Lowden *op. cit.*, pp. xv–xvi

Chapter 4: Stitching Things Together

p. 99   'The two commanders looked like . . .' This account has been written with reference to an interview with Don Evans – a Staff-Sergeant at FAAA – 16 May 2007 and WO 219/4998 Operation Market: Planning Papers, The National Archives, Kew

p. 101   'like threading seven needles with one piece . . .' quoted in A.D. Harvey *Arnhem* Cassell 2001, p. 31

p. 101   'to blast my way down the main road . . .' Horrocks *op. cit.*, p. 210

p. 101   'as most of the available resources . . .' ibid., p. 209

p. 103   'I was deeply troubled by the possibility . . .' James M. Gavin *On to Berlin – Battles of an Airborne Commander 1943–1946* Viking Press New York 1978, p. 149

p. 104   'Your Primary task is to capture the Arnhem . . .' Operation 'Market' Instructions No. 1 to: Maj-Gen R.E. Urquhart from Lt-Gen F.A.M. Browning 13 Sep 1944, author's archive

p. 105   'There was no doubt that the RAF . . .' quoted in Harvey *op. cit.*, p. 45

p. 105   'I assumed that the British . . .' quoted in Ryan *op. cit.*, p. 126

p. 106   'But the Germans, how about the Germans . . .' quoted in William F. Buckingham *Arnhem 1944* Tempus Stroud 2002, p. 67

p. 106   '13 officers, 73 NCOs . . .' SSPz. Gren. A.u.E. Btl. 16 in den Kämpfen bei ARNHEIM 17.9.44–7.10.44, author's archive

p. 107   'We understood that Germany . . .' interview with Wolfgang Amsel, 22 June 2006

p. 108 'The whole II SS Corps was especially . . .' quoted in Kershaw *op. cit.*, p. 41

p. 108 'gave up three APCs . . .' quoted ibid., p. 39

p. 109 '[The operation] depended on the unbelievable notion . . .' quoted in Ryan *op. cit.*, p. 116

p. 110 'They said, as I remember . . .' quoted in Harvey *op. cit.*, p. 34

p. 110 'The enemy is fighting determinedly . . .' Operation 'Market' Summary of Intelligence No.1. 13 Sept 1944, author's archive

p. 111 'The planning of the operation . . .' Major-General R.E. Urquhart *Arnhem* Pan 1960, p. 19

p. 111 'in the division there was a certain reserve . . .' Urquhart *op. cit.*, pp. 20–21

p. 111 'The total German force, including both remnants . . .' WO 371/341, National Archives, Kew

p. 112 'I knew that we were opposed . . .' Horrocks *op. cit.*, p. 210

p. 112 'political aptitude and ruthless ambition . . .' Buckingham *op. cit.*, p. 9

p. 113 'cautioned me against . . .' quoted in Powell *Devil's Birthday op. cit.*, p. 38

p. 113 'Montgomery could have cancelled the operation . . .' ibid., p. 48

p. 113 'In retrospect, it seems crazy . . .' quoted in Martin Middlebrook *Arnhem 1944 – The Airborne Battle* Penguin 1995, p. 62

p. 114 'By the time we went on Market Garden . . .' quoted in John Baynes *Urquhart of Arnhem – The Life of Major-General R.E. Urquhart CB, DSO* Brassey's 1993, p. 100

p. 114 'Nerves had frayed and discipline . . .' Geoffrey Powell *Men at Arnhem* Leo Cooper Barnsley 1998, p. 14

p. 114 'had the effect . . . of sharpening our state . . .' quoted in Baynes *op. cit.*, p. 79

p. 115 'an airborne division was a force . . .' Urquhart *op. cit.*, p. 26

p. 115 'The snag with bringing a complete newcomer . . .' Frost *op. cit.*, p. 73

p. 116 'We found the airborne boys . . .' quoted in Middlebrook *op. cit.*, p. 22

p. 116 'As a whole, the division contained . . .' quoted in Baynes *op. cit.*, p. 72

p. 117 'These were a bunch of very tough customers' quoted in Nordyke *All American op. cit.*, p. 408

p. 117 'particularly tough on the replacements . . .' Major Dick Winters with Colonel Cole C. Kingseed *Beyond Band of Brothers* Berkley New York 2006, pp. 120–21

p. 117 'Our ranks had been filled with replacements . . .' David Webster Kenyon *Parachute Infantry – An American Paratrooper's Memoir of D-Day and the Fall of the Third Reich* Delta Books 1994, p. 49

p. 119 'The variety of headgear was striking . . .' quoted in Powell *The Devil's Birthday op. cit.*, p. 84

p. 119 'This is a tale that you will tell . . .' ibid., p. 84

p. 119 'parked for miles all over the countryside . . .' *op. cit.*, quoted in Ryan, p. 155

p. 120 'September 14: Things are mighty hot . . .' Rapport and Northwood *op. cit.*, p. 259

p. 120 '[On the morning of the 16th] troops were issued . . .' Nordyke *All American op. cit.*, p. 424

p. 120 'The briefings were over . . .' Geoffrey Powell *Men at Arnhem op. cit.*, p. 15

p. 121 'The remainder of the morning was free . . .' Nordyke *All American op. cit.*, p. 424

p. 121 'in case there was time for a quick game' quoted in Middlebrook *op. cit.*, p. 72

p. 121 'sweated out the jump; hoping the chute . . .' quoted in Ryan *op. cit.*, p. 155

p. 121 'jamming Stens and Bren guns' Powell *Men at Arnhem op. cit.*, p. 15

p. 121 'who warned us that if we refused . . .' Sims *op. cit.*, p. 29

p. 121 'At night, you had your own thoughts . . .' Guarnere and Heffron *op. cit.*, pp. 98–9

p. 122 'Confirm Market Sunday 17th . . .' quoted in Ryan *op. cit.*, p. 162

p. 122 'The morning was cool, with a thick fog . . .' Donald R. Burgett *The Road to Arnhem – A Screaming Eagle in Holland* Dell New York 2001, p. 28

p. 122 'Sunday started off just like any other day . . .' Sims *op. cit.*, p. 31

p. 123 'I got up with mixed feelings . . .' Frost *op. cit.*, pp. 203–4

p. 123 'We pulled each other up . . .' interview with Len Wright, 9 October 1994

p. 124 'It was as though the stimulation of their senses . . .' interview with Len Wright, 9 October 1994

p. 124 'Someone dished out great mugs of tea . . .' Sims *op. cit.*, p. 31

p. 124 'I sought a spiritual motto to fit the occasion . . .' Nordyke *All American – All the Way op. cit.*, p. 428

p. 125 'helmet, boots and gloves . . .' Stephen Ambrose, Foreword to Burgett *Currahee! – A Screaming Eagle in Normandy*, pp. ix–x

p. 125 'A haversack containing maps . . .' Powell *Men at Arnhem op. cit.*, pp. 20–21

p. 126 'we were marched over the field . . .' Blockwell *op. cit.*, p. 94

p. 127 'Even at this late stage . . .' interview with Len Wright, 9 October 1994

p. 127 'We were all in bucket-seats . . .' Burgett *The Road to Arnhem op. cit.*, p. 35

p. 127 'The time waiting for the aircraft to take off . . .' Frost *op. cit.*, pp. 205–6

p. 128 'Then it was our turn . . .' Burgett *The Road to Arnhem op. cit.*, pp. 35–6

p. 128 '[We sat down and] tightened our safety belts . . .' Blockwell *op. cit.*, pp. 94–5

p. 129 'I put the crockery on the kitchen table . . .' interview with Jane Mayhew, 16 July 2006

p. 129 'C-47, Short Stirling, Horsa, Hamilcar . . .' interview with Jim Russell, 13 August 2006

p. 129 'This was the genuine airborne thrust . . .' Frost *op. cit.*, p. 198

Chapter 5: Jumping the Rhine (I)

p. 131 'The pilot of the C-47 held a steady course . . .' based on the following material: Captain John D. Phillips, the commander of 3rd platoon, Company E, 2nd Battalion, 505th PIR, 82nd US Airborne Division Advanced Infantry Officers Course 1947–48 Personal Experience, The Infantry Center, Fort Benning GA and correspondence (author's archive)

p. 132 'continuous enemy motorized movement . . .' quoted in Kershaw *op. cit.*, p. 45

p. 132 'heavy enemy supply traffic with headlights . . .' ibid., p. 45

p. 132 '[I] entered the plane but it was empty . . .' quoted in George E. Koskimaki *Hell's Highway – A Chronicle of the 101st Airborne in the Holland Campaign, September–November 1944* Ballantine Books New York 2007, p. 70

p. 133 'I was beginning to relax a little . . .' quoted in Lowden *op. cit.*, p. 99

p. 133 '16,200 parachutists . . .' Figures from Clay Blair *op. cit.*, p. 332

p. 133 'It was a lovely Sunday morning . . .' Horrocks *op. cit.*, p. 210

p. 134 'At 1435 hours Lieutenant Keith Heathcote . . .' Fitzgerald *op. cit.*, p. 490

p. 134 'Nine tanks were knocked out . . .' ibid., p. 490

p. 135 'Willis [the driver] has some shrapnel in both forearms . . .' quoted in Taylor *op. cit.*, p. 92

p. 135 'The Typhoons came cutting in . . .' Fitzgerald *op. cit.*, p. 492

p. 135 'I have never seen Guardsmen . . .' quoted ibid., p. 490

p. 136 'I saw a young German soldier staggering . . .' quoted in Taylor *op. cit.*, p. 92

p. 136 'Dressed in their best Sunday uniforms . . .' Sims *op. cit.*, p. 38

p. 137 'an advance on Arnhem . . .' SSPz. Gren. A.u.E. Btl. 16 in den Kämpfen bei ARNHEIM 17.9.44–7.10.44, author's archive

p. 138 'We must delay them at all costs . . .' ibid.

p. 139 'As we reached the crossroads . . .' Tom Hoare *Rouge Diablos* Avon 1995, p. 40

p. 140 'like almost everyone else . . .' quoted in Ryan *op. cit.*, p. 162

p. 140 'They were moving in single file . . .' Urquhart *op. cit.*, p. 49

p. 140 'It was a terrifying experience . . .' Sims *op. cit.*, p. 40

p. 140 'The firing ceased as the German . . .' ibid., p. 40

p. 141 'I could now hear the plop . . .' Urquhart *op. cit.*, p. 50

p. 142 'When I convinced him . . .' Frost *op. cit.*, p. 216

p. 143 'As soon as my men fired the first . . .' T. Moffatt Burriss *Strike and Hold – A Memoir of the 82d Airborne in World War* II Brassey's Washington DC 2000, p. 106

p. 143 'many empty uniforms were found at positions . . .' Captain Carl W. Kappel, The Operations of Company 'H', 504th Parachute Infantry (82nd Airborne Division) in the Invasion of Holland 17–21 September 1944 Advanced Infantry Officers Course 1947–48 Personal Experience, The Infantry Center, Fort Benning, GA

p. 143 'The forest was as quiet as a grave . . .' interview with Don Shanks, 19 April 2006

p. 144 'We dug our individual holes . . .' Lebenson *op. cit.*, pp. 147–8

p. 144 'I raised my carbine and fired . . .' Phil Nordyke *All American – All the Way: The Combat History of the 82nd Airborne Division in World War II* Zenith Press St Paul MN 2005, p. 456

p. 145 'We sent scouts and moved within Nijmegen's . . .' Dwayne T.

Burns and Leland T. Burns *Jump into the Valley of the Shadow – The World War II Memories of a Paratrooper in the 508th PIR, 82nd Airborne Division* Casemate, Philadelphia PA 2006, pp. 116–17

p. 146 'A German MG-42 opened up . . .' quoted in Phil Nordyke *All American Way op. cit.*, p. 460

p. 146 'Here within two hours, two of my basic . . .' ibid., p. 462

p. 147 'they had the situation well in hand' ibid., p. 465

p. 147 'At this point the group . . .' quoted in Koskimaki *op. cit.*, pp. 114–15

p. 148 'Suddenly, without warning, explosions ripped . . .' Don Burgett *The Road to Arnhem op. cit.*, p. 49

p. 148 'The bloodied remnants of A Company . . .' ibid., pp. 52–3

p. 149 'A very young German soldier was lying . . .' quoted in George Koskimaki *Hell's Highway op. cit.*, pp. 116

p. 149 'We were closing in on the bridge . . .' correspondence written by Sergeant Hugh Pritchard with Tom Simmons, 1 August 1947, author's archive

p. 150 'we passed the charred remains . . .' diary of Corporal David Summers, 1st battalion, 502 PIR dated 17 September 1944, author's archive

p. 150 'two German tanks, one had been following . . .' quoted in George Koskimaki *Hell's Highway op. cit.*, p. 195

p. 151 'We seized Veghel quite quickly . . .' ibid., p. 166

p. 151 'I don't know where the other companies were . . .' ibid., p. 240

p. 152 'if I were a German commander . . .' correspondence with David R. Smith, letter dated 12 December 1995

p. 153 'dizziness, throbbing head, and the return . . .' quoted in Ian Kershaw, *Hitler 1936–1945: Nemesis* Penguin 2000, p. 726

p. 153 'The First Parachute Army is pulling . . .' quoted in Helmut, Heiber and David Glantz (eds) *Hitler and his Generals –*

Military Conferences 1942–1945 Enigma Books New York 2004, p. 416

p. 154 '18/0200–0900hrs MMG, infantry . . .' Draft Account 3rd Parachute Battalion 'C' Company – Lt Len Wright, author's collection

p. 154 'the Germans put down a sustained . . .' Sims *op. cit.*, pp. 56–7

p. 155 'a couple of our fellows excelled themselves . . .' Appendix 'J' to War Diary HQ, British Airborne Corps for September 1944 – Summary of Statement by Lt D.J. Simpson, RE 1 Para Bn

p. 156 'the odds against an outcome . . .' Frost *op. cit.*, p. 224

p. 156 'My section's first encounter with the enemy armour . . .' Hoare *op. cit.*, p. 42

p. 156 'To take over seemed to be the only thing . . .' Anthony Deane-Drummond *Arrows of Fortune* Leo Cooper Barnsley 1992, pp. 103–4

p. 157 'I came out of the back door . . .' Urquhart *op. cit.*, pp. 72–3

p. 157 'We laid Lathbury on the floor . . .' ibid., pp. 73–4

p. 158 'This enormity in hirsute handlebars . . .' ibid., p. 75

p. 158 'We all dived into a lavatory on the ground . . .' Anthony Deane-Drummond *op. cit.*, pp. 104–5

p. 159 'Two minutes after landing I suddenly realized . . .' quoted in R. Brammall *The Tenth – A Record of Service of the 10th Battalion, the Parachute Regiment 1942–1945 and the 10th Battalion, the Parachute Regiment (T.A.) (County of London) 1945–1965* Eastgate Ipswich 1965, p. 52

p. 160 'Every time we tried to move forward . . .' notes of an interview conducted with James Blue by Peter Rider, 10 November 1948, author's archive

p. 161 'I talked to one glider pilot . . .' quoted in Lowden *op. cit.*, p. 102

p. 161 'Hollywood could not have created a better scene . . .' Burns *op. cit.*, pp. 121–2

p. 163 'A round entered my right jaw . . .' quoted in Koskimaki *op. cit.*, pp. 132–3

p. 163 'I do remember trying to flush out snipers . . .' ibid., p. 129

p. 163 'The advance continued for . . .' Captain Lloyd E. Willis, The Operations of the 506th Parachute Infantry Regiment, (101st Airborne Division) in Holland 17 September to 9 October 1944 Advanced Infantry Officers Course 1947–1948 Personal Experience, The Infantry Center, Fort Benning, GA

p. 164 'My parents had been told that the Americans . . .' interview with Pauel Velay, 3 March 2007

p. 165 'September 18th was one of the darkest days . . .' quoted in Koskimaki *op. cit.*, p. 170

p. 165 'to within one hundred yards of our battalion lines . . .' Narrative of Market Garden for 502nd Parachute Infantry Report Operation Market Garden, Donovan Research Library, US Army Infantry School, Fort Benning, GA

p. 165 'The reaction of the enemy . . .' Brereton *op. cit.*, p. 348

Chapter 6: Perimeters

p. 167 'The battle was draining . . .' interview with Len Wright, 9 October 1994

p. 169 'the separate explosions now merged . . .' Sims *op. cit.*, pp. 66–7

p. 169 'The German SP crashed out . . .' ibid., p. 74

p. 170 'A blast of hot air hit me in the back . . .' ibid., p. 75

p. 171 'LC Horton was wounded . . .' quoted in Brammall *op. cit.*, p. 62

p. 171 'We went in straight and level . . .' ibid., p. 64

p. 172 'From foxholes and slit trenches . . .' Urquhart *op. cit.*, p. 74

p. 174 'They fairly brought the whip . . .' *One Aspect of the Battle of Nijmegen Bridge, Tues–Wed 19/20 Sep 1944* by Major H.F. Stanley, 1st (Motor) Bn Grenadier Guards, author's archive

p. 174 'All the way the battalions were greeted . . .' Fitzgerald *op. cit.*, p. 499

p. 174 'My orders had said that the Nijmegen . . .' Adair *op. cit.*, p. 164

p. 175 'The Battle Group heading for the main bridge . . .' Stanley *op. cit.*, mother's archive

p. 175 'We were opposed by really tough troops . . .' Adair *op. cit.*, p. 166

p. 176 'It went all quiet for a moment . . .' quoted in Koskimaki *op. cit.*, p. 180

p. 176 'Around noon we became conscious . . .' ibid., p. 183

p. 177 'more than we had ever seen at one time' quoted in Ambrose *Band of Brothers op. cit.*, p. 127

p. 178 'We had liberty to attack the Allies . . .' correspondence between Simon Rees and Kurt Student dated 15 May 1956

p. 178 'Both sides had hope . . .' interview with Len Wright, 9 October 1994

p. 179 'We found it difficult to do anything . . .' ibid.

p. 180 'The enemy had by now moved . . .' quoted in Middlebrook *op. cit.*, p. 311

p. 180 'My world swirled and blurred . . .' interview with Len Wright, 9 October 1994

p. 180 'There was a sudden savage crash . . .' Frost *op. cit.*, p. 230

p. 180 'I was quite affected by the blast . . .' quoted in Middlebrook *op. cit.*, p. 312

p. 182 'With the help of one of the bomb-happy . . .' Frost *op. cit.*, p. 231

p. 183 'No one hesitated. The men rose . . .' Powell *Men at Arnhem op. cit.*, p. 120–1

p. 184 'On one of my trips . . .' Urquhart *op. cit.*, p. 120

p. 186 'Non-surgical casualties were virtually . . .' Derrick Randall http://www.bbc.co.uk/ww2peopleswar/stories/78/a5516778.shtml

p. 186 'By this time General Urquhart and his staff . . .' ibid.

p. 187 'Our path was blocked . . .' Brereton *op. cit.*, pp. 349–50

p. 188 'We were told that British armour . . .' interview with Thomas Abt, a lieutenant in 406 Landesschützen Division, 24 February 2007

p. 188 'It was like a Laurel and Hardy movie . . .' Moffatt Burriss *op. cit.*, p. 112

p. 189 'As soon as we launched the first boats . . .' ibid., p. 113

p. 190 'I surrendered along with several others . . .' interview with Urs Ebersbach, 25 February 2007

p. 191 'General Horrocks knew that only infantry . . .' Adair *op. cit.*, p. 167

p. 192 'I went to bed a happy man . . .' Horrocks *op. cit.*, p. 221

p. 192 'I was seated alongside Claude . . .' quoted in Taylor *op. cit.*, p. 100

p. 193 'In the grey morning light . . .' Urquhart *op. cit.*, p. 128

p. 193 'A tough-looking SS soldier . . .' quoted in John Waddy *A Tour of the Arnhem Battlefields 17–26 September 1944* Leo Cooper Barnsley 1999, p. 76

p. 194 'It blew me over backwards . . .' quoted in Middlebrook *op. cit.*, p. 344

p. 195 'They came across – running and shouting . . .' ibid., p. 344

p. 195 'As soon as it was daylight . . .' quoted in Waddy *op. cit.*, p. 131

p. 196 'lack of initiative of British junior . . .' Urquhart *op. cit.*, p. 132

p. 196 'Thus started one of the most exciting . . .' ibid., p. 130

p. 197 'When we saw fresh paratroopers . . .' quoted in Kershaw *op. cit.*, p. 242

p. 197 'so much noise and tracer . . .' quoted in George F. Cholewczynski *Poles Apart – The Polish Airborne at the Battle of Arnhem* Sarpedon New York 1993, p. 140

p. 197 'We were under fire from machine guns . . .' quoted in Middlebrook *op. cit.*, p. 404

p. 198 'I hoped that this fresh infantry division . . .' Horrocks *op. cit.*, p. 222

p. 199 'Field Marshal Model has ordered . . .' quoted in Kershaw *op. cit.*, p. 249

Chapter 7: Touching the Rhine

p. 201 'Sergeant Karl Krahl had expected ...' account written with reference to an interview with Karl Krahl held 23 February 2007

p. 203 'Stunned by this determined blow ...' Major-General H. Essame *The 43rd Wessex Division at War 1944–1945* William Clowes 1952, p. 125

p. 205 'I had been told that ...' quoted in Waddy *op. cit.*, p. 171

p. 206 'Above all, do try ...' Urquhart *op. cit.*, p. 143

p. 206 'You had to be careful when ...' interview with Joe Roberts, 16 April 1986

p. 206 'The snipers were more numerous ...' Urquhart *op. cit.*, pp. 142–3

p. 207 'One of our pilots ...' quoted in Middlebrook *op. cit.*, pp. 356–7

p. 207 'We heard the tank several times ...' ibid., pp. 363–4

p. 208 'Men, there's nothing to get excited about ...' quoted in Ambrose *Band of Brothers op. cit.*, p. 131

p. 209 'Had the Germans realized that my force ...' Tim Saunders *Hell's Highway* Leo Cooper Barnsley 2001, p. 166

p. 209 'It was touch-and-go all the time ...' Rapport and Northwood *op. cit.*, p. 352

p. 209 'The village looked like a Kerr Eby ...' Webster *op. cit.*, p. 119

p. 209 'Men who were there don't need ...' Rapport and Northwood *op. cit.*, p. 359

p. 210 'Our slit trench – for we never dug ...' Webster *op. cit.*, p. 100

p. 211 'The tanks were firing point-blank at us ...' Rapport and Northwood *op. cit.*, p. 355

p. 211 'The attack began with a heavy mortar ...' interview with Karl Krahl, 23 February 2007

p. 213 'it was a worrying day for me' Horrocks *op. cit.*, p. 226

p. 213 'Looking back I am certain . . .' Horrocks *op. cit.*, p. 228

p. 214 'was alive with water spouts and explosions . . .' Cholewczynski, *op. cit.*, p. 179

p. 214 'It was bloody typical . . .' interview with Sergeant 'Jimmy' Riddle, 14 January 2007

p. 214 'The Group's journey to Uden . . .' quoted in Saunders *Hell's Highway op. cit.*, p. 163

p. 215 'inadequate to meet the requirements . . .' ibid., p. 172

p. 215 'Our platoon leader was visibly shaken . . .' ibid., p. 175

p. 217 'We went straight up the highway . . .' ibid., p. 176

p. 217 'What impressed me so much . . .' Horrocks *op. cit.*, pp. 228–9

p. 218 'At almost our darkest hour . . .' quoted in Adair *op. cit.*, p. 167

p. 218 'We were beginning to give up hope . . .' Blockwell *op. cit.*, p. 131

p. 219 'Food was now the dominant problem . . .' Powell *Men at Arnhem op. cit.*, p. 154

p. 220 'The firing across the gardens was getting heavier now . . .' Blockwell *op. cit.*, p. 133

p. 220 'About noon the Germans attacked once again . . .' Powell *Men at Arnhem op. cit.*, p. 180

p. 221 'a crumbling ruin and yet, confined within . . .' Stuart Mawson *Arnhem Doctor* Orbis 1981, pp. 133–4

p. 222 'Many attacks during day by small parties . . .' Urquhart *op. cit.*, p. 157

p. 223 '[Mackenzie] was certain in his own mind . . .' ibid., p. 159

p. 223 'I can find no fault with the attempts . . .' quoted in Middlebrook *op. cit.*, p. 411

p. 224 'The floor was already packed tightly . . .' Kate A. ter Horst *Cloud Over Arnhem* Airborne Museum Oosterbeek, 1999 p. 9

p. 225 'The hours drag by . . .' ibid., p. 36

p. 225 'eventually these houses too became overcrowded . . .' Derrick Randall http://www.bbc.co.uk/ww2peopleswar/stories/78/a5516778.shtml

p. 225 'I did not want to encourage the Germans . . .' Urquhart *op. cit.*, p. 161

p. 228 'We had dug in along the bank . . .' quoted in Middlebrook *op. cit.*, p. 422

p. 229 'There were now about 2500 of us left . . .' Urquhart *op. cit.*, p. 172

p. 229 'However exhausted the poor devil . . .' Powell *Men at Arnhem op. cit.*, p. 155

p. 230 'The enemy established themselves . . .' quoted in Middlebrook *op. cit.*, p. 426

p. 231 'The bombardment suddenly stopped . . .' interview with Otto Egger, 17 April 1996

p. 232 'Monday 25th seemed much as usual . . .' Derrick Randall http://www.bbc.co.uk/ww2peopleswar/stories/78/a5516778.shtml

p. 232 'As the exhausted paratroopers . . .' Horrocks *op. cit.*, p. 230

p. 233 'A clatter of mortar bombs came down . . .' quoted in John Fairley *Remember Arnhem Pegasus Journal* Aldershot 1978, p. 193

p. 233 'After an hour . . . on the riverbank . . .' quoted in Fairley *op. cit.*, p. 193

p. 233 'By the light of the tracer . . .' Urquhart *op. cit.*, pp. 182–3

p. 234 'A total of 3,910 officers and men . . .' Figures from Buckingham *op. cit.*, pp. 7–8

Chapter 8: Riposte

p. 237 'Field Marshal Bernard Montgomery . . .' account written with reference to Major L.F. Ellis with Lieutenant-Colonel A.E. Warhurst *Victory in the West Volume II The Defeat of Germany* HMSO 1968; Alistair Home with David Montgomery *Monty – The Lonely Leader, 1944–45* HarperCollins New York 1994; Nigel Hamilton *Monty: The*

Field Marshal 1944–1976 Sceptre 1987 and notes taken by Major Peter Wraysfield, Royal Artillery

p. 239 'I told him that since Eisenhower . . .' Montgomery *Memoirs*, p. 300

p. 239 'Montgomery was criticizing the fact . . .' excerpt from 'Marshall's Recollections', author's archive

p. 240 'The political difficulty of restraining . . .' quoted in Robin Neillands *The Battle for the Rhine, 1944 Arnhem and the Ardennes: the Campaign in Europe* Weidenfeld & Nicolson 2005, p. 210

p. 240 'unconscionable strategic demands . . .' Omar Bradley *A General's Life*, p. 341

p. 242 'I do not like the layout of the coming offensive . . .' Alan Brooke Diary, entry 8 November 1944

p. 242 'I was never able to convince myself . . .' Arthur Tedder *With Prejudice* Cassell 1966, p. 600

p. 242 'I feel that Monty's strategy for once . . .' Horne *op. cit.*, p. 272

p. 242 'All operations will come to a standstill . . .' quoted in Neillands *The Battle for the Rhine op. cit.*, p. 226

p. 242 'All I remember is the mud and the lack of cover . . .' Robin Neillands, ibid., pp. 158–9

p. 243 'We would load the wagons up with ammunition . . .' interview with Brian Milburn, 12 August 2002

p. 244 'We took a beating in Holland . . .' Guarnere and Heffron *op. cit.*, p. 147

p. 244 'rather depressed at the state of the war . . .' Ramsay Diary, 28 November PRO CAB106/1124

p. 244 'No sooner had they risen from their foxholes . . .' quoted in Neillands *The Battle for the Rhine op. cit.*, p. 245

p. 245 'To put it candidly my plan to smash . . .' Omar Bradley *A General's Life*, p. 343

p. 245 'We have definitely failed to implement . . .' quoted in Neillands *The Battle for the Rhine op. cit.*, p. 267

p. 246 'US Ninth Army: 10,056 . . .' Figures taken from Hastings *op. cit.*, p. 225

p. 246 'What did it matter to an American GI . . .' quoted in Neillands *The Battle for the Rhine op. cit.*, p. 208

p. 247 'It was not a pleasant time . . .' interview with Alan Hudson, 28 March 2007

p. 247 'No matter how hard we tried to keep dry . . .' interview with Donald Kennedy, 16 November 1999

p. 248 'Here it is all damp and dreary . . .' Tom Pocock *Alan Moorehead* The Bodley Head 1990, p. 195

p. 248 'We tried to make sure that the men . . .' interview with Charlie Harris, 20 March 2007

p. 249 'I had had enough by Christmas . . .' interview with Tommy Hobson, 2 May 2006

p. 250 'It was bad for us. Poor conditions . . .' interview with Richard Ritterbecks, 17 November 2006

p. 250 'Having fought in Normandy and all the way . . .' interview with Herbert Piplak, 19 November 2006

p. 250 'I believe we have committed . . .' quoted in Hastings *op. cit.*, p. 222

p. 251 'Few thought that Germany had any hope . . .' WO218/311 17 January 1945, National Archives, Kew

p. 251 'I had decided that I would fight . . .' WO 208/5536, National Archives, Kew

p. 251 'I am conducting operations . . .' quoted in a letter to the author from Major Peter Wraysfield dated 16 August 1994

p. 252 'When you analyse how difficult . . .' quoted in Hastings *op. cit.*, p. 160

p. 252 'I hope the American public will realize . . .' Home *op. cit.*, p. 298

p. 253 'A stooped figure with a pale and puffy face . . .' William Richardson and Seymour Friedlin *Fatal Decisions* Michael Joseph 1956, p. 225

p. 254 'This plan hasn't got a damned . . .' quoted in Steven H. Newton *Hitler's Commander – Field Marshal Walther Model – Hitler's Favorite General* Da Capo Press Cambridge MA 2006, p. 329

p. 254 'When I received this plan . . .' ibid., p. 329

p. 254 'I had merely to cross a river, capture Brussels . . .' quoted in Andrew Williams *D-Day to Berlin* Hodder & Stoughton 2004, p. 186

p. 255 'It looks as if we may now have to pay the price . . .' quoted in Max Hastings *op. cit.*, p. 238

p. 256 'I hope you understand that . . .' quoted in D'Este *op. cit.*, p. 666

p. 257 'We must make certain that [the enemy] is not free . . .' quoted in Hastings *op. cit.*, p. 391

p. 258 'I thought you were the one . . .' quoted in D'Este *op. cit.*, p. 667

p. 258 'trying to arrange the blankets smoothly . . .' ibid., p. 672

p. 259 'It's a typical Monty set-up . . .' quoted in Robin Cross *Fallen Eagle – The Last Days of the Third Reich* Caxton Editions 1995, p. 145

p. 259 '3–5 February 1945 . . .' quoted in Barry Turner *Countdown to Victory – The Final European Campaigns of World War II* Hodder & Stoughton 2004, p. 175

p. 260 'My orders were that under no circumstances . . .' quoted in Neillands *The Battle for the Rhine op. cit.*, p. 212

p. 260 'The weather had been so bad recently . . .' interview with Heinz Kempa, 17 July 2006

p. 260 'We had spent weeks preparing . . .' interview with Mick White, 1 May 2006

p. 261 'At one minute to five that morning . . .' quoted in Turner *op. cit.*, p. 180

p. 262 'There were craters and fallen trees . . .' quoted in Tim

Saunders, *Operations Plunder and Varsity: The British and Canadian Rhine Crossing* Leo Cooper Barnsley 2006, p. 17

p. 262 'You have now accomplished the first part . . .' quoted in Cross *op. cit.*, p. 150

p. 263 'It was a terrible situation . . .' interview with Heinz Kempa, 17 July 2006

p. 263 'I want him to hang on to the West Wall . . .' quoted in Saunders *Operation Plunder op. cit.*, p. 22

p. 263 'I could see my hopes of a long life rapidly dwindling' quoted in Cross *op. cit.*, p. 153

p. 264 'If you have a map before you . . .' ibid., p. 153

p. 265 'Where are you going to go from Remagen?' quoted in Williams *op. cit.*, p. 306

p. 265 'I can outfight that little fart anytime' quoted in Tony Hall (ed. John Pimlott) *March to Victory* Salamander 1994, p. 136

p. 266 'Without the benefit of aerial bombardments . . .' quoted in Tony Hall *op. cit.*, p. 136

Chapter 9: The Deluge

p. 269 'Winifred Steets tried not to expect . . .' account written with reference to an interview and correspondence with Hans-Dieter and Winifred Steets, 21 June 2006

p. 270 'I am busy getting ready for the next battle . . .' Montgomery, letter to Phyllis Reynolds (guardian of his son David), Montgomery Papers, quoted in Hamilton *Monty: The Field Marshal op. cit.*, p. 409

p. 271 'The fighting gets closer . . .' diary of Sophie Becker, 16 March 1945, author's archive

p. 271 'The most difficult thing for our commanders . . .' interview with Klaus Beich, 25 June 2006

p. 273 'The Field Marshal was immediately told the worst . . .' letter from Wilhelm Hagemenn to Peter Mills, 23 August 1951, author's archive. I am grateful to Sheila Mills for providing me with a copy of this letter in 1994.

p. 273 'If the German army was anything like my unit . . .' interview with Heinz Kempa, 17 July 2006

p. 274 'The fighting needed to be passionate . . .' letter from Wilhelm Hagemenn to Peter Mills, 23 August 1951, author's archive

p. 274 'It was demoralizing to have to fight . . .' interview with Herbert Piplak, 20 November 2006

p. 274 'The explosions were so concentrated . . .' quoted in Derek S. Zumbro *Battle for the Ruhr – The German Army's Final Defeat in the West* University Press of Kansas Lawrence KS 2006, p. 130

p. 275 'I should not have been there . . .' interview with Peter Kress, 29 June 2006

p. 275 'The fate of the German people . . .' extract from *Hitler's Speeches 1945*, author's archive

p. 276 'In four to eight weeks . . .' quoted in Neillands *The Conquest of the Reich op. cit.*, p. 155

p. 276 'Hitler became particularly uncomfortable . . .' Siegfried Westphal *The German Army in the West* Cassell 1951, p. 194

p. 277 'Each of the generals had his own very clear plans . . .' quoted in Hamilton *Monty op. cit.*, p. 409

p. 277 'was to be sufficient to provide room . . .' Operational Order No.1 – Operation Plunder, author's archive

p. 278 'Our intelligence was very poor . . .' letter to Klaus Beich from Alfred Schlemm, 30 October 1956, copied during interview with Beich on 25 June 2006

p. 280 'Montgomery had the most difficult of assignments . . .' quoted in Peter Allen *One More River – The Rhine Crossings of 1945* J.M. Dent 1980, p. 219

p. 281 'From their location it seemed clear . . .' quoted in Allen ibid., p. 219

p. 281 'In 6th Airborne we reckoned we had nothing . . .' quoted in Neillands *The Conquest of the Reich – From D-Day to VE-Day: A Soldiers' History* Weidenfeld & Nicolson 1995, p. 159

p. 282 'I was left in no doubt . . .' From an extract sent to the author by Brigadier James Hill, 3 January 2006

p. 283 'As he went on to describe . . .' quoted in Allen *op. cit.*, p. 221

p. 283 'Gentlemen the artillery and air support is fantastic . . .' quoted in Allen *op. cit.*, p. 222

p. 284 'We received orders to take down a church . . .' interview with Heinrich Balck, July 2006

p. 284 'I had been asked to provide . . .' interview with Heinz Kempa, 17 July 2006

p. 285 'We received the usual complaints . . .' interview with Michael Williams, 28 August 2006

p. 286 'Our soldiers would prefer that the Germans . . .' quoted in Zumbro *op. cit.*, p. 126

p. 286 'It was this sort of unglamorous work . . .' Letter from General Sir Miles Dempsey to Major Daniel Stein dated 12 April 1945, author's archive

p. 286 'A sand table 8ft by 6ft was prepared . . .' Andrew Rawson *The Rhine Crossing – 9th US Army and 17th US Airborne* Leo Cooper Barnsley 2006, pp. 29–30

p. 287 'Although we practised over and over again . . .' quoted in Allen *op. cit.*, p. 224

p. 287 'We were told that there was potentially tricky . . .' interview with Rick Andrews, 18 July 2002

p. 288 'The time spent before a set-piece . . .' interview with David Moores, 21 July 2002

p. 289 'I think, although my knowledge of military history . . .' quoted in Allen *op. cit.*, p. 240

p. 289 'Never in the history of human warfare . . .' ibid., p. 241

p. 289 'We were too enthused . . .' ibid., p. 241

p. 289 'It was not so much ...' interview with David Moores, 21 July 2002

p. 290 'Everything pointed towards ...' interview with Bill Potts, 8 August 2006

p. 290 'I tried not to think ...' interview with Rick Andrews, 18 July 2002

p. 291 'The most debilitating aspect of being a replacement ...' interview with Nobby Clarke, 23 September 2006

p. 291 'Today I will die ...' diary of Alistair Trewin, author's archive

p. 291 'If I was going to die ...' interview with John Bird, 16 July 2006

p. 291 'The enemy possibly thinks he is safe behind this great ...' Hamilton *Monty: The Field Marshal op. cit.*, p. 426

p. 292 'The noise was ferocious ...' interview with Brian MacDonald, 18 March 2006

p. 292 'We had all blackened our faces ...' quoted in Allen *op. cit.*, p. 243

p. 293 'Finding our way was easy ...' Neillands *The Conquest of the Reich op. cit.*, p. 157

p. 293 'Our Buffalo skidded on the top ...' quoted in Allen *op. cit.*, p. 246

p. 293 'We couldn't see anything properly ...' quoted ibid., p. 246

p. 294 'It was like fireworks ...' quoted ibid., p. 248

p. 294 'Bomber command delivered a crushing blow ...' quoted in Saunders *Operation Plunder op. cit.*, p. 30

p. 295 'The RAF had devastated the town ...' Neillands *The Conquest of the Reich op. cit.*, p. 158

p. 296 'The cellar ceiling had fallen in ...' interview with Hans-Dieter Steets, 21 June 2006

p. 297 'Plunder began more successfully ...' letter from General Sir Miles Dempsey to Major Daniel Stein, 12 April 1945, author's archive

Chapter 10: Jumping the Rhine (II)

p. 299 'On the morning of 24 March 1945 . . .' account written with reference to Alan Brooke Diary entry 23 March 1945, 24 March 1945; Martin Gilbert *Road to Victory – Winston S. Churchill 1941–1945* Heinemann 1986; John Colville Diary entry 24 March 1945; Nigel Hamilton *Monty: Master of the Battlefield 1942–1944*

p. 301 'An airborne division is a single entity . . .' quoted in Blair *op. cit.*, p. 125

p. 301 'In that moment I knew . . .' interview with Peter Harris, 12 March 2006

p. 301 '24 March: Weather fine . . .' Diary of Ronnie Joyce, author's archive

p. 302 'We were ferried across the Rhine . . .' account by Paul Gerber dated 12 July 1963, author's archive

p. 303 'The air was pregnant with tense . . .' Neillands *The Conquest of the Reich op. cit.*, p. 217

p. 303 'our priority is to protect the developing . . .' quoted in Blair *op. cit.*, p. 126

p. 303 'I was more nervous on the Rhine . . .' interview with Teddy Smith, 16 May 2005

p. 304 'I was getting into my jeep . . .' quoted in Allen *op. cit.*, p. 252

p. 304 'Most of the lads settled down . . .' Ernest J. Rooke-Matthews file 92/37/1 IWM 'One Third of My Life'

p. 305 'where the Germans could be relied . . .' Denis Edwards, *The Devil's Own Luck From Pegasus Bridge to the Baltic 1944–45* Leo Cooper Barnsley 1999, p. 101

p. 305 'I could see columns of transport below . . .' quoted in Stephen L. Wright *The Last Drop: Operation Varsity, March 24–28 1945* Stackpole Books Mechanicsburg PA 2008, p. 80

p. 306 'of the very real possibility . . .' interview with Otto Leitner, 2 May 2005

p. 307 'The red "stand-by" light was on ...' quoted in Neillands *The Conquest of the Reich op. cit.*, pp. 161–2

p. 307 'with so many aircraft it was difficult ...' interview with Otto Leitner, 2 May 2005

p. 308 'one piece of metal tore a hole ...' quoted in Allen *op. cit.*, pp. 269–70

p. 308 'We had dug a slit trench on the fringes ...' interview with Rolf Siegel, 23 November 2006

p. 309 'The Jerries were firing at us but nobody ...' interview with Ken Williams, 18 July 1994

p. 309 'Speed and initiative is the order ...' quoted in Lieutenant-Colonel Bernd Horn and Michel Wyczynski *Para versus the Reich – Canada's Paratroopers at War 1942–45* The Dundurn Group Toronto 2003, p. 193

p. 309 'As soon as the paratroopers ...' interview with Rolf Siegel, 23 November 2006

p. 312 'I only did what every last man ...' quoted in Horn and Wyczynski *Para op. cit.*, p. 193

p. 312 'By 1330 hrs we were dug-in ...' Neillands *The Conquest of the Reich op. cit.*, pp. 165–6

p. 313 'My battalion was ordered to establish itself ...' quoted in Allen *op. cit.*, p. 273

p. 314 'I saw this big tree coming up to hit me ...' Eric Barley and Yves Fohlen *Para Memories – 12th Yorkshire Parachute Battalion in Europe and the Far East During the Second World War* Parapress Tunbridge Wells 1996, p. 123

p. 314 'Immediately on landing we swapped ...' quoted in Wright *op. cit.*, p. 168

p. 315 'Bullets zipped through one side ...' Edwards *op. cit.*, p. 179

p. 316 'There was an almighty "Bang!" ...' quoted in Wright *op. cit.*, p. 149

p. 316 'I ordered my second pilot to open up ...' ibid., p. 153

p. 317 'There was a shout that two German tanks . . .' Neillands *The Conquest of the Reich op. cit.,* pp. 166–7

p. 318 'to warn the inhabitants . . .' correspondence with Fraser Edwards, 10 February 2007

p. 318 'Immediate contact was made with 3 and 5 Para . . .' quoted in Wright *op. cit.,* p. 160

p. 320 'The enemy was firing from positions . . .' quoted in Allen *op. cit.,* p. 276

p. 320 'The German position was pretty hopeless . . .' ibid., p. 276

p. 322 'The C-46 was burning when we hooked up . . .' *Stars and Stripes* 26 March 1945

p. 322 'American paratroopers hanging dead from the trees . . .' quoted in Wright *op. cit.,* p. 212

p. 322 'I started looking for terrain features . . .' quoted in Allen *op. cit.,* p. 275

p. 324 'Several gliders were set on fire and streamed . . .' quoted in Andrew Rawson *The Rhine Crossing – 9th US Army and 17th US Airborne* Leo Cooper Barnsley 2006, p. 89

p. 325 'After all our Rhine defences . . .' quoted in a letter to Klaus Beich from Alfred Schlemm dated 30 October 1956, copied during interview with Beich on 25 June 2006

p. 327 'I ordered my platoon to fix bayonets . . .' Extract from 6th British Airborne Memories, author's archive

p. 327 'It was not long before . . .' ibid.

p. 328 'Most of us anticipated a German counterattack . . .' quoted in Wright *op. cit.,* p. 212

p. 329 'At about 8 o'clock on the Sunday morning . . .' quoted in Neillands *The Conquest of the Reich op. cit.,* p. 170

p. 329 'The Rhine and all its fortress lines . . .' quoted in Wright *op. cit.,* p. 290

Conclusion

p. 333 'It is my opinion that Montgomery . . .' Hoare *op. cit.*, p. 1

p. 333 'Market Garden was a gamble . . .' correspondence with Brad Wiley, letter dated 3 March 2006

p. 334 'used to make a beautiful airborne plan . . .' quoted in Middlebrook *op. cit.*, p. 8

p. 334 'We knew that the risks were great . . .' Gavin *op. cit.*, p. 191

p. 334 'The battle was a decided victory . . .' quoted in Lloyd Clark *Arnhem – Operation Market Garden, September 1944* Sutton Stroud 2003, p. 234

p. 334 'Operation Market Garden accomplished . . .' O. H. Ellis Vol II p. 237

p. 335 'we might have held our bridgehead . . .' quoted in General Sir Charles Richardson *Send for Freddie – The Story of Montgomery's Chief of Staff, Major-General Sir Francis de Guingand, KBE, CB, DSO* William Kimber 1987, pp. 165–6

p. 335 'one of the most imaginative [plans] of the war . . .' quoted in Hamilton *Monty: The Field Marshal op. cit.*, p. 56

p. 336 'some overbearing need . . .' Charles B. MacDonald *The Last Offensive, United States Army in World War II. The European Theater of Operations* Center of Military History (Washington DC) 1973 p. 324

p. 336 'a remarkable success . . .' quoted from a manuscript during an interview with Geoffrey Powell, 6 May 1993

p. 336 'a breathtaking attack . . .' ibid.

p. 337 'the men with whom I served were of the highest calibre . . .' Tom Hoare *op. cit.*, p. 61

Glossary

ADC – aide de camp
AT Gun – anti-tank gun
BAR – Browning automatic rifle
CO – commanding officer
CP – command post
CQMS – company quarter-master sergeant
CSM – company sergeant major
DUKW – amphibious truck
DZ – drop zone
FAAA – First Allied Airborne Army
FOO – forward observation officer
GOC – General Officer Commanding
LC – lance corporal
LCT – landing craft tank
LZ – landing zone
MDS – medical dressing station

MG – machine gun

NCO – non-commissioned officer

OB West – German Army Command in the West

OBLI – Oxfordshire and Buckinghamshire Light Infantry

OC – officer commander

OKH Oberkommando des Heeres – German Army High Command

OKW – Oberkommando der Wehrmacht – German Supreme Command of the Armed Forces

ORs – other ranks

PFC – private first class

PIAT – projector infantry anti tank

PIR – Parachute Infantry Regiment

RAP – regimental aid post

RV – rendezvous

SHAEF – Supreme Headquarters Allied Expeditionary Force

SPG – self-propelled gun

Bibliography

Primary sources

United Kingdom

WO 171/1240 8 Bn Parachute Regiment War Diary 1944 (National Archives, Kew)

WO 171/1257 3/Irish Guards (Armoured) War Diary (National Archives, Kew)

WO 208/5536 Interrogation Reports on German Prisoners of War (National Archives, Kew)

WO 208/5537 Interrogation Reports on German Prisoners of War (National Archives, Kew)

WO 208/5538 Interrogation Reports on German Prisoners of War (National Archives, Kew)

WO 208/5539 Interrogation Reports on German Prisoners of War (National Archives, Kew)

WO 171/406 1st Airborne Division Reconnaissance Squadron War Diaries Arnhem Sept 44 (National Archives, Kew)

Air 29/520 No. 1 Parachute Training School Ringway (National Archives, Kew)

WO 166/10465 HQ Airborne Troops War Diary (National Archives, Kew)

WO 166/10470 1 Bn Glider Pilot Regiment War Diary (National Archives, Kew)

AIR 69/1093 'Airborne Forces' by Major-General F.A.M. Browning (National Archives, Kew)

WO 219/552 1 Allied Airborne Army: Organization and Order of Battle. Establishment of Combined Airborne Headquarters (National Archives, Kew)

WO 219/2860 Formation of 1 Allied Airborne Army (National Archives, Kew)

WO 219/739 82 US Airborne Division training for future operations (National Archives, Kew)

WO 219/5000 Operation Market: Employment of 101 Airborne Division (National Archives, Kew)

Box 29/E/01 Glider Pilot Regiment Operation Tonga, Mallard, Neptune: Interview with Staff-Sergeant Geoff Barkway conducted in 1986 (Museum of Army Flying, Middle Wallop)

Personal account of the action at Pegasus Bridge by Major John Howard (Museum of Army Flying, Middle Wallop)

IWM File 99/23/1 W/O Ronald Oliver RAF (Imperial War Museum)

IWM File 98/23/1 Captain C.V. Duffield Coldstream Guards (Imperial War Museum)

IWM File 98/3/1 Captain Michael Bendix 5/Coldstream Guards 32 Guards Brigade, Guards Armoured Division. Extracts from: Memoirs of Captain Michael Bendix OBE CStJ JP DL FLS FIB (Imperial War Museum)

IWM File 97/19/1 Captain W.C. Brown File (Imperial War Museum)

IWM File 92/37/1 Ernest J. Rooke-Matthews, 'One Third of My Life' (Imperial War Museum)

United States

RG 407 Box 24154–ML 487 Vol. 2 War Diary 7th Army High Command '6 June 1944–31 July 1944 (National Archives, Washington)

Captain John D. Phillips, Commander of 3rd platoon, Company E, 2nd Battalion, 505th PIR, 82nd US Airborne Division Advanced Infantry Officers Course 1947–48 Personal Experience (Donovan Research Library, US Army Infantry School, Fort Benning, GA

Captain Lloyd E. Willis, The Operations of the 506th Parachute Infantry Regiment, (101st Airborne Division) in Holland 17 September–9 October 1944 Advanced Infantry Officers Course 1947–48 Personal Experience. (Donovan Research Library, US Army Infantry School, Fort Benning, GA)

Captain Carl W. Kappel, The Operations of Company 'H', 504th Parachute Infantry (82nd Airborne Division) in the Invasion of Holland 17–21 September 1944 Advanced Infantry Officers Course 1947–48 Personal Experience (Donovan Research Library, US Army Infantry School, Fort Benning, GA)

Narrative of Market Garden for 502nd Parachute Infantry Report Operation Market Garden (Donovan Research Library, US Army Infantry School, Fort Benning, GA)

Germany

Heydte, Oberst von der, '*Kämpfe des Fallschirmjaeger Regiment 6 mit amerik Fallschirmjaegern in Holland im September 1944* (Bundesarchiv, Freiburg)

Schacht, Gerhard I.G. '*Abschrift.* '*die Käempfe der Gruppe Walther von 13.9.44 bis zum 12.10.44 in Süed Holland* (Bundesarchiv, Freiburg)

Tettau, von, '*Abschrift.* '*Gefechtbericht ueber die Schlacht bei Arnheim 17–26.9.44* (Bundesarchiv, Freiburg)

Zangen, Gustav, 15. Armee: Amerikanischen Grossangriff aus dem Bruckenkopf Remagen 23–30.3.45 (Bundesarchiv, Freiburg)

Author's archive

SSPz. Gren. A.u.E. Btl. 16 in den Kämpfen bei ARNHEIM 17.9.44–7.10.44

'One Aspect of the Battle of Nijmegen Bridge, Tues. – Wed. 19/20 Sep 1944' by Major H. F. Stanley, 1st (Motor) Bn Grenadier Guards

Appendix 'J' to War Diary HQ, British Airborne Corps for September, 1944 – Summary of Statement by Lt D.J. Simpson, RE 1 Para Bn.

Report No. 139, Historical Officer, Canadian Military Headquarters: 1st Canadian Parachute Battalion in France (6 June–6 September 1944) dated 7 Jul 1945

Hitler's Speeches 1945 London n.d.

Draft Account 3rd Parachute Battalion 'C' Company – Lieutenant Len Wright

Captain R.H. Clark MC *My Time with Airborne Forces*

Microsoft *Close Combat Conduct 2: A Bridge too Far* (1997)

Diaries, correspondence and interviews

Thomas Abt

Wolfgang Amsel

Rick Andrews

Heinrich Balck

Sophie Becker

Klaus Beich

John Bird

Tony Brady

Frank 'Nobby' Clarke

James Cleminson

Bob Collins

Elles Dean

Anthony Deane-Drummond
Urs Ebersbach
Denis Edwards
Fraser Edwards
Otto Egger
Don Evans
John Frost
Wilhelm Hagemenn
Lars Hahn
Charlie Harris
Peter Harris
James Hill
Tommy Hobson
Volker Holzman
John Howard
Alan Hudson
David Jones
Ronnie Joyce
Heinz Kempa
Donald Kennedy
Peter Kress
Julius Lange
Otto Leitner
Stanley Livermore
Brian MacDonald
Jimmy Mason
Heinrich Mayer
Jane Mayhew
Peter Merchant
Billy Meyers
Brian Milburn
David Moores

Wally Parr
Herbert Piplak
Bill Potts
Geoffrey Powell
Hugh Pritchard
Ron Reeve
Fenton Richards
'Jimmy' Riddle
Richard Ritterbecks
Joe Robert
Jim Russell
Don Shanks
Rolf Siegel
James Sims
David R. Smith
Teddy Smith
Hans-Dieter Steets
Winifred Steets
Daniel Stein
Kurt Student
David Summers
Andrew Taylor
Alistair Trewin
John Waddy
Harold Watkins
Mick White
Brad Wiley
Ken Williams
Michael Williams
Brian Wilson
Charles Wilson
Len Wright

Internet

Nuremberg Papers, www.nizkor.org/hweb/imt/tgmwe-15 /tgwe-15-145-07.shtml, accessed 16 May 2006

Derrick Randall *Experiences of a Medical Officer at Arnhem* http://www.bbc.co.uk/ww2peopleswar/stories/78/a5516778.shtml, accessed 12 March 2007

Published Sources

Articles

Bordewich, Fergus M. *The Ambush that Changed History* http://www.smithsonianmag.com/issues/2005/september/ambush.htm

Corrigan, Major Gordon, MBE 'Haig and Montgomery – A Comparison', The Douglas Haig Fellowship Records 11 (2005 and 2006)

McGhee, Major James T. *In the Shadow of the Elites: The 9th SS Panzer Division Hobenstaufen* http:// militaryonline.com/wwii/articles/ 9SSHHobenstaufen.aspx

Wallwork, James H. *No Higher Test of Piloting Skill*, Supplement to *Aeroplane Monthly*, May 1994

Books

Note: Place of publication is London unless stated otherwise.

Adair, Major-General Sir Allan *A Guards' General* Hamish Hamilton 1986

Allen, Peter *One More River – The Rhine Crossings of 1945* J.M. Dent 1980

Ambrose, Stephen E. *Pegasus Bridge: June 6, 1944* Touchstone New York 1985

Ambrose, Stephen E. *Band of Brothers* Pocket Books 2001

Anderson, Dudley *Three Cheers for the Next Man to Die* Robert Hale 1983

Arthur, Max *Forgotten Voices of the Second World War* Ebury Press 2004

Barber, Neil *The Day the Devils Dropped In – The 9th Parachute Battalion in Normandy – D-Day to D+6* Pen and Sword Barnsley 2002

Barley, Eric and Fohlen, Yves *Para Memories – 12th Yorkshire Parachute Battalion in Europe and the Far East During the Second World War* Parapress Tunbridge Wells 1996

Baynes, John *Urquhart of Arnhem – The Life of Major-General R.E. Urquhart CBE, DSO* Brassey's 1993

Blair, Clay *Ridgway's Paratroopers – The American Airborne in World War II* Naval Institute Press Annapolis MD 2002

Blennemann, Dirk et al. *Hitler's Army – The Evolution and Structure of German Forces* Da Cao Press Cambridge MA 1996

Blockwell, Albert (ed. Maggie Clifton) *Diary of a Red Devil – By Glider to Arnhem with the 7th King's Own Scottish Borderers* Helion 2005

Boscawen, Robert *Armoured Guardsmen: A War Diary, June 1944–April 1945* Leo Cooper Barnsley 2001

Bradley, Omar N. *A Soldier's Story of the Allied Campaigns from Tunis to the Elbe* Eyre & Spottiswoode 1951

Brammall, R. *The Tenth – A Record of Service of the 10th Battalion, The Parachute Regiment 1942–1945 and the 10th Battalion, The Parachute Regiment (T.A.) (County of London) 1945–1965* Eastgate Ipswich 1965

Brereton, Lewis H. *The Brereton Diaries – The War in the Air in the Pacific, Middle East and Europe 3 October 1941–8 May 1945* William Morrow New York 1946

Bruce, Colin John *War on the Ground: 1939–1945* Book Club Associates 1995

Bryant, Arthur *Triumph in the West 1943–46* Collins 1959

Buckingham, William F. *Arnhem 1944* Tempus Stroud 2002

Bullock, Alan *Hitler – A Study in Tyranny* Penguin 1962

Burgett, Donald R. *Currahee! – A Screaming Eagle in Normandy* Dell New York 1967

Burgett, Donald R. *The Road to Arnhem – A Screaming Eagle in Holland* Dell New York 2001

Burns, Dwayne and Burns Leland T. *Jump into the Valley of the Shadow –*

The World War II Memories of a Paratrooper in the 508th PIR, 82nd Airborne Division Casemate, Philadelphia PA 2006

Burriss, T. Moffatt *Strike and Hold – A Memoir of the 82d Airborne in World War II* Brassey's Washington DC 2000

Carius, Otto *Tigers in the Mud – The Combat Career of German Panzer Commander Otto Carius* Stackpole Books Mechanicsburg PA 2003

Cholewczynski, George F. *Poles Apart – The Polish Airborne at the Battle of Arnhem* Sarpedon New York 1993

Churchill, Winston S. *The Second World War, Volume VI: Triumph and Tragedy* Penguin 1985

Clark, Lloyd *Arnhem – Operation Market Garden, September 1944* Sutton Stroud 2003

Clark, Lloyd *The Orne Bridgehead* Sutton Stroud 2004

Colville, John *The Fringes of Power – Downing Street Diaries 1939–1955* Weidenfeld & Nicolson 2004

Cooper, Alan *Wot! No Engines? Royal Air Force Glider Pilots & Operation Varsity* Woodfield West Sussex 2002

Cooper, Matthew *The German Army 1933–1945 – Its Political and Military Failure* Macdonald & Janes 1978

Crookenden, Napier *Dropzone Normandy – The Story of the American and British Airborne Assault on D Day 1944* Ian Allan 1976

Cross, Robin *Fallen Eagle – The Last Days of the Third Reich* Caxton Edition 1995

Danchev, Alex and Todman, Daniel (eds) *War Diaries 1939–1945 Field Marshal Alan Brooke* Weidenfeld & Nicolson 2001

Deane-Drummond, Anthony *Arrows of Fortune* Leo Cooper Barnsley 1992

D'Este, Carlo *A Genius for War: A Life of General George S. Patton* HarperCollins 1995

D'Este, Carlo *Eisenhower – Allied Supreme Commander* Cassell 2004

Detwiler, Donald S. *et al.* (ed.) *World War II German Military Studies, Vols 2,3, 10 and 11* Garland 1979

Devlin, Gerard M, *Paratrooper! The Saga of Parachute and Glider Combat Troops During World War II* Robson 1979

Dixon, Norman F. *On the Psychology of Military Incompetence* Futura 1988

Doherty, Richard *Ireland's Generals in the Second World War* Four Courts Press Dublin 2004

Edwards, Denis *The Devil's Own Luck: From Pegasus Bridge to the Baltic 1944–45* Leo Cooper Barnsley 1999

Eisenhower, Dwight *Crusade in Europe* Heinemann 1948

Ellis, Major L. F. with Lieutenent-Colonel A.E. Warhurst *Victory in the West: Volume II, The Defeat of Germany* HMSO 1968

Essame, Major-General H. *The 43rd Wessex Division at War 1944–1945* William Clowes 1952

Fairley, John *Remember Arnhem: Pegasus Journal* Aldershot 1978

Fest, Joachim *Inside Hitler's Bunker – The Last Days of the Third Reich* Pan 2005

Fitzgerald, Major D.J.L. *History of the Irish Guards in the Second World War* Gale & Polden 1949

Ford, Ken *The Rhine Crossings 1945* Osprey Oxford 2006

Fraser, David *Alanbrooke* Hamlyn 1983

Frost, Major-General John *A Drop Too Many* Sphere 1983

Fullick, Roy *Shan Hackett – The Pursuit of Exactitude* Leo Cooper Barnsley 2003

Gable, Kurt *The Making of a Paratrooper – Airborne Training and Combat in World War II* University Press of Kansas KS 1990

Gale, R.N. *With the 6th Airborne Division in Normandy* Sampson Low Marston 1948

Gavin, James M. *On to Berlin – Battles of an Airborne Commander 1943–1946* Viking New York 1978

Gilbert, Martin *Road to Victory – Winston S. Churchill 1941–1945* Heinemann 1986

Gill, Ronald and Groves, John *Club Route in Europe – The History of 30 Corps from D-Day to May 1945* MLRS 2006 (1st edn 1946)

Golden, Lewis *Echoes from Arnhem* William Kimber 1984

Green, Alan T. *1st Battalion the Border Regiment – Arnhem* Museum of the Border Regiment and the King's Own Royal Border Regiment 1991

Gregory, Barry and Batchelor, John *Airborne Forces 1918–1945* Phoebus 1979

Grossjohann, Georg *Five Years, Four Fronts – A German Officer's World War II Combat Memoir* Presidio New York 1999

Guarnere, William 'Wild Bill' and Heffron, Edward 'Babe' with Robyn Prost *Brothers in Battle, Best of Friends – Two WWII Paratroopers from the Original Band of Brothers Tell their Story* Berkley Caliber New York 2007

Hackett, General Sir John *I Was a Stranger*, Chatto & Windus 1977

Hagen, Louis *Arnhem Lift* Severn House 1977

Hamilton, Nigel *Monty: Master of the Battlefield 1942–1944* Hamish Hamilton 1983

Hamilton, Nigel *Monty: The Field Marshal 1944–1976* Sceptre 1987

Hamilton, Nigel *Monty – The Battles of Field Marshal Bernard Montgomery* Hodder & Stoughton 1994

Harclerode, Peter *Para! Fifty Years of the Parachute Regiment* Arms & Armour 1992

Harclerode, Peter *Wings of War – Airborne Warfare 1918–1945* Weidenfeld & Nicolson 2005

Hargreaves, Richard *The Germans in Normandy* Pen & Sword 2006

Hart, Stephen Ashley *Colossal Cracks – Montgomery's 21st Army Group in Northwest Europe, 1944–45* Stackpole 2007

Harvey, A.D. *Arnhem* Cassell 2001

Hastings, Max *Armageddon – The Battle for Germany 1944–45* Pan 2005

Heaps, Leo *Escape from Arnhem – A Canadian Among the Lost Paratroopers* Macmillan Toronto 1945

Heiber, Helmut and Glantz, David M. (eds) *Hitler and his Generals – Military Conferences 1942–1945* Enigma New York 2004

Higham, Robin *Air Power – A Concise History* Macdonald 1972

Hoare, Tom *Rouge Diablos* Avon 1995

Horn, Bernd Lieutenant-Colonel and Wyczynski, Michel *Para Versus the Reich – Canada's Paratroopers at War 1942–45* Dundurn Toronto 2003

Horne, Alistair with David Montgomery *Monty – The Lonely Leader, 1944–45* HarperCollins New York 1994

Horrocks, Lieutenant-General Sir Brian *A Full Life* Collins 1960

Howard, John and Bates, Penny *The Pegasus Diaries – The Private Papers of Major John Howard DSO* Pen Sword Military 2006

Irving, David *Hitler's War 1942–1948* Macmillan 1977

Jackson, Julian *France – the Dark Years 1940–1944* Oxford University Press Oxford 2001

James, Julian *A Fierce Quality – A Biography of Brigadier Alastair Pearson* Leo Cooper Barnsley 1989

Joll, James *Europe since 1870 – An International History* Penguin 1983

Jones, Colonel Robert E. *History of the 101st Airborne Division – Screaming Eagles – The First 50 Years* Turner Paducah KY 2005

Keegan, John (ed.) *Churchill's Generals* Warner 1992

Kent, Ron *First In! Parachute Pathfinder Company – A History of the 21st Independent Parachute Company, the Original Pathfinders of the British Airborne Forces, 1942–1946* Batsford 1979

Kershaw, Ian *Hitler 1936–1945: Nemesis* Penguin 2000

Kershaw, Robert *It Never Snows in September – The German View of MARKET GARDEN and the Battle of Arnhem, September 1944* Shepperton Ian Allan 1994

Killblane, Richard and McNiece, Jake *The Filthy Thirteen – From the Dustbowl to Hitler's Eagle's Nest: The 101st Airborne's Most Legendary Squad of Combat Paratroopers* Casemate Philadelphia PA 2006

Koskimaki, George E. *Hell's Highway – A Chronicle of the 101st Airborne in the Holland Campaign, September–November 1944* Ballantine Books New York 2007

Kurowski, Franz *Infantry Aces – The German Soldier in Combat in WWII* Stackpole Mechanicsburg PA 1994

Kurowski, Franz *Hitler's Last Bastion – The Final Battles for the Reich 1944–1945* Schiffer Military Histroy Atglen PA 1998

Larrabee, Eric *Commander In Chief – Franklin Delano Roosevelt. His Lieutenants, and their War* André Deutsch 1987

Lebenson, Len *Surrounded by Heroes – Six Campaigns with Division Headquarters, 82d Airborne Division, 1942–1945* Casemate Philadelphia PA 2007

Liddell Hart, B.H. *The Other Side of the Hill* Pan 1978

Lowden, John L. *Silent Wings at War – Combat Gliders in World War Two* Smithsonian Institution Press Washington 1992

Lucas, James *Battle Group! German Kampfgruppen Action of World War Two* Cassell 2000

MacDonald, Charles B. *The Last Offensive, United States Army in World War II. The European Theater of Operations* Center of Military History (Washington DC) 1973

Marsden, Walter *The Rhineland* Batsford 1973

Martin, Lieutenant-General H.G. *The History of the Fifteenth Scottish Division 1939–1945* Blackwood 1948

Mawson, Stuart *Arnhem Doctor* Orbis 1981

Meacham, Jon *Franklin and Winston – A Portrait of a Friendship* Granta 2004

Mead, Richard *Churchill's Lions – A Biographical Guide to the Key British Generals of World War II* Spellmount Stroud 2007

Middlebrook, Martin *Arnhem 1944 – The Airborne Battle* Penguin 1995

Milbourne, Andrew *Lease of Life* Museum Press n.d.

Ministry of Information *By Air to Battle – The Official Account of the British First and Sixth Airborne Divisions* HMSO 1945

Mitcham, Jr Samuel W. *Hitler's Legions – The German Army Order of Battle, World War II* Dorset Press New York 1985

Mitcham, Jr Samuel W. *Retreat to the Reich – The German Defeat in France, 1944* Praeger Westport CT 2000

Mitchell, William *Memoirs of World War I* Random House New York 1960

Montgomery of Alamein, Field Marshal Viscount *Normandy to the Baltic* Hutchinson 1947

Montgomery, Bernard Law *The Memoirs of Field Marshal the Viscount of Alamein, K.G.* Collins 1958

Moorehouse, Roger *Killing Hitler – the Third Reich and the Plots against the Führer* Jonathan Cape 2006

Morrow (Jnr), John H. *The Great War in the Air – Military Aviation from 1909 to 1921* Airlife Shrewsbury 1993

Neillands, Robin *The Conquest of the Reich – From D-Day to VE-Day: A Soldiers' History* Weidenfeld & Nicolson 1995

Neillands, Robin *The Battle for the Rhine, 1944 – Arnhem and the Ardennes: the Campaign in Europe* Weidenfeld & Nicolson 2005

Newton, Steven H. *Hitler's Commander – Field Marshal Walther Model, Hitler's Favorite General* Da Capo Press Cambridge MA 2005

Nordyke, Phil *All American – All the Way – The Combat History of the 82nd Airborne Division in World War II* Zenith Press St Paul MN 2005

Nordyke, Phil *Four Stars of Valor – The Combat History of the 505th Parachute Infantry Regiment in World War II* Zenith Press St Paul MN 2006

Otway, Lieutenant-Colonel T.B.H. *Airborne Forces – The Second World War 1939–45 Army* Imperial War Museum 1990

Overy, Richard *Why the Allies Won* Jonathan Cape 1995

Packe, Michael *First Airborne* Secker & Warburg 1948

Pay, D.R. *Thunder from Heaven – Story of the 17th Airborne Division 1943–1945* Battery Press Nashville TN 1947

Pershing, John J. *My Experiences in the World War* Hodder & Stoughton 1931

Pocock, Tom *Alan Moorehead* The Bodley Head 1990

Powell, Geoffrey *The Devil's Birthday – The Bridges to Arnhem 1944* Buchan & Enright 1984

Powell, Geoffrey (originally published in 1976 under the pseudonym Tom Angus) *Men at Arnhem* Leo Cooper Barnsley 1998

Prüller, Wilhelm *Diary of a German Soldier* Faber & Faber 1963

Rapport, Leonard and Northwood, Arthur *Rendezvous with Destiny – A History of the 101st Airborne Division* 101st Airborne Division Association Fort Campbell KY 1948

Rawson, Andrew *The Rhine Crossing – 9th US Army and 17th US Airborne* Leo Cooper Barnsley 2006

Rees, Goronwy *The Rhine* Weidenfeld & Nicolson 1967

Report by The Supreme Commander to the Combined Chiefs of Staff on the Operations in Europe of the Allied Expeditionary Force 6 June 1944 to May 1945 HMSO 1946

Reynolds, Michael *Sons of the Reich – II SS Panzer Corps in Normandy, Arnhem, Ardennes and on the Eastern Front* Spellmount Staplehurst 2002

Richardson, General Sir Charles *Send for Freddie – The Story of Montgomery's Chief of Staff, Major-General Sir Francis de Guingand, KBE, CB, DSO* William Kimber 1987

Ryan, Cornelius *A Bridge too Far* Hodder & Stoughton 1974

Saunders, Hilary St George *The Red Beret – The Story of the Parachute Regiment at War 1940–1945* Michael Joseph 1950

Saunders, Tim *Hell's Highway* Leo Cooper Barnsley 2001

Saunders, Tim *The Island – Nijmegen to Arnhem* Leo Cooper Barnsley 2002

Saunders, Tim *Operations Plunder and Varsity: The British and Canadian Rhine Crossing* Leo Cooper Barnsley 2006

Seaton, Albert *The Fall of Fortress Europe 1943–1945* Batsford 1981

Sims, James *Arnhem Spearhead – A Private Soldier's Story* Imperial War Museum 1978

Smythe, Donald *Pershing – Generals of the Armies* Indiana University Press Bloomington IN 1986

Stainforth, Peter *Wings of the Wind – The Story of the 1st Parachute Division* Viking Press 1952

Steer, Frank *Arnhem – The Fight to Sustain – The Untold Story of the Airborne Logisticians* Leo Cooper Barnsley 2000

Steer, Frank *Arnhem – The Landing Grounds and Oosterbeek* Leo Cooper Barnsley 2002

Steer, Frank *The Bridge – Arnhem* Leo Cooper Barnsley 2003

Stein, George H. *The Waffen SS – Hitler's Elite Guard at War 1939–1945* Oxford University Press Oxford 1966

Stimpel, Hans-Martin *Die deutsche Fallschirmtruppe 1942–1945* Mittler Hamburg 2001

Summersby, Kay *Eisenhower was my Boss* Werner Laurie 1949

Taylor, A.J.P. *The Course of German History – A Survey of the Development of Germany since 1815* Hamish Hamilton 1945

Taylor, Vivian *The Armoured Micks 1941–45* Regimental Headquarters Irish Guards 1997

Ter Horst Kate A. *Cloud over Arnhem* Airborne Museum Oosterbeek, 1999

Tieke, Wilhelm *In the Firestorm of the Last Years of the War*, trans. Frederick Steinhardt, J.J. Fedorowicz Winnipeg 1999

Tugwell, Maurice *Airborne to Battle – A History of Airborne Warfare 1918–1971* William Kimber 1971

Turner, Barry *Countdown to Victory – The Final European Campaigns of World War II* Hodder & Stoughton 2004

Urquhart, Major-General R.E. *Arnhem* Pan 1960

van Creveld, Martin *Supplying War* Cambridge University Press, Cambridge 1977

van Roekel, Chris *The Torn Horizon – The Airborne Chaplains at Arnhem* Jan and Wendelta ter Horst and Chris van Rockel Kontrast Oosterbeek 1998

van Teeseling, Peter-Alexander *Over and Over – Eyewitness Accounts of the Battle of Arnhem* Kontrast Oosterbeek 2000

Vandiver, Frank E. *Black Jack – The Life and Times of John J. Pershing* Vol. II A&M University Press Houston 1977

Verney, Major-General G.L. *The Guards Armoured Division – A Short History* Hutchinson 1955

Waddy, John *A Tour of the Arnhem Battlefields 17–26 September 1944* Leo Cooper Barnsley 1999

Warren, Dr John C. *Airborne Operations in World War II, European Theater – USAF Historical Studies: No. 97* USAF Historical Division, Research Studies Institute, Air University Maxwell Air Force Base Maxwell AL September 1956

Webster, David Kenyon *Parachute Infantry – An American Paratrooper's Memoir of D-Day and the Fall of the Third Reich* Delta Books 1994

Weeks, John *The Airborne Soldier* Blandford Press Poole 1982

Weigley, Russell F. *Eisenhower's Lieutenants – The Campaign of France and Germany 1944–1945* Sidgwick & Jackson 1981

Westphal, Siegfried *The German Army in the West* Cassell 1951

Whitaker, Brigadier-General Denis and Whitaker, Shelagh *Rhineland – The Battle to End the War* Stoddart Toronto 2000

Whiting, Charles *West Wall: The Battle for Hitler's Siegfried Line* Spellmount Staplehurst 1999

Williams, Andrew *D-Day to Berlin* Hodder & Stoughton 2004

Williamson, Gordon *Loyalty is my Honor: Personal Accounts from the Waffen SS* Brown 1999

Wilson, Robert L. and Wilson, Philip K. *A Paratrooper's Panoramic View – Training with the 464th Parachute Field Artillery Battalion for Operation Varsity's Rhine Jump with 17th Airborne Division* Authorhouse Bloomington IN 2005

Winters, Major Dick with Kingseed, Colonel Cole C. *Beyond Band of Brothers* Berkley New York 2006

Wright, Stephen L. *The Last Drop: Operation Varsity March 24–28, 1945* Stackpole Books Mechanicsburg, PA 2008

Wurst, Spencer F. and Wurst, Gayle *Descending from the Clouds – A Memoir of Combat in the 505 Parachute Infantry Regiment, 82d Airborne Division* Casemate Havertown PA 2004

Zumbro, Derek S. *Battle for the Ruhr – The German Army's Final Defeat in the West* University Press of Kansas Lawrence KS 2006

Index

Note: Individual units are listed under their respective armies. Subheadings are arranged in alphabetical order, with the exception of those for individuals and operations, which are in chronological order.